Ministries of Compassion
among Russian Evangelicals,
1905–1929

Ministries of Compassion among Russian Evangelicals, 1905–1929

MARY RABER

Foreword by Ian M. Randall

◖PICKWICK *Publications* • Eugene, Oregon

MINISTRIES OF COMPASSION AMONG RUSSIAN EVANGELICALS,
1905–1929

Copyright © 2016 Mary Raber. All rights reserved. Except for brief quotations in critical publications or reviews, no part of this book may be reproduced in any manner without prior written permission from the publisher. Write: Permissions, Wipf and Stock Publishers, 199 W. 8th Ave., Suite 3, Eugene, OR 97401.

Pickwick Publications
An Imprint of Wipf and Stock Publishers
199 W. 8th Ave., Suite 3
Eugene, OR 97401

www.wipfandstock.com

PAPERBACK ISBN 13: 978-1-4982-8070-9
HARDCOVER ISBN 13: 978-1-4982-8072-3

Cataloguing-in-Publication data:

Raber, Mary.

Ministries of compassion among Russian evangelicals, 1905–1929 / Mary Raber ; foreword by Ian M. Randall.

xiv + 260 pp. ; 23 cm. Includes bibliographical references and index.

ISBN: 978-1-4982-8070-9 (paperback) | ISBN: 978-1-4982-8072-3 (hardcover)

1. Baptists—Russia—History—20th century. 2. Russia—Church history—20th century. 3. Salvation Army—Russia—History. 4. Stundists. 5. Molokans. 6. Prokhanov, I. S. (Ivan Stepanovich), 1869–1935. I. Randall, Ian M. II. Title.

BX4849 R32 2016

Manufactured in the U.S.A.   05/13/2016

Scripture taken from the Holy Bible, New International Version. Copyright © 1973, 1978, 1984 by International Bible Society. Used by permission of Zondervan Publishing House.

Cover: Residents of the homeless shelter at Dom Evangeliia in St. Petersburg (*Gost'* No. 12 [December 1914]).

Contents

Foreword by Ian M. Randall | vii
Preface | xi
Glossary and Abbreviations | xiii

Introduction | 1
1. Russian Evangelical Ministries of Compassion before 1905 | 22
2. Russian Evangelicals from 1905 to 1929: Varied Ministries, Common Convictions | 52
3. Aid within the Evangelical Community—D. I. Mazaev, V. G. Pavlov, and V. V. Ivanov | 84
4. Urban Rescue Ministry—W. A. Fetler | 113
5. War, Revolution, and Famine, 1914 to 1923 | 144
6. Christian Economic Communities—I. S. Prokhanov | 174
Conclusion: The Legacy of Russian Evangelical Ministries of Compassion | 200

Bibliography | 213
Index | 229

Foreword

IVAN S. PROKHANOV, ONE of the significant evangelical leaders in Russia in the period which is the focus of this book, wrote an autobiography titled *In the Cauldron of Russia, 1869–1933* (published in New York in 1933). Perhaps more revealing than the title is the sub-title, *The Life of an Optimist in the Land of Pessimism*. Mary Raber's study of the compassionate ministries of Russian evangelicals (those within the Russian Baptist Union and the Evangelical Christian Union) in the period from 1905 to 1929 strikingly illuminates a movement that was optimistic, but not unrealistic. As they looked at the world in which they lived, with all its struggles, these evangelicals responded in ways that were determinedly outward-looking. Whereas some in other parts of the world-wide evangelical community were withdrawing from social involvement in the 1920s—the "great reversal"—Russian evangelicals committed themselves to activities designed to contribute to the good of wider Russian society. Indeed, this book argues that from the 1870s to the 1920s the Russian evangelicals "tended to emphasize engagement and action over formal theology" and in their compassionate ministry they "exhibited a basically positive attitude to the world."

This is a story that has not previously been told. Work has more recently been done on the history of the various compassionate ministries undertaken by the Christian community in Russia, but the focus has been on the Russian Orthodox tradition and virtually no research has been undertaken on the involvements of Russian evangelicals. Yet in the period examined here, the late Imperial and early Soviet era, Russian evangelicals were of considerable significance, both in terms of their influence and their numerical growth. This significance is analyzed well in an important scholarly volume by Heather J. Coleman, *Russian Baptists and Spiritual Revolution, 1905–1929*.[1] Coleman is aware of the part played by compassionate ministry

---

1. Heather J. Colemen, *Russian Baptists and Spiritual Revolution, 1905–1929* (Bloomington: Indiana University Press, 2005).

among the evangelicals, but that is not the focus of her investigation. Mary Raber's work, based on extensive use of Russian-language sources, among them sources not available before, is ground-breaking. She opens up a subject that has not been touched in academic study. The picture she paints is of a high degree of social involvement, something of which even present-day evangelicals in the former USSR are largely unaware.

This study ably fulfils its intention to present a comprehensive picture of the compassionate ministries of Russian evangelicals in the so-called "Golden Age," which was a period in which these evangelicals experienced relative freedom. It began with Emperor Nicholas II's Decree of 17 April 1905, "On the strengthening of the beginnings of religious toleration," and came to an end with the Soviet law "On religious associations," on 8 April 1929, which made it illegal for religious groups—which had to be registered—to engage in any activity other than worship. Their social endeavors, which had offered many benefits to society, were prohibited from 1929 onwards and were not to be possible again until the end of the Communist period. One of the strengths of Mary Raber's work is that she knows the wider history of Russia and consequently is well able to place the contributions in historical context. Also, she has lived and worked for a number of years among evangelicals in the former Soviet Union and has an understanding of the life of the tradition which is not possible without that experience.

Although the main focus here is on the years 1905 to 1929, the first chapter examines the pre-1905 period. The remarkable evangelical movement that grew initially among members of the Russian nobility from the 1870s has become better known through studies such as Gregory Nichols's work on the development of Russian evangelical spirituality.[2] However, Mary Raber sheds further light on the amazing range of ministries undertaken by men and women from high society in Russia, the Pashvokite movement (after V. A. Pashkov) as it became known. She then goes on to argue that three broad patterns of evangelical compassionate ministry may be distinguished from 1905 to 1929. The first is aid shared among evangelicals themselves. Here the book brings vividly to life the thinking and work of three influential leaders, D. I. Mazaev, V. G. Pavlov, and V. V. Ivanov. Raber argues that the second main emphasis of compassionate ministry was serving the urban poor. She examines the forceful and entrepreneurial W. A. Fetler, who trained at the Pastors' College (later Spurgeon's College) in London and was indebted to his experience of the Welsh Revival and the work of the Salvation Army. The third major area of compassionate ministry, it is

---

2. Gregory L. Nichols, *The Development of Russian Evangelical Spirituality: A Study of Ivan V. Kargel (1849–1937)* (Eugene, OR: Pickwick Publications, 2011).

contended, was the formation of economic communities and labor cooperatives following the 1917 Bolshevik Revolution. Here Raber shows how I. S. Prokhanov's creative leadership was crucial. Indeed, I suggest he deserves a full-length scholarly biographical study.

As well as providing an in-depth analysis of these influential evangelical leaders, of their contexts, and of the way their outlooks shaped the evangelical community, this book probes the underlying convictions of Russian evangelicals. Mary Raber's conclusion is that although each of the areas of ministry throughout the period was distinct, the common theological convictions were that preaching the gospel was the primary calling, that the gospel had the power to eradicate human suffering, that witness should consist of good works as well as words, and that compassion was the concern of all members of the community, regardless of their gender, economic status, or age. By drawing from evangelical publications of the time, Raber shows in detail how these emphases were promoted and implemented.

There has been and continues to be much debate about the extent to which Russian evangelicals were an indigenous movement and the extent to which they were an importation from the West. Recent scholarship, such as Constantine Prokhorov's *Russian Baptists and Orthodoxy, 1960-1990*,[3] has shown that common interpretations are often inadequate. Polarized views, often based on presuppositions, are particularly unhelpful. Mary Raber convincingly identifies and evaluates the way in which Russian evangelicals drew models from the West, with a good example being urban rescue ministry in the style of the Salvation Army, while also drawing on indigenous Russian sectarian tradition. There was a willingness to make use of ideas that were seen to be appropriate to different circumstances.

When I wrote the Foreword to *Dance or Die: The Shaping of Estonian Baptist Identity under Communism*, by Toivo Pilli,[4] I noted that in recent decades there had been sustained historical examination, by scholars such as David Bebbington and Mark Noll, of evangelical experiences in the English-speaking world. I suggested at that time that relatively little had yet been done—certainly that had been made more widely available—on evangelicals in Eastern Europe. For that and other reasons I was delighted to commend Toivo Pilli's scholarly work. Since then the situation has changed. One development has been that a community of scholars has emerged connected with what is now the International Baptist Theological Study Centre

3. Constantine Prokhorov, *Russian Baptists and Orthodoxy, 1960-1990: A Comparative Study of Theology, Liturgy, and Traditions* (Carlisle, UK: Langham Monographs, 2013).

4. Toivo Pilli, *Dance or Die: The Shaping of Estonian Baptist Identity under Communism* (Milton Keynes, UK: Paternoster, 2008).

(formerly in Prague, now in Amsterdam) and their work has played an important part in the transformation of the study of evangelicals in Eastern Europe. Mary Raber has made an outstanding contribution to this scholarly advance: in this superb volume she has argued convincingly for a fresh understanding of the identity of Russian evangelicals in the early twentieth century.

Ian M. Randall
Cambridge Centre for Christianity Worldwide

Preface

FROM 1993 TO 2007 one of my tasks as a Mennonite Central Committee voluntary service worker in Ukraine and Russia was to assist groups that were attempting to address the crushing social needs that accompanied the collapse of the Soviet Union. In many ways, especially during the early 1990s, it was a frightening, uncertain time. Suddenly the social safety net that had functioned adequately for decades was gone. Industries failed. People's savings were wiped out by inflation. As families broke up, homeless children in many cities found warmth by clustering around the artificial campfire of the eternal flame at the local World War II memorial.

Yet for a number of the evangelical Christians my co-workers and I encountered, in spite of genuine day-to-day hardship, it was also a hopeful, joyous time. For the first time in living memory they were able to speak freely about their faith and to undertake new ministries. Where previously they had been marginalized outsiders, suddenly they had valuable contributions to make to the wider society. While a sense of loss and confusion prevailed, it seemed extraordinary to us that many evangelical Christians were among those who had some notion of how to pick up the shattered pieces of their society and begin to build a viable future. Frequently, their involvement took the form of serving those in need: setting up children's shelters, rehabilitation projects for alcoholics, or counseling networks for AIDS patients.

Not all of their efforts succeeded and the dynamics of daily life have changed a great deal over the years. Yet care for people in need remains a significant part of evangelical life for many in the former Soviet Union. It is ongoing contact with individuals and groups involved in such ministries that made me curious about how Russian evangelicals had coped with social need in the past. Recovering that history—largely forgotten during Soviet times—was an obvious dissertation topic when I enrolled as a doctoral student at International Baptist Theological Seminary in Prague (now the IBTS

Centre in Amsterdam). I am grateful for the opportunity to publish my research and sincerely hope that somehow its wider availability will both inform and encourage.

I am very grateful to Dr. Ian M. Randall, author of the Foreword, who gently supervised me from the beginning of the proposal stage in 2005 until his retirement in the summer of 2013. Dr. Toivo Pilli then patiently stayed with me until completion. Dr. Walter Sawatsky, a co-worker and friend for many years, stood by throughout with helpful criticism and resource suggestions.

It has been a pleasure to be a part of the IBTS community both in Prague and in Amsterdam. I thank Dr. Lina Andronoviene, Dr. Keith Jones, and Dr. Parush Parushev, and especially Katharina Penner, Zdenko Sirka, and Pieter van Wingerden, as well as the library staffs they represent. I have also greatly appreciated the good company of my fellow students.

Sources for this research are scattered across the United States and the former Soviet Union, so I am indebted to the people who helped me find them: the staff of the St. Louis (Missouri) Public Library; Taffey Hall at the Southern Baptist Historical Library and Archives in Nashville, Tennessee; the Slavic library staff at the University of Illinois at Champaign/Urbana; Aleksei Sinichkin at the Evangelical Christian-Baptist archives in Moscow; and the staff at the Salvation Army International Heritage Centre in London. Dr. Sharyl Corrado, Dr. Gregory Nichols, and Dr. Albert J. Wardin, Jr. were most generous in handing on items they had accumulated over years of research. Thanks are also due to an anonymous collector of Russian evangelical periodicals in Odessa, Ukraine, and to Valentina Chernova and Elvera Siegel who loaned me personal manuscripts and books. Needless to say, the historical, bibliographic, orthographic, and other mistakes in this book are all my own and have nothing to do with any of the people who kindly helped me along the way.

Many people and institutions provided me with a place to write: Andrew and Philippa Chalkley; Odessa Theological Seminary (Ukraine); Dr. Peter F. Penner; Danuta Raciborska; Jerri Lake and Stephen Rayburn; and my own family. I have been employed by two agencies during this project, Mennonite Mission Network and Mennonite Central Committee, represented by supervisors Tim Foley and Ionka Hristozova, respectively. They have been supportive and tolerant throughout.

Finally, I thank my brother Thomas and my sister Martha for caring for our parents and maintaining a home for me to return to from time to time.

Glossary and Abbreviations

funt: measure of weight, approximately 1.10 pounds
guberniia: "governorate" or province
oblast': territorial unit introduced in the 1920s
pud: measure of weight, approximately 36 pounds
uezd: local district, subdivision of a guberniia
ABFMS: American Baptist Foreign Mission Society
AUCEC-B: All-Union Council of Evangelical Christians-Baptists
E-AAA: Euro-Asian Accrediting Association
EC-B: Evangelical Christians-Baptists
EKh-B: Evangel'skie khristiane-baptisty (Evangelical Christians-Baptists)
GARF: Gosudarstvennyi arkhiv Russkoi Federatsii (The State Archives of the Russian Federation)
SBHLA: Southern Baptist Historical Library and Archives
SAIHC: Salvation Army International Heritage Centre
VSEKh-B: Vserossiiskii soiuz Evangel'skikh Khristian-Baptistov (All-Union Council of Evangelical Christians-Baptists)

NOTE ON TRANSLITERATION

In this study a standard transliteration of Russian words into English is followed except where a name already has an established English rendering. Thus, the more familiar Fyodor Dostoevsky and Leo Tolstoy appear here rather than Fedor Dostoevskii and Lev Tolstoi. In the same way, emperors' names are given as Alexander or Nicholas while others with the same names are identified as Aleksandr or Nikolai.

Introduction

ONE EVENING A TRAVELER arrived at the home of Dei Ivanovich Mazaev (1855–1922), a prosperous sheep rancher in southern Russia, and asked to spend the night. Mazaev instructed his household staff to give the man a meal and a bed. While he was eating, the stranger turned the conversation to spiritual topics and the salvation of the soul. Knowing that their Baptist employer would be interested, the servants called Mazaev into the kitchen, and he began to question his guest. Who was he? Where had he come from and where was he going? The man answered that he was from the village of Liubomirka, in Kherson guberniia (central Ukraine), and that his name was Ivan Grigor'evich Riaboshapka (1831–1900).

Although Mazaev had never met Riaboshapka before, he knew a great deal about him. Riaboshapka was probably the most effective Russian Baptist evangelist of the nineteenth century—the classic example of a peasant Stundist[1] who had taught himself to read the Scriptures, repented, and in 1870 was baptized.[2] Delighted to discover this distinguished brother in his kitchen, Mazaev invited Riaboshapka into his own room and asked why he had not identified himself immediately? Riaboshapka answered, "I knew that you would receive me as a brother, nay, as Riaboshapka, but I felt like finding out how you receive simple strangers, and now I know that

---

1. "Stundist" is usually used as an uncomplimentary term dating from the mid-nineteenth century referring to a Russian or Ukrainian peasant who, like a German-speaking Pietist, attends a *Bibelstunde* (Bible hour) or *Gebetstunde* (prayer hour) apart from regular worship services.

2. I. G. Riaboshapka is remembered to this day as the founder of numerous Baptist congregations in Ukraine. For sketches of his life, see M. S. Karetnikova, "Russkoe bogoiskatel'stvo" (The Russian God-search), 72–78, and A. V. Karev, "Russkoe evangel'sko-baptistskoe dvizhenie" (The Russian Evangelical-Baptist movement), 100–101 in Karetnikova, *Al'manakh, vypusk 1*; "Ivan Grigor'evich Riaboshapka," http://www.blagovestnik.org/bible/people/p0021.htm.

according to the commandment of Christ you kindly receive all strangers, not only your own people."³

It is worth mentioning that there are other stories still in circulation about Riaboshapka's travels in which the wise peasant-preacher confronts various people with scriptural truth, including Orthodox hierarchs and even the tsar.⁴ Whether such stories are based in fact or not, they serve the purpose of pointing up the power and sufficiency of the Bible, even in the hands of a simple interpreter. In this case, Riaboshapka's gentle test of Mazaev's hospitality was obviously based on the parable of the sheep and the goats in Matthew 25:31–46. Jesus promised that whoever welcomes strangers, cares for those in need, or comforts the sick or prisoners, is, in fact, serving Jesus himself: "whatever you did for one of the least of these brothers of mine, you did for me" (Matthew 25:40). Yet, assuming that this story reflects an actual encounter, a question remains. Why would Riaboshapka take it upon himself to verify Mazaev's hospitality in particular? If it is true that the first meeting between the two men actually took place in Mazaev's home, a likely window for that event would be sometime between Mazaev's baptism in December 1885⁵ and December 1886 when he became president of the missionary-sending group that formed the nucleus of what later was known as the Russian Baptist Union.⁶ The missions group was organized in May 1884 and about two years later its president, Johannes (Ivan) Wieler (1839–1889), was forced to flee Russia.⁷ In a very short time Mazaev had gained sufficient recognition among his fellow believers to move into the empty leadership position. Perhaps at least part of that swift recognition depended on the approval of Riaboshapka in his informal capacity as a Baptist elder statesman. Did he decide to call on Mazaev to see whether such a recent convert was capable of managing the delicate and dangerous position of missions committee president? As it turned out, he was: Mazaev served in that capacity from 1886 to 1920, except for a brief interval from 1909 to 1911.

---

3. N. I. Levindanto, "Pamiati Deia Ivanovicha Mazaeva" (In memory of Dei Ivanovich Mazaev), *Bratskii vestnik,* Nos. 2–3 (1953) 98.

4. For example, on 9 November 2012 several such Riaboshapka stories were related to a group of students from Odessa Theological Seminary by Pavel Shapoval, Senior Presbyter of the Baptist church in Pomoshchnaia, Kirovograd oblast; Ukraine.

5. Levindanto, "Pamiati Deia Ivanovicha Mazaeva," 95; Gavriil Ivanovich Mazaev (Dei Ivanovich's brother) gives the date as 1884, but this may be a typographical error ("Vospominaniia," [Recollections], 24).

6. Demchenko, "Missionerskoe sluzhenie," 2; Levindanto gives 1887 as the year when Mazaev became president of the Baptist Union ("Pamiati Deia Ivanovicha Mazaeva," 95).

7. Sawatsky, *Soviet Evangelicals,* 44.

However, besides wanting to be sure of the scriptural obedience of the potential leader, Riaboshapka's interest in Mazaev's reception of a stranger also suggests a key element of the Russian evangelicals' spirituality and understanding of mission. Simply put, from the early days of their movement the Russian evangelicals believed that they were required to care for people both within and outside of their own circle, according to the example of Christ. Certainly they are better known for their energetic verbal witness. Their consistent support of numerous evangelistic preachers and the effort they devoted to producing and distributing Christian literature[8] indicate that they were deeply committed to spreading the word of salvation by faith. However, compassionate ministry was always an integral part of the overall picture. Indeed, it may even be said that the evangelicals tended to regard preaching itself as an act of compassion because they had such high expectations of the effect of the gospel on every aspect of people's lives. Evidently, Riaboshapka wanted to be sure that Mazaev shared a concern for the welfare even of strangers who crossed his path.

It is remarkable that Riaboshapka did not test other aspects of Mazaev's belief. Like many of the early Baptist leaders, Mazaev came from a Molokan background, one of Russia's numerous indigenous sects. The Molokans rejected the sacraments, but held a high view of Scripture. The key to their conversion, therefore, was to convince them of the importance of baptism according to the Bible.[9] Yet Riaboshapka did not inquire about Mazaev's views on baptism, or any other points of doctrine or church practice. Instead, he wanted to know how Mazaev treated strangers. Furthermore, although they could be very generous to those outside their own community,[10] the Molokans were especially noted for the thoroughness with which they practiced mutual aid amongst themselves.[11] Perhaps it was important to Riaboshapka to find out whether Mazaev had left his Molokan sensibilities behind and embraced the Russian evangelicals' concern for all people.

Thus, the story of Riaboshapka's visit to Mazaev suggests that compassionate ministry was important to Russian evangelicals from an early date.

---

8. Descriptions of the evangelicals' many evangelistic activities are given in Sinichkin, *Vse radi missii*; see also Sawatsky, *Soviet Evangelicals*, 39–42.

9. Sawatsky, *Soviet Evangelicals*, 32. For detailed accounts of Molokan beliefs see Bonch-Bruevich, *Materialy k istorii i izucheniu russkogo sektanstva i raskola*; Klibanov, *Istoriia religioznogo sektanstva v Rossii*; Breyfogle, *Heretics and Colonizers*.

10. Fedot Petrovich Kostromin, *Baptist* 4 (15 February 1909) 22–23; Prokhanoff, *Cauldron*, 34.

11. S. Atav, *Otechestvennye zapiski* (Native sketches) No. 4 (1870) 621–23, quoted by Conybeare, *Russian Dissenters*, 315; Shubin, *A History of Russian Christianity, Vol. III*, 138–39.

Moreover, it continued to be an evangelical emphasis throughout the history of their movement. It must always be kept in mind that many limitations were imposed on the Russian evangelicals by the wider society, whether imperial or Soviet. This was especially true during the tenure of Konstantin Petrovich Pobedonostsev (1827–1907) as Ober-prokuror (Director General) of the Most Holy Synod from 1880 to 1905, when laws were enacted to curb the activities of evangelicals and many of their leaders suffered exile or imprisonment.[12] Although for a time in the early years of Soviet rule they enjoyed improvements in their situation to the extent that they were regarded as something like allies who had suffered during the tsarist regime and even as potential revolutionary material, the evangelicals were never free from government harassment.[13] Yet in spite of constant setbacks, the Russian evangelicals maintained definite ideas about how to "go about doing good" (Acts 10:38) and realized them quite consistently, although never on a large scale because of their ambiguous status as a so-called sectarian group. Even between 1905 and 1929, sometimes called the "Golden Age" of Russian evangelical activity and growth,[14] believers experienced the push-pull effect of intermittent periods of relative freedom and restriction, yet their basic commitment to compassionate ministry—expressed in a variety of undertakings—remained constant. It was not until the Soviet law "On religious associations" was put into effect on 8 April 1929 that all aspects of religious life beyond worship in a registered congregation were brought to a close.[15]

This important aspect of Russian evangelical life has been mentioned only in passing by previous studies. Detailed attention has been given to the complex development of the movement as a whole,[16] the evangelicals' relationship to the state,[17] their emphasis on evangelistic preaching, literature publication and distribution,[18] and their role as a modernizing element in

---

12. For the texts of legislation concerning Russian sectarians during the late nineteenth century, see Iasevich-Borodaevskaia, *Bor'ba za veru*.

13. Sawatsky, *Soviet Evangelicals*, 37–39.

14. See, for example, Constantine Prokhorov, "The 'Golden Age' of the Soviet Baptists in the 1920s," in Corrado and Pilli, eds., *Eastern European Baptist History: New Perspectives*, 88–101.

15. Sawatsky, *Soviet Evangelicals*, 46; Coleman, *Russian Baptists*, 217.

16 Steeves, "The Russian Baptist Union"; Sawatsky, *Soviet Evangelicals*; Savinskii, *Istoriia russko-ukrainskogo baptizma*; Puzynin, *The Tradition of the Gospel Christians*.

17. Blane, "Relations between the Russian Protestant Sects and the State"; Reshetnikov, *Ukrainskie baptisty i rossiiskaia imperiia*; Nikol'skaia, *Russkii protestantizm*.

18 Sinichkin, *Vse radi missii*.

Russian society.[19] However, thus far no attempt has been made to present a history of their practice of compassionate ministry. Besides verbal witness, what did the Russian evangelicals actually do to fulfill Christ's command to help people in need? How does a persecuted minority go about serving others? What did they teach their own members about this aspect of Christian mission? What were their main models? How did the tumultuous events of the early twentieth century in Russia affect their compassionate ministry? Finally, what does the practice of compassionate ministry tell us about Russian evangelical identity? The purpose of this research is to reconstruct a coherent narrative of Russian evangelical compassionate ministry between 1905 and 1929 and to analyze what such activity reveals about the movement in general.

HISTORICAL BACKGROUND AND MOTIVATION FOR RESEARCH

It is well known that no religious groups in the Soviet Union were officially permitted to do such things as care for the sick in hospitals, visit prisoners, or help orphans, because social welfare was understood to be the responsibility of the state. More concerned with matters of survival in an officially atheistic society, the legacy of Christian compassionate ministry seemed to have been forgotten by the churches during the Soviet period. What is more, since presumably there was no need for private charities in the Soviet Union, it was generally assumed that the impulse to engage in such activities had disappeared as well. However, one of the surprises of the late 1980s and early 1990s was the reappearance of charitable organizations in the USSR, which historian Adele Lindenmeyr has likened to the blooming of flowers thought to be extinct on the prairies of the American Midwest.[20] That is, something regarded as long gone reappeared unexpectedly. In fact, the contrast between the assumption that Soviet society had transcended the need for charitable organizations altogether and their sudden resurgence was so great, that attempts had to be made to justify their existence on ideological grounds.[21] In the late 1980s the churches, too, recovered their call to compassionate ministry. In April 1988, the year when one thousand years of Christianity were celebrated in the Soviet Union, President Mikhail Gorbachev met with several Orthodox Church representatives at the Kremlin.

---

19. Coleman, *Russian Baptists*.
20. Lindenmeyr, *Poverty is Not a Vice*, 3.
21. Such an attempt was made by Tretyakov, *Philanthropy in Soviet Society*.

Significantly, the church leaders requested the freedom to engage once again in compassionate ministry.[22]

During the late 1980s one of the important words in circulation in the Soviet Union along with *glasnost'* ("openness") and *perestroika* (reconstruction) was the word *miloserdie*, usually translated in English as "mercy," or "compassion." *Miloserdie* describes a certain quality of the human heart, a gracious attitude of kindness and pity capable of expressing itself in positive acts of service. It is a quality that many people felt was missing from Soviet society and that was needed desperately. *Miloserdie* was discussed in conversations and newspaper articles as a delicate principle of human life that had been shunted aside and then lost in the turmoil and callousness of Soviet history. At a worship service dedicated to compassionate ministry at the Central Baptist Church in Moscow in 1988, V. N. Kozyrev, head doctor of the Kashchenko Psychiatric Hospital in that city commented, "Out of the cobwebs of oblivion, words full of human warmth have surfaced: Love, Compassion [*miloserdie*], Kindness—and we have begun to measure our lives accordingly."[23] In fact, the word *miloserdie* had been officially banned in 1920 as the title of nursing sisters (sisters of mercy) and was obliterated from the names of educational and medical institutions as well.[24] Its sister concept, charity (*blagotvoritel'nost',* or "creating good") literally disappeared from the dictionary during the Soviet period.[25]

However, since the 1980s the practice and understanding of Christian *miloserdie* has rapidly regained ground in the former Soviet Union. It is the all-encompassing term currently applied in the Russian language to a wide range of activities, from simple almsgiving, to the support of social service institutions, to monastic orders that care for people in need. A website of the Russian Orthodox Church-Moscow Patriarchate, www.miloserdie.ru, offers information on thousands of charitable projects and voluntary service opportunities around the Russian Federation, besides historical sketches and reflective articles on such topics as terminal illness, drug addiction, and homelessness. What is more, great efforts have been made to recover the history of *miloserdie* in the Russian Empire. The Museum of Entrepreneurs, Patrons, and Charitable Workers in Moscow was founded to memorialize the life of the city's merchant class, repressed in Soviet times, and its active

---

22 Davis, *A Long Walk to Church*, 64–65.

23. Viktoria Mazharova, "Byl bolen, i vy posetili Menia," (I was sick and you visited Me), *Bratskii vestnik* 6 (1988) 70.

24. "Miloserdie—popovskoe slovo" (Compassion is a priestly word), http://www.miloserdie.ru/in.php?ss=2&s=12&id=13302.

25. Ivanova and Ivanova, *Zarubezhnyi opyt*, 14; see also Tretyakov, *Philanthropy in Soviet Society*, 5–10.

sponsorship of charity and the arts.[26] Interest has been renewed in the lives of once-famous innovators in the area of social reform. In the village of Vozdvizhenskoe, in northeastern Ukraine, on the second floor of a school building, a roomful of photos and artifacts has been collected relating to the life of Nikolai Nikolaievich Nepliuev (1851–1908), a nobleman who gave away his estate to create a "workers' brotherhood" (*trudovoe bratstvo*).[27] Extensive information sources on compassionate ministry have also been collected. The on-line *Entsiklopediia blagotvoritel'nosti Sankt-Peterburga* (Encyclopedia of St. Petersburg charity)[28] details the hundreds of organizations and services that existed in the capital especially during the second half of the nineteenth century. These are only three instances of many more lost legacies that are presently being pieced together in the former Soviet Union.

Yet, although much has already been done to restore and publicize information about compassionate ministries, it must be noted that most of that effort has been related to the mainstream Orthodox tradition. Less attention has been given to searching out the contributions of other groups, including Russian evangelicals, and to placing them in the broader Russian context. Recently Heather J. Coleman has examined the social implications of the Russian evangelical movement in *Russian Baptists and Spiritual Revolution, 1905–1929*. However, although Coleman acknowledges the practice of compassionate ministry among the evangelicals, its details are beyond the scope of her work. Meanwhile, Adele Lindenmeyr has analyzed the role of charitable organizations in Russia (*Poverty is not a Vice: Charity, Society, and the State in Imperial Russia*), but also has not described the activities of evangelicals. Since the collapse of the Soviet Union, the study of previously unavailable archival materials has led to important research that presents much new information about sectarian life in Imperial Russia and the Soviet Union, such as O. Iu. Redkina, *Sel'skokhoziaistvennye religioznye trudovye kollektivy v 1917-i-1930-e gody na materialakh evropeiskoi chasti RSFSR* (Agricultural religious labor collectives from 1917 to the 1930s, based on materials from the European part of the RSFSR) and Nicholas B. Breyfogle, *Heretics and Colonizers: Forging Russia's Empire in the South Caucasus*, but compassionate ministry has only been mentioned in passing. Likewise, recent political and social changes and rekindled interest in the role of religion have made it possible for historians to produce valuable

26. *Muzei predprinimatelei, metsenatov i blagotvoritelei* is located near the Oktiabrskaia Metro station, 119049 Moscow, ul. Donskaia, d. 9.

27. A brief summary of Nepliuev's contribution is given by Avdasev, *Trudovoe bratstvo N. N. Nepliueva*.

28 See http://encblago.lfond.spb.ru

regional histories of the evangelical movement in recent years, including Viktor Dik, *Svet Evangeliia v Kazakhstane, Istoriia vozveshcheniia Evangeliia i rasprostraneniia obshchin baptistov i mennonitov v Kazakhstane (pervaia polovina XX veka)* (The light of the Gospel in Kazakhstan, The history of the proclamation of the Gospel and the spread of Baptist and Mennonite congregations in Kazakhstan [first half of the twentieth century]) and Ivan Shnaider, *Evangel'skie obshchiny v Aktiubinskoi stepi, Sto let pervoi obshchine baptistov v Aktiubinske* (Evangelical congregations in the Aktiubinsk steppes, On the one-hundredth anniversary of the first Baptist congregation in Aktiubinsk). However, in these works as well, compassion is afforded only a few lines. Thus, compassionate outreach among evangelicals remains a subject that is relatively untouched.

Certainly one reason for the gap is that the evangelicals were simply better known for their preaching and publishing activity rather than for compassionate ministry as such. Their interest in encouraging people to read the Bible, repent, and be converted was what most clearly distinguished them from the Orthodox mainstream understanding of Christian living, which generally tended to emphasize traditional religious observance. In addition, their contribution was comparatively small, owing to their minority status and the restrictions they faced. In fact, it is possible that the restrictions against them have not yet completely ended. There is some evidence that evangelicals may have been intentionally excluded from at least one collection of historical information on compassion. The Pashkovite movement, which took its name from Colonel Vasilii Alekseevich Pashkov (1831–1902), a St. Petersburg aristocrat who responded to the evangelistic preaching of William Granville Waldegrave, Lord Radstock (1833–1913), had a well-founded reputation for compassionate ministry.[29] Yet the current on-line *Encyclopedia of St. Petersburg Charity* does not mention Pashkov. Nor does it mention Iuliia Denisovna Zasetskaia (d. 1883), who organized what is purported to be the first night shelter in the capital in 1873. She became a Radstockist-Pashkovite and eventually left Russia.[30] On the other hand, the *Encyclopedia* includes an article on Maria Mikhailovna Dondukova-Korsakova (1827–1909), the founder of an order of sisters of mercy who devoted herself to prison ministries. Although she was part of the Radstockist-Pashkovite circle beginning in 1876, she returned to Orthodoxy later on.[31] Perhaps that is one of the reasons Dondukova-Korsakova is included

29 See Heier, *Religious Schism;* Corrado, "Colonel Vasiliy Pashkov"; McCarthy, "Religious Conflict."

30. The writer Nikolai Leskov identified Zasetskaia as the founder of the first night shelter, quoted by McCarthy, "Religious Conflict," 131–33.

31. D. Severiukhin, "Dondukova-Korsakova Mariia Mikhailovna, Kniazhna."

in a comprehensive list of compassionate ministries in St. Petersburg while Zasetskaia is not. Be that as it may, documenting the compassionate activity of a religious minority will help to present a fuller and therefore more realistic picture of Russian social life during the late nineteenth and early twentieth centuries.

The gap in information about evangelical compassionate ministry does not only exist in the wider society. Present-day evangelicals remain largely unaware of this aspect of their own history. Like the Orthodox, evangelicals have also engaged in numerous and creative compassionate ministries since the collapse of the Soviet Union. Almost as soon as it was permitted in 1988, a group of volunteers from the Central Baptist Church in Moscow began to do supplementary care among geriatric patients at Kashchenko Psychiatric Hospital.[32] Numerous similar undertakings quickly followed in many places throughout the country. On 22 and 23 January 1989, the Baptist church in Syktyvkar (Komi, ASSR) held concerts of classical and contemporary Christian music to benefit victims of the 1988 earthquake in Armenia.[33] Also in 1989, Baptists in Zaporizhzhia (Ukraine) provided materials and labor to repair and redecorate the *dom maliutki* (home for children up to the age of three) in their city. At a celebration held in August 1989 commemorating the two-hundredth anniversary of Mennonite settlement in that area, an offering of 7,260 rubles was collected to benefit the home.[34] Prison and hospital visitation became common activities. During the 1990s children's homes, rehabilitation centers for alcoholics and drug addicts, and halfway houses for former prisoners were started up by evangelicals.[35] Inevitably the initial enthusiasm of the 1990s has waned and especially since the economic downturn of 2008 it has been considerably more difficult to maintain the institutions that were founded by evangelicals a decade earlier. Nevertheless, to the present day it is quite common for churches and other evangelical organizations to assist government-run children's homes, counsel AIDS patients, or provide home care services for the elderly in their neighborhoods. I have frequently heard evangelical Christians thank God for compassionate ministries saying, "We were never before allowed to do this," meaning

---

32. Vera Kadaeva, "Seminar molodykh sluzhitelei rossiiskoi federatsii," (Seminar of young ministers of the Russian Federation), *Bratskii vestnik* 6 (1988) 58.

33. S. V. Nikolaev, "Po dorogam severnogo kraia," (Along the roads of the northern region), *Bratskii vestnik* 3 (1989) 77.

34. "Iz zhizni pomestnykh tserkvei," (From the life of local churches), *Bratskii vestnik*, 6 (1989) 86.

35. I became aware of many of these ministries and was directly involved with some of them through my work as a volunteer with Mennonite Central Committee, based mostly in Ukraine, from 1993 to 2007.

during Soviet times. That statement is correct; however, their more distant antecedents remain largely unknown.

It has sometimes been assumed that because of persecution evangelicals were prevented from engaging in any compassionate ministry at all. The main exception is the Pashkovite movement, whose compassionate activity is familiar to Russian evangelicals, especially since the publication of Russian-language historical materials, such as the second volume of Karetnikova's *Al'manakh* series of articles and primary sources (2001) and especially her translation of Sharyl Corrado's Master's thesis, "The Philosophy of Ministry of Colonel Vasiliy Pashkov" (2000). In a later article Corrado has pointed out that Pashkovite compassionate ministry continued beyond Pashkov's exile in 1884[36]; nevertheless, in this aspect of their movement the Pashkovites have been treated as something of an isolated phenomenon. The history of compassionate ministry among Russian evangelicals after the height of the Pashkovite movement has not yet been described in detail, especially the vigorous 1905 to 1929 era. This twenty-four year period between the time when religious toleration was first declared until it was completely revoked, encompassed war, revolution, and famine—all factors that affected compassionate ministry. In addition, the contribution of other historical strands with bearing on the evangelicals, especially the Molokans, has not been considered, although the Molokan emphasis on mutual support is part of the background of the establishment of evangelical institutions such as charitable funds and homes for orphans and the elderly. Filling in these gaps concerning the history of the evangelical movement is potentially helpful to the current generation of believers as they seek to contribute to the needs of present-day society.

LIMITATION OF RESEARCH

The title of this study is *Ministries of Compassion among Russian Evangelicals, 1905 to 1929*. Those years have been chosen as the focus, following the lead of Heather J. Coleman (*Russian Baptists and Spiritual Revolution, 1905–1929*), because of two pieces of legislation. Emperor Nicholas II's decree of 17 April 1905, "On the strengthening of the beginnings of religious toleration," broadly speaking, initiated a new era that lasted until the Soviet law "On religious associations" brought it to a close on 8 April 1929. That law forbade religious groups to engage in any activity except for worship

---

36. Corrado, "The Gospel in Society: Pashkovite Social Outreach in Late Imperial Russia," in Corrado and Pilli, eds., *Eastern European Baptist History: New Perspectives*, 68.

conducted by legally registered congregations. It should be noted that the transition was not necessarily abrupt in those areas more distant from European Russia where Soviet power took longer to consolidate. Nevertheless, in general terms, the dates 1905 to 1929 effectively bracket the single longest continuous period of relative freedom for Russian evangelicals—and consequently the time of greatest concentrated activity for them—until the breakup of the Soviet Union more than sixty years later.

The term "compassion" is meant to translate the Russian word *miloserdie*, which encompasses a wide range of activities intended to relieve human suffering without regard for any kind of compensation. I have generally avoided using the term "charity," because of its association with charitable organizations, with which Russian evangelicals (except for many of the Pashkovites) had relatively little involvement. Likewise, the terms "social service" or "social ministry" are little used because they suggest professional status and even bureaucracy that were not characteristic of Russian evangelical compassion.

Meanwhile, the word "Russian," as applied to evangelical believers in this research, does not strictly distinguish an ethnic or linguistic group, but for the sake of convenience is used more broadly to include all the people, regardless of nationality, who identified themselves with the evangelical movement within the geographical boundaries of the Russian Empire and the Soviet Union. Thus, although William A. Fetler (1883–1957), whose urban rescue mission activities are described in chapter 4, was a Latvian by birth, he is here treated as "Russian," both because he was a subject of the Russian Empire and because he was one of the leading pastors in the Russian Baptist Union. Conversely, although worthy of detailed treatment, the compassionate activity of the Mennonites and other non-Orthodox ethnic/religious groups such as the German Baptists are not included here because collectively and organizationally they did not necessarily identify themselves with the Russian movement. True, these groups were part of the Russian Empire and the Soviet Union and certain individuals from among them even gave important leadership to the Russian evangelical movement at crucial points.[37] However, during the period under consideration for the most part the Mennonites, in particular, remained separate. As settlers who came to Russia in the late eighteenth century at the invitation of Empress Catherine II (ruled 1762–1796), the Mennonites were granted special rights and

---

37. Johann Wieler, Hermann Fast (1860–1935), and J. J. Dyck (Iakov Dik, 1890–1919) are three examples mentioned in this study. Note also that German Baptists and Mennonite Brethren took active part in the meeting that is regarded as the founding of the Russian Baptist Union at Novo-Vasil'evka in May 1884 (see Nichols, *Russian Evangelical Spirituality*, 124–30).

lived in colonies apart from the Russian masses. They spoke German rather than Russian, and maintained their own church life, schools, hospitals, and other charitable institutions,[38] which are well documented.[39] However, the experience of the Mennonites is cited at several points when it overlaps with that of the Russian evangelicals. Also, the compassionate ministry of Pentecostals is not included because of the relatively late date of their appearance in Soviet Russia (1921).

The term "evangelical" contains many layers of meaning[40] and especially requires a more detailed explanation in the Russian context. In this study, "evangelical" (with a small "e") translates the word *evangel'skii* and is intended to encompass more than a single group or denomination.[41] Here it will refer to Christian communities consisting of people from a number of different religious backgrounds that took shape in the mid-nineteenth century almost simultaneously in at least three major locations—South Russia (Ukraine), the Caucasus, and St. Petersburg. Representing social classes ranging from the peasantry to the aristocracy, and inspired by the availability of the Russian New Testament (1862) and German Pietist and English evangelical preaching,[42] they began to gather in small groups outside of regular worship services to read the Bible and pray together. David W. Bebbington's well-known list of evangelical emphases—conversion, the cross, the Bible, and activism[43]—usefully underlines the main characteristics that distinguished them from their neighbors in the state-recognized churches, especially the Russian Orthodox Church. Chiefly through Bible study, Russian evangelicals began to question the teachings of what they had come to regard as a lifeless Orthodox Church that only retained the outward semblance of Christianity.[44] In contrast, they taught that individuals should seek direct contact with God, repent of their sin, and convert to a

38. C. K., "Russia," in *The Mennonite Encyclopedia*, Vol. IV, 381–392; see also Leland D. Harder, "Acculturation," *GAMEO* 1990 (http://gameo.org/index.php?title=Acculturation&oldid=90715).

39. See, for example, the numerous articles in the *Global Anabaptist-Mennonite Encyclopedia On-Line*, www.gameo.org.

40. A detailed study of the complexities of the term "evangelical" is given in Hutchinson and Wolffe, *A Short History of Global Evangelicalism*, 1–24.

41 Cf. Sawatsky, *Soviet Evangelicals*, 18. Coleman, on the other hand, has identified the entire Russian evangelical movement as "Baptist," which does not seem sufficiently inclusive. Note that the Russian word *evangelicheskii* is also translated as "evangelical," but refers to specific Christian confessions within Russia, such as the Evangelical Lutheran Church.

42. Sawatsky, *Soviet Evangelicals*, 30–35.

43. Bebbington, *Evangelicalism in Modern Britain*, 2–17

44 Sawatsky, *Soviet Evangelicals*, 30–31; Heier, *Religious Schism*, 36–37.

holy life—all made possible through the death of Jesus Christ on the cross. Their new status as forgiven children of God led to endeavors to spread the message further, through preaching and good works.[45]

Their status in Russia was ambiguous. At first, many of them retained their original religious affiliation, which might be Orthodox, Lutheran, Molokan, or something else. The formation of a separate community took time. However, their growing presence presented a challenge both to church and state in Russia because, "[The evangelicals] . . . were Russians who had chosen what was perceived as a non-Russian path."[46] In Ukraine they were usually labeled Stundists; many of them could be considered "Baptist" in that they accepted baptism by immersion through contact with Mennonite Brethren, who were themselves influenced by Johann Gerhard Oncken.[47] Others, chiefly in St. Petersburg, referred to themselves simply as "believers," or as evangelical (*evangel'skie*) Christians,[48] sometimes translated "Gospel Christians."[49] Those in the Caucasus had historical ties to European Baptists and identified themselves as such.[50] Thus, the 1884 conference considered the beginning of the Russian Baptist Union was formally titled, "The Russian Conference of the Union of Believers, Baptized Christians, or as they are called, Baptists, of South Russia and the Caucasus,"[51] acknowledging the rather different identities of these groups. As the movement grew, however, and especially as these like-minded Christians began to come into closer contact with one another, it became more important that they share a common name. However, issues of baptism, closed or open communion, ordination, and personality conflicts continued to divide them. In general, the Baptists were more concerned with establishing a recognizable denomination. They refused communion to any who had not been baptized on profession of faith and taught that the elements must be administered by an ordained presbyter. Other evangelicals were less concerned with the

45. Nichols has demonstrated each of Bebbington's emphases in the life of Ivan Kargel, the most influential Russian evangelical theologian during the period under consideration (*Russian Evangelical Spirituality*, 8–9).

46. Coleman, *Russian Baptists*, 3.

47. Sawatsky, *Soviet Evangelicals*, 33–34.

48. Heier, *Religious Schism*, 54.

49. See Puzynin, *The Tradition of the Gospel Christians*.

50. In 1867 Martin Kalweit (1833–1918), a newly-baptized German from the Baltics, baptized the Molokan Nikita Isaevich Voronin (1840–1905) near Tiflis (present-day Tbilisi) and a consciously Baptist congregation developed there. One of the earliest leaders in Tiflis, Vasilii Gur'evich Pavlov (1854–1924), was ordained as a missionary to Russia in 1876 by the "Father of Continental Baptism," Johann Gerhard Oncken (1800–1884) after a year of theological studies in Hamburg.

51. Nichols, *Russian Evangelical Spirituality*, 124.

formalities of clerical office; they wished to downplay differences and keep the movement open to all Christians sympathetic to evangelical emphases.[52] Some objected to the name "Baptist" on principle as foreign, and un-Russian.[53] Thus, the formal name and doctrinal distinctives of the evangelicals remained rather fluid until the legislation of 1905 and 1906 made it possible for non-Orthodox Russian confessions to be registered. In 1907 Ivan Stepanovich Prokhanov (1869–1935), who had a keen interest in building a broadly inclusive evangelical movement, led the way in gathering various groups together at a meeting in St. Petersburg to prepare a joint declaration to the government. However, the effort failed when the Baptist delegation, led by D. I. Mazaev, refused to acknowledge that children could be considered part of their parents' confession.[54] In 1908 Prokhanov organized the Russian Evangelical Union, intended to bring like-minded individuals together in a body that would be a counterpart to the Evangelical Alliance.[55] Then, in 1909 he registered the All-Russian Evangelical Christian Union (or simply Evangelical Christian Union), a church union which, although baptistic in doctrine, served as an umbrella organization for congregations that, for whatever reason, were not inclined to identify themselves exclusively as Baptist.[56] Prokhanov's critics accused him of wishing to dominate the entire movement by taking these administrative steps.[57] The same charge could be leveled against the staunchly Baptist Dei Mazaev.[58]

Be that as it may, in this research when the name Evangelical Christian appears (capital "E," capital "C") it refers specifically to individuals and institutions connected with that church union. It should be kept in mind that for most of the period under examination (1905 to 1929), broadly speaking, the evangelicals were represented by two alternately cooperating and competing unions: the Russian Baptist Union (formally called the Russian Union of Evangelical Christians-Baptists since 1903) and the Evangelical Christian Union. Several attempts were made to bring them together, notably in 1920,

---

52. Sawatsky, *Soviet Evangelicals*, 78–84.

53. Coleman, *Russian Baptists*, 44–45.

54. Sawatsky, *Soviet Evangelicals*, 78–79.

55. Prokhanoff, *Cauldron*, 149–52; for more analysis of the Evangelical Union in Russia, see Kahle, *Evangel'skie khristiane v Rossii i Sovetskom soiuze*, 102–6.

56. Nichols, *Russian Evangelical Spirituality*, 174–75, 178–79.

57. Coleman, *Russian Baptists*, 45; for a sharply polemical account of the differences between Baptists and Evangelical Christians from a slightly later Baptist point of view (1921), see N. I. Peisti and R. A. Fetler, "Raznitsa mezhdu Baptistami i tak nazyvaemymi 'Evangel'skimi Khristianami'" (The difference between Baptists and the so-called "Evangelical Christians"), *Blagovestnik*, Nos. 3–4 (1921) 47–49.

58. Sawatsky, *Soviet Evangelicals*, 78–79.

but organizational unity eluded these two bodies until 1944 when they were brought together by the Soviet state to form the All-Union Council of Evangelical Christians-Baptists (AUCEC-B).[59]

STRUCTURE

The structure of the research is as follows: *Chapter 1* presents the pre-1905 period, especially the experience of the Pashkovites in the context of compassionate ministry as it was practiced in late nineteenth century Russia. *Chapter 2* gives a brief overview of the development of the evangelical movement with reference to compassionate ministry and describes the three broad patterns of compassionate ministry that may be distinguished during the period 1905 to 1929. Each one is identified with certain evangelical leaders whose biographies shed some light on the different emphases they represent. The first area of service is aid shared among the evangelicals themselves, which was of particular concern to D. I. Mazaev, Vasilii Gur'evich Pavlov, and Vasilii Vasilievich Ivanov (1848–1919) who put much effort into maintaining dedicated funds for the relief and support of evangelical believers in need, particularly preachers and their families, and taught on money and giving through numerous articles especially in the journal *Baptist* (The Baptist). Church-based institutions for the support of orphans and the elderly also belong to this category. The second main emphasis of compassionate ministry strove to serve the urban poor. This type of ministry was characteristic of W. A. Fetler, who was educated at Pastors' College in London and inspired by the Welsh Revival and the work of the Salvation Army. The third major area of compassionate ministry was the formation of economic communities and labor cooperatives in the years immediately following the Bolshevik Revolution (1917). The long-term goal of such communities was to eliminate poverty altogether. The most energetic and consistent supporter of such communities among the evangelical leaders was I. S. Prokhanov. Although these three areas of emphasis are quite different from one another, they are all undergirded by the same set of convictions concerning compassionate ministry, which are also outlined in chapter 2. *Chapter 3* discusses aid within the evangelical community. Background is given on the mutual support practiced before 1905, especially with reference to the Molokan roots of many of the evangelical leaders. The history of dedicated church funds and church-based institutions is also

---

59. For more details on unity issues and the formation of the AUCEC-B, see Sawatsky, *Soviet Evangelicals*, 78–99; and especially Steeves, "The Russian Baptist Union."

given. *Chapter 4* has to do with evangelical service among the urban poor in the form of rescue ministry, the relationship between the Salvation Army and the Russian evangelicals, and the latter's involvement in the temperance movement. *Chapter 5* outlines the changes that took place in compassionate ministry during the period from 1914 to 1923, which encompassed World War I, the Bolshevik Revolution, the Civil War, and the famine of 1921 to 1923. During this time evangelicals confronted unprecedented disasters in ways that were consistent with their convictions. *Chapter 6* describes the efforts of evangelicals to respond to the state's invitation to establish agricultural communes. They regarded these communities as instruments to obliterate poverty and demonstrate Christian ideals of thrift, industry, and service that would ultimately transform all of society. *Chapter 7* draws conclusions concerning the identity and legacy of the Russian evangelical movement based on their compassionate ministry.

SOURCES

Because of the social turmoil of the period studied, the marginalized status of evangelicals in both imperial and Soviet times, and also because of the Soviet state's intention to destroy all religious life, sources for this research, while sufficiently plentiful, are also scattered and fragmentary. Paradoxically, some primary sources are more extensive and easily accessible in the United States than in the countries of the former Soviet Union, especially the many evangelical publications of the period that provided the richest source of information for this study. The journal *Khristianin* (The Christian) first appeared in 1906 under the editorship of I. S. Prokhanov. *Bratskii listok* (Fraternal leaflet, 1906) and *Molodoi vinogradnik* (The young vineyard, 1908) were soon added as its supplements. *Khristianin* was quickly followed by *Baptist* (1907), first edited by D. I. Mazaev, and later by V. G. Pavlov and V. V. Ivanov, and *Gost'* (The visitor, 1910), overseen by W. A. Fetler. Later Prokhanov added *Utrenniaia zvezda* (Morning star, 1910) and V. G. Pavlov introduced *Slovo istiny* (Word of truth, 1913). In short, the Russian evangelicals were prolific writers and publishers. Besides theological articles, sermons, and translations of the same by Western authors, these publications printed news items and letters sent in by readers all across the Russian empire and the Soviet Union. In addition, the publications circulated the regular reports of church-supported missionary-evangelists and detailed accounts of union congresses. Often such letters and reports contained references to compassionate ministry as it was practiced across the country. In addition, records of contributions to church union funds were printed in the journals. The gleaning of this material served as the main resource for the reconstruction of the history of compassionate ministry among Russian evangelicals from 1905 to 1929, as well as a summary of their teaching on the subject. Most of the contemporary Russian evangelical journals are available on microfilm in the Slavic collection of the University of Illinois library at Champaign/Urbana. In addition, the Historical Library and Archives of the Southern Baptist Conference in Nashville, Tennessee has a great deal of correspondence, meeting minutes, and other data on microfilm about the Russian evangelicals, especially concerning the 1921 to 1923 famine—another example of information that has been largely unavailable to researchers within the former Soviet Union.

Nevertheless, the Russian evangelicals were conscious of the value of historical data concerning their movement and began to collect and publish the personal memoirs of believers who had spent time in exile at least as early as the 1910s.[60] During the Soviet period, members of the evangelical community quietly continued archival work and historical research, with manuscripts circulating in the form of *samizdat* (self-published materials). Short biographies and historical surveys also appeared during the Soviet years in the official journal of the AUCEC-B, *Bratskii vestnik* (Fraternal messenger, first issued in 1945). The archive of the AUCEC-B is now managed by the Russian Union of Evangelical Christians-Baptists in Moscow and contains many such items. During the perestroika era it became possible for the All-Union Council of Evangelical Christians-Baptists to publish the first comprehensive historical survey of the evangelical movement produced within the Soviet Union, *Istoriia Evangel'skikh khristian-baptistov v SSSR* (History of the Evangelical Christians-Baptists in the USSR, 1989). The trend continued throughout the 1990s with the publication of research by Soviet-era evangelical historians in book form, such as the survey by S. N. Savinskii, *Istoriia russko-ukrainskogo baptizma: Uchebnoe posobie* (The history of Russian-Ukrainian baptism: A textbook, 1995), and *Gerusy-Giriusy (Goris)*[61] (1996), a travelogue and collection of memoirs about evangelicals in exile in the Trans-Caucasus region during the 1890s by Iu. S. Grachev. Beginning in 1997 M. S. Karetnikova compiled and edited a series of five books containing historical articles, her own lectures, and other documents on the evangelical movement. Especially the first two volumes of her *Al'manakh po istorii russkogo baptizma* (Almanac on the history of Russian Baptism, 1997 and 2001) have added useful background to this study.

60. See *Baptist* 1 (January 1908) 20–22; 2 (February 1908) 19–23; 4 (15 February 1909) 22–23; 7 (April 1909) 6–10; 8 (April 1909) 12; 9 (May 1909) 13–17; 10 (May 1909) 6–9.

61. Goris in Armenia is the present-day name of what was once Gerusy or Giriusy.

The opening of state archives subsequent to the collapse of the Soviet Union has greatly increased the amount of historical material available to researchers and there has been an upsurge in interest in the history and role of religion in the Russian Empire and the USSR. A book of previously inaccessible archival sources, *Istoriia Evangel'sko-Baptistskogo dvizheniia v Ukraine* (The history of the Evangelical-Baptist movement in Ukraine) was compiled by S. I. Golovashchenko and published in 1998. Somewhat later, new technology made it possible for rare books and fragile *samizdat* to be shared with a wide readership. In the early 2000s the Euro-Asian Accrediting Association (E-AAA), which represents about fifty theological educational institutions mostly in the countries of the former Soviet Union, assembled five CDs of historical materials, including many previously unavailable books, manuscripts, and items from newly-opened state archives, as well as a CD of all the issues of *Bratskii vestnik*.[62] Wilhelm Kahle's biography of I. S. Prokhanov, *Evangel'skie khristiane v Rossii i Sovetskom Soiuze: Ivan Stepanovich Prokhanov (1869–1935) i put' evangel'skikh khristian i baptistov* (Evangelical Christians in Russia and the Soviet Union: Ivan Stepanovich Prokhanov [1869–1935] and the path of the Evangelical Christians and Baptists, 1978), which was translated from German to Russian during the Soviet era is an example of one such work now available on CD. An additional source for journals of the period and previously unavailable books is the historical website of the Russian Union of Evangelical Christians-Baptists (ecbarchive.org). Again, little of this information has previously been examined from the point of view of compassionate ministry.

Other primary sources that mention compassionate ministry among evangelicals in Russia from 1905 to 1929 include the memoirs of some of its practitioners who published in the West, such as Jenny E. De Mayer (*Adventures with God in Freedom and in Bond*, 1948); Sofia Liven (*Dukhovnoe probuzhdenie v Rossii*, [Spiritual revival in Russia], first published 1967); and I. S. Prokhanoff (sic) (*In the Cauldron of Russia, 1869–1933*, 1933). Nikolai Salov-Astakhov's novelized writings, such as *Judith* (first published 1941), and *Palatochnaia missiia* (The tent mission, Russian translation published 2006) set out the basic history of the Tent Mission during the Civil War. Additional information came from the contemporary accounts of foreign observers in Russia, including Chas. T. Byford (*Peasants and Prophets [Baptist Pioneers in Russia and Southeastern Europe]*, 1914); Dr. Archibald McCaig (*Wonders of Grace in Russia*, 1926); J. A. Packer (*Among the Heretics in Europe*, 1912); and W. T. Stead (*Truth about Russia*, 1888). Biographies of

---

62. *Istoriia Evangel'skogo dvizheniia v Evrazii* Nos. 1.1, 2.0, 3.0, 4.0, 5.0, *Elektronnaia khristianskaia biblioteka* (Odessa: E-AAA); *Bratskii vestnik*, *Elektronnaia khristianskaia biblioteka* (Odessa: E-AAA).

some of the Russian evangelical leaders provided more details, such as John Fetler's biography of his father, W. A. Fetler (*Sluzhenie Rossii* [Ministry to Russia], Russian translation published 1997); Robert Sloan Latimer's work on Dr. Friedrich Baedeker (*Dr. Baedeker and His Apostolic Work in Russia*, 1907); and Mrs. Edward Trotter's study of Lord Radstock (*Lord Radstock: An Interpretation and a Record*, n.d.). Two novelized biographies by Vladimir Popov published in 1996 were also used: (*Stopy blagovestnika* [Footsteps of an evangelist]) about V. G. Pavlov and (*Stranitsy zhizni* [Pages of life]) about I. S. Prokhanov.

Prior to the collapse of the Soviet Union valuable sources on the general history of the evangelical movement include Hans Brandenberg's *The Meek and the Mighty: The Emergence of the Evangelical Movement in Russia* (1977); Samuel Nesdoly's doctoral dissertation, "Evangelical Sectarianism in Russia: A Study of the Stundists, Baptists, Pashkovites, and Evangelical Christians, 1855–1917" (1971); Walter Sawatsky's *Soviet Evangelicals since World War II* (1980); and Paul D. Steeves's doctoral dissertation, "The Russian Baptist Union, 1917–1935: Evangelical Awakening in Russia" (1976). The best-known Soviet-era study of the Pashkovites is Edmund Heier, *Religious Schism in the Russian Aristocracy* (1970).

Since the 1980s, new scholarship, utilizing unexamined resources or bringing known ones together in fresh combinations, has confirmed much earlier work while also challenging certain assumptions and adding depth and texture to the study of the Russian evangelical movement. Tat'iana Nikol'skaia's excellent survey, *Russkii protestantizm i gosudarstvennaia vlast' v 1905–1991 godakh* (Russian Protestantism and state power, 1905–1991 [2009]) is based on previously unavailable archival material and was helpful in establishing the overall background of compassionate ministry for this study. Sharyl M. Corrado's Master's thesis on the Pashkovites, "The Philosophy of Ministry of Colonel Vasiliy Pashkov" (2000) brings together German-, English-, and Russian-language primary sources to present a detailed picture of the movement, including their compassionate activity. Since late-Soviet times Vladimir Popov has published numerous articles on various aspects of Russian evangelical history. He has brought to light their previously unexamined involvement with economic communities and political parties in "Sibirskaia utopia baptistov" (The Siberian utopia of the Baptists, 2010); "Evangel'skoe dvizhenie v Rossii i politicheskie partii" (The evangelical movement in Russia and political parties, 2011); and "Khristianskie kommuny I. S. Prokhanova i gorod Solntsa" (The Christian communes of I.S. Prokhanov and the city of the Sun, 2011). Albert W. Wardin Jr.'s survey, *On the Edge: Baptists and Other Free Church Evangelicals in Tsarist Russia, 1855–1917* (2013) effectively calls attention to the ties between

German Baptists and the Russian evangelicals. Andrei Puzynin's doctoral dissertation, *The Tradition of the Gospel Christians: A Study of their Identity* (2008) presents what is sometimes referred to as "Russian Baptist history"[63] with greater emphasis on the Evangelical Christians, showing the influence on them of both Orthodoxy and English evangelicalism. Gregory Nichols's book, *The Development of Russian Evangelical Spirituality: A Study of Ivan V. Kargel (1849–1937)* (2011) demonstrates the influence of Holiness teaching on the Russian evangelicals. All of these post-Soviet studies indicate that the history of the Russian evangelicals continues to be worthy of exploration.

In addition, since perestroika, scholars both within and outside of the former Soviet Union have rediscovered religion as a lens through which to view Russian and Soviet history. Again, the availability of new data has led to numerous studies. Excellent resources for understanding the broader Orthodox context within which the evangelicals lived, including Orthodox approaches to compassionate ministry, are Jennifer Hedda, *His Kingdom Come* (2008); Geoffrey A. Hosking, ed. *Church, Nation and State in Russia and Ukraine* (1991); Nadiezda Kizenko, *A Prodigal Saint: Father John of Kronstadt and the Russian People* (2003); Vera Shevzov, *Russian Orthodoxy on the Eve of Revolution* (2004); and Sergei I. Zhuk, *Russia's Lost Reformation: Peasants, Millennialism, and Radical Sects in Southern Russia and Ukraine, 1830–1917* (2004). Two recent doctoral dissertations by American scholars, Mark McCarthy, "Religious Conflict and Social Order" (2004) about the Pashkovites, and Matthew Lee Miller, "American Philanthropy among Russians: The Work of the YMCA, 1900–1940" (2006) were also consulted. Of course, the previously mentioned books by Heather J. Coleman (*Russian Baptists and Spiritual Revolution, 1905–1929*) and Adele J. Lindenmeyr (*Poverty is Not a Vice: Charity, Society, and the State in Imperial Russia*) also belong to this category. The neglected role of sectarians in Russian history is examined by Nicholas B. Breyfogle, *Heretics and Colonizers: Forging Russia's Empire in the South Caucasus*. O. Iu. Redkina explores in great detail the proliferation of religiously-based communes during the 1920s in *Sel'skokhoziaistvennye religioznye trudovye kollektivy v 1917–i–1930-e gody na materialakh evropeiskoi chasti RSFSR* (Agricultural religious labor collectives from 1917 to the 1930s, based on materials of the European part of the RSFSR [2004]).

The availability of new sources has also led to post-Soviet studies of Russian social history that are relevant to evangelical compassion, such as Tom Aitkin, *Blood and Fire, Tsar and Commissar: The Salvation Army in*

---

63. Note again that Heather J. Coleman identifies the entire Russian evangelical movement as "Baptist" (*Russian Baptists and Spiritual Revolution*).

Russia, 1907–1923 (2007); Patricia Herlihy, *The Alcoholic Empire: Vodka and Politics in Late Imperial Russia* (2002); William B. Husband, *Godless Communists: Atheism and Society in Soviet Russia, 1917–1932* (2000); Catriona Kelly, *Children's World: Growing Up in Russia, 1890–1911* (2007); Bertrand M. Patenaude, *The Big Show in Bololand: The American Relief Expedition to Soviet Russia in the Famine of 1921* (2002); Daniel Peris, *Storming the Heavens: The Soviet League of the Militant Godless* (1998); and Kate Transchel, *Under the Influence: Working-Class Drinking, Temperance, and Cultural Revolution in Russia, 1895–1932* (2006).

Finally, because of the connection between Russian and English evangelicals, especially in the matter of compassion, I also consulted sources on the history of English evangelicalism. The main historical survey is David W. Bebbington, *Evangelicalism in Modern Britain: A History from the 1730s to the 1980s. I Will Pour out My Spirit: A History and Theology of Revivals and Evangelical Awakenings* by R. E. Davies; *History of Evangelism: Three Hundred Years of Evangelism in Germany, Great Britain, and the United States of America* by Paulus Scharpf; and *Rhythms of Revival: The Spiritual Awakening of 1857–1863* by Ian M. Randall, all helped to clarify the relationship between preaching and compassion. Peter J. Morden's 'Communion with Christ and His People': *The Spirituality of C. H. Spurgeon* and Ian M. Randall's article, "'The Breath of Revival': The Welsh Revival and Spurgeon's College," were useful in understanding two of the important influences on W. A. Fetler and his rescue work in St. Petersburg. Especially relevant to the history of compassion is Kathleen Heasman, *Evangelicals in Action: An Appraisal of their Social Work in the Victorian Era*.

The present study represents something of a synthesis of the above-mentioned sources, as well as many others. It seeks to fill a gap in the study of the evangelical movement in Russia by presenting a comprehensive picture of their compassionate ministry from 1905 to 1929. From the beginning of their movement, compassionate ministry played an important part in the evangelicals' witness to society. Although it was never extensive because of their marginal status, the evangelicals nevertheless maintained a consistent intent and effort to serve people in need. They also had a lively expectation that acceptance of the gospel would introduce positive changes in people's lives that would ultimately serve to improve society as a whole. Three main patterns of activity may be discerned: aid within the evangelical community, urban rescue ministry, and the establishment of economic communities. Although each of these areas of service is quite distinct, they were all supported by the same set of theological convictions.

1

Russian Evangelical Ministries of Compassion before 1905

THIS CHAPTER WILL SKETCH the historical and cultural background of ministries of compassion in Russia during the late nineteenth and early twentieth centuries and place the evangelicals in that context. Many of the patterns for ministries of compassion among the Russian evangelicals between 1905 and 1929 were set during the second half of the nineteenth century as their movement took on a coherent shape. An organic part of their evangelistic activity from the very beginning was the practice of ministries of compassion, responding in various ways to a range of human need. The particular focus of this chapter is on Pashkovism, after Colonel Vasilii Alekseevich Pashkov, a Russian aristocrat who responded to the evangelistic preaching of William Granville Waldegrave, Lord Radstock.

The Pashkovites, many of whom were from the upper classes, were greatly inspired in compassionate ministry by Lord Radstock, who first visited St. Petersburg during the winter of 1873 to 1874. However, a number of the aristocrats were already active in the charitable work that was practiced in Russia at the time, even before they gathered around Radstock. Their work as sisters of mercy, providing medical and educational services to peasants on their own estates, or organizing sewing cooperatives for poor women, were all done according to existing patterns. It was their conversion to an evangelical approach to Christianity through Radstock and their subsequent commitment to preaching the gospel as part of their service that made their activities distinct. As Pashkov and his close associate, Count Modest Modestovich Korf (1843–1937) explained to the emperor, their greatest desire was to help people "understand the love of Christ which passes our understanding."[1] In contrast to some traditional Orthodox thinking, Radstock, Pashkov, and their followers taught that Christ's love is appropriated by faith, not by good works. Instead of a means of earning salvation, the Pashkovites regarded good works as its fruit: those who believed and were saved would inevitably do good works.[2] Thus, compassionate ministries were a sign of their relationship to Christ and an organic part of their witness.

The situation of the evangelicals changed abruptly in 1884 when Colonel Pashkov and Count Korf were exiled from Russia. After 1884 the evangelical movement in St. Petersburg took on a semi-underground character; nevertheless, many of the old activities continued while another generation of evangelicals rooted in Pashkovism developed new forms of service, also drawing on models that were practiced in the wider society. The Pashkovites also gave attention to compassionate ministry practiced abroad by such organizations as the Salvation Army and the YMCA. However, the combination of two aspects—easing human need and spreading the gospel in Russia—remained one of their basic characteristics. The model of the Pashkovites would continue to inform the activities of evangelicals after religious toleration was introduced by imperial decree in 1905, especially in St. Petersburg. This was an important part of the inheritance the evangelicals brought into what has been called their Golden Age (1905 to 1929).

COMPASSIONATE MINISTRY AND RUSSIAN IDENTITY

During the second half of the nineteenth-century in Russia it seems to have been impossible to avoid the question, "What is to be done?"[3] According to the philosopher Nicholas Berdyaev, the search for social solutions in Russia

---

1. D. I. Bogoliubov, "Pashkovtsy" (Pashkovites) in M. A. Kalnev, *Russkie sektanty, ikh uchenie, kul't i sposoby propagandy* (Russian sectarians, their teaching, cult, and methods of propaganda), (Odessa, 1911), 93, quoted by Corrado, "Colonel Vasiliy Pashkov," 48.

2. Heier, *Religious Schism*, 45; see also "Pashkovtsy" (Pashkovites) in *Entsiklopedicheskii slovar'* (Encyclopedic dictionary), vol. 23, (St. Petersburg: I. A. Efron, 1898), 64, quoted by Corrado, "Colonel Vasiliy Pashkov," 60–61; Puzynin, *The Tradition of the Gospel Christians*, 75.

3. The questioned originated with Nikolai Chernyshevskii who published a novel in 1863 entitled *Chto delat'?* (What is to be done?). It was echoed later by the writer Leo Tolstoy (*Tak chto zhe nam delat'?*/What then must we do? 1886) and the revolutionary V. I. Lenin (*Chto delat'?*/What is to be done? 1902). In effect, throughout the second half of the nineteenth century, the question was constantly being asked in different ways by members of the intelligentsia, the church, and the ruling classes.

was intensely moral and idealistic, based on a sense of guilt and the desire to set all of humanity free from suffering and injustice.[4] Furthermore, it was widely perceived that something was seriously wrong with Russia that had to be addressed. Russia's humiliating defeat in the Crimean War (1854 to 1856) had revealed the country's backwardness. It seemed evident that the existing order had failed and many believed that "not only serfs, but society more generally must be 'emancipated' from the shackles of state tutelage."[5] Accordingly, during the Era of Great Reforms (approximately 1861 to 1880) policies were launched to eradicate the empire's distressing and widespread poverty, ignorance, and injustice. The most famous of the reforms introduced during the reign of Emperor Alexander II (ruled 1855–1881) was the emancipation of the serfs in 1861. The emperor also initiated a general trend toward decentralization, social involvement, and the personal responsibility of individual citizens. Key to these goals was the founding of the *zemstvo*, an elected local governing body that was to take over responsibility for basic education and the provision of medical and other social services.

Ultimately, the reforms were not an outstanding success, and are even considered by some historians to have been "highly dysfunctional and destructive."[6] Although technically "liberated" and working their own land, peasants were still bound to their traditional village communes, which were required to take collective responsibility for paying off the debt owed to the government for the lump sum paid to former masters as reparations for the loss of their serfs. Rather than transforming serfs into independent small farmers, emancipation instead had the effect of reinforcing ancient land tenure patterns and burdening the rural population with debt.[7] In general, liberal critics of the reforms felt that they did not go far enough in ameliorating social conditions. Meanwhile, conservative critics held that the reforms created instability and even contributed to the increasing radicalism that led to the assassination of Emperor Alexander II in 1881.[8]

However, the period was of consequence for the development of new social attitudes, especially the formation of voluntary organizations for philanthropic or educational purposes. At the start of the Great Reforms in the 1860s there were ninety-two charities and 249 charitable institutions in the whole of Russia, but by 1871 those figures had risen to 798 and 809,

---

4. Berdyaev, *Russkaia ideiia*, 53.

5. Gregory L. Freeze, "Reform and Counter-Reform, 1855–1890," in Freeze, ed. *Russia: A History*, 201.

6. Ibid., 228.

7. Fitzpatrick, *The Russian Revolution*, 17.

8. Husband, *The Human Tradition in Modern Russia*, 1–2.

respectively.⁹ An increase in literacy, greater mobility, ideas about individualism, the practice of voluntarism, and other aspects of modernity slowly began to affect Russian society on many levels during this period. "New initiatives . . . came mainly from members of the educated elite . . . many of them openly dedicated to high-minded public causes, to social progress, and to forging positive links between 'the people' (*narod*) and 'society.'"[10] The Russian Orthodox Church was also affected by these changes. Although generally regarded as a backward and even reactionary institution, during the Era of Reform the church also made efforts, especially within the parish of St. Petersburg, to enlighten and serve the population in new ways. Emphasis was made on establishing closer contact with the people through accessible preaching and literature. Voluntary organizations in the form of numerous Orthodox brotherhoods and parish societies, often led by charismatic priests, attempted to meet the needs of the poor. Orthodox temperance societies combined spiritual uplift with a social agenda. Personal devotional practices—pilgrimages, frequent confession, and the veneration of local icons—flourished.[11]

Thus, the Russian evangelical movement took shape during a period when the nation perceived itself to be in crisis and was actively experimenting with a variety of solutions. The participation of the citizenry in shaping change, particularly through the formation of numerous voluntary organizations, was a significant phenomenon of the era. It is not surprising that the evangelicals, too, would take part in the process, creating new patterns for religious life that were not directly rooted in nationality or tradition, but were based on a voluntary model. As older forms of social interaction disappeared, an intense public debate took place concerning Russian identity.

Adele Lindenmeyr has demonstrated that one of the arenas for this debate had to do with care for the poor as the traditional view of individual religious compassionate activity, centered around direct almsgiving, began to give way to private charitable organizations, the founding of institutions, voluntarism, and other elements of a civil society.[12] A dichotomy developed between traditional views of poor relief that had prevailed in Russia for centuries and modernizing trends that sought to make compassion

---

9. Kelly, *Children's World*, 163–64.

10. Reginald E. Zelnik, "Revolutionary Russia 1890–1914," in Freeze, *Russia, A History*, 236.

11. For a brief overview, see Simon Dixon, "The Church's Social Role in St. Petersburg, 1880–1914," in Hosking, *Church, Nation and State in Russia and Ukraine*, 167–92; for in-depth treatments, see Hedda, *His Kingdom Come*; Kizenko, *A Prodigal Saint*; Shevzov, *Russian Orthodoxy on the Eve of Revolution*.

12. See Lindenmeyr, *Poverty is Not a Vice*.

"scientific," which were generally identified as Western. By "scientific" were meant such practices as formal administration, planning, budgeting, and record keeping. Russian traditionalists disparaged the practice of identifying and helping only the "deserving poor," as opposed to serving everyone indiscriminately. Stereotyping is inevitable here, but the basic idea put forth by Russian traditionalists in the nineteenth century was that in the West poverty was regarded as the fault of the poor themselves, while the Russians viewed them as family members, the victims of misfortune who must be loved, pitied, and helped.[13] The traditional Russian approach to charity drew on the church fathers' teaching that "every charitable act must be personal, spontaneous, direct, and inspired by unconditional, uncritical love and compassion for the recipient."[14] Also, many Russian thinkers identified traditional charity as a way of eradicating social differences.[15]

The Russian evangelicals were part of the same social context, but because of their marginalized status they were never at the center of the debate over the best methods of charity and traditional or "scientific" ideals, although like many other Russians of the period they clearly admired Western charitable models, reporting on them frequently in their publications.[16] While the Russian evangelicals also tended not to distinguish between the deserving and undeserving poor[17] and agreed that compassionate ministry had the power to unite divided social classes and had to be personal to be effective,[18] above all they believed that the inner transformation of individuals, brought about by a conscious acceptance of the gospel, was the plan of God and therefore the only way to improve society.[19] For this reason, evangelism was their answer to the question, "What is to be done?"

13. For a contemporary article elaborating on this theme, see K. P. Iarosh,' "Zabota o blizhnem: Ocherki blagotvoritel'nosti" (Concern for a neighbor: Sketches of charity), *Russkii vestnik* (Russian herald) 213 3 (1891) 39–74, 214 5 (1891) 170–205.

14. Lindenmeyr, *Poverty is Not a Vice*, 11.

15. Ibid.

16 Dixon, "The Church's Social Role in St. Petersburg," 175–76; *Khristianin* 1 (1906) 66–68; *Khristianin* 2 (February 1906) 66–68; *Khristianin* 3 (March 1906) 66; *Bratskii listok* 6 (1906) 6–7; F. Balikhin, "Moia poezdka za granitsu" (My trip abroad), *Baptist* 1 (June 1907) 16; *Baptist* 11 (November 1908) 35; *Iunyi khristianin* 1 (1909) 1–8; *Baptist* 4 (15 February 1909) 8–9; "Parad p'ianits" (A parade of drunkards), *Baptist* 52 (22 December 1910) 416; *Gost'* 1 (January 1917) 16; *Khristianin* 6 (1925) 29–30; *Khristianin* 2 (1926) 4–6; *Khristianin* 3 (1926) 19–20; I. Motorin, "Vefil'" (Bethel), *Khristianin* 4 (1926) 61–63; *Khristianin* 7 (1927) 57–60; *Khristianin* 9 (1927) 59.

17. Prokhanoff, *Cauldron*, 31–32; V. V. Ivanov, "O delakh" (On works), *Baptist* 5 (March 1909) 7.

18. V. Pavlov, "Kto moi blizhnyi?" (Who is my neighbor?), *Baptist* 4 (April 1908) 3.

19. Ivanov, "O delakh," 7.

More than simply preaching the gospel in words, their evangelistic efforts included all possible methods, from Scripture distribution to founding and running children's homes.

"PHILANTHROPY" AND THE EVANGELICAL CONNECTION

Compassionate ministry and Western evangelicalism were often linked in Russian experience. Lindenmeyr places the beginning of "scientific charity" during the reign of Alexander I (ruled 1801–1825) when liberalizing tendencies transformed the idea of "compassion" (*miloserdie*) into "philanthropy" (*chelovekoliubie*), that is, the notion that human beings could promote the general welfare without specific reference to Orthodoxy, or indeed to formal religion of any kind. In 1816 the Imperial Philanthropic Society was formed; it functioned as a kind of "twin" of the Russian Bible Society (founded in 1813). Both societies were inter-confessional and had many of the same members; both were headed by the Ober-Prokuror of the Most Holy Synod, Prince Aleksandr Golitsyn (1773–1844), who was rather sympathetic to Protestantism.[20] Lindenmeyr notes that Russian "philanthropists" were well aware of Western charitable models and copied them, but does not mention that many of those models were inspired by Western evangelicals, Dissenters, and Pietists.[21]

Contact between Western religious groups, such as Quakers and other Dissenters, and the Russian ruling class has a long history that has often included an element of compassionate ministry. For example, on two occasions in the mid-seventeenth century, George Fox (1624–1691), founder of the Religious Society of Friends (Quakers) wrote to Tsar Alexis I (ruled 1645–1676) concerning famine conditions in Poland. In 1768 Empress Catherine II invited Quaker Dr. Thomas Dimsdale (1712–1800) to St. Petersburg to inoculate her and members of her family against smallpox. Emperor Alexander I encountered the Friends in 1814 in London and a few years later invited Quaker Daniel Wheeler (1771–1840) to develop a plan to drain and develop the St. Petersburg marshes. Wheeler and his family remained in Russia for the next fifteen years, working at reclaiming marsh land for agriculture.[22]

---

20. Lindenmeyr, *Poverty is not a Vice*, 106; see also Sawatsky, "Prince Alexander N. Golitsyn."

21. Lindenmeyr, *Poverty is not a Vice*, 107.

22. McFadden and Gorfinkel, *Constructive Spirit*, 19–22.

Another early visitor was English Dissenter John Howard (?1726–1790), who came to Russia once in 1781 and again in 1789. A prison reformer, he made a special study of Russian prisons while tending to the sick in field hospitals, quarantine hospitals, and prisons. He died near Kherson (Ukraine) of a fever contracted from a patient. For many years a monument erected to him was one of the city's landmarks. To this day, a small headstone in an abandoned cemetery carries the inscription of the original monument in Russian and Latin: "Whoever you may be, your friend lies here."[23] From 1890 until 1927 the main street of Kherson was named for John Howard.[24]

The brothers John (1776–1858) and Walter Venning (1781–1821), English evangelicals, helped to establish the St. Petersburg Prison Guardian Society in 1819, which was supported by Emperor Alexander I and had branches in nine different cities. The Society worked to improve the living conditions of prisoners, distributed Scripture, and provided instruction in religion and literacy, as well as trades. Like John Howard, Walter Venning died of a fever contracted in a St. Petersburg jail. Mark McCarthy points out the significance of the women's auxiliary of this organization, because Elizaveta Ivanovna Chertkova (1834–1923) and Maria Grigorievna Peiker (1827–1881), two important figures in the Pashkovite movement, were active in the auxiliary by the time Lord Radstock first came to St. Petersburg late in 1873.[25] The Prison Guardian Society studied the reforming work of Quaker Elizabeth Fry (1780–1845) and followed out her recommendations.[26] Later Fry was consulted on the matter of improving conditions at the St. Petersburg lunatic asylum, of which John Venning was made governor while the Dowager Empress Maria Fedorovna (1759–1828) was patron. Venning translated Fry's letters into French for the Dowager, who then had them translated into Russian and passed along for implementation. Following Fry's recommendations, sightseeing at the asylum was prohibited; inmates were allowed to wear their own clothes instead of uniforms; family visits were accommodated in private rooms; training was given to caregivers selected for their patience and kindness; and Scripture was made available to all.[27]

In summary, well before the Pashkovites appeared in the 1870s, there was some historical precedent in Russia for identifying evangelicals with

---

23. Visited by the author in 2006.

24. Lindenmeyr, *Poverty is not a Vice*, 113; see also Hollingsworth, "John Venning"; Pivorovich and Diachenko, *Ulitsami starogo Khersona*, 47–49.

25. McCarthy, "Religious Conflict," 25.

26. Fry, Fry, and Cresswell, *A Memoir of the Life of Elizabeth Fry*, 372–75.

27. Ibid., 377–79.

compassionate ministry. In this respect, the contribution of Lord Radstock deserves further comment. The first visit of William Waldegrave, Lord Radstock to St. Petersburg in the winter of 1873 to 1874 could be regarded as one more in a series of many Russian encounters with evangelical Christianity that took place during the nineteenth century, but his arrival was definitely the catalyst for a focused and distinct evangelical movement in the capital. He made a powerful impression, especially in aristocratic circles where he became very popular. Lord Radstock was highly regarded by many Russians for his sincerity. He avoided discussing dogma and promoted no particular denomination, but instead focused on presenting simple Bible messages and inviting individuals to "find Christ."[28] Despite his unpretentious (his critics would say simplistic) approach, Radstock's ultimate goal was lofty, indeed. According to Edmund Heier, "he preached the Gospel as a means to the realization of the ideal society and, as a consequence, for the salvation of mankind."[29] Radstock's ethos was carried on by his converts, especially V. A. Pashkov. From about 1878, the Radstock movement became known as "Pashkovism" and its aristocratic followers "did not hesitate to dream big dreams . . . Pashkov joined Radstock to pursue the goal of 'bringing to faith the entire population of Russia . . .'"[30] Early on, the Pashkovites exerted themselves to "revive neglected Christian ideals"[31] among the Russian population. To this end, in his palace ballroom that could accommodate as many as one thousand people, Colonel Pashkov began to hold evangelistic meetings that drew people from all social classes.[32] In 1875 Maria Peiker founded the journal *Russkii rabochii* (The Russian workman) modeled after *The British Workman,* which circulated moral and spiritual stories, many of them in translation from German or English[33] to the increasingly literate populace.[34] Anticipating the later, better-known efforts by the writer Leo Tolstoy (1828–1910) to provide improving reading material to the Russian masses, in 1876 the Pashkovites founded *Obshchestvo pooshchreniia dukhovno-nravstvennogo chteniia* (Society for the encouragement of spiritual-moral reading) to print spiritual stories and articles in brochure

---

28. Heier, *Religious Schism,* 34, 47; Corrado, "Colonel Vasiliy Pashkov," 48, 58, 71.
29. Heier, *Religious Schism,* 33.
30. Corrado, "Colonel Vasiliy Pashkov," 47, cf. 52, 69.
31. Heier, *Religious Schism,* 108.
32. Nichols, *Russian Evangelical Spirituality,* 63.
33. Corrado, "Colonel Vasiliy Pashkov," 132–36.
34. For a detailed study of the development of literacy in Russia, see Brooks, *When Russia Learned to Read.*

form, which were then sold at affordable prices.[35] The Pashkovites gave particular emphasis to Bible reading, and saw to it that thousands of Bibles were circulated among the population, with passages that called attention to God's grace and justification by faith hand marked in colored ink.[36]

Such activities were clearly intended to change people's thinking, to bring them closer to God, to improve them morally and spiritually. Some observers had considerable faith in the movement's ability to benefit the nation. Two of Pashkov's distinguished relatives, A. E. Timashev, the Minister of Internal Affairs, and General Trepov, the governor of St. Petersburg, are credited with exclaiming, "If Pashkov succeeds we [Russian society] are all saved."[37]

Besides inspiring their desire to bring others to Christ, Radstock's evangelical influence on the Russians also encompassed compassionate activity. His preaching ministry is associated with the Anglo-American "prayer revival" that began in the late 1850s.[38] Social concern and the active participation of the laity in evangelism and missions are considered to be among that revival's distinguishing marks, although not all accounts agree as to whether it served to improve morality in general.[39] In any case, William Booth (1829–1912), the founder of the Salvation Army, and Thomas Barnardo (1845–1905), founder of Barnardo Homes for children were among those converted through the revival. The founding of the Student Volunteer Movement and the ensuing expansion of the work of China Inland Mission are also connected with it.[40] All of these names and organizations would be among those that were known to the Russian evangelicals and admired by them for many years. Following the pattern of increased lay involvement, Lord Radstock's evangelistic preaching ministry and indeed his whole life were intertwined with compassionate ministry. According to Mrs. Edward Trotter, Radstock came from two generations of Christians with evangelical

---

35. Nichols, *Russian Evangelical Spirituality*, 64; Corrado, "Colonel Vasiliy Pashkov," 128–29.

36. Dalton, "Recent Evangelical Movements in Russia, 114; R. S. Latimer, *Dr. Baedeker and His Apostolic Work in Russia*, quoted by Corrado, "Colonel Vasiliy Pashkov," 136–37.

37. Waldemar Gutsche, *Westliche Quellen des Russichen Stundism* (Western sources of Russian Stundism), 64, cites A. E. Timashev, while Heier, *Religious Schism*, 113, cites General Trepov, both quoted by Nichols, *Russian Evangelical Spirituality*, 63.

38. Liven, *Dukhovnoe probuzhdenie v Rossii*, 6; Davies, *I Will Pour out My Spirit*, 161–62; Randall, *Rhythms of Revival*, 120–21.

39. Randall, *Rhythms of Revival*, 113–14.

40. Scharpff, *History of Evangelism*, 169, 172, 191; Randall, *Rhythms of Revival*, 118–19.

interests who were active in supporting missionary efforts and caring for the needs of the poor.⁴¹

After a serious fever during the Crimean War and a dramatic recovery, Radstock converted to both personal faith and compassionate ministry. In 1884 he was instrumental in founding and sustaining an Emigrants' Home in London to accommodate workers from abroad who lived in poverty and were subject to all kinds of exploitation. Between 1903 and 1904 Radstock established homes for working class girls in England and for English ballet girls in Paris, as well as the Victoria Hostel for Women in London. Far from merely dispensing largesse, he cut down on his own food and fuel in order to support these ministries. He is said to have had the ability to bring together rich and poor.⁴²

In many ways, Radstock modeled practical Christianity for his Russian followers. According to the writer Nikolai Leskov, he taught that "they should do good works and serve their lesser brethren."⁴³ Clearly, Radstock brought with him an ethic and example of self-sacrifice that greatly influenced his audience. The novelist Fyodor Dostoevsky (1821–1876), for example, although he was unmoved by Lord Radstock's preaching and felt that it posed a danger to Russian Orthodoxy, nevertheless admitted in 1876 that, "[Radstock] performs miracles over human hearts; people cling to him; many are astounded: they are looking for the poor in order, as quickly as possible, to bestow benefits upon them; they are almost ready to give away their fortunes." Immediately the writer adds dismissively: "Of course, this could only [happen] among us in Russia; abroad it seems he is not so much noticed."⁴⁴ Yet in Russia he was noticed. Chief among those who were "almost ready to give away their fortunes" was V. A. Pashkov. An English eyewitness, Professor Emile J. Dillon described Pashkov as abandoning a life of refinement and giving away money to the poor:

> . . . his right hand seldom knowing what his left was doing, and, throwing open his sumptuous palace on the blue Neva, he invited the . . . masses to come and hear the Gospel of Jesus . . . he spent [his fortune] most generously, on the poor and suffering, with a secrecy and tact to which I have never seen a parallel.⁴⁵

---

41. Trotter, *Lord Radstock*, 4–7.

42. Ibid., 10–19; 26–28; 43–44; 120–21.

43. Leskov, *Schism in High Society*, 64, quoted by Puzynin, *The Tradition of the Gospel Christians*, 62.

44. Dostoevskii, *Dnevnik pisatelia za 1876 g.*, 87.

45. Dillon, "A Russian Religious Reformer," 332.

Nor was Pashkov's transformation unique. Sofia Liven, the daughter of Princess Natalia Liven, related that as a result of Radstock's preaching her aunt, Vera Fedorovna Gagarina, began to dress modestly, visit the sick and prisoners, and generously distribute both Scripture and financial help to the poor.[46] Count Vladimir Alekseevich Bobrinskii (1824–1898) changed the way he treated the peasants on his estate.[47] Count M. M. Korf, the seven Kruze sisters, E. I. Chertkova, Maria Peiker and her daughter Aleksandra, and many others were transformed into devoted Radstockist/Pashkovite activists who gave away money, circulated Scripture and Christian literature, and helped the sick and prisoners. Compassionate ministry was a natural and integral part of Pashkovite activity. It is certain that the generous aid offered to the poor served to make Pashkovism popular—indeed, the movement's critics accused Pashkov, especially, of buying converts—but the ultimate goal was that people, and therefore society, would be transformed by the gospel.[48]

PASHKOVITE CONTINUITY WITH EXISTING MINISTRIES OF COMPASSION

However, Radstock's influence was not the only thing at work in the lives of the Russians who responded to his message. Long before his arrival aristocrats, including some of those who would later be identified as Pashkovites, lent their support to social causes and charitable projects. V. A. Bobrinskii, for example, took part in the Society for the Improvement of Housing for the Working and Needy Population of St. Petersburg (founded 1858), and was a founding member of the Society of Agricultural Colonies and Industrial Shelters (founded 1866).[49] Princess Natalia Liven had undergone something of a preliminary religious conversion years before Radstock arrived in St. Petersburg, when she attended an evangelical meeting at the home of the Blackwood family in England. In many ways, the career of Stevenson Arthur Blackwood (1832–1893) paralleled that of Lord Radstock. Following a Crimean War conversion, he also disassociated himself from high society and became a lay evangelist, preaching to railway and postal workers.[50] As

---

46. Liven, *Dukhovnoe probuzhdenie*, 28.

47. McCarthy, "Religious Conflict," 138 n. 382.

48. Heier, *Religious Schism*, 109–15.

49 *Entsiklopediia blagotvoritel'nosti Sankt-Peterburga*, http://encblago.lfond.spb.ru/showObject.do?object=2853475715.

50 See http://studymore.org.uk?arcel1872.htm; and The British Postal Museum and Archive, http://postalheritage,org.uk/page/leadership.

mentioned above, Maria Peiker, the first editor of the Pashkovite journal, *Russkii rabochii,* and E. I. Chertkova were auxiliary members of the Prison Guardian Society, which had some evangelical antecedents and was one of many charitable organizations to which any well-born lady might have belonged. Peiker made a commitment to Christ through the preaching of the American evangelist Dwight L. Moody (1837–1899), an encounter that possibly took place in London in 1872 when Moody was preaching there and she was attending an international conference on prison reform.[51] Thus, the context for Pashkovism in Russia was prepared by different agents.

More significantly, there was already plenty of cultural and religious precedent in Russia for people to practice a sacrificial lifestyle on the basis of their convictions. For example, the "repentant nobleman" who identifies himself with the suffering people and attempts to atone for the evils committed against them by his class had long been a familiar figure in Russia.[52] Catherine de Hueck Doherty (1896–1985), who founded the Madonna House Apostolate in Canada, was born in Russia and told the story of her father's friend who gave away his property to the poor and became a beggar and *iurod,* a "fool for Christ," in order to atone for people having called God a fool.[53] The careers of anarchist Prince Pyotr Kropotkin (1842–1921), author of *Mutual Aid*; Prince Dmitri Khilkov (1858–1915), who sold off his land to his peasants and accompanied Dukhobor immigrants to Canada in 1898; and the writer Leo Tolstoy, who strove to identify himself with the peasants, all quickly come to mind. A remarkably successful practical example is Nikolai Nikolaevich Nepliuev who gave up his diplomatic career and organized an agricultural "labor brotherhood" (*trudovoe bratstvo*) on his estate in the 1890s.[54]

Edmund Heier points out that Lord Radstock arrived in Russia at the height of the most idealistic phase of the Populist movement when thousands of intellectuals were "going to the people" on a mission of solidarity and enlightenment.[55] Writing about the characteristics of the nineteenth century intelligentsia, Father Aleksandr Men' explains: "The main inheritance, inadvertently accepted from Christianity by the intelligentsia was dedication to high moral ideals, a readiness for sacrifice in the name of the good of the people."[56] Although they do not seem to have carried the same

---

51. Liven, *Dukhovnoe probuzhdenie,* 25, 38; McCarthy, "Religious Conflict," 81.
52 Berdyaev, *Russkaia ideia,* 53, 85.
53. Doherty, *Poustinia,* 34–36.
54. See Avdasev, *Trudovoe bratstvo.*
55. Heier, *Religious Schism,* 6–7.
56. Men', *Russkaia religioznaia filosofiia,* 102.

burden of guilt that apparently motivated some others, it is not difficult to draw parallels between the social concerns of the Pashkovites and those of many of their contemporaries.

Two areas of compassionate ministry in particular demonstrate the continuity of Pashkovite activity with existing commitments, albeit with a distinctly evangelical emphasis: the work of sisters of mercy and the founding of sewing cooperatives. It was common practice for aristocratic women to serve as sisters of mercy (*sestry miloserdiia*) in hospitals and military units, including the Empress Alexandra Fedorovna (1872–1918) during the First World War.[57] Many women active in the Pashkovite movement ministered in this way. Pastor Hermann Dalton of the Reformed Church in St. Petersburg described the work done by evangelical aristocrats during the Russo-Turkish War (1877 to 1878):

> I observed a plainly-dressed lady reading the Word of God to a dangerously wounded soldier and recognised the good Samaritan to be no other than the Princess Y—, who had volunteered for the service, and was known there only under the ordinary name and simple attire of a Sister of Mercy.[58]

Dalton also described a group of aristocratic women reading Scripture on a train journey, who, "after the fashion of Miss Florence Nightingale" were serving as voluntary nurses at the front.[59] Dalton must have known that these particular women were associated with the Pashkovite movement, but their ministry was also typical of many women who were not. According to Brenda Meehan-Waters, most of the well-known orders of sisters of mercy began to flourish at the time of the Crimean War, and there are competing claims as to whether the Russians or the French were actually the first to establish orders of nursing sisters.[60] Some orders were later affiliated with the Red Cross, which came to Russia in the 1860s. Their priority was military service and nurses' training. Other communities remained church-related and gave greater attention to spiritual life and instruction while taking care of the sick and orphans.

57. Zvereva, *Avgusteishie sestry miloserdiia*.
58. Dalton, "Recent Evangelical Movements in Russia," 109–10.
59. Ibid.
60. Meehan-Waters, "From Contemplative Practice to Charitable Activity: Russian Women's Religious Communities and the Development of Charitable Work, 1861–1917," in McCarthy, *Lady Bountiful Revisited*, 142–45; see also http://imosm.narod.ru/nikol.html; Kristina Petrochenkova, "Kniaginia-svoboda i ee sestry" (Princess freedom and her sisters), http://www.miloserdie.ru/index.php?ss=2&s=12&id=9896; I. Zakhonov, *Nikolai Pirogov: Khirurg, pedagog, reformator* (Nikolai Pirogov: Surgeon, pedagogue, reformer), http://www.triz-ri.ru/themes/profi/profi13.asp.

One of the best known and most beloved Russian sisters of mercy, the noble Maria Mikhailovna Dondukova-Korsakova, was a follower of Radstock for a time, although she later returned to Orthodoxy.[61] However, N. I. Peisti (more readily recognized in the West as the evangelist N. J. Poysti), whose Swedish father and Russian mother were Pashkovites, recalls Dondukova-Korsakova as one of the "regulars" who gathered in the Peisti apartment in St. Petersburg.[62] As early as 1861 she founded an unofficial order of nursing sisters on one of her father's estates. In addition, the sisters ran a library and conducted an elementary school and literacy classes for adults with Bible reading on Sundays. Her initial work as a sister of mercy obviously predates Radstock's arrival in St. Petersburg; however, it is not clear to what extent the movement may have influenced her continuing work, or how she may have influenced others. For example, the early work she did on her family estate sounds very much like the work of Pashkovites who also founded hospitals and schools on their property. It is interesting that Dondukova-Korsakova's special calling was prison visitation and toward the end of her life she befriended even the revolutionist Vera Figner (1852–1942), who was one of the conspirators in the 1881 assassination of Emperor Alexander II.[63]

The ministry of caring for poor women represents another point of continuity between Pashkovite activity and existing charities. Iuliia Denisovna Zasetskaia, daughter of the 1812 war hero and poet, Denis Davydov, set up sewing cooperatives for poor women in several St. Petersburg neighborhoods. When she left Russia permanently in the early 1880s, she passed along the ministry to Princess Vera Fedorovna Gagarina, Aleksandra Ivanovna Pashkova (V. A. Pashkov's wife), her sister Elizaveta Chertkova, and other women. Zasetskaia's departure could be connected to increased restrictions on the Pashkovites. In his memoirs, M. M. Korf maintained that prior to 1882 the movement's activities were centered on evangelizing at large meetings and the sewing groups were started after that date as a less obvious method of gathering women together in order to acquaint them

---

61. Severiukhin, "Dondukova-Korsakova Mariia Mikhailovna, Kniazhna"; see also Porter, *The Diaries of Sofia Tolstoy*, 314.

62. Goroshko, *N. I. Peisti*, 23. In this reference her name is given as "Dantukova-Korsakova," which may be due to an error in translating Peisti's memoir.

63. Kristina Petrochenkova, "Kniazhna Dondukova-Korsakova—drug padshikh zhenshchin i terroristok" (Princess Dondukova-Korsakova—friend of fallen women and [female] terrorists). http://www.miloserdie.ru/index.php?ss=2&s=12&id=9758; Lindenmeyr, *Poverty is not a Vice*, 15–16, 126.

with the gospel.⁶⁴ However, it seems likely that Zasetskaia began the work even earlier on her own initiative.

Twice a week sewing classes were held at each location, accompanied by Bible reading. In addition, women enrolled in the project could collect piecework at the rooms which they would then complete at home and return for pay. Completed items were sold from the "Malachite Hall" in the Liven palace until too much damage was done by visitors chipping out bits of malachite from the decorations for souvenirs. After that, space was rented for a store. Later on two other shops were opened that dealt in more exclusive items made by women who had been taught fine sewing and embroidery by another Pashkovite. A laundry service was added as well. The organizers of the sewing collectives also visited the women in their homes and arranged special holiday events for them and their children.⁶⁵

Zasetskaia and the others would have had earlier models to follow. Similar efforts to help poor women support their families through honest labor date back to at least 1865 with the founding of the Society for Support of Poor Women in St. Petersburg. Like the Pashkovite women would do later on, the Society offered vocational training and piecework that was later sold in a special shop. Various branches of the society sought to provide housing and additional educational opportunities for women in need.⁶⁶ Perhaps the society's founders were not unaware of Nikolai Chernyshevskii's revolutionary novel *Chto delat'?* (What is to be done? 1863), which described the founding and operation of a women's independent sewing cooperative in great detail.⁶⁷ In other words, Pashkovite activity in and of itself was not necessarily unique; rather, they quite naturally drew on existing models of service. It was their evangelical aspirations that set them apart. Whether serving as sisters of mercy or helping poor women find employment, the Pashkovites always took care to impart Bible knowledge and pray with the people whom they served.

Pashkovite compassionate activity also had much in common with the work of other Protestant churches and individuals in St. Petersburg. In 1876 Pastor H. F. Dalton became the first leader of the Evangelical Society for the Religious and Moral Education of St. Petersburg Protestants (*Evangelicheskoe obshchestvo religioznogo i nravstvennogo popecheniia protestantov v*

---

64. "M. M. Korf," *Bratskii vestnik* 5 (1947) 43–44.
65. Liven, *Dukhovnoe probuzhdenie*, 37–40; 65.
66. *Entsiklopedia blagotvoritel'nosti Sankt-Peterburga*, http://encblago.lfond.spb.ru.
67. Chernyshevskii, *Chto delat'?* 148–55; 162–72; 175–77.

Peterburge),⁶⁸ which in many ways corresponded to the work to the Pashkovite Society for the Encouragement of Spiritual Moral Reading founded in the same year. Through its charitable fund established in 1879 the Evangelical Society operated a shelter, facilities for those recovering from injuries or illnesses, and two Sunday schools. The mission charter described its purpose as "drawing members who have fallen into sin or poverty closer to the Protestant church." In addition to caring for the poor, the Society produced a weekly newspaper, work that continued until 1906.⁶⁹ The charitable outreach of the Lutheran community was also well developed, with numerous associations and institutions, and even enjoyed the patronage of members of the royal family who had converted to Orthodoxy from Lutheranism.⁷⁰ Some St. Petersburg Protestants were active Pashkovites as well, such as Dr. Karl Karpovich von Mayer, who served as head doctor of the Lutheran Evangelical Hospital (founded 1859). He acted as treasurer and informal advisor of "the committee" of Pashkovite women who ran the sewing collectives for poor women.⁷¹

It should be noted, however, that the legally recognized, non-Orthodox Christian confessions in Russia were forbidden by law to engage in evangelism among the Orthodox population; therefore, the Protestant churches in St. Petersburg focused their services on people in their own communities. In contrast, Pashkovite compassionate ministry was directed toward everyone, regardless of nationality or religious affiliation, in order to reach as many as possible with a new understanding of the message of Christ.

In some instances the Orthodox were inspired by Pashkovite activities. Jennifer Hedda states that one of the main reasons for the founding of the Society for the Dissemination of Moral-Religious Enlightenment in the Spirit of Orthodoxy (founded 1881) was to counteract the spirit of Pashkovism. Indeed, the Orthodox society organized a number of parish-based charitable efforts, such as the 1901 all-female Religious-Educational Union, whose members did hospital and prison visitation.⁷² That is, even if sometimes the activities of evangelical and Orthodox groups were much the same, the sponsorship and commitment to evangelism were different.

---

68. Litsenberger gives the founding date as 1875 and calls it the Evangelical Union (*soiuz*) for the Religious and Moral Education of St. Petersburg Protestants (*Evangelichesko-liuteranskaia tserkov'*, 156); A. P. Kerzum, "Evangelichesko-missionerskoe blagotvoritel'noe obshchestvo" (Evangelical-missionary charitable society), http://encblago.lfond.spb.ru.

69. McCarthy, "Religious Conflict," 87–88, n. 252.

70. Litsenberger, *Evangelichesko-liuteranskaia tserkov',* 151.

71. Liven, *Dukhovnoe probuzhdenie,* 37–38.

72. Hedda, *His Kingdom Come,* 87–97.

PASHKOVITES, EVANGELICAL ASPIRATIONS, AND COMPASSIONATE MINISTRY

The purpose of all Pashkovite ministries was to bring as many people as possible of all social classes and nationalities to Jesus Christ. At the same time, they believed not only in eternal salvation, but also in the good effects of conversion in the present. Simply stated, they were convinced that people's lives manifestly improved when they received the gospel. According to Sofia Liven: "All the rough sins fell away: drunkenness, swearing, and immorality immediately ceased. Apartments became clean and peace reigned in homes. There was still a lot to learn, but the foundation of a new life was laid, and where there is life, there is growth."[73] E. J. Dillon added:

> The peasant, listless, lazy, lying, and greedy . . . became zealous, painstaking, truthful, and unselfish; Poles, Russians, and Germans, Greek Churchmen, Roman Catholics, and Lutherans felt drawn together by a bond of brotherhood stronger than that of nature, and all Russia seemed springing up into new life."[74]

In other words, the Pashkovites anticipated the total transformation of society through the gospel. They expected that order and peace would replace squalor; new habits would replace destructive ones; and, finally, new relationships would cut across the old dividing lines of class and nationality.

According to Edmund Heier, the goal of the Pashkovites was ". . .a religious renovation and with it a transformation of Russia on an ethical and moral basis."[75] To this end, as noted above, much of their energy was directed toward the printing and distribution of Christian literature, including Scripture. However, the literature did not circulate in a vacuum. It was embodied in concrete deeds of mercy, systematically carried out by followers of the evangelical movement.

The Pashkovites hoped and worked for the transformation of individual lives. Their charitable activity, although continuous with existing forms of service, was also distinguished by its variety, creativity, and energy. A good example is an inexpensive dining room Pashkov organized especially to accommodate poor students and provide a counter influence to the nihilism and revolutionary activity of the period.[76] Here again, inexpensive dining rooms for students were not uncommon in St. Petersburg at

---

73 Liven, *Dukhovnoe probuzhdenie*, 14.
74 Dillon, "A Russian Religious Reformer," 332.
75 Heier, *Religious Schism*, vii.
76. Ibid., 116–17.

the time.⁷⁷ At the Pashkovite dining room, however, the atmosphere was markedly cheerful and the food was good. For ten kopeks one could buy a bowl of soup or buckwheat served in a room decorated with Scripture verses (until a new ruling required that the texts be removed). Sometimes up to one thousand meals a day were served.⁷⁸ Some sources report another two or three dining rooms. Pashkov also opened a women's shelter in the Vyborg neighborhood and tea rooms especially for cab drivers and coachmen. A sort of Christian labor exchange functioned to match employers with sober, conscientious workers.⁷⁹

Iuliia Zasetskaia, who organized the women's sewing cooperatives, was acquainted with many important literary and philosophical figures of the day, such as Nikolai Leskov and the philosopher Vladimir Solov'ev (1853–1900). She opened a night shelter in St. Petersburg's Haymarket in 1873, possibly the first one in the city,⁸⁰ and ran it herself. She met Fyodor Dostoevsky there when he was writing a report about the shelter for publication in *The Citizen*. The two became good friends, although they argued constantly about religion. According to Leskov, Zasetskaia asked several Orthodox priests to come to the shelter once a week to explain the gospel to the people there. They responded that they could not work with such "rabble" and asked Zasetskaia why she even bothered. No doubt it was such disappointing encounters that contributed to Zasetskaia's formal break with the Orthodox Church. Dostoevsky tried to convince her to return, but without success.⁸¹ However, it is important to note that presenting the gospel message was an integral part of her compassionate work.

Much Pashkovite ministry went on outside St. Petersburg on private estates. Like Maria Dondukova-Korsakova, aristocrats distributed Christian literature among the peasants and established schools and hospitals on their own properties. Pashkov owned several estates, for example at Vetoshkino in the Urals, where the family organized a hospital, a school, and a homeless shelter.⁸² On another of his properties, Pashkov engaged two British Congregationalists as managers, Edward and Henry Hilton, where they helped build schools and arranged for religious lessons to be given by local clergy.⁸³ With the help of Aleksandra Peiker, Countess Perovskaia opened a hospital

---

77. Miller, "American Philanthropy among Russians," 13.
78. Liven, *Dukhovnoe probuzhdenie*, 36.
79. McCarthy, "Religious Conflict," 134, 137.
80. Ibid., 131–33.
81 Heier, *Religious Schism*, 58–62; McCarthy, "Religious Conflict," 133, 170.
82 http://pripyanye.livejournal.com/539.html.
83. Stead, *Truth about Russia*, 344–53; McCarthy, "Religious Conflict," 138.

on her property.⁸⁴ Count Bobrinskii and Count Zinov'ev assisted peasants in their regions with grain and livestock donations.⁸⁵ In all these examples of social projects, the Pashkovite emphasis was on spiritual transformation as much as material help. The presentation of the gospel message was central, but was consistently backed up by compassionate ministry. The combination had the potential to replicate itself in the lives of converts, as the following story illustrates.

In the course of his hospital visitation, Colonel Pashkov became acquainted with N. E. Gorinovich, a young Nihilist who had been blinded and disfigured with sulfuric acid in 1876 by fellow revolutionaries who suspected him of betraying them to the police. At first the young man refused to speak to the visitor, who went on talking and reading to the other patients loud enough so that Gorinovich could hear. After some time, however, he accepted Christ and was taken to live on the Bobrinskii estate. Eventually he married, and he and his wife opened a shelter for blind children. Their daughter Vera became the first Russian Salvation Army officer in 1913 and worked among the poor in the Army's St. Petersburg slum post.⁸⁶

Pashkovite compassionate ministry was characterized by strong personal commitment, as well as a clear emphasis on the inner renewal of individuals and society through the gospel. Pashkovism's effect on society could also be seen in its egalitarian ideal and practice. All observers, even critics of the movement, frequently called attention to the variety of people who were attracted to the evangelistic meetings held at Pashkov's mansion. Eyewitness A. S. Prugavin described the scene:

> With curiosity I looked around at [the people], seated on chairs, armchairs, and sofas, [and] standing along the wall. And there was, indeed, something to look at. You could hardly see such variety anywhere else. Here were factory workers, and lackeys, and cooks, and female clerks, and officers, and day-laborers, and gymnasium students, and Junkers; here is a fine lady, and female students, and clerks, and heavy laborers, and merchants . . . Here is a smart uniform with aiguillettes next to a postal worker with a name plate, a little further on are the dirty, ragged sheepskin jackets of the working people, knee-length cloth jackets [i.e. of the nouveau riche], and light, tight-fitting coats . . .⁸⁷

---

84. Liven, *Dukhovnaia probuzhdenie*, 65.

85. McCarthy, "Religious Conflict," 138.

86. Trotter, *Lord Radstock*, 195; Prokhanoff, *Cauldron*, 69; Liven, *Dukhovnaia probuzhdenie*, 17–20; Aitken, *Blood and Fire*, 161–62.

87. A. S. Prugavin, *Raskol vverkhu*, 204.

Critics of the movement believed that Pashkov's teaching became popular simply because of his practice of handing out food and money following the prayer meetings,[88] an accusation that followed him even after his exile from Russia in 1884.[89] Rumors circulated that Pashkov paid cab-drivers and the peasants on his estates so much a head to listen to his sermons.[90] However, in many cases, the movement truly served to bring people from different social classes together in a new and genuine spirit. From a historical perspective there is no reason to doubt the sincerity of the Pashkovite aristocracy's motives. Once Count Korf is said to have asked Princess Natalia Liven why her beautiful Malachite Hall smelled like a stable? She replied that she had just held a prayer meeting there that included not only the nobility, but also their coachmen.[91] The Livens' senior caretaker, Ivan Il'ich R., was respected as an effective personal evangelist.[92] At the first national gathering of evangelicals called together by V. A. Pashkov and M. M. Korf in 1884 Baptists, Stundists, Molokans, Mennonites, and others, met for several days in St. Petersburg. For Baptist V. G. Pavlov the "brightest memory" of the occasion was the sense of fellowship that transcended class, especially at the table: "A peasant sat next to a count, and well-born ladies served the simple brothers."[93]

Compassionate ministry also had the effect of exposing members of the upper classes to the realities of life among the poor. When Sofia Liven and her sister, the daughters of Princess Natalia Liven, were a little older, they took over one of the sewing projects and accompanying visitation. Sofia commented: "In this way, we became acquainted with the poorest parts of the city and saw poverty in its unvarnished form. These visits were a good school that taught us to relate to souls that were not inclined to listen to spiritual truths."[94]

By some accounts, social reconciliation did not always happen. A. S. Prugavin wrote that real fellowship and concern between rich and poor was more common in the early days of the Pashkovite movement; by the late 1880s much of the original enthusiasm had died away. Prugavin gave a tongue-in-cheek description of a Pashkovite meeting in Moscow at the

88. Heier, *Religious Schism*, 114–15.

89. Just one example is Pobedonostsev, "Pis'ma Aleksandru III" (Letters to Alexander III), 30 July 1887, http://krotov.info/libr_min/p/pobed.html#68.

90. Stead, *Truth about Russia*, 360.

91 McCarthy, "Religious Conflict," 153–54.

92. Liven, *Dukhovnoe probuzhdenie*, 65–66.

93. V. G. Pavlov, "Vospominaniia ssylnogo" (Recollections of an exile), in Karetnikova, *Al'manakh, vypusk 1*, 197–98.

94. Liven, *Dukhovnoe probuzhdenie*, 38.

home of one Liudmila Pavlovna. Here, indeed, rich and poor were gathered together, but the poor were all huddled up in one corner. The privileged in attendance commented on everyone's equality in Christ, while the simple people awkwardly edged into the corridor.[95]

Be that as it may, it is still true that the evangelical movement sometimes managed to transcend class in ways that were rather unusual for Russia. As will be shown, rich and poor evangelicals continued to interact for many years, with aristocrats supporting and defending their poorer fellow believers at least until the First World War. Besides their commitment to evangelism and their personal sacrificial spirit, social egalitarianism is a feature that added to the identity of Pashkovite compassionate ministry.

CONTINUATION OF PASHKOVITE MINISTRY

There is much discussion concerning the long-term effects of the Pashkovite movement after the exile of V. A. Pashkov and M. M. Korf in 1884. Eager to realize the dream of coming together in a brotherhood of common Christian reforming interests, in April 1884 Pashkov and Korf organized and financed a large meeting of like-minded Christians in St. Petersburg. However, on the third day of the meeting, the delegates failed to appear. The organizers learned that there had been a mass arrest and everyone had been obliged to leave the capital. Shortly afterward Pashkov and Korf were asked to sign a document promising that they would give up practicing spontaneous prayer, preaching, and gathering together with Stundists. When they refused, they were forced to leave the country.[96]

Obviously, the movement had to adjust to the absence of its leaders. Sofia Liven remarked that "Almost none of the educated brethren remained." Some key persons, such as V. A. Bobrinskii, retired from the St. Petersburg scene. It remained for less refined preachers to carry on the meetings, "and although they conveyed to us the truths of God simply and reverently, keeping strictly to the Scripture, their sermons nevertheless were often insufficiently understandable."[97] Accordingly, Konstantsiia Sergeevna Kozlianinova, Aleksandra Peiker, and other educated women sometimes

---

95. Prugavin, *Raskol vverkhu*, 223–41.

96. A. V. Karev, "Russkoe evangel'sko-baptistskoe dvizhenie" (Russian Evangelical-Baptist movement), 131–32, and Pavlov, "Vospominaniia ssylnogo," 197–98 in Karetnikova, *Al'manakh, vypusk 1* are only two examples of many places where this story is recounted.

97. Liven, *Dukhovnoe probuzhdenie*, 55.

took the lead as preachers and in small group meetings.[98] Over the next few decades, Pashkovism, partly represented in St. Petersburg by the remaining group of aristocratic women, developed into a semi-underground movement that was more and more closely identified with the Baptists, although some descendants of the Pashkovite movement were uncomfortable with that designation and preferred to identify themselves as "Evangelical Christians." However, an important point of continuity remained in the form of ministries of compassion that continued as Pashkov's commitments were carried out by others and believers addressed themselves anew to the needs around them. According to Sharyl Corrado:

> The Pashkovite story is often considered to end in 1884, when Pashkov and Korff were banished abroad, much of the literature removed from circulation, and public meetings forbidden. Yet quietly, privately, or in cooperation with Orthodox and secular aid societies, Pashkovites continued to reach out to their communities and country. Prison and hospital visitation in the capital continued. Large donations were still given to worthy causes. Bible distribution continued in prisons throughout Siberia . . . Those raised in the movement eventually began their own ministries throughout Russia and even internationally.[99]

Pashkov continued to be involved in the Russian evangelical movement from afar through correspondence and providing financial support.[100] A letter from K. P. Pobedonostsev, Ober-prokuror of the Most Holy Synod, to Emperor Alexander III in 1887, warned that in spite of Pashkov's exile, his aristocratic supporters "are not ashamed to bribe the poor people with gifts and material assistance." Moreover, Pobedonostsev complained that Pashkov continued to spread his teaching through his "agents," which he was capable of doing because of his great wealth. The Ober-prokuror observed that "zealous sectarians" had been put in charge of Pashkov's several estates, notably the one in the village of Matcherka in Tambov guberniia, where the Polish factory director appointed thirteen Molokans to supervisory positions.[101]

98. Ibid., 55–56.

99. Sharyl Corrado, "The Gospel in Society: Pashkovite Social Outreach in Late Imperial Russia," in Corrado and Pilli, eds., *Eastern European Baptist History*, 68. Hedda, on the other hand, assumes that after 1884 Pashkovism merely "developed into a distinct sect . . . [which] eventually came to resemble Shtundism" (*His Kingdom Come*, 91).

100. Nichols cites numerous examples in *Russian Evangelical Spirituality*.

101. Pobedonostsev, "Pis'ma" 30 July 1887, http://krotov.info/libr_min/p/pobed.html#68.

The original Pashkovite ministries continued to operate, albeit in a more muted form. The sewing cooperatives and shops continued until the First World War.[102] Regular financial reports concerning them were sent to Pashkov, such as one that begins rather archly: "Along with many St. Petersburg philanthropic societies, there is one that exists and busily works, the so-called 'circle.' It is less well-known than the other societies, but the reason for that, of course, is not because of its inactivity."[103] In other words, in a capital city overflowing with charitable organizations, "the circle"—composed of Pashkovite women—was still quietly continuing its work, busy, but unwilling to draw the attention of the authorities. The charitable institutions founded on Pashkovite estates also continued. In the latter part of her life, Aleksandra Peiker devoted herself to patients in the hospital she had helped to set up on Countess Vera Perovskaia's estate.[104] At least one of the inexpensive dining rooms continued to operate for at least another decade, subsidized from abroad by Pashkov. When Baptist leader V. G. Pavlov lost one of his children to drowning and his wife and three more of his five children to cholera in 1892 during his second exile in Orenburg, the evangelist Fedor Prokhorovich Balikhin (1854–1919) reported Pavlov's situation to the congregation in St. Petersburg. Aleksandra Egorovna Gil'debrandt, at that time the manager of the dining room, went to Orenburg and married Pavlov on 2 January 1893.[105] Tom Aitken is reasonably sure that the Salvation Army took over the Pashkovite dining rooms to use as meeting halls in 1917.[106] Foreign visitors, such as Salvation Army Brigadier Mildred Duff, found evangelical believers of this later period busy with ministries such as home visitation. During Duff's 1899 trip to Russia, she was conducted around the working class neighborhoods of St. Petersburg by a woman impressive enough to be identified simply as "She" with a capital "S." During her tour, Duff observed believers' efforts to teach carpentry and sewing to children.[107] Well into the twentieth century, members of the old Pashkovite circle continued to be noted for their compassionate ministry, such as "Madam Yasnovsky" [sic, that is, Baroness Maria N. Iasnovskaia], who was among the roster of Russian delegates enthusiastically introduced at the Baptist World Alliance congress in 1911 in Philadelphia: "The daughter of a Russian baron; brought

---

102. Liven, *Dukhovnoe probuzhdenie*, 40.
103. Pashkov Papers, Fiche I,5.
104. Liven, *Dukhovnoe probuzhdenie*, 56–57.
105. Pavlov, "Vospominaniia ssylnogo," 210; Popov, *Stopy blagovestnika*, 58.
106. Aitken, *Blood and Fire*, 75, 224.
107. Duff, "Furlough Days in Russia," *All the World* 20.5 (1899) 255–56.

up in a wealthy home, converted under Lord Radstock, she works in Russian society for the prevention of the white slave traffic."[108]

While a degree of freedom remained for evangelicals in St. Petersburg, largely because aristocrats were among its members, over time the situation became more difficult for Stundists, Baptists, and Molokans in the south. New legislation intended to curb the spread of Stundism led to numerous arrests and exiles in the 1890s. A former police officer from Kharkov, Vasilii Nikolaevich Ivanov, became a convert and traveled widely in Ukraine and the Caucasus to encourage frightened believers and carry material aid to exiles.[109] Elena Ivanovna Shuvalova (1830–1900), a Radstock convert, was married to the chief of police and frequently interceded with the authorities for the release of prisoners exiled for their religious beliefs, sometimes inviting officials to her home for dinner in order to plead her case.[110] Prayer meetings went on in the coachman's basement room in her home.[111] When the preacher Savelii Alekseevich Alekseev and his wife were exiled to the Caucasus, Princess Gagarina housed and educated their son.[112] Later, highly placed friends interceded for the Latvian preacher W. A. Fetler when he was sentenced to exile in Siberia in 1915.[113]

Prison visitation was continued by Friedrich Baedeker, who visited Russia numerous times between 1875 and 1901. An Anglicized German and Radstock convert, during the 1890s Baedeker received a permit granting him access to all the prisons in the Russian Empire, through the intervention of Pashkovites and their sympathizers. With Ivan Veniaminovich Kargel (1849–1937), Baron Paul Nicolay (1860–1919), or the Armenian evangelical leader Patwakan Tarajantz acting as translators, Baedeker visited hundreds of prisons and distributed thousands of Scripture portions across Russia.[114] His prison work also included material aid and encouragement for exiled Baptists, Stundists, Molokans, and others. Indeed, it could almost be said that as persecution increased during the 1890s, "prison ministry" for many Russian evangelicals came to mean caring for fellow believers in

---

108. *The Baptist World Alliance Second Congress*, 237.

109. Prokhanoff, *Cauldron*, 65–68.

110. Liven, *Dukhovnoe probuzhdenie*, 59–60; Heather Vose, "The Ministry of Women in the Baptist Churches in the USSR," in Brackney and Burke, *Faith, Life and Witness*, 129–38.

111. Liven, *Dukhovnoe probuzhdenie*, 58.

112. Ibid., 59–60.

113. J. Fetler, *Sluzhenie Rossii*, 46.

114 For detailed information on Dr. Baedeker's prison ministry in Russia, see Latimer, *Dr. Baedeker and His Apostolic Work in Russia*; Langenskjöld, *Baron Paul Nicolay*, 75; Nichols, *Russian Evangelical Spirituality*, 162–66.

exile. Other foreign visitors to exiles in this period include the Quakers Joseph Neive and John Bellow who went to the Caucasus between 1892 and 1893 accompanied by Hermann Fast, the Mennonite brother-in-law of N. E. Gorinovich, the revolutionary who had become a Christian through V. A. Pashkov's preaching.[115] Of course, prison ministry in the sense of outreach to criminals also continued through Baedeker and others. Between 1896 and 1905 Baron Paul Nicolay made numerous journeys to visit prisons throughout the Russian Empire.[116] In about 1905 Adam Karlovich Podin (1862–1941), an Estonian Baptist with Latvian background who trained as a missionary in London, was asked by a government official to visit prisons throughout Siberia. The request came from "a highly placed official in St. Petersburg, a Baptist . . .," according to the English Baptist visitor Chas. T. Byford, but the official likely had Pashkovite connections. Equipped, like Baedeker before him, with a permit granting him general access, Podin carried many thousands of New Testaments and other literature to prisons throughout the empire. He continued that ministry for at least seven years.[117]

Thus, even after the exile of Pashkov and Korf, the Pashkovite forms of compassionate ministry—dining rooms, sewing cooperatives, activity among the peasants on private estates, house-to-house visitation in the cities, and prison visitation—continued quietly. Protected by their higher social position, Pashkovites nevertheless also made it their business to aid poorer evangelicals who were more likely to suffer arrest and exile.

NEW MINISTRY IN THE PASHKOVITE TRADITION

New forms of ministry also appeared during the post-1884 era, carried out by a new generation of evangelical activists with roots in the old Pashkovite community. As was typical of the earlier generation, the younger Pashkovites also made use of existing models of ministry, but with added evangelical content. During this time there were many groups and individuals in Russia that began innovative social experiments. Some of the new generation of Pashkovites took on these forms and turned them to evangelical witness.

---

115. Cornelius Krahn, "Fast, Herman (1860–1935)," *Global Anabaptist Mennonite Encyclopedia Online*, 1956; Grachev, *Gerusy-Giriusy (Goris)*, 15.

116 Langenskjöld, *Baron Paul Nicolay*, 75–81.

117. Byford, *Peasants and Prophets*, 127–34; Toivo Pilli, "Adam Podin: An Estonian Baptist with International Links and Pan-Evangelical Vision," in Lalleman et al, *Grounded in Grace*, 103–17.

An example of a "new Pashkovite" who was active in the post-1884 period is Laura Grundberg, by nationality a Swede, who founded a home for orphaned children in 1889 in Kellomäki (then part of the Grand Duchy of Finland; present day Komarovo, Russia). According to an article she wrote in 1908, Grundberg became an evangelical believer in 1883 through Pashkov's preaching. Although she wanted to become a missionary in China, she concluded that her role was to serve "little ones" closer to home. Another woman, Mrs. Wenberg, joined her. They started with four Estonian sisters in 1889, and then Finnish, Russian, Polish, and Jewish children joined what she called (for some reason) in English, a "baby home" (*bebi khom*).[118] One of Grundberg's purposes in founding the home was to raise children to serve as missionaries.[119] Establishing a children's home may have been an ambitious, but not overly unusual undertaking in Russia, but her interest in preparing missionaries clearly shows that Grundberg, like other Pashkovites, gave evangelical content to traditional compassion. One of the first children in the orphanage, Anna (Agneta or Aniuta) Renberg, born in Estonia in 1883 and orphaned in 1889, studied in London from 1903 to 1904 at a missionary college and then went to China under China Inland Mission. Her letters to the Evangelical Christian community in St. Petersburg were featured from time to time in the *Bratskii listok* supplement to the journal *Khristianin*.[120] Likewise, Anna (Aniuta) Smirnova, a Russian girl who was born in 1886 and came to the home in 1889, grew up to train as a medical missionary in London in about 1908. At the same time another child in the home was preparing to train for missionary service in China as well.[121]

The home experienced many difficulties, including hunger, cold, illness, death, and police surveillance. When they moved to a larger residence they had space to "hold meetings"—obviously of an evangelical type—and consequently had problems with the authorities. Many times, according to Grundberg, they were without money and feared having to close down, however, as she emphasized, the Lord always provided. Sometimes complete strangers helped; some help they received from abroad.[122]

Another example of the younger Pashkovite generation who added evangelical content to existing forms of compassionate service was Evgeniia

118. Laura Grundberg, "Detskii priiut" (Children's shelter) and "Bebi-khom (Detskii priut)," (Baby-home [Children's shelter]) *Bratskii listok* 9 (September 1908) 1–3.

119. Ibid., 5.

120. See, for example, *Bratskii listok* 9 (September 1908) 6–16; 11 (November 1908) 3–7; 10 (1909) 1–4; 4 (April 1910) 9–12.

121. Grundberg, "Bebi-khom," 2–3.

122. Ibid., 4–6.

(Jenny) de Mayer, who carried out her many ministries as a Red Cross sister during this period. Her father was Karl Karpovich von Mayer, the Pashkovite head doctor of the Lutheran Evangelical Hospital. A committed evangelical believer, Jenny de Mayer nevertheless enjoyed the protection of highly placed people, including a lady-in-waiting to both the Empress Alexandra Fedorovna and the Dowager Empress Maria Fedorovna (1847–1928).[123] From 1899 to 1900 de Mayer directed an orphanage for children born to deportees in the women's prisons along the long road through Siberia to the island of Sakhalin. After an interval of service with a Red Cross unit in South Manchuria during the Boxer Rebellion, she returned to Sakhalin in 1901 and organized a House of Industry (*Dom trudoliubiia*) for discharged prisoners who were to remain on the island and earn their own living. Some of them had been in prison for as long as twenty-five years. At this time the House of Industry movement was at its height in Russia. It was inspired in large part by the popular Father Ioann Sergiev of Kronstadt,[124] a St. Petersburg parish priest who challenged the authorities to provide shelter and honest labor for those who could not find regular employment. He established the first House of Industry in Kronstadt in 1882. Four years later Baron Otto O. Buksgevden (1839–1907) established the Evangelical House of Industry under the auspices of the Lutheran Church specifically to serve the needs of Protestant men. More Houses of Industry were organized in other Russian cities and in 1895 the Guardianship of Houses of Industry and Workhouses was established under the patronage of the new Empress Alexandra Fedorovna. Although it was in part a government agency, the Guardianship relied almost exclusively on the initiative of private citizens to start up and run Houses of Industry—a factor that surely worked to de Mayer's advantage.[125]

She set up five workshops for about one-hundred tailors, shoemakers, carpenters, bookbinders, and rug-makers, with broom-making offered as an occupation for the oldest clients. Later a group of about twenty women took up spinning to supply the rug-making enterprise. De Mayer began with Red Cross funds, but also worked hard to secure orders for the goods produced by the House of Industry. Help, however, continued to come from the outside, including a donation of fifteen thousand rubles from Empress

123. De Mayer, *Adventures with God*, 72–73.

124. He is better known in English as Father John of Kronstadt.

125. Lindenmeyr, *Poverty Is not a Vice*, 175–76. Concerning Father John of Kronstadt and the House of Industry, see Kizenko, *A Prodigal Saint*, 75–78, and Kristina Petrochenkova, "Dom trudoliubiia sv. Ioanna: 'Uchrezhdenie pervykh khristian vremen apostol'skikh" (House of industry of St. John: "An establishment of the first Christians of apostolic times," http://www.miloserdie.ru.

Alexandra Fedorovna, who entrusted her mistress of ceremonies, Madame Naryshkina, with the sum, mentioning de Mayer by name. In 1903 de Mayer's health broke down and she entrusted the continuing work of the House of Industry to members of the island government staff, although she continued to be responsible for funding. Her inspiring ministry career continued with work in the Moscow slums, as a literature colporteur in Central Asia, and accompanying Muslim pilgrims on their way to Mecca.[126]

Evangelical compassionate ministry was also practiced in the south of Russia. A Pashkovite and the widow of a military officer, Iuliia Nikolaevna Karpinskaia, came to Kyiv in 1899 and applied for permission to open "People's kindergartens" *(Narodnye detskie sady)* for the purpose of seeing to the religious-moral education and physical well-being of poor children in the city.[127] By the 1890s kindergartens and other facilities for the care of very young children were fairly common in large Russian cities, sometimes operated as private institutions and sometimes as day-care centers for the convenience of mothers employed at a factory or other business.[128] In fact, Karpinskaia opened several such establishments that were caring for about two-hundred children, when a complaint was lodged against her in 1899 because she had no diploma in pedagogy and because some of the teachers she employed were Jewish, as were about half of the pupils.[129] The kindergartens closed because of a lack of funds, but trouble began again when Karpinskaia opened another kindergarten in June 1901 for which she evidently had not received permission. In 1902 a complaint was made to the Ministry of the Interior by Metropolitan Feognoz of Kyiv and the ministry turned to the governor-general. Karpinskaia was accused of coming to Kyiv in order to get in touch with the local Stundists and gather them together in a single group with the Pashkovites. In fact, Stundists did gather in her apartment to pray. The authorities intended to close down the kindergarten. Eventually the complaints led to a court trial and Karpinskaia was fined five rubles, which she refused to pay on the grounds that she could not afford it. However, it appears that the kindergarten continued to function nevertheless, and as of May 1902 was caring for thirty-four boy and thirty-two girl pupils, aged seven to twelve. They were from the lower classes and were charged nothing for their education. The children were given lessons in basic literacy and Orthodox children learned catechism (*Zakon Bozhii*), although

---

126. De Mayer, *Adventures with God*, 167–78.

127. Golovashchenko, *Istoriia Evangel'sko-Baptistskogo dvizheniia*, 121–22.

128. D. Ia. Severiukhin, "Detskie sady" (Kindergartens), http://encblago.lfond.spb.ru/showObject.do?object=2815935235.

129. Zhuk, *Russia's Lost Reformation*, 224–25.

there was no qualified catechism instructor. Karpinskaia herself taught the Gospels to the "sectarian children" with a "sectarian slant."[130] Karpinskaia hired Stundist peasant women to teach needlework and other handcrafts.[131] In September 1902 the kindergarten was closed down, as Karpinskaia was declared guilty of "spreading Stundism," and "must be deprived of the possibility of having a harmful influence on Orthodox children."[132]

Sergei Zhuk connects Karpinskaia with the interest Ukrainian Stundists showed in education, especially literacy, which was extremely important for people whose religious life centered on the Bible. Zhuk also cites the case of Olga Zenkova, the daughter of an army colonel, who began a clandestine school for Stundist children in her Kyiv home in 1903. He does not indicate whether Zenkova was also an evangelical believer, although it seems likely that she was, given the risk that she took.[133] Clearly, Karpinskaia belongs to the general trend of Pashkovite ministry after 1884, as they continued to practice compassionate ministries that were already familiar to the wider society, but with an evangelical emphasis. It is also worth noting Karpinskaia's Pashkovite egalitarian and, in a way, ecumenical approach to service, mingling Jews and Christians, and offering Orthodox catechism lessons as well as Bible instruction for children from non-Orthodox families.

The examples of Laura Grundberg, Jenny de Mayer, and Iuliia Karpinskaia show that evangelical compassionate ministry continued after the 1884 exile of V. A. Pashkov and M. M. Korf. As before, the evangelicals creatively employed forms of ministry that were already familiar in the Russian context, but filled them with evangelical meaning, using them as a platform to preach their understanding of the gospel.

CONCLUSION

Throughout the nineteenth century Russian society was deeply concerned with the solution to a variety of problems and changes brought about by industrialization and the emancipation of the serfs. One of the important arenas for the debate on "what is to be done?" was the area of charity, whether it was better to subscribe to traditional notions of care for the poor or to organize what was known as "scientific" charity. The religious movement called Pashkovism was not directly part of that debate; instead, the

---

130. Golovashchenko, *Istoriia Evangel'sko-Baptistskogo dvizheniia*, 122.

131. Zhuk, *Russia's Lost Reformation*, 225.

132. Golovashchenko, *Istoriia Evangel'sko-Baptistskogo dvizheniia*, 122.

133. Zhuk, *Russia's Lost Reformation*, ch. 4 n. 60, n.p; Iasevich-Borodaevskaia, *Bor'ba za veru*, 125.

Pashkovites proposed an alternative based on the spiritual transformation of the individual, which they believed would inevitably lead to the transformation of society. Compassionate ministry was one of the tools they used to achieve that transformation. The Pashkovites participated in ministry that was familiar to people of their social class (sisters of mercy, organizing services for peasants on their own estates, participating in existing charitable organizations), but added evangelical content by distributing Scripture and other Christian literature and leading people to conversion. They had some measure of success in bridging the gap between upper and lower classes.

With the exile of Colonel V. A. Pashkov in 1884, the movement underwent considerable changes. Nevertheless, compassionate ministries remained an important part of evangelical activity, linking the identity of pre- and post-1884 Pashkovites. Many of the original ministries (sewing cooperatives, inexpensive dining rooms for poor students, ministries on private estates, and prison visitation) continued in a quieter form, while new ministries were launched (a children's home, a house of industry, student ministries, etc.). After 1905 the compassionate ministry models continued to have an effect, especially on urban ministries in St. Petersburg, though the social and political context was changing rapidly.

2

Russian Evangelicals from 1905 to 1929
Varied Ministries, Common Convictions

THE PREVIOUS CHAPTER BRIEFLY surveyed compassionate ministry in Russia in general and among the Pashkovites in particular during the era before 1905 and the introduction of religious toleration, which began with Emperor Nicholas II's Decree of 17 April 1905, "On the strengthening of the beginnings of religious toleration." During the period from 1905 to 1929 such ministries continued to play an important role. To be sure, in the atmosphere of freedom brought about by the legislation of 1905 and 1906, many possibilities for ministry competed for the evangelicals' attention and limited financial resources, such as theological education, the construction of prayer houses, and the support of traveling evangelists. Clearly, however, their commitment to compassionate ministry was present from the beginning of the era.

In January 1906 the journal *Khristianin* (The Christian), the first legal evangelical publication since *Ruskii rabochii* (The Russian workman) closed down in 1885, was officially launched.[1] Certain items in the journal suggest ways that compassionate ministry was lived out by evangelicals at an early stage. In May 1906, just a few months after the journal was first published, *Khristianin* noted the receipt of an unsolicited contribution from Tavriia guberniia (in present-day Ukraine) toward the founding of a clinic (*lechebnitsa*), "for the sick of all social classes." The small sum was set aside by the founder and editor, I. S. Prokhanov, as were another three rubles sent at about the same time by two church members in Baku designated for a chil-

---

1 Sinichkin, *Vse radi missii*, 163–64.

dren's shelter.² Perhaps in response to contributions sent so trustingly and spontaneously from church members, by August 1906 *Khristianin* had set up a number of special funds, including one earmarked "for the construction of hospitals, shelters, orphans' homes and other charitable institutions [to] be run in a purely evangelical spirit."³ Just two months later, in October 1906, *Bratskii listok* (Fraternal leaflet, the supplement to *Khristianin*) mentioned a shelter for children that had already been founded by the St. Petersburg Evangelical Christians in Raivola, along the Finnish Railway. Significantly, the journal recorded that two "sisters," that is, female believers, identified only as "D." and "B." had sent a gift to the shelter consisting of a length of cloth, a sugar bowl, and six silver teaspoons. The wording of the announcement is somewhat ambiguous and may signify either that the gift was given in commemoration of the decree of 17 April 1905, or that the shelter itself was actually founded in commemoration of the decree.⁴ Be that as it may, the gift, the mention of 17 April, and the early presence of the children's shelter taken together indicate that evangelicals quickly made a connection between their new freedom and the opportunity to practice compassionate ministry.

Throughout the 1905 to 1929 period, their commitment to practical service remained the same, but new circumstances also brought about important changes in the Russian evangelicals' approach to caring for people in need. The new post1905 freedoms allowed believers to formalize and strengthen church unions, which led to the organization of institutions and funds that were administered especially for the purpose of serving the evangelical community itself. In addition, the newly-legalized evangelical press provided a forum for discussing such topics as money, giving, and good works. For the first time evangelicals were able to reflect on their theological convictions and also educate newcomers to the movement on their attitudes concerning material wealth. Also, foreign evangelical organizations connected with compassionate ministry and social concern, namely the Salvation Army and the YMCA, were physically present in Russia for the first time and served as an inspiration and a model for local believers, even as they in turn provided the newcomers with a base of operations. Not only that, but between 1905 and 1929 unprecedented social changes took place in Russia that both demanded new responses to human need and provided the framework for a response. In particular, from 1914 until the

2 *Bratskii listok* 5 (1906) 32.

3 I[van] S[tepanovich] P[rokhanov], "Brat'ia! K molitve" (Brothers! To prayer), *Bratskii listok* 8 (August 1906) 3.

4 *Bratskii listok* 10 (1906) 18–19.

early 1920s, war, revolution, and famine created the necessity for new, mass forms of compassionate intervention, while the social experimentation of the Soviet 1920s made it possible for evangelicals to participate in new kinds of communities which were intended to transform society altogether. This chapter will provide a framework for examining the ministries that were practiced by evangelicals between 1905 and 1929, describing three quite different basic trends that were nevertheless all undergirded by a common set of principles.

THE "GOLDEN AGE" OF RUSSIAN EVANGELICALISM— 1905 TO 1929

Before examining the main patterns of compassionate ministry practiced by Russian evangelicals between 1905 and 1929, it is necessary to sketch both the general history of the movement during that period and the place of such ministries within it. Two pieces of legislation, one imperial and the other Soviet, but both issued in the month of April, make up the twenty-four year period sometimes remembered as the Golden Age of the Russian evangelical movement. The aforementioned decree of 17 April 1905 opened the door to a wide range of missionary activity, including compassionate ministry, public preaching, education, publishing, and church building construction. The Golden Age concluded with the Soviet law of 8 April 1929, "On religious associations," which brought an end to all believers' activities beyond the conduct of worship in registered meeting places.[5]

Some researchers claim deep historical roots for Russian evangelicalism, finding ancestors as early as the fourteenth or fifteenth centuries,[6] or relating it to the numerous sects that grew out of the seventeenth century schism in Russian Orthodoxy.[7] Yet all agree that the modern expression of evangelicalism in Russia began in the middle of the nineteenth century. Religious revival among German-speaking colonists and the presence of missionary preachers, the emancipation of the serfs in 1861, the availability of Scripture in a variety of languages from about 1813 (especially the second edition of the Russian New Testament in 1862) were all among the

---

5. Coleman, *Russian Baptists*, 217.

6 Savinskii, *Istoriia russko-ukrainskogo baptizma*, 10–12; M. S. Karetnikova, "Russkoe Bogoiskatel'stvo" (The Russian God-search), 3–84 and A. V. Karev, "Russkoe evangel'sko-baptistskoe dvizhenie" (The Russian Evangelical-Baptist Movement), 89–90, in Karetnikova, *Al'manakh, vypusk 1*; cf. Pastor Wilhelm Fetler, "Russia and the Gospel," *The Missionary Review of the World* (October 1912) 740.

7 Savinskii, *Istoriia russko-ukrainskogo baptizma*, 12–15.

catalysts in a religious awakening that took place almost simultaneously in several different locations in the Russian Empire, most notably South Russia (Ukraine), the Caucasus, and St. Petersburg.

Almost from the beginning, however, the movement was opposed by the authorities to a greater or lesser degree in different contexts. The exile of V. A. Pashkov and M. M. Korf in 1884 and the semi-underground existence that ensued for the St. Petersburg evangelicals were described in the previous chapter. Restriction reached its height in 1894 with the introduction of laws aimed at the systematic suppression of the *shtundisty* (Stundists). These were usually Russian or Ukrainian peasants who were disparagingly nicknamed after the German *Bibelstunde* (Bible hour) or *Gebetstunde* (prayer hour), because of their practice of gathering outside of regular worship services in small groups for a time of Bible reading and prayer like their Pietist neighbors. By the mid 1890s, according to the law, people branded as Stundists were not permitted to gather together for worship; they could not be employed; their children were to be removed to the homes of Orthodox relatives or handed over to members of the clergy. For some of them, a life of arrest and imprisonment became routine. Many spent years in exile, either within the Empire or abroad.[8]

The status of evangelical believers changed rather abruptly in 1905. Pressured by strikes, assassinations, and the defeat of Russia in the war with Japan, Emperor Nicholas II acquiesced to a series of political and social concessions. Of prime importance to the evangelicals was, of course, the Decree of 17 April. Its appearance meant that evangelicals were able to gather together freely for worship, and if evangelism ("proselytism") was still regarded with suspicion, there were no longer penalties for a Russian who wished to leave the Orthodox Church. Other important legislation followed. The October Manifesto (1905) established a legislature (the Duma) and proclaimed freedom of conscience, speech, and assembly. A year later (17 October 1906) another decree set out the procedure for the formal registration of evangelical congregations.[9] All this paved the way for greater freedom to minister among their fellow-citizens.

Almost as soon as religious freedom was declared, the Russian evangelicals launched ambitious plans. From the vantage point of 1911, reflecting on the rapid gains that began in 1905, the Baptist leader of Baku, V. V. Ivanov, referred to this period as "the epoch of the open storm," in the

---

8 For the texts of legislation concerning Russian sectarians during the late nineteenth century, see Iasevich-Borodaevskaia, *Bor'ba za veru*; see also Brandenburg, *The Meek and the Mighty*, 114–27; Coleman, *Russian Baptists*, 13–26.

9 Coleman, *Russian Baptists*, 27–46.

military sense of storming, or assault.¹⁰ Many exiles returned home and took up preaching; the first legal periodicals appeared; national congresses assembled; missionaries were appointed; training courses for preachers were started; and prayer houses were built. As for compassionate ministries, evangelicals formalized their activities by organizing designated funds for the support of members of their own communities in need and also to support church-based institutions. They also addressed themselves to the needs of the urban population by participating in rescue ministries and the Russian temperance movement. Above all, during this period the evangelical movement grew. It will be recalled that during this period most evangelicals belonged to one of two church unions. Heather Coleman cites a government survey on sectarianism published in 1912, establishing that over the seven years between April 1905 and January 1912, Russian Baptists (members of a union unofficially founded in 1884) added 21,140 members to their ranks, that is, about one-third of their total membership at the time (66,788). During the same period the Evangelical Christian Union (founded in 1909 by I. S. Prokhanov) also grew by approximately one-third, adding 9,175 people to its total of 29,988.¹¹

Yet it was not an easy time. The St. Petersburg Baptist preacher, W. A. Fetler, in a speech to the Baptist World Alliance gathered at Philadelphia in the summer of 1911, compared the past and present situation of evangelicals in Russia to the difference between eating stale crusts and eating fresh, black bread. Although the Russian evangelicals might prefer white bread with butter and cheese, they were grateful for the "bread" that was available when they remembered the "bread" they used to eat, meaning their previous almost total lack of freedom.¹² In other words, after 1905 evangelicals were comparatively free and active, but they still had to deal with intermittent persecution on the part of the authorities as well as their fellow citizens. A regular feature of *Khristianin* was the documentation of violations against believers collected by legal activist Ivan Petrovich Kushnerov of Kyiv, who had devoted himself to the defense of persecuted sectarians since the mid-1890s.¹³ The new freedoms gradually gave way to increasing

---

10 V. V. Ivanov, "Polozhenie Baptistov" (The situation of Baptists), *Baptist* 9 (23 February 1911) 69.

11 Coleman, *Russian Baptists*, 27.

12 *The Baptist World Alliance Second Congress*, 21.

13 For information on Kushnerov, see *Khristianin* 2 (1908) 11–12 and Coleman, *Russian Baptists*, 32, 43. Examples of documentation of persecution include *Bratskii listok* 2 (1907) 33, 35–40; *Bratskii listok* 7 (1907) 10; *Bratskii listok* 4 (1908) 5–7; "Zverstva v Rossii" (Brutalities in Russia), *Bratskii listok* 7 (July 1910) 4, 9–10; I. P. Kushnerov, "Zabytaia zapoved' Gospoda Iisusa" (The forgotten commandment of the Lord Jesus),

pressure. Restrictions introduced in 1910 kept evangelicals from holding outdoor meetings, curtailed special meetings for children and youth, and even sometimes led to prayer houses being closed entirely. After 1911 Baptists were no longer permitted to call together congresses. Over the New Year holiday in 1912, the Evangelical Christian Union held its last congress until 1917.[14]

The uncertain status of evangelicals in the wider community inevitably affected their compassionate ministries as well. An English Baptist observer, Chas. T. Byford, related the story of four nursing sisters who were baptized by V. G. Pavlov in about 1912, most likely in Odessa. Immediately, all four women lost their jobs and Pavlov went to prison for two months. In other words, women who could be described as "mainstream" participants in a form of compassionate ministry were deprived of that activity as soon as they joined the evangelicals. Two of them, known only as "Claudia and Mary," continued to work with Pavlov, "among the sick and sorrowing members of his great and growing Church."[15] That is, because they were often excluded from the rest of Russian society, evangelicals of necessity tended to emphasize caring for their own.

With the start of World War I in 1914 a surge of patriotic unity raised hopes for renewed religious freedom. Evangelicals welcomed the opportunity to demonstrate their willingness to assist in the war effort and thus prove their loyalty. In numerous locations congregations fitted out their prayer houses to serve as infirmaries for the wounded or contributed to the equipping of similar facilities. Evangelical women's circles were organized to knit and sew for the soldiers.[16] Some evangelicals went to the front as nursing sisters or as medical orderlies;[17] others ministered to war refugees and soldiers' families.[18] However, within months after the start of the war, an

---

Bratskii listok 8 (August 1910) 1–2.

14 For information on the escalating tensions between Baptists and Orthodox during 1910 and 1911, see Coleman, *Russian Baptists*, 109–14.

15 Byford, *Peasants and Prophets*, 96.

16 See, for example, V. V. Ivanov, "Na pomoshch' rannenym voinam" (To the aid of wounded soldiers), *Baptist,* 15–16 (1914) 17–18; "Rabota Balashovskikh Baptistov" (The work of Balashov Baptists), *Baptist,* 21–22-23–24 (1914) 5–6.

17 *Gost',* 1 (January 1915) 7; E. B., "Iz pis'ma sestry miloserdiia s fronta" (From the letter of a sister of mercy at the front), *Gost',* 5 (May 1917) 10–11; Salov-Astakhov, *Palatochnaia missiia,* 11; A. A. Toews, "Dyck, Jakob J. (1890–1919)." *Global Anabaptist Mennonite Encyclopedia Online.* 1956, http://gameo.org/index.php?title=Dyck,_Jakob_J._(1890–1919)&oldid=94462.

18 E. N. K[uteinikova], "'Sem'ia' detei v Levashove' iz opyta raboty v kruzhkakh molodezhi pri Dome Evangeliia" (The "family of children in Levashov" from the work experience in the Dom Evangeliia youth groups), *Gost',* 6 (June 1917) 86–87; "Nechto

almost total blackout descended again when prayer houses were closed and many leaders were sent into exile as "German elements," dangerous to the state. By 1916 both the Baptist Union and the Evangelical Christian Union were temporarily shut down.[19] Clearly, this was a serious hindrance for the compassionate ministry of evangelicals.

The evangelical movement rallied again with the February Revolution of 1917 and the abdication of Emperor Nicholas II. Amnesty was declared for all exiles and political prisoners, which meant that hundreds of evangelical pastors returned to their congregations. All Russian citizens were granted equal rights and freedom of assembly, speech, press, and religion. A few evangelical leaders proposed political programs.[20] In November 1917 when the Bolsheviks took power, their first concern was the destruction of the Orthodox Church as complicit in the injustices of the tsarist regime. To a certain extent, as elements that had suffered at the hands of the Empire and longed for the formation of a new society, some Soviet authorities regarded the evangelicals as something like allies and even potential revolutionary material.[21] However, the situation quickly grew ominous. In 1919 a nameless "fervent female servant of God in Petrograd,"[22] wrote a letter on behalf of a "circle of women" there to Christians in England detailing the distressing changes that were taking place in Russian society and asking for prayer. The writer was particularly concerned about the sufferings of children who were daily dying of hunger and disease, but also being taught in the schools to reject God.[23] Many evangelical leaders suffered multiple imprisonments. Ivan Nikitovich Shilov (1887–1942), who was ordained pastor of the flagship Baptist church in Petrograd, Dom Evangeliia (House of the Gospel) in 1919, was first arrested in 1920 and then four subsequent times for longer or shorter periods until he died doing hard labor in a forestry camp in Eastern Siberia.[24] During this time especially the institutional expression of com-

---

o priiute v Levashove" (Something about the shelter in Levashov), *Gost'* 11 (November 1917) 175; Larsson, "The Army in Russia," 57–58; Aitken, *Blood and Fire*, 169–74, 191.

19 Coleman, *Russian Baptists*, 115–123.

20 Nikol'skaia, "Russkii protestantizm na etape utverzhdeniia legalizatsii," 176–79.

21. Sawatsky, *Soviet Evangelicals*, 3637; Coleman, *Russian Baptists*, 154–79.

22 The letter could possibly have been written by M. N. Iasnovskaia or perhaps Sofia Liven. Note that in 1914 for patriotic reasons the Germanic name "St. Petersburg" was changed to its Slavic equivalent, "Petrograd." Ten years later, in 1924, Petrograd became Leningrad in honor of the Bolshevik leader V. I. Lenin (1870–1924).

23 "Vozzvanie russkikh zhenshchin k moliashchimsia detiam Bozhiim povsiudu" (The call of Russian women to the praying children of God everywhere), *Drug*, (November 1919) 82–86.

24 Sevast'ianov, "Pleiada sluzhitelelei," 5.

passionate ministries among evangelicals was tolerated less and less. By the early 1920s the government had taken over the running of the Baptist home for children and the elderly in Balashov, and replaced the Christian personnel in other evangelical institutions for children as well.[25]

At the same time, however, the unprecedented social upheaval of this period required a new response to human need on the part of the evangelicals. Faced with the potential death by starvation of at least 20 percent of their total membership,[26] as well as the suffering of others during the famine of 1921 to 1923, Russian evangelicals coordinated the distribution of approximately US $600,000 worth of food and other forms of material aid brought in from Western Europe and the United States.[27] Also, in the volatile atmosphere of the 1920s, there was space for evangelicals to experiment with agricultural communes and cooperative labor enterprises. Despite its atheistic policies, because of the unsettled, experimental nature of the new regime in some ways the evangelicals could work more freely in the 1920s than they were able to at certain times under the tsars. Certainly, the Soviet government applied pressure to the evangelicals, especially in the matter of their position on military service. In 1919 provision had been made for conscientious objector status.[28] Rather surprisingly, that policy continued until the mid 1930s;[29] however, in 1923 the government demanded that the evangelicals renounce pacifism.[30] Nevertheless, during the 1920s, the church unions were revived and congresses were held. Evangelicals preached and

25 SBHLA, The Historical Papers of Mrs. I. V. Neprash, "Zapis' No. 23, Zasedanie Kollegii Vserossiiskogo Soiuza," 18 March 1922; Toews, *Mennonite Martyrs*, 93–94; see also Saloff-Astakhoff, *Little Lame Walter* and *Real Russia*, 71–72.

26 SBHLA, The Historical Papers of Mrs. I. V. Neprash, "Zapis' No. 19," 24 February 1922, states that 44,000 Baptists were threatened by the famine in the Volga region; Steeves estimates that 20 percent of all Baptists were endangered ("The Russian Baptist Union," 174). Evangelical Christian congregations were also threatened according to *Utrenniaia zvezda*, 3–4–5 (March–April–May 1922) 2. The estimate of the number of sufferers increased significantly as the famine zone expanded to include Ukraine and the Caucasus.

27 SBHLA, ABFMS Correspondence, "International Conference on Baptist Relief and Mission Work in Europe," Baptist World Alliance, 1 August 1922, 348; J. H. Rushbrooke, "European Relief," Foreign Missions Board Report, Southern Baptist Conference, 1923, 121; J. H. Rushbrooke (London) to Rev. Dr. J. H. Franklin (New York) 20 December 1923; "General Review of the Year," American Baptist Foreign Mission Society, 1923, 25.

28. Sawatsky, *Soviet Evangelicals*, 115–20.

29. Guy F. Hershberger, Albert N. Keim and Hanspeter Jecker, "Conscientious Objection" *Global Anabaptist Mennonite Encyclopedia Online*, 1990, http://gameo.org/index.php?title=Conscientious_Objection&oldid=103534.

30. Coleman, *Russian Baptists*, 191–97.

baptized, conducted educational programs, formed choirs and orchestras, and established cultural patterns for church life that have been sustained to the present day.[31] Also, in spite of government interference, as well as civil war, epidemics, and famine in the earliest years, the 1920s also saw remarkable growth in the Russian evangelical movement. Statistics are inexact and possibly rather inflated, but according to one estimate, there may have been as many as five-hundred thousand Baptists and Evangelical Christians by the end of the decade. If believers' children and other relatives are counted, it would mean that more than one million Soviet citizens could have been considered part of the evangelicals' wider circle.[32]

Yet, although evangelicals presented themselves as loyal citizens who were grateful for religious freedom and acknowledged many parallels between their goals and those of the Soviet state, by 1927, as Josef Stalin (1879–1953) was consolidating his power, there was less and less room for alternative approaches in an atmosphere of increasing ideological strictness. The law of 8 April 1929, "On religious associations," forbade religious groups to participate in a long list of activities, such as organizing meetings or outings for different age groups, engaging in any form of compassionate ministry, or forming economic associations. The following month an amendment to the constitution allowed only "freedom of religious confession," but not "propaganda"—in other words evangelism. Only the right to anti-religious propaganda remained. By the end of the 1920s the process of drawing all aspects of community life into the hands of the state was nearly complete. Private social or charitable institutions, such as orphanages, hospitals, and schools, ceased to exist. By 1929, the evangelical Golden Age had reached its end.[33]

MAIN EMPHASES OF EVANGELICAL COMPASSIONATE MINISTRIES, 1905 TO 1929

Thus, the commitment of Russian evangelicals to compassionate ministry continued throughout the entire period under discussion, although, of course, the actual outworking of that commitment was necessarily adapted to various circumstances, especially given the alternating periods of relative

---

31. Ibid., 154–79.

32. Ibid., 162–63; cf. Constantine Prokhorov, "The 'Golden Age' of the Soviet Baptists in the 1920s" in Corrado and Pilli, *Eastern European Baptist History*, 88.

33. Sawatsky, *Soviet Evangelicals*, 46; Coleman, *Russian Baptists*, 217. Note that religious freedom lasted a few years longer away from the center in more remote areas of the Soviet Union.

freedom or restriction. Overall, it is possible to distinguish three distinct approaches to compassionate ministries among the evangelicals from 1905 to 1929, each identified with certain leaders. These approaches are: first, aid within the evangelical community itself, represented by D. I. Mazaev, V. G. Pavlov, and V. V. Ivanov (sometimes also known as Ivanov-Klyshnikov);[34] second, urban rescue ministry, represented by W. A. Fetler; and third, the establishment of economic communities, represented by I. S. Prokhanov. As will be demonstrated below, all of the leaders described shared the same basic set of convictions about the Christian responsibility to help people in need, but because of their rather different contexts and goals, they tended to emphasize different aspects of that responsibility.

The first major type of compassionate ministry among evangelicals of the period was aid practiced among church members, especially sustaining pastors and missionaries. This was considered crucial because of the importance of preaching the gospel, which they understood as the key to transforming people's lives. In other words, if, as the evangelicals believed, evangelism was their most significant task, then it was essential to care for the needs of the evangelist. In addition, because of their rather marginalized status, it was also important for church members to take responsibility for caring for those within their own midst. This approach was most typical of Baptist leaders such as D. I. Mazaev, V. G. Pavlov, and V. V. Ivanov. Mazaev and Pavlov both served as president of the Russian Baptist Union and all three leaders served at different times as editor of the main Baptist publication, *Baptist*.[35]

Mazaev, Pavlov, and Ivanov were committed to building a strong, distinctively Baptist denominational organization. Mazaev was once described by a Swedish missionary as "Baptist from head to foot,"[36] and expressed that identity in vigorous organizational activity and systematic teaching on money and giving in support of Christian ministry which appeared on the pages of *Baptist*. The actual writer who most frequently reflected on those themes in *Baptist* was V. V. Ivanov; nevertheless, I have also put forward D. I. Mazaev and V. G. Pavlov as representative of the first stream because in their role as editors they would have been in agreement with Ivanov and solicited the articles he wrote, and as union presidents would have led the way in planning the church's program. Doubtless because of V. G. Pavlov's experience of exile (two four-year periods of exile in Orenburg, 1887 to 1891 and

---

34. N. V. Odintsov, "Obrazets dlia vernykh" (An example for the faithful), *Baptist* 2 (1929) 10.

35. Sinichkin, *Vse radi missii*, 155–59.

36. Sawatsky, *Soviet Evangelicals*, 79.

1891 to 1895, after which time he sought refuge in Tulcea, Romania until he returned to Russia in 1901),[37] he was keenly interested in building a support structure capable of sustaining Baptist missionaries and pastors.

In addition, the practice of compassionate ministry within the Russian evangelical community owed something to patterns established among indigenous Russian sectarian groups, namely the Dukhobors and especially the Molokans, a group that separated from the Dukhobors during the 1770s. D. I. Mazaev, V. G. Pavlov, V. V. Ivanov, and I. S. Prokhanov, as well as other leaders, all came from the Molokan community.[38] Generally speaking, Dukhobors and Molokans rejected all material manifestations of Christianity, including the Lord's Supper, baptism, images, and the church hierarchy and emphasized equality in their dealings with one another and the wider society, a teaching that led them sometimes to reject government authority and military service.[39] In terms of their attitude to compassionate ministry, "the sectarians were pariah groups who tended to turn inward and work together as a community, providing vital economic and social support to each other."[40] That is, first of all they tended to emphasize their responsibility to the well-being of members of their own group. The evangelical understanding of compassionate ministry was considerably broader than that of the Molokans, but the evangelicals' commitment to supporting preachers and their families, as well as the hindrances they experienced on the part of the authorities often caused them to concentrate on serving members of their own community.

To meet their goals, the Russian Baptist Union tended to focus on the establishment of denominational institutions, such as a home for orphans and elderly in Balashov (near Saratov), and the maintenance and administration of assistance funds, most of which continued to exist until a few years after the Bolshevik Revolution. Mutual assistance continued during the 1920s in the form of small business cooperatives and a credit union, *Bratskaia pomoshch'* (Fraternal assistance) was founded in 1922 specifically for church members.[41]

Although part of the Russian Baptist Union, Wilhelms Andreis Vettlers, better known in English as William A. Fetler, and later in life as Basil

---

37. V. G. Pavlov, "Vospominaniia ssylnogo" (Recollections of an exile) in Karetnikova, *Al'manakh, vypusk 1*, 199–218.

38. Sawatsky, *Soviet Evangelicals*, 32.

39 For detailed accounts of Dukhobor and Molokan beliefs see Bonch-Bruevich, *Materialy k istorii i izucheniu russkogo sektanstva i raskola*; Klibanov, *Istoriia religioznogo sektanstva v Rossii*; Breyfogle, *Heretics and Colonizers*.

40 Breyfogle, *Heretics and Colonizers*, 122.

41. Popov, "Evangel'skie trudovye arteli," 27

Malof, represented the second emphasis in compassionate ministry which I have called urban rescue ministry. He shared in Baptist denominational life, but he was an enthusiastic revival preacher rather than an institution builder. Fetler was inspired by ministry models he encountered in England as a student at Pastors' College from 1903 to 1907. Fetler learned from the legacy of C. H. Spurgeon and followed the practices of the Welsh Revival of 1904 to 1905, evangelist Rodney "Gypsy" Smith (1860–1947), and the Salvation Army.[42] From his arrival in St. Petersburg in 1907 until his exile from Russia in 1915,[43] Fetler and the members of the congregation at Dom Evangeliia actively evangelized among the growing numbers of urban poor, holding night meetings, running a shelter for men who wished to change their way of life, operating an inexpensive dining room, and other similar ministries.[44]

The industrial revolution in Russia began later than it did in Western Europe, accelerating gradually after the emancipation of the serfs in 1861, and then peaking sharply during the 1890s. Eighty-five percent of Russia's industries were established after 1861, and nearly half of those appeared between 1891 and 1902. Between 1890 and 1914 the number of industrial laborers in Russia grew from about 1,424,000 to 3,743,800.[45] As in Western Europe, industrialization was accompanied by a steady movement of the population into urban centers, although in Russia the process took place more slowly because it was difficult for peasants to leave the land permanently. Many laborers were temporary, migrating to factories or mines for shorter or longer periods while maintaining ties with their home villages. Nevertheless, the general trend tended to keep millions of Russian peasants, most of them young, working for months at a time in urban settings.[46] As in the West, urbanization was, on the one hand, full of promise, offering greater earning power and new experiences. However, it also carried social consequences. City living and factory work required new skills. Even for seasonal workers, family and village ties tended to unravel with the passage of time. Without access to traditional means of social support, many were unable to cope with the demands of city life. People were crowded into dangerous and

---

42. J. Fetler, *Sluzhenie Rossii*, 10–15.

43. *Bratskii listok* 8 (1907) 20; Wardin, "William Fetler," 238–39; Fetler's own account of his 1915 arrest appears in J. Fetler, *Sluzhenie Rossii*, 42–46.

44. *Baptist* 18 (28 April 1910) n.p.; *Baptist* 19 (5 May 1910) n.p.; *Baptist* 23 (2 June 1910) n.p; *Gost'* 3 (January 1911) 37; Packer, *Among the Heretics*, 39–40; Oncken et al, "The Baptist Work in Russia," 188; Wardin, "William Fetler," 237.

45 Engel, *Between the Fields and the City*, 102.

46 Fitzpatrick, *The Russian Revolution*, 18–19.

filthy slum neighborhoods, such as Khitrovka in Moscow.[47] An injury, an illness, or a pregnancy could render a worker unemployable, forcing many into begging, theft, or prostitution to survive. As poverty deepened, it was more and more difficult to overcome one's circumstances. Disease and vice overtook thousands. Widespread social concern for the plight of so many people led to a spike in the establishment of charitable organizations during the second half of the nineteenth century, accompanying the growth of industry and the increase in the urban population during the same period. According to a statistic published in 1900, there were 13,918 charitable organizations in the Russian Empire, 95 percent of which had been founded between 1861 and 1899,[48] many of which were intended to serve the needs of the urban poor. Likewise, the Russian temperance movement flourished between 1895 and 1914, and numerous church- and government-sponsored organizations were formed to fight against alcoholism, especially among the lower classes.[49]

W. A. Fetler and other evangelicals, such as I. S. Prokhanov[50] and some of the remaining St. Petersburg Pashkovites, such as Elizaveta Chertkova and Baroness M. N. Iasnovskaia,[51] were actively involved in reaching the urban poor during this period. Indeed, Fetler's compassionate ministries in some ways represented a continuation of Pashkovite interest in serving the poor, although in a rather different vein. Whereas many of the aristocratic Pashkovites added an evangelical emphasis to ministries that were typical for people of higher social classes, Fetler's approach was like that of the Salvation Army, utilizing popular culture, especially music, as an attraction, and introducing techniques that were new to Russia, such as night meetings, intended to draw drunkards and prostitutes.[52] Fetler and others also promoted the Russian temperance movement, while linking it with evangelical motifs of repentance and spiritual transformation.[53] Urban rescue ministry continued to be practiced in Russia through the early 1920s.

---

47 For a graphic description of Khitrovka see Vladimir Giliarovskii's essay "Khitrovka" in *Moskva i moskvichi*, 42–70.

48 Ivanova and Ivanova, *Zarubezhnyi opyt*, 43–44.

49 Transchel, *Under the Influence*, 47.

50 A. I. Kareva, "Moi vospominaniia" (My recollections) in Karetnikova, *Al'manakh, vypusk 2*, 184.

51 *The Baptist World Alliance Second Congress*, 237; Stewart, *A Man in a Hurry*, 39; J. Fetler, *Sluzhenie Rossii*, 29.

52 *Baptist* 4 (20 January 1910) 29–30; Packer, *Among the Heretics*, 39; Fetler, "Russia and the Gospel," 745.

53. *Baptist* 4 (20 January 1910) 29–30.

Third, the evangelicals were attracted to the idea of creating economic communities, usually agricultural communes, where they anticipated that poverty and vice would be eradicated altogether. V. A. Pashkov and M. M. Korf had pursued the idea in 1883, and possibly even several years earlier.[54] I. S. Prokhanov, under the combined influence of his Molokan roots, his contact with the agricultural community established by N. N. Nepliuev, and possibly his knowledge of Mennonite colony life, was instrumental in setting up an evangelical community in Crimea called Vertograd in 1894.[55] Before the Bolshevik Revolution, Prokhanov and the Evangelical Christians (the church union he organized in 1909) were also involved in urban rescue ministries similar to those promoted by Fetler.[56] Beginning in 1906, like Mazaev, Pavlov, and Ivanov, Prokhanov also established, promoted, and administered church-based assistance funds and charitable institutions.[57] Ultimately, however, Prokhanov is distinguished from other evangelical leaders by his articulation of a broader social agenda, especially his promotion of alternative communities during the 1920s. The Bolshevik Revolution presented new opportunities for the cause of communal living, particularly in the early years when the desperate need for food supplies permitted agricultural experimentation. In 1921 a special government committee facilitated the settlement of sectarians and Old Believers on newly nationalized lands.[58] Sectarian communes, scores of them founded by evangelicals, continued to exist in one form or another in Soviet Russia at least until the late 1920s, with a few surviving into the 1930s.[59] Yet, although theoretically communal living was encouraged by the state, over time it became clear that from an ideological point of view, communes were socially radical, that is, potentially difficult to control.[60] Especially as the battle against all forms of religious expression gained momentum, communes formed by religious groups, including those organized by evangelicals, were targeted for dissolution.

54. AUCEC-B Archives, Drawer 3, ISP Folder 7.3a, Savchenko, "Ekspeditsiia v kommunu Vertograd," 1; Popov, *I. S. Prokhanov*, 134.

55. Prokhanoff, *Cauldron*, 88–90.

56. *Iunyi khristianin* 1 (1909) 1–8; Kareva, "Moi vospominaniia," 184.

57. P[rokhanov], "Brat'ia! K molitve," *Bratskii listok* 8 (August 1906) 2–3; *Khristianin* 4 (1910) n.p.

58 Popov, "Khristianskie kommuny I. S. Prokhanova i gorod Solntsa" (Christian communes of I. S. Prokhanov and the City of the Sun), in Beliakova and Sinichkin, *105 let legalizatsii russkogo baptizma*, 135.

59 Berezhnoi, "Byt' souchastnikom Evangeliia," 6; Red'kina, *Sel'skokhoziaistvennye religioznye trudovye kollektivy*, 566–89.

60. Wesson, *Soviet Communes*, 91.

Although other evangelicals, notably the Baptist Union, were behind the founding of numerous communes and cooperatives,[61] Prokhanov was the leader who wrote most comprehensively on the topic. In 1918 he published a brochure entitled *Evangel'skoe khristianstvo i sotsial'nyi vopros* (Evangelical Christianity and the social question) that outlined a pattern for the development of different kinds of communities.[62] Prokhanov understood communal living as part of an all-embracing social transformation that would elevate people's spiritual life and also allow their physical needs to be met. Basing his ideas on the model of the Jerusalem church in the Book of Acts, Prokhanov drew attention to the biblical testimony that "there were no needy persons among them," i.e. the Christians (Acts 4:34), and asserted that only Christians had the spiritual capacity to realize a new society.[63] Eventually, Prokhanov took the initial steps toward establishing an entire city to be called Evangel'sk, or City of the Sun. A site for the city was allocated in the Altai region on the border with Mongolia in 1927, but by May 1928 the project was liquidated on instructions from the Politburo.[64]

Thus, from 1905 to 1929 there were three basic evangelical approaches to social need in Russia: aid in the form of dedicated funds and the development of institutions shared within the community; rescue ministry aimed at the needs of the urban poor; and the total transformation of society through the founding of economic communities. Although there was some overlap between the practitioners of each approach, it is possible to identify each one in the main with a particular leader who pursued that form of ministry as a parallel stream. Baptist Union leaders D. I. Mazaev, V. G. Pavlov, and V. V. Ivanov emphasized church-based assistance funds and institutions; the pastor of Dom Evangeliia, W. A. Fetler, practiced rescue ministry; Evangelical Christian Union leader I. S. Prokhanov promoted economic communities. Furthermore, each was located in its own particular relatively favorable time frame. Assistance among fellow believers only became publicly practicable after 1905 and lasted until the early 1920s. Urban rescue ministry reached its height in the 1910s and survived through the early 1920s. Economic communities were a matter of interest for evangelicals since the nineteenth century, but became viable in a juridical sense from about 1921 and lasted until nearly the end of the decade. Meanwhile, right in the middle of the

61. Popov, "Khristianskie kommuny," 136.

62. Popov, "Evangel'skie trudovye arteli," 28; Redkina, *Sel'skokhoziaistvennye religioznye trudovye kollektivy*, 126.

63 Prokhanov, "Novaia ili Evangel'skaia zhizn,'" 96–124; I. S. Prokhanov, "Chto nam delat'" (What must we do) *Khristianin* 1 (1928) 6–15; Popov, "Evangel'skie trudovye arteli," 28–32.

64 Popov, "Khristianskie kommuny," 137.

1905 to 1929 Golden Age, between 1914 and 1923 major social disasters created by war, revolution, and famine made new demands on evangelicals and the 1917 Bolshevik Revolution brought about drastic ideological changes concerning the practice of compassionate ministry. Nevertheless, in spite of the difference in timing and emphasis between the three basic approaches, the differing contexts and concerns of the leaders who represent each approach, and in spite of their rapidly changing environment, the Russian evangelicals maintained quite a consistent understanding of compassionate ministry throughout the period from 1905 to 1929. The basic convictions on which they were in substantial agreement are illustrated by the following points.

THE TRANSFORMING POWER OF THE GOSPEL

Evangelism—preaching the good news of Jesus Christ to all creation, according to his command (Matthew 28:19–20)—was considered by all the leaders to be the most important work to which all Christians must give their greatest attention. Russian evangelicals believed that not only the eternal future of human beings depended on the willingness of believers faithfully to carry the gospel everywhere, but also something of their well-being in the present. This is because they perceived the effect of the gospel to be far-reaching, striking at the very root of all misery, which is sin, "the mother of the social question . . . the cause of death, all the sufferings and all the needs of people."[65] If sin was not dealt with, all efforts to improve social conditions were nothing more than "pitiful bandages," that cover up but do not heal wounds.[66] Like the Pashkovites, the later generation of evangelicals was interested in the transformation of society as a whole. They perceived Russia to be in the throes of great suffering, socially, materially, and spiritually, and they believed that they held the key to the solution of all the nation's problems. A writer identified by the initials "Kh. I. K." declared the church's mission to be the following: "There are 140 million Russian people. We must go forward to meet this spiritually suffering people with the true Gospel of Christ."[67] Some evangelical leaders involved themselves briefly in politics, notably I. S. Prokhanov who proposed Christian political parties in 1905 and again in 1917.[68] However, the Russian evangelicals believed that

65. "Drug iunoshi, Sotsial'nyi vopros" (The friend of youth. The social question), *Molodoi vinogradnik* 1 (January 1911) 2.

66. Ibid., 2.

67 Kh. I. K., *Bratskii listok* 6 (1906) 4.

68. For a concise summary of these and other attempts, see Vladimir Popov,

the transformation of systems was not possible without individual transformation and relied on preaching the gospel to influence society.[69] The gospel was the ultimate answer to human suffering, as V. V. Ivanov reflected:

> How much joy has the gospel brought to individual families and individual hearts of sinners and unhappy people! Through the preaching of the Gospel thousands of drunkards have become sober; wantons [male and female] have become chaste. Through the Gospel beggars have become rich. The Gospel, like the sun, drives away all darkness and ignorance and makes people useful to their families, to society, and to the Kingdom of God on earth.[70]

Evangelicals also believed that Christianity held the solution to alienation between social classes. In a speech given on 13 May 1907 at a "spiritual concert" at the Baptist church in Baku in aid of orphans (probably created by the famine of 1906),[71] V. G. Pavlov pointed to changed attitudes through the "law of love" as the only lasting solution for social and political problems:

> ... there is no other way out of our worsening class and economic struggle between capital and labor, between rich and poor ... Only the observation of this commandment by everyone can make us happy and give us the opportunity to perfect our lives in every respect ... .[72]

Thus, the Russian evangelicals saw the gospel as the ultimate solution to all human need, whether on the personal or national level. That being the case, they believed that it was essential to meet the needs of the preachers who carried the greatest responsibility for evangelism. In 1909 V. V. Ivanov proudly pointed out that the Russian Baptist Union annually collected upwards of ten thousand rubles for the support of twenty evangelists.[73] That

---

"Evangel'skoe dvizhenie v Rossii i politicheskie partii" (The evangelical movement in Russia and political parties), in Raber and Penner, *History and Mission in Europe,* 161–76.

69. For a useful summary of the Russian evangelical view of politics, see Nesdoly "Evangelical Sectarianism in Russia," 307–47.

70 V. V. Ivanov, "O delakh," *Baptist* 5 (March 1909) 7.

71 For background on the 1906 famine, see Liudmila Zhukova and Galina Ul'ianova, "'Ne imeia rodnogo ugla...' Istoricheskii opyt bor'by s besprizornost'iu detei" (With no corner of one's own... The historical experience of the battle against lack of supervision among children), http://miloserdie.ru, 1–2.

72 V. G. Pavlov, "Kto moi blizhnyi?" (Who is my neighbor?), *Baptist* 4 (April 1908) 3; see also "Drug iunoshi, Sotsial'nyi vopros," 4.

73 Ivanov, "O delakh," 7.

is, a significant part of the evangelicals' giving was centered on helping their own people, especially evangelists.

THE EVANGELICAL DILEMMA: WORDS OR WORKS?

Compassionate ministry was always considered essential by Russian evangelical believers despite external criticism that accused them of focusing only on words and neglecting works of charity and help. Both the criticism and the believers' response to it illustrate different kinds of theological thinking and biblical interpretation. An important concept was the way that the key Protestant tenet of "faith alone" was understood. One criticism frequently leveled against the evangelicals was that they did no good works at all and taught others to do the same because they believed that salvation is by faith alone. In some cases, this impression was probably well founded. In March 1900 *Missionerskoe obozrenie* (Missionary review), an Orthodox publication founded in 1896, described two encounters between two factory workers, one a "Pashkovite" named Gavriil Kozmin and the other an Orthodox Christian, Stepan Ivanovich Ivanov. When Kozmin came to work at a ship-building factory in St. Petersburg, he began to spread Pashkovite teaching among his fellow workers until he was challenged to a public dispute by Ivanov. One of the topics they discussed in their two meetings was the essence of faith. Kozmin asserted that his faith could be summed up in one word: "Believe." Ivanov countered by quoting James 2:19: even demons believe, but faith shows itself in good works. With this and several other arguments Ivanov defeated Kozmin, who soon afterwards left St. Petersburg for Sevastopol.[74]

Kozmin's misunderstanding of Christian teaching must have been fairly widespread, because in two of his articles V. V. Ivanov complained that some people, who had left behind the Orthodox understanding of gaining merit by doing good works, simply used that as an excuse never to do anything at all![75] In fact, he wrote, many of them seemed to think that giving alms was a direct denial of the teaching on salvation by grace. Ivanov argued that, on the contrary, giving and good works are not excluded by the message of salvation through the blood of Christ.[76] Ivan Prokhanov added that a person who hopes in faith without works is just as unfortunate as the

---

74 "Dve besedy pravoslavnago mirianina s pashkovtsem" (Two conversations of an Orthodox layman with a Pashkovite), *Missionerskoe obozrenie* 10 (1900) 427–33.

75 Ivanov, "O delakh," 6–7.

76 V. V. Ivanov, "Slovo k veruiushchim" (A word to believers), *Baptist* 6 (December 1907) 5.

one who hopes in works apart from faith in Christ and summed it all up by stating that Scripture teaches that the point of doing good is not to "pay" for one's salvation, but to express gratitude to God, to proclaim God's love for people, and to serve as a sign of a lively faith.[77] In fact, Russian evangelicals taught that people are called to bless and help one another.[78]

Another important reason for the evangelicals' reputation for neglecting compassionate ministry was, according to V. V. Ivanov, that they no longer contributed to such things as the upkeep of monasteries, or paid fees for prayers or memorial services. All these traditional Orthodox practices of doing good were dismissed by Ivanov as having been "spontaneously determined by people who were not enlightened by the Word of God."[79] Having established the importance of good works, evangelicals concurred that it is necessary to perform only those deeds that God has given people to do according to the Bible, namely spread the gospel (including contributing support to evangelists) and care directly for the poor.[80] What the wider society might interpret as neglecting good deeds was actually the evangelicals' way of setting priorities: faith and word first, and then—closely linked with these—everyday help and good works.

THE RIGHT ATTITUDE TO SERVICE AND WEALTH

Despite external criticism, the Russian evangelicals believed that keeping biblical principles in mind would ensure that they approached good works with an attitude of sensitivity, humility, and compassion. They taught that one's attitude to compassionate ministry was as important as what one actually did. In the first place, all giving had to be done "in secret" before God, rather than for the sake of other people's praise, according to Christ's words in Matthew 6:3: "do not let your left hand know what your right hand is doing." V. V. Ivanov rejected as too literal the Molokan practice of placing offerings under a towel spread on a table so that no one could see how much each person gave. Rather, he said, Christians should be moved by love and sympathy for those in need and not by any hope of public honor for their generosity.[81]

77 Prokhanov, *Verouchenie evangel'skikh khristian*, 23.

78. "Zhizn' dana na dobrye dela," (Life is given for good works), *Molodoi vinogradnik* 3 (March 1911) 22.

79. Prokhanov, *Verouchenie*, 23; Ivanov, "O delakh," 7.

80. Ivanov, "O delakh," 7–8; Prokhanov, *Verouchenie*, 23.

81 "Propoved' V. V. Ivanova" (The sermon of V. V. Ivanov), *Bratskii listok* 2 (1907) 27.

V. G. Pavlov stressed that love is not merely the command to "do no harm" but an active, outgoing principle. As he pointed out, "It is possible not to offend one's neighbor, but [still] not do him any good."[82] Thus, Russian evangelicals understood Christian compassion as something lively, intentional, and active, in contrast to a lifeless obligation. The parable of the Good Samaritan (Luke 10:25–37) served as the prime illustration of this principle. Referring to Christ's parable about a man who was attacked by robbers, beaten, stripped, and left for dead, in his 1907 speech Pavlov asked rhetorically, "How would you want to be treated if you were the victim?" He encouraged his listeners to be attentive to the needs of people around them: "Will we pass by like the priest and the Levite, who day and night studied Holy Scripture and saw the service of God merely in the fulfillment of temple rituals and not in the service of their suffering neighbor? Or will we, like the merciful Samaritan, extend to them a helping hand and bind up their wounds and return them to life?"[83] Pavlov added that help for the starving should involve more than merely buying a ticket to a charity event or gathering up a few extra crumbs to toss in their direction. Rather, the helper should identify with those needing help.[84]

In keeping with espousing the right attitude to those in need, evangelicals expressed a preference to err on the side of generosity. I. S. Prokhanov made it his practice to fulfill literally Christ's command to "Give to anyone who asks" (Matthew 5:42) because of an incident that had affected him deeply as a child. He and his brother were outside playing on a midwinter day in Vladikavkaz when they saw a beggar, "evidently a drunkard," who asked a neighbor on horseback for the price of a night's lodging in a shelter. The neighbor refused, saying that no doubt the beggar was lying and would only use the money for drink. Young Prokhanov pitied the man but had no money to give him. The next day, some other boys called the brothers to see a man who had frozen to death in the market overnight. To his horror, Prokhanov recognized the beggar who had been turned away. Many years later he reflected:

> If we were omniscient ... we might be justified [in turning down a request for money], but as our knowledge of man is extremely limited and we may make a mistake by refusing a really needy person who can through that refusal perish, we must not refuse anybody . . . If some of those whom we help abuse our help, the responsibility for that rests entirely with them . . . But if we

82. Pavlov, "Kto moi blizhnyi?" 2.
83. Ibid.
84. Ibid.

judge those who ask for help and give to some while we refuse others, we may make a mistake in both ways—by giving to those who will abuse and by refusing those who are really in need. Therefore, the wisest thing, according to Christ, is to "give to him that asketh."[85]

In a 1909 article, V. V. Ivanov stated that Russian Baptists are called to giving on the basis of texts such as 1 Corinthians 16:1 (concerning collecting offerings for "God's people"); Galatians 2:10 (instructions on "remembering the poor"); and James 1:27 (on looking after widows and orphans). He gave the example of the Baku Baptist congregation caring for a widow and helping a brother through an illness and added that the Baku Baptists, without regard for confession of faith and nationality, refused none of the poor in giving alms "according to their capability."[86] That is, evangelicals were expected to give to everyone as freely as their circumstances permitted.

Russian evangelicals also taught that people must help one another based on their common creation. In V. G. Pavlov's 1907 speech in Baku, he pointed out that human beings cannot neglect one another because all are descended from Adam and Eve: "We humans make up one great family, regardless of the shape of our bodies, the color of our skin, our language, and religion."[87] Evangelicals also believed that human beings have a responsibility to one another because of the humanity of Christ and in imitation of him. Iakov Stepanov, in a 1908 letter to the editor, called on readers of *Baptist* to respond to a call for material help from a church in Voronezh guberniia. He noted that, "Christ, in his earthly life, being in human flesh, had need of bread and also hungered and thirsted and how He rejoiced when some served Him with their material goods and fed Him." Stepanov added that since Christ showed mercy to the hungry, Christians should serve them as well.[88] In a sermon delivered in St. Petersburg in 1906, Grigorii Akimovich Boichenko agreed: "Jesus . . . did not only preach the Gospel of the Kingdom of God . . . but also did works of compassion . . . We also must do the works of the one who sent us . . . The Lord did not only say, 'I am the light of the world, but also, 'You are the light of the world.'"[89]

The right attitude in the evangelicals' understanding also involved good stewardship and generosity regarding material wealth. They reflected upon their approach to material resources, as their publications give evidence.

85. Prokhanoff, *Cauldron*, 31–32.
86. Ivanov, "O delakh," 7.
87. Pavlov, "Kto moi blizhnyi?" 3.
88 Iakov Stepanov, *Baptist* 5 (1908) 41.
89. *Bratskii listok* 11 (1906) 2.

Russian evangelicals believed and taught that personal wealth should be used to further God's Kingdom. A number of evangelicals were people of means. D. I. Mazaev was a wealthy rancher; Z. I. Smirnov was a merchant who was able to subsidize most of the construction of the large prayer house in Balashov;[90] and at least some of the Tiflis Baptists prospered. In fact, questionable methods of making money were the cause of a congregational split with the differing parties led by Nikita Isaevich Voronin and V. G. Pavlov in 1880.[91] In any case, becoming an evangelical tended to improve people's circumstances as a matter of course because their habits changed. They no longer smoked, drank, or laid out money for funeral observances and consequently had more disposable income.[92] Perhaps this is one of the reasons why Stundist leaders such as Riaboshapka prospered and were grumbled against as *kulaki* (rich peasants).[93] But, according to V. V. Ivanov, the question remained as to whether their money was only intended to be stored up for this life? On the contrary, he insisted, Christians must do good with whatever money they have.[94] Whatever their financial circumstances, evangelicals were expected to be generous in supporting the "Lord's work." In fact, Russian evangelicals regarded stinginess as "just as much a sin as drunkenness, depravity, and murder, although in a more refined form."[95] Moreover,

> The brother and sister whose conscience allows them to spend thousands on themselves, on pleasure trips, and on luxurious living, while so many are lost without salvation, are, in our opinion, apostates and worse than unbelievers. It seems to us that the brother and sister who are stingy and grasping, if they do not mend their ways, should be excluded from the congregation of believers . . .[96]

Russian evangelicals also expected that poverty would be no barrier to giving. Almost without exception the journals of this period quaintly referred to offerings as the "mite," or "the widow's mite" after the story of

---

90 V. G. Pavlov, "Pis'mo s puti," (A letter from the journey), *Baptist* 2 (8 January 1910) 16.

91 Wardin, *On the Edge*, 157–58.

92 Ivanov, "Slovo k veruiushchim," 5–8.

93 F. A. Shcherbina, "Malorusskaia shtunda" (The Little Russian shtunda), *Nedelia* 2 (1877) 57–58, quoted by Wardin, *On the Edge*, 143.

94 Ivanov, "Slovo k veruiushchim," 58; "Ispytaite menia" (Test me), *Baptist* 12 (December 1908) 3.

95 *Gost'* 2 (December 1910) 12.

96 Ibid.

how Jesus praised a widow who put two small coins into the temple treasury because she gave "all she had" (Mark 12:41–44; Luke 21:1–4). The image is of something very small and insignificant being gathered up from all the simple people in order to accomplish something pleasing to God that is greater than the sum of its parts.[97] That people of slender means did generously contribute to various funds promoted on the pages of the journals is evident from the lists of contributors, sometimes accompanied by an affecting description, such as the "poor, blind sister," or the "sick little one" (*bol'naia kroshka,* literally "sick crumb"), both of whom gave small sums to each of five church funds.[98] Anonymous offerings were a regular part of worship.[99]

Evangelicals were expected to live simply in order to be able to give freely to people in need. As in the Book of Acts, it was expected that wealthy believers would look to the needs of those less well off. "The Word of the Lord does not only comfort the spiritual suffering [of the poor] directly, but by means of people who have accepted Christ and have wealth, it helps them in their . . . needs. The Love of Christ acts in the members of His Church and causes them to help the needy brother."[100] An open letter to "sisters" from A. I. Smirnova-Goliaeva of Balashov, which was published by *Baptist* in 1914, illustrated the point. The author's double surname testifies to her wealth and prestige: evidently she was related by blood or marriage both to Z. I. Smirnov, the merchant who subsidized the building of the Balashov Baptist church and Il'ia Andreevich Goliaev (1859–1942), the presbyter,[101] or at least to their families. In her letter Smirnova-Goliaeva presented a true-life fable on the basis of Matthew 6:19: "Do not store up for yourselves treasures on earth, where moth and rust destroy, and where thieves break in and steal." She owned a large quantity of valuables and expensive, although evidently outmoded clothing, which she stored in trunks and wardrobes. She congratulated herself on being such a good housekeeper because she knew how to store everything safely. In spite of all her vigilance, however, moths seriously damaged the clothing and twice thieves broke into her storeroom. She asked herself what the meaning of these events might be and remembered what the Lord had said in Matthew 6:19. She continued,

---

97 For example, see I. S. Prokhanov *Bratskii listok* 8 (1906) 3; D. I. Mazaev, "Vozzvanie" (The calling), *Baptist* 1 (January 1908) 25; Iakov Stepanov to Dei Mazaev 17 March 1908, *Baptist* 5 (May 1908) 41; "Obrashchenie k dobrym serdtsam" (An appeal to kind hearts), *Baptist* 12 (December 1908) 38; *Baptist* 3 (1 February 1909) 8.

98 *Bratskii listok* 10 (1906) 16.

99 Packer, *Among the Heretics,* 35.

100 "Rokovaia zhertva," (A fateful sacrifice), *Khristianin* 1 (January 1906) 35.

101. Pavlov, "Pis'mo s puti," 16; *Bratskii listok* 10 (October 1910) 7.

"I was very ashamed that I did not have pity for the poor and did not want to give away my . . . things to sisters in need who had nothing to wear to the meeting [i.e. worship service] on holidays." Smirnova-Goliaeva warned other wealthy women that they needed to admit before the Lord that, "we . . . behave very unjustly to our poor sisters and we pack our trunks and wardrobes with silk and expensive materials and keep it all for moths and thieves, while our poor sisters need essential clothing." The point is that God will judge their behavior: "If my conscience now judges me because I kept my expensive things for moths and thieves, then how severely will the Lord judge us when we keep our clothing in storerooms and our money in banks . . . ?"[102] The moral of the story is that wealth is not to be hoarded, but used to bless others, with the clear expectation that judgment will follow.

Likewise, Agaf'ia Ivanovna Kapranova, an effective traveling evangelist in the Caucasus who also worked in hospitals as a literature colporteur,[103] sent in a revealing item that was published in *Baptist* in March 1909. In it she continued the theme of judgment for hoarding wealth, but in a more mystical way. Kapranova described a dream she had at a time when she was greatly concerned about money: "I often thought about how we would live; we had little to live on and nothing with which to help the poor." In her dream she had died and was met by a man dressed in white. Suddenly she was aware of a five kopek coin she had clutched in her hand and understood that it was not only useless to her, but also unclean. In fact, when she tried to throw it away her guide shouted that she must not throw away unclean things there because the place where she stood was holy. "I was terribly frightened, not knowing what to do." Kapranova wrote, "It would be a burden in my hand for all of eternity." She regretted not having disposed of the coin before: "I remembered that on earth many had asked me for it, especially one hungry person begged me for it, but I didn't give it to him, thinking that I would need it and now I had carried it with me into eternity." Kapranova's angelic guide then softened his tone and explained: "Why did you bring [the coin] here? There on earth it is needed and gives people bread; you must give everything away before you enter eternity."

---

102 A. I. Smirnova-Goliaeva, "K sestram" (To the sisters), *Baptist*, Nos. 15–16 (1914) 17.

103 The article identifies the author as A. Kaprova, but this is certainly a typographical error. For more on Kapranova see *Bratskii listok* 11 (1906) 5; Ivanov, "Ispytaite menia," 4; F. Trosnov, "Vecheri khristianskoi liubvi SPB. Obshchiny evangel'skikh khristian" (Evenings of Christian love SPB. Congregations of Evangelical Christians), *Bratskii listok* 9 (September 1910) 24; McCaig, *Wonders of Grace*, 104–8; Demchenko, "Missionerskoe sluzhenie."

At that moment a trumpet sounded, signaling that in three days the Lord would descend to judge the earth. Kapranova wanted desperately to warn her relatives to give away everything so that they would be ready to meet the Lord: "I remembered my husband, all my relatives and acquaintances, how all of them are rushing around, hurrying to accumulate more . . . and stash it in the bank, while all around so many are dying of hunger and need." She realized that the rich are actually in a dreadful spiritual state:

> Horror took possession of me . . .when I remembered how on earth people oppress one another for the sake of money; each one tries to trade more cheaply with his neighbor and gather more money. Oh, people do not know that this money will be a heavy burden for them in eternity, especially when they see the hungry people who died because of them and I wanted very much to shout to the earth, "Give it away! Give it away while there is still time so that you would not come here with money! Oh, how unnecessary it is here and how badly it interferes!"

Fortunately, she was awakened by her own cry. In conclusion, Kapranova admitted, "The dream hasn't completely cured me," but now at least she realized that money does not last for eternity.[104] The vivid description needs little commentary. Obviously, the editors of *Baptist* were in agreement with the message of Kapranova's dream: money was actually dangerous if it was not kept moving along and channeled into good causes—in this case, the relief of hunger. Evangelicals understood that wealth had to be passed on. The consequences for not doing so were dire. A quote from St. John Chrysostom printed in the journal *Gost'* in 1910 confirmed this view: "A treasure is a risky thing in a house; in the hands of a beggar it is safe."[105] The evangelical approach regarded all people as equal before God; in practical matters it resulted in an equal challenge to all to be generous according to their means. Every member of the evangelical community was called to participate in the ministries of compassion and giving. This attitude also reinforced their practice of working together.

COMPASSIONATE MINISTRY IS A COMMON TASK

Russian evangelicals believed that compassionate ministry was an area of service open to all members of the believing community, not only to the leadership or specially appointed practitioners. In particular, for the

104 A. Kaprova, "Son" (The dream), *Baptist* 5 (March 1909) 4–5.
105 *Gost'* 1 (November 1910) 4.

evangelicals, ministering to those in need was one of the spheres of service to which women were called. In his booklet on the teaching of the Evangelical Christian Union I. S. Prokhanov identified one main type of women's ministry as broadly "charitable," namely underwriting the expenses of both evangelistic ministry and service to the poor. Wealthy women could simply contribute, as the women did who supported Christ and the disciples (Luke 8:3), while the less affluent could participate in sewing circles and similar enterprises. Prokhanov also described the ministry of deaconesses who share in the distribution of material aid and generally care for the needs of the congregation, especially among women.[106]

The Pashkovite sewing cooperatives were rather different from the women's "missionary circles" or sewing circles that began to be mentioned in the Russian evangelical press in about 1908 and continued throughout the 1920s. Instead of providing employment for poor women, the sewing circles' main function was to do handwork either to sell to support evangelists, to supply the needs of evangelists and other church workers themselves, or simply to give away to those in need.[107] By the 1920s, in some places, women were maintaining quite sophisticated assistance ministries beyond sewing circles. In 1926 in Kyiv a group of Evangelical Christian women that had been feeding twenty-five to thirty-five people every week at worship gatherings had purchased a bigger stove and were making plans to cook every day for up to one-hundred people. The same group had pooled their money to buy furniture for a poor family living in a basement and regularly did sewing and laundry for believers in prison as well as for traveling evangelists.[108]

In addition, rescue work, hospital and home visitation, and ministry to children, were often promoted as forms of ministry suitable for youth groups. In a speech on the organization of such groups at a national Baptist congress for youth held in 1909 in Rostov-na-Donu, Mikhail Danilovich. Timoshenko (?1880–1938) named home visitation and material assistance to the poor as an appropriate sphere of activity for the young.[109] The youth group at First Evangelical Christian Church of St. Petersburg organized a "summer *priut*" ("summer shelter"—probably something like a camp) for

---

106 Prokhanov, *Verouchenie*, 72-76; see also *Khristianin* 6 (1924) 113–15.

107 Examples of reports on women's missionary circles may be found in *Bratskii listok* 12 (1908) 6–7; *Bratskii listok* 2 (1909) 4; *Khristianin* 7 (1925) 50–51; 2 (1926) 59; 3 (1926) 56–57; 6 (1927) 44–45; 9 (1927) 55; 11 (1927) 58; 2 (1928) 57; 5 (1928) 65.

108 A. Mazina, "Pervyi prazdnik sester obshchin Kievskogo otdela V.S.E.Kh." (The first celebration of the sisters of the congregations of the Kiev department of the AUEKh), *Bratskii listok* 3 (1926) 56–57.

109. Timoshenko, *Pervyi vserossiiskii molodezhnii congress*, 19.

poor children in 1909.[110] Later it was the youth of Dom Evangeliia who undertook the organization and staffing of a small children's home for several months in 1917.[111] There are many examples of young people's groups from both Baptist and Evangelical Christian congregations who made it their regular practice to visit doss houses, railroad stations, hospitals, and taverns to witness and to minister to people in whatever practical ways they could.[112]

The common task of compassionate ministry also resulted in evangelicals looking beyond their own circles for inspiration and models. Specifically, in their publications they observed and reported on the ministries of foreign evangelicals. Not surprisingly, considering their marginalized status in Russia, they admired and identified themselves with fellow evangelicals abroad and regarded their own ministries as being part of a worldwide movement. The sense of kinship was mutual. Brigadier Mildred Duff of the Salvation Army paid a holiday visit in 1899 to unnamed Russian friends whom she considered, "more than three-quarters Salvationists themselves."[113] Through occasional foreign visitors, and also through V. A. Pashkov's own connection with missions and social service ministries during his exile abroad, a lively awareness of foreign compassionate ministry was sustained among Russian evangelicals that lasted from the 1880s until the end of the 1920s. While living in Western Europe, among those with whom Pashkov corresponded and supported was Thomas Barnardo, the founder of the East End Juvenile Mission (1870), later known as the Barnardo Homes.[114] Pashkov also kept in touch with George Mueller of Bristol, the influential founder of a number of children's homes. Mueller visited Russia in 1874 and again from January to March 1883, at which time he

---

110 *Iunyi khristianin* 2 (1909) 1–4; A. N. "Sredi detei" (Among the children), *Molodoi vinogradnik* 12 (1909) 21.

111 E. N. K., "'Sem'ia' detei v Levashove," *Gost'* 6 (June 1917) 86; *Gost'* 11 (November 1917) 175.

112. A. Dobrynin," "Iz" zhizni kharkovskago iunosheskago kruzhka evangel'skikh khristian" (From the life of the Kharkov Evangelical Christian youth group), *Molodoi vinogradnik* 2 (February 1911) 20; *Gost',* 10 (October 1917) 156; *Gost'* 11 (November 1917) 175; Kareva, "Moi vospominaniia," 176, 183; "Iz deiatel'nosti soldatskogo khristianskogo kruzhka gor. Moskvy" (From the activity of the Christian Soldiers' Circle in Moscow), *Gost',* 7 (July 1917) 108–9; "Ot rukovoditelei soldatskogo khristianskogo kruzhka Moskvy" (From the leaders of the Christian Soldiers' Circle of Moscow), *Gost'* 10 (October 1917) 155; E. N. K. "Iz zhizni obshchiny doma Evangeliia" (From the life of the Dom Evangeliia congregation), *Gost'* 10 (October 1917) 155–56; G. Babera, "Dom Evangeliia," *Golos istiny* 5 (44) (May 2003) 30.

113. Brigadier Duff, "Furlough Days in Russia," 255.

114 Pashkov papers, Fiche I.5 (Letter 27 September 1886).

baptized Pashkov.[115] After 1905 the Russian evangelicals published many articles on the subject of compassionate ministries practiced abroad. They were especially well aware, for example, of the Salvation Army.[116] Sermons by George Mueller and articles about his work appeared frequently in the evangelical press.[117] Indeed, his ministry continued to inspire the Russian evangelical imagination throughout the twentieth century until the days of perestroika. There were also reports on the work of Thomas Barnardo.[118] The Bethel complex established by Friedrich von Bodelschwingh (1831–1910), with services for those suffering from epilepsy, the homeless, the mentally ill, and others, was described in detail by Ivan Motorin in 1926.[119] During a trip to the United States in the late 1920s, I. S. Prokhanov took time to be photographed with Charles Sheldon (1857–1946),[120] author of *In His Steps*, a novel about members of a congregation in the American Midwest who determine to make no decision without first asking, "What would Jesus do?" As a result, the characters in the novel involve themselves in a number of different social service-type ministries, a scenario that proved to be of interest to many outside of evangelical circles as well, including Father Grigorii Petrov (1866–1925), who translated Sheldon's book into Russian.[121] Father Petrov was an associate of Nikolai Nepliuev, who influenced Prokhanov's attitude to Christian economic communities.[122]

Two foreign organizations with which the Russian evangelicals had fruitful connections were the Salvation Army and the Young Men's Christian Association (YMCA). By the early twentieth century the Salvation Army was actively seeking entry to Russia, an undertaking that was eagerly supported by Russian evangelicals.[123] General William Booth visited Russia in

115 Pashkov papers, Fiche I.5; Liven, *Dukhovnoe probuzhdenie*, 63; Nichols, *Russian Evangelical Spirituality*, 120–21.

116 Duff, "Furlough Days in Russia," 255; F. Balikhin, "Moia poezdka zagranitsu" (My trip abroad), *Baptist* 1 (June 1907) 16; *Baptist* 11 (November 1908) 35; *Baptist* 52 (22 December 1910) 416; *Iunyi khristianin* 1 (1909) 1–8; "Parad p'ianits" (Parade of drunkards), *Baptist* 52 (22 December 1910) 416.

117 *Khristianin* 2 (February 1906) 66–68; *Baptist* 4 (15 February 1909) 8–9; *Gost'* 1 (January 1917) 16; *Khristianin* 6 (1925): 29–30; *Khristianin* 2 (1926): 4–6; *Khristianin* 3 (1926): 19–20; *Khristianin* 7 (1927) 57–60; *Khristianin* 9 (1927) 59–62.

118 *Khristianin* 1 (1906) 66–68; *Khristianin* 3 (March 1906) 66; *Bratskii listok* 6 (1906) 6–7.

119 Ivan Motorin, *Bratskii listok*, 4 (1926) 61–63.

120. *Khristianin* 3 (1927) 8.

121. Hedda, *His Kingdom Come*, 112.

122. "Pamiati N. N. Nepliueva" (In memory of N. N. Nepliuev), *Khristianin* 1 (1908) 46.

123. "Parad p'ianits," 416.

1909 as part of a decade-long attempt to set up a permanent post. According to Tom Aitken, Booth was "the latest in a long line of foreign preachers from whom [the Pashkovites] hoped to derive the leadership and identity they had lost,"[124] after Radstock, Pashkov, and Korf had left Russia for good in the 1880s. The identity of the evangelical movement in St. Petersburg and elsewhere in the Empire was certainly in flux during this complex period, but it is inaccurate to suggest that the Russian evangelicals were actually looking to foreigners to provide leadership, which would have been impossible in any case. Princess Natalia Liven, Elizaveta Chertkova, and other influential women remained the backbone of the evangelical movement in St. Petersburg. Although Liven and Chertkova were evidently subject to exile at the same time as Pashkov and Korf, they were protected by Emperor Alexander III on the grounds that they were widows.[125] Meanwhile, by the mid-1880s Ivan Kargel was the leading pastor of the St. Petersburg evangelicals[126] and from about 1888 I. S. Prokhanov was relating to the community when he came to the capital as a student. Rather, although the Russian evangelicals obviously were eager to help bring the Salvation Army (and the YMCA) into the country, and recognized them as believers of their own kind, visitors to Russia such as Booth depended on the resident evangelicals to provide them with the support that would allow them to stay and minister.

In 1899 the Salvation Army found a back door into Russia through the post they organized in the Grand Duchy of Finland, which at that time was part of the Russian Empire. They found good friends among the former Pashkovites in St. Petersburg. Elizaveta Chertkova, Natalia Liven, Baron Paul Nicolay, Aleksandra Peiker, Princess K. Golitsyna, and Princess Gagarina[127] were among those who offered energetic support. From 1910 to 1912 the Army maintained a discreet, unofficial presence in St. Petersburg, holding meetings at the palaces of the former Pashkovites and at other preaching stations around the city, almost certainly those set up by W. A. Fetler.[128] Local evangelicals continued to lobby for the Salvation Army's official admission to Russia, and when they were permitted to participate in the All-Russian Hygiene Exhibition in 1913, Colonel Karl Larsson, the Army representative, was housed at Dom Evangeliia. When the Army began to produce and sell its journal, its publication address was given as that of Dom

---

124 Aitken, *Blood and Fire*, 72.
125. Corrado, "Colonel Vasiliy Pashkov," 169.
126 Latimer, *With Christ in Russia*, 39.
127. Aitken, 76–78.
128. Ibid., 134–35.

Evangeliia.¹²⁹ The Army, with an increasing number of Russian recruits, remained active in Russia throughout World War I, yet only became official after the February (1917) Revolution. The Army was a respected evangelical practitioner of compassionate ministry until it was finally excluded from Soviet Russia in 1923.¹³⁰

Another Western Christian group that sought permanent entrance to Russia and gradually found it with the help of the Pashkovites in the post-1884 period was the YMCA. Its entry was also through the Grand Duchy of Finland with the help of Baron Paul Nicolay, who had been involved in a number of missionary endeavors, including travels with Friedrich Baedeker.¹³¹ Aleksandra Peiker also took active part in the student movement, which had a compassionate ministry component because of the poverty of a great many students in Russia.¹³² Indeed, ministry to students had been an important Pashkovite emphasis.¹³³ In 1899 Nicolay met John R. Mott (1865–1955), the leader of the Student Christian Volunteer Movement at a YMCA conference in Helsinki and took the American on a brief trip to St. Petersburg. The result was the founding of the Russian Students' Christian Movement (RSCM) in November 1899, and also of a club intended for young Russian workers called *Maiak* (Lighthouse) in 1900. In its later phase after World War I and the Bolshevik Revolution, the RSCM had a strong positive influence on a generation of Orthodox theologians who matured in Western Europe.¹³⁴ As with the Salvation Army, the YMCA/RSCM served to connect the Russian evangelicals with the wider world and also to increase their ranks within their own country.

Thus, although their political and financial circumstances did not permit Russian evangelicals to undertake massive social service efforts such as were possible in the West, as a group they were nevertheless aware and

---

129 See the front page of *Vestnik spaseniia* (Herald of salvation) 1(July 1913). Details on the hygiene exhibit and *Vestnik spaseniia* in Russia are given by Larsson, "The Army in Russia," 20–23; Ivanova and Ivanova, *Zarubezhnyi opyt*, 80–82; Aitken, *Blood and Fire*, 144–150.

130 AUCEC-B Archives, Drawer 5, Folder 21, "Istoriia tserkvei Evangel'skikh khristian 1917–1929" (History of Evangelical Christian churches 1917–1929), Istoricheskiie vospominaniia, N. Vysotskii (Historical recolections, N. Vysotskii), (Moscow, 13 May 1981), 1; Larsson, "The Army in Russia," 99; Aitken, *Blood and Fire*, 242, 230–31.

131 Langenskjöld, *Baron Paul Nicolay*, 55, 59, 73–81.

132. Ibid. 5455; Miller, "American Philanthropy among Russians," 12–14.

133. Heier, *Religious Schism*, 116–17.

134 According to Matthew Lee Miller, both the Orthodox historian Anton Kartashev and the respected American YMCA patron of Russian Orthodoxy Paul B. Anderson, point to the Pashkovites as the originators of the RSCM; see Miller, "American Philanthropy among Russians," 212, 293–94.

admiring of what their fellow believers were doing elsewhere. They clearly identified themselves with leaders in compassionate ministry abroad such as Booth and Mueller. The spirit of cooperation added important theological and practical insights into the compassionate ministry efforts of Russian evangelicals. They were not alone in their service.

CONCLUSION

During the period of their Golden Age (1905 to 1929), Russian evangelicals maintained a steady involvement and interest in compassionate ministries, in spite of resistance on the part of church and government authorities. Three major emphases in the practice of compassionate ministries may be observed among them. All three are undergirded by the evangelicals' overriding concern for preaching the gospel and bringing sinners to repentance. They regarded evangelism as the ultimate act of compassion, because it had the potential to free people from sin and thus transform their lives, making them into useful, productive, sober citizens. Not only that, but the gospel had the power to transform all of Russia, removing class conflict and political strife by replacing social divisions with love.

The first main emphasis was mutual aid practiced within the evangelical community—the founding of church-based institutions and charitable funds to minister to the needs of fellow believers. If evangelism was to be practiced, evangelicals believed that the church had a responsibility to support its own people, especially missionaries, preachers, and their families.

The second emphasis of the Russian evangelicals was urban rescue ministry, devoted to reaching the people who were suffering the most as a result of the social dislocation created by rapid urbanization. This category especially had to do with intervention directed at drunkards and prostitutes, but also with serving other impoverished and vulnerable members of society, such as children and students.

Their third emphasis was the establishment of ideal communities, the idea being that by modeling life after that of the Jerusalem Church described in the Book of Acts, poverty could be eradicated and a creative, hard-working, fulfilling life made possible for all.

Although each approach was typical of different evangelical leaders, the three emphases are not mutually exclusive. In addition to their primary concern for evangelism, all the approaches held several other convictions in common. All agree that faith without works is dead; in other words, ministries of compassion were an expected and necessary part of the Christian life. However, the evangelicals believed that the only deeds with which they needed to concern themselves were those that are biblical; that is, they were to evangelize and take care of people in need and not contribute to causes based on mere tradition or social convention. Moreover, evangelicals agreed that compassionate ministries have to do with an outgoing attitude of concern for others, a spirit of generosity, involvement, and sympathy rather than the cold execution of a duty. They taught that an important part of the necessary attitude is the believer's understanding of money, which was not to be hoarded or misspent but to be used freely to help others and to further the spread of the gospel. Ministries of compassion were to be practiced by all believers, with some expectation that it is the special province of women and even youth. Finally, ministries of compassion were a topic of ongoing interest, as the Russian evangelicals observed social services that were practiced by evangelicals abroad and interacted with foreigners who ministered within Russia.

3

Aid within the Evangelical Community—D. I. Mazaev, V. G. Pavlov, and V. V. Ivanov

THIS CHAPTER WILL EXAMINE the first broad category of compassionate ministry practiced among Russian evangelicals, namely the support shared within the evangelical community itself. Russian evangelicals did, indeed, extend acts of mercy to those outside their own circles as a matter of course. The swiftness with which they included compassionate ministry in their plans following the imperial decree of 17 April 1905 indicates that they considered service to people in need an organic part of their mission.[1] Even before 1905 evangelicals contributed to the wider Russian society in times of national need. During the Russo-Turkish War (1877 to 1878), the Tiflis Baptists supported two men (Nikolai Poroshin and Emel'ian Skorokhodov) and two women (Anastasiia Pavlova and Ekaterina Kapranova) from their congregation to tend the wounded at the front. For this act the congregation as a whole was awarded a medal by the Red Cross in 1880.[2]

Nevertheless, although Russian evangelicals maintained that Scripture commands that all Christians practice compassion (see 1 Corinthians 16:1; Galatians 2:10; James 1:27), in his report on Russian Baptists to the European Baptist Congress in Berlin in 1908, V. G. Pavlov stated that, "Our first and

---

1. *Bratskii listok* 5 (1906) 32; I[van] S[tepanovich]. P[rokhanov], "Brat'ia! K molitve" (Brothers! To prayer), *Bratskii listok* 8 (1906) 3; *Bratskii listok* 10 (1906) 18–19.

2. V. G. Pavlov, "Pravda o baptistakh" (The truth about Baptists) in Karetnikova, *Al'manakh, vypusk 1*, 245-46; Sinichkin adds that Martin Kal'veit was given the right to wear the medal by a vote of the Tiflis congregation (*Vse radi missii*, 120).

most important assignment consists in the preaching of the Gospel."[3] This does not mean that they regarded salvation strictly as a matter of individual souls being admitted to heaven. As described in the previous chapter, while the evangelicals were convinced of the eternal dimension of the gospel's power, they also believed that social ills are remedied through it. In a 1908 article D. I. Mazaev commented on the opening of a Molokan-sponsored library and reading room in Tiflis (present-day Tbilisi). The library's charter outlined a two-fold goal: to contribute to cultural-economic improvement and spiritual-moral knowledge, particularly among the young. While Mazaev was supportive of the project, he noted that the first goal was useful for the present life only, while spiritual-moral development, although focused on the future, had consequences in the present as well: "Cultural-economic development may feed our body, but cannot satisfy the soul, while spiritual-moral development satisfies the soul and brings inestimable blessing to the body."[4] Mazaev did not elaborate here, but it is a fair assumption that he was not referring to specific health benefits of the gospel, but rather to the conviction that it had the power to change people's lives for the better, drawing them out of poverty and vice. The ultimate expectation was that society as a whole would benefit through the preaching of the gospel.

Given the transformative power that they attributed to the gospel both for eternal salvation and for life in the present, it was of first importance to the evangelicals to support evangelism, which, by extension, included sustaining those whose main calling was to preach.[5] From the time of the Baptists' organizational meeting in Novo-Vasil'evka (Tavriia guberniia, in present-day Ukraine) in 1884, the evangelicals gave attention to supporting preachers.[6] To the same end, during the period after 1905 they built up their own administrative structures and institutions that were primarily intended to minister to the needs of those within the church, especially those who were actively engaged in spreading the gospel. Furthermore, in order to sustain their commitment, they developed an informal but coherent educational system through articles printed in their own publications, teaching believers about the Christian attitude to money and encouraging them to give generously to the funds and institutions founded by the evangelical churches.

3. V. Pavlov, "Nachalo, razvitie i nastoiashchee polozhenie baptizma sredi russkikh" (The beginning, development, and present situation of baptism among the Russians), *Baptist*. 11 (November 1908) 38.

4. D[ei]. M[azaev], "Biblioteka-chital'nia" (Library-reading room), *Baptist* 3 (March 1908) 20.

5. Pavlov, "Nachalo," 39.

6. Sinichkin, *Vse radi missii*, 79–85.

Several factors informed this type of compassionate ministry. First of all, its main architects, whose contributions will be sketched in this chapter, were all of Molokan background: D. I. Mazaev, V. G. Pavlov, and V. V. Ivanov. Besides adhering to biblical models, the Russian evangelical practice of compassionate ministry among church members also owed something to patterns of mutual support established among this indigenous Russian sectarian group, perhaps as well to the Dukhobors from which the Molokans were descended. Second, it is important to remember that although they were more or less tolerated after 1905, the evangelicals were not necessarily welcome participants in the wider Russian society. New laws on religion were not always uniformly applied and after 1905 the evangelicals kept careful watch over their legal status and regularly documented cases of injustice on the part of the authorities.[7] Nor did they forget their experience of persecution and exile prior to 1905. Even in their new-found freedom they recorded stories of the sufferings of the previous generation[8] and sought support for the survivors among them.[9] These factors suggest that one motivation for mutual aid was that evangelicals were concerned for their own preservation. While not necessarily directly stated in their publications, it is nevertheless clear that, based on their own experience, some of the evangelical leadership sought to develop ways of looking out for their own in a society that was not concerned with their welfare. Third, and finally, based on the Bible, evangelicals expected the church to be a community of mutual support according to the pattern established in apostolic times, especially according to the Book of Acts, which describes the members of the Jerusalem congregation as contributing to everyone's needs: "Selling their possessions and goods, they gave to anyone as he had need" (Acts 2:45) and "There were no needy persons among them" (Acts 4:34). The evangelicals viewed the church as a place where the poor were not only comforted by the gospel, but also where they could expect to find

---

7. Examples of documentation of persecution include *Bratskii listok* 2 (1907) 33, 35–40; *Bratskii listok* 7 (1907) 10; *Bratskii listok* 4 (1908) 5–7; "Zverstva v Rossii" (Brutalities in Russia), *Bratskii listok* 7 (July 1910) 4, 9–10; I. P. Kushnerov, "Zabytaia zapoved' Gospoda Iisusa" (The forgotten commandment of the Lord Jesus), *Bratskii listok* 8 (August 1910) 1–2.

8. See, for example, "Materialy dlia istorii russkikh baptistov iz zapisok ssyl'nago" (Materials for the history of Russian Baptists from the notes of an exile), *Baptist* 1 (January 1908) 20–22; *Baptist* 2 (February 1908) 19–23; *Baptist* 4 (15 February 1909) 22–23; *Baptist* 7 (April 1909) 6–10; *Baptist* 8 (April 1909) 12; *Baptist* 9 (May 1909) 13–17; *Baptist* 10 (May 1909) 6–9.

9. *Bratskii listok* 10 (1906) 21; I. Liasotskii, "Iz zapisok ssylnago" (From the notes of an exile), *Baptist* 2 (February 1908) 21–22.

help from members of the congregation who were better off.[10] In short, the comprehensive vision of leaders such as Mazaev, Pavlov, and Ivanov was the creation of a self-sustaining community with a level of commitment to one another reminiscent of the Molokans and in which particular attention was given to caring for the needs of those who preached the gospel.

MUTUAL AID AMONG RUSSIAN EVANGELICALS PRIOR TO 1905

Before describing the development of mutual aid after the decree on religious toleration, it is necessary to outline some of its antecedents. Of particular importance are the practices of mutual support practiced among Russian sectarians, especially the Molokans and their Dukhobor predecessors. Generally speaking, Dukhobors and Molokans rejected all material manifestations of Christianity, including the Lord's Supper, baptism, images, and the church hierarchy and emphasized equality in their dealings with one another and the wider society.[11] In terms of their attitude to compassionate ministry, Breyfogle states that "the sectarians were pariah groups who tended to turn inward and work together as a community, providing vital economic and social support to each other."[12] That is, first of all they emphasized their responsibility to the well-being of members of their own group. The origins of the Dukhobors are hazy, although they are evidently rooted among the numerous groups associated with the schism that took place in the Russian Orthodox Church in the seventeenth century.[13] The name "Dukhobor" ("Spirit wrestler") first occurred in the 1750s. Whether they were fighting against the Spirit, as their opponents maintained, or fighting together with the Spirit against evil, as they themselves asserted, is a matter of perspective.[14] They were resisted as heretics from the time they first appeared, but by 1792, during the reign of Emperor Paul I, they were subject to systematic persecution and banished to Siberia. The danger they were perceived to present to society consisted, curiously, in their good conduct, industry, morality, and freedom from drunkenness—all traits that

---

10. "Rokovaia zhertva" (A fateful sacrifice), *Khristianin* 1 (January 1906) 35.

11. For detailed accounts of Dukhobor and Molokan beliefs see Bonch-Bruevich, *Materialy k istorii i izucheniu russkogo sektanstva i raskola*; Conybeare, *Russian Dissenters*; Klibanov, *Istoriia religioznogo sektanstva v Rossii*; Breyfogle, *Heretics and Colonizers*.

12. Breyfogle, *Heretics and Colonizers*, 122.

13. M. S. Karetnikova, "Russkoe bogoiskatel'stvo" (The Russian God-search) in Karetnikova, *Al'manakh, vypusk 1*, 48.

14. Ibid., 51.

made them attractive and therefore a threat, drawing people away from the official church.[15] After Emperor Alexander I was enthroned in 1801, one of his first acts was to permit the Dukhobors to return from exile. In 1802 Dukhobors already in the New Russia territory (present-day Ukraine) were granted permission to resettle in the region of Molochnye vody near Melitopol.' Alexander's policy was two-fold: to ensure religious toleration for Russian citizens, but also to isolate a dissenting group from contact and possible influence on their Orthodox neighbors. Other groups of Dukhobors were settled elsewhere in the Empire on similar terms.[16] In 1805 a favorably-disposed observer described the Dukhobors in this way:

> Their cardinal tenet was mutual love. They had no private property, and the goods of each were those of all. In their settlement at Milky Waters [i.e. Molochnye vody] they practised real communism, had a common treasury, common flocks and herds, and in each of their villages, common granaries, from which each was supplied according to his needs.[17]

During the Molochnye vody period, the Dukhobor leader, Savelii Kapustin, organized a common fund referred to as the *Sirotskii dom* (Orphan home). As Dukhobors were later resettled elsewhere in the Russian Empire, chiefly in the Caucasus, the Orphan Home continued and developed as an institution, and "held an important place in the Dukhobor psyche as the physical and spiritual core of the community."[18] It consisted of communal money, sometimes administered in the form of interest-free loans, but could also include grain, land, livestock, and buildings, donated annually by members of the community and distributed by the leader. The ancient Russian peasant *mir*, or commune also allocated resources to its members, but the Dukhobor practice of holding common property appears to be distinct.

The Molokans separated from the Dukhobors under the leadership of Simeon Uklein sometime in the 1770s. The name "Molokan" or "milk-drinker" was probably coined by their enemies because of their neglect of the fasts of the Russian Orthodox Church, continuing to drink milk during Lent, for example. The Molokans accepted the name, citing 1 Peter 2:2: "Like newborn babies, crave pure spiritual milk, so that by it you may grow up in your salvation."[19] Like their Dukhobor forebears, the Molokans rejected all material forms of religious practice; unlike the Dukhobors, they placed

---

15. Conybeare, *Russian Dissenters*, 268.
16. Breyfogle, *Heretics and Colonizers*, 25, 27–30.
17. Conybeare, *Russian Dissenters*, 267.
18. Breyfogle, *Heretics and Colonizers*, 223–24.
19. Karetnikova, "Russkoe bogoiskatel'stvo," 67.

Aid within the Evangelical Community—Mazaev, Pavlov, and Ivanov 89

greater emphasis on the centrality of the Bible—the Word of God—rather than the Spirit as the source of spiritual enlightenment.[20] They experienced persecution and exile as the Dukhobors did, and like them were also granted amnesty during the reign of Alexander I.[21] In terms of their practice of mutual aid, Molokans had no institution comparable to the Orphan Home, although they readily offered support to fellow Molokans and also were known to maintain some form of common fund for community members in need.[22] F. V. Livanov, a visitor to a Molokan village near Riazan in 1862, observed that they took care of their own needy.[23] Likewise, Frederick C. Conybeare references S. Atav, who stated in 1870 that "there never was a case of a Molokan household being ruined. Positively they would never allow such a thing to happen. If a calamity befalls one of them, all are prepared to assist him."[24] Hardworking and frugal in their habits, Molokans tended to be more affluent than their Orthodox neighbors. Wealth, however, was not something they believed was to be used for one's personal benefit, but to benefit others in the community.[25] Conybeare records the case of a wealthy Molokan, M. A. Popov of Samara, who in about 1820 gave away his property to the poor and called on others to do the same.[26]

Although they could be hostile to those who left the community (D. I. Mazaev was ostracized by his own father for three years when he was baptized in 1885)[27] Molokans could also be helpful to Baptists and other believers in exile, making no distinction between their own group and others in need. Baptist Fedot Petrovich Kostromin wrote of his exile to Gerusy (present-day Goris, Armenia) in 1890: "When the Molokans from the village of Bazarchai heard about us, they were touched with pity and came to help with whatever they had, because their ancestors had also been exiled there and they, having collected flour, butter, and cheese, brought these things to us."[28]

20. Ibid., 66–67.

21. Ibid., 69.

22. For details on the Molokan approach to common property and monetary funds, see Klibanov, *Istoriia religioznogo sektanstva*, 135–43.

23. Shubin, *A History of Russian Christianity, Vol. III*, 138–39.

24. S. Atav, *Otechestvennye zapiski* 4 (1870) 621–23, quoted by Conybeare, *Russian Dissenters*, 315.

25. Conybeare, *Russian Dissenters*, 315.

26. Ibid., 327–28.

27. G. I. Mazaev, "Vospominaniia," 24; the 1885 date of Mazaev's baptism is given by N. A. Levindanto, "Pamiati Deia Ivanovicha Mazaeva" (In memory of Dei Ivanovich Mazaev), *Bratskii vestnik*, Nos. 2–3 (1953) 95.

28. Fedot Petrovich Kostromin, *Baptist* 4 (15 February 1909) 22–23.

Molokans also practiced hospitality to strangers. I. S. Prokhanov remembered an elderly man named Gavrilich who worked as a watchman and gardener in the family's orchard. As a young man Gavrilich had been a soldier and was captured by Chechens in the Caucasus. He remained there as a slave for twenty-five years until he was freed by Russian troops. He came to a Molokan gathering in Vladikavkaz where the Prokhanov family was in attendance. It was the custom at worship meetings to announce the presence of strangers to the congregation and ask that they be given a place to stay. On this occasion the elder announced that an old man, a Chechen prisoner, was present, and Prokhanov's father immediately invited him home and gave him a job.[29]

Molokans were known to participate in national compassionate campaigns. A foreign observer, Jonas Stadling, who reported on the relief work organized by the novelist L. N. Tolstoy and his family during the 1891 Russian famine noted that, "Among the Russians it was mainly sectarian people who aided the starving. A Molokan lady, a widow, quietly did much work among the poor, according to her means."[30] Molokans worked with Baptists in Baku to set up a field hospital (*lazaret*) for the wounded at the beginning of World War I.[31]

In summary, probably in part because of their experience of persecution and exile, Dukhobors and Molokans relied on one another to ensure their survival. The Dukhobors maintained communal property in the institution of the Orphan Home; Molokans did not necessarily hold common property, but were nevertheless known for their strong support of their own community. They accumulated wealth, but expected to use it for the benefit of others. In addition, the Molokans welcomed exiles and strangers, and also took part in compassionate activity carried out by the wider society. As will be described in more detail below, these traits were among those that were actively promoted among Russian evangelicals, specifically the Russian Baptist Union. Through V. G. Pavlov there was a strong inclination to follow patterns of worship and organization set by the German Baptists; however, leaders such as V. V. Ivanov sought to preserve what they viewed as a simpler spirituality more faithful to their Molokan background. In fact, Ivanov averred that Russian Baptism was Molokan in origin.[32] A sense of communal responsibility like that of the indigenous sectarians, therefore,

---

29. Prokhanoff, *Cauldron*, 34.

30. Stadling, "The Famine in Eastern Russia," 561.

31. V. V. Ivanov, "Na pomoshch ranenym voinam" (To the aid of wounded soldiers), *Baptist*, Nos. 15–16 (1914) 17–18.

32. Coleman, *Russian Baptists*, 96; Wardin, *On the Edge*, 156.

was part of the attitude they wished to promote. It is worth noting that the early Stundist communities had the same practices, collecting freewill offerings for the benefit of members in need, for traveling preachers, and for legal assistance for those in prison.[33]

In addition to the mutual aid experience of Russian sectarian groups, support for missionary preachers was an established part of evangelical concern before 1905, drawing on the practical experience of the Mennonite Brethren, notably Johann (Ivan) Wieler. Indeed, the close-knit nature of the Mennonite community as a whole may have influenced the Russian evangelicals in the matter of mutual support as well. A few weeks after the exile of V. A. Pashkov and M. M. Korf from Russia in 1884, a meeting was called in Novo-Vasil'evka, which essentially organized the workings of a missions committee, but is also considered the founding of the Russian Baptist Union. Johann Wieler, a Mennonite Brethren leader, was elected president of the committee, and a support fund for evangelists was set up.[34] According to this arrangement, two fully-supported evangelists would receive five-hundred rubles a year, plus housing expenses, with the understanding that the preacher would be on the road for eight months of the year. An evangelist who was active for four months at a time would receive 175 rubles, with travel expenses drawn from a separate fund. It was expected that all preachers who received money from these funds would work in their assigned ministry territories and report regularly on their activities and expenditures. The executive committee took responsibility for collecting money to support evangelists and pooled their resources every three months. Ordinary church members took active part in supporting the missions committee, evidenced by the story of the women of the Novo-Vasil'evka congregation who each set aside the egg-money from just one chicken. In the course of a year they contributed thirty-seven rubles to the fund.[35] Thus, from the beginning, the evangelicals strove to support their own missionaries.

In many cases, however, missionary activity eventually led to exile.[36] Support for those exiled or imprisoned for their faith formed an important part of evangelical patterns of compassion during the period before 1905. I. S. Prokhanov's father, Stepan Antonovich, often aided prisoners

33. Wardin, *On the Edge*, 134.
34. Ibid., 146.
35. Sinichkin, *Vse radi missii*, 79–85.
36. Exile and imprisonment were common enough that it would be interesting to know how some leaders avoided it, such as D. I. Mazaev or the evangelist F. P. Balikhin. Wardin suggests that Mazaev's wealth and geographical obscurity probably protected him (*On the Edge*, 256).

of conscience passing through Vladikavkaz. Sometimes he was alerted to their presence by his young son, who frequently visited the prison, asked if there were evangelical believers among those being sent into exile, and then summoned his father to help.[37] The pressure of persecution increased during the 1890s when K. P. Pobedonostsev served as Ober-prokuror of the Most Holy Synod. Sozont Evtikhievich Kapustinskii of Kyiv was exiled to Transcaucasia in 1890.[38] Martin Kal'veit, who baptized the first Russian convert, Nikita Voronin, in 1867, was exiled for five years to Gerusy in 1891.[39] At about the same time, I. G. Riaboshapka, and F. P. Kostromin were exiled to the same location for five years. Eventually Kostromin, a Cossack who had fought in the Crimean War, spent a total of sixteen years in exile. His wife was not permitted to join him. Their eight children were removed and placed in different monasteries, none of them knowing where the others were.[40] V. V. Ivanov was banished to Slutsk in 1895.[41] The father of I. S. Prokhanov was sent to Gerusy in the mid-1890s.[42] Another exile, Ivan Liasotskii, reported that in December 1896 there were thirty exiled Baptists in Gerusy.[43] V. G. Pavlov was sent to Orenburg and Simon Stepanov went to Siberia.[44]

Prisoners in transport were bound with chains and were frequently forced to travel to their places of exile on foot. Sometimes exile locations were chosen because they were remote and inhospitable, offering little chance to make a living. The rocky soil of Gerusy, for example, where many exiles lived in caves, was almost impossible to cultivate, meaning that they were essentially consigned to slow starvation. Idleness and hunger oppressed the exiles and their families.[45] In their weakened condition, some succumbed to disease, such as the family of V. G. Pavlov who died of cholera in 1892, or the wife of S. E. Kapustinskii, who died of typhus probably in the

---

37. Prokhanoff, *Cauldron*, 41.

38. Pavlov, "Pravda o baptistakh," 261.

39. Grachev, *Gerusy-Giriusy*, 42.

40 *The Baptist World Alliance Second Congress*, 238; Byford, *Peasants and Prophets* 114; Grachev, *Gerusy-Giriusy*, 49–50.

41. VSEKhB, *Istoriia Evangel'skikh khristian-baptistov v SSSR*, 527; Byford states that Ivanov was banished to Transcaucasia in 1894 and served time on a treadmill, but Russian-language sources do not mention this (*Peasants and Prophets*, 106–107).

42. Prokhanoff, *Cauldron*, 15.

43. Grachev, *Gerusy-Giriusy*, 54.

44. *The Baptist World Alliance Second Congress*, 237.

45. Vladimir Bonch-Bruevich, *Sredi sektantov*, quoted by Grachev, *Gerusy-Giriusy*, 34–39.

same year.⁴⁶ Over time, some exiles were able to piece together ways of making a living. The wife of exile S. K. Nezdolyi managed to get a job cooking for a local official; Nezdolyi himself found employment in the post office.⁴⁷ Some exiles subsisted by gardening or beekeeping.⁴⁸

However, it is obvious that in such a setting the help of fellow evangelicals was essential to survival, especially at the beginning of the exile period. In St. Petersburg, Countess Elena Ivanovna Shuvalova, a Radstock convert, was married to the chief of police and frequently interceded with the authorities for the release of prisoners exiled for their religious beliefs, sometimes inviting officials to her home for dinner in order to plead her case.⁴⁹ Friedrich Baedeker's travels in Russia during the last quarter of the nineteenth century involved bringing aid and encouragement to religious exiles—Molokans, Stundists, and Baptists.⁵⁰ The English Quakers Joseph Neive and John Bellow interceded for religious exiles with Emperor Alexander III and went to the Caucasus from 1892 to 1893, accompanied by Hermann Fast (1860–1935), a Mennonite associate of I. S. Prokhanov.⁵¹ As mentioned above, Molokan communities were known to assist Baptist exiles, and wealthier brethren, such as D. I. Mazaev also sent help.⁵² Vasilii Nikolaevich Ivanov (d. 1908) a former policeman from Kharkiv, traveled extensively in Ukraine (Malorossia) and Siberia to bring material assistance and encouragement to exiles.⁵³ A believer named Ivan Kupriianov contrived to deliver a sewing machine to Anastasiia Tsiglerova, the wife of an exile in Gerusy, so that women could sew for their families and also make

---

46. V. G. Pavlov, "Vospominaniia ssylnogo" (Recollections of an exile), in Karetnikova, Al'manakh, vypusk 1, 208–209; Grachev, Gerusy-Giriusy, 77.

47. Grachev, Gerusy-Giriusy, 72–73.

48. Ibid., 77.

49. Concerning Shuvalova's ministry, see Liven, Dukhovnoe probuzhdenie, 59–60; Heather Vose, "The Ministry of Women in the Baptist Churches in the USSR" in Brackney and Burke, Faith, Life and Witness, 129–138; Karetnikova, "Istoriia Peterburgskoi tserkvi evangel'skikh khristian-baptistov, beseda vos'maia" (History of the St. Petersburg Evangelical Christian-Baptists church, eighth talk), in Karetnikova, Al'manakh, vypusk 2, 66–67.

50. See Latimer, Dr. Baedeker; V. V. Ivanov, Bratskii listok 1 (1907) 3–4; V. G. Pavlov, "Nachalo," 37; Grachev, Gerusy-Giriusy, 74–75.

51 Cornelius Krahn, "Fast, Herman (1860–1935)," Global Anabaptist Mennonite Encyclopedia Online, 1956; Stepan Korneevich Nezdolyi, Avtobiografiia (Autobiography), quoted by Grachev, Gerusy-Giriusy, 15, 69–70.

52. Fedot Petrovich Kostromin, Baptist 4 (15 February 1909) 22–23.

53. "Konchina br. Vasiliia Nikolaevicha Ivanova" (The death of Brother Vasilii Nikolaevich Ivanov), Bratskii listok 12 (December 1908) 1–4; Prokhanoff, Cauldron, 65–68.

a little money.⁵⁴ During the famine of 1891 V. G. Pavlov and his fellow exiles in Orenburg were helped with a supply of flour sent by believers in St. Petersburg.⁵⁵

On another occasion, evangelicals in St. Petersburg collected two thousand rubles for exiles which they entrusted to a certain Brother Dolgopolov, a church elder, to deliver to S. E. Kapustinskii in Transcaucasia. On a steep mountain road he was overtaken by bandits who conducted him to their chieftain. Dolgopolov explained that he was delivering funds from St. Petersburg to fellow believers in exile. It developed that the chieftain was familiar with Kapustinskii and offered to delegate members of his band to deliver the money lest Cossacks in the area rob him. Seeing that he had no choice, Dolgopolov agreed to this arrangement and settled down to wait until the bandit emissaries returned to their headquarters. Meanwhile, the bandits dispatched by the chieftain located Kapustinskii and his hungry children and learned from him that all the other exiles in the area were also living in dire need. Thereupon, one of the bandits extended the packet of money to Kapustinskii and said, "Take what Allah has sent to you and your brothers. This is what your brothers in Petersburg have sent you. Take paper and write them an answer." Presently they brought Kapustinskii's letter back to Dolgopolov, who immediately returned to the capital.⁵⁶

Thus, prior to 1905, the practices of the indigenous sectarian community, particularly Molokans, contributed to the later understanding of mutual aid among evangelicals. Some structures were in place to support missionary preachers even before the 1884 meeting in Novo-Vasil'evka. Finally, in a variety of ways and sometimes through surprising agents, evangelicals took responsibility for caring for their own exiles and prisoners.

MUTUAL AID AMONG RUSSIAN EVANGELICALS AFTER 1905

In the post-1905 era the experience of prisoners and exiles and the cultivation of a sense of responsibility to them, as well as to church ministers in general, continued to be a strong motivating factor for evangelical compassion. Developing consistency in the matter of caring for fellow evangelicals, especially for preachers, and building up habits of support for churches and church institutions made up a significant part of the ministries of D. I. Mazaev, V. G. Pavlov, and V. V. Ivanov. All three were raised as Molokans

---

54. Grachev, *Gerusy-Giriusy*, 69.
55. Pavlov, "Vospominaniia ssylnogo," 208.
56. Grachev, *Gerusy-Giriusy*, 79–83.

Aid within the Evangelical Community—Mazaev, Pavlov, and Ivanov 95

and would have been familiar with sectarian patterns of mutual support. All three also strongly identified themselves as Baptists. D. I. Mazaev was president of the Baptist Union from 1886 to 1920, except for the brief time that V. G. Pavlov served in that capacity (1909 to 1910). All three leaders edited the journal *Baptist,* which was founded in 1907 and served as the major educational organ as well as the central clearing house for assistance funds. Mazaev served as editor from 1907 to 1909 in Rostov-na-Donu, after which the editorship moved with V. G. Pavlov to Odessa from 1910 to 1911. Mazaev took up the editorship again in 1912, but the journal was closed down by the authorities during 1913. *Baptist* then reopened during 1914 when Ivanov edited it from Baku before it closed again. It reappeared briefly during 1917, again under Mazaev's editorship, and then ceased publication until 1925. After that, it continued to appear regularly until it was closed once and for all in 1929.[57] In their capacity as Baptist Union leaders, editors, and writers, Mazaev, Pavlov, and Ivanov were well-positioned to shape policy concerning mutual aid and to teach about money and giving.

D. I. Mazaev is an example of a wealthy evangelical who made it his business to support his fellow believers and taught others to do the same. The Molokan community to which his family belonged was divided over the question of baptism. As an adult Mazaev was impressed by the preaching of M. D. Koloskov and V. G. Pavlov during 1883 and 1884; both were Molokans who had become Baptists.[58] Eventually Mazaev was baptized at the age of thirty in 1885 together with his wife, his brother Gavriil and his wife, and several others.[59] Just two years after the structure for sending and supporting missionaries had been set up at Novo-Vasil'evka in 1884, Johann Wieler suggested Mazaev as president of the organization.[60] Mazaev is remembered for having presided at annual semi-underground congresses during the early years of his tenure, until the increasing pressure of the Pobedonostsev era put an end to these gatherings.[61] The word "congress" perhaps overstates the case during those difficult years;[62] nevertheless, small groups of Baptists conscientiously met to hear reports and appoint missionaries from 1884 until 1891.[63] D. I. Mazaev had a large house with space for his family and

57. Sinichkin, *Vse radi missii,* 155–59.
58. VSEKhB, *Istoriia,* 536.
59. Levindanto, "Pamiati Deia Ivanovicha Mazaeva," 95. Gavril Mazaev gives the date as 1884, but that may be a typographical error (G. I. Mazaev, "Vospominaniia," 24).
60. Wardin, *On the Edge,* 252.
61. VSEKhB, *Istoriia,* 536.
62. See Kahle, *Evangel'skie khristiane v Rossii i Sovetskom Soiuze,* 61.
63. Demchenko, "Missionerskoe sluzhenie," 1–3.

servants and also owned a considerable amount of land where his workers lived.⁶⁴ Ivanov and others were critical of Mazaev for his controlling leadership and his affluent personal lifestyle,⁶⁵ but Mazaev also showed concern for believers in exile, such as F. P. Kostromin. On one occasion, Mazaev sold a sheepskin to an Armenian for twelve rubles and instead of pocketing the money, instructed the buyer to give the money to Kostromin.⁶⁶ More ambitiously, in 1887 Mazaev provided for the resettlement of twenty-five persecuted Baptist families by giving them land on his property along the lower Don and seed to begin farming. Later the group moved to the Omsk region.⁶⁷ Mazaev's prosperity did not endure beyond the turmoil of 1917. He experienced a bandit raid on his estate in October of that year. Later, when the Civil War came close to Rostov, Mazaev was separated from his wife and family as people were fleeing the city. He was a refugee for about a year and at last returned, exhausted and in rags, to Mozdok where he was taken into the home of another Baptist leader, V. G. Mamontov. Mazaev did not dwell on his great losses, even though he lived in extreme poverty to the end of his days and was even seen among the beggars in the Mozdok marketplace, not an unusual fate during the 1921 to 1923 famine.⁶⁸

Likely because of his own harsh experience, especially during his second period of exile, V. G. Pavlov was an advocate for former exiles and for pastoral support in general.⁶⁹ Pavlov was raised in a Molokan family in the Caucasus. In 1870, at the age of sixteen, he joined the small Baptist congregation in the city of Tiflis (present-day Tbilisi). In 1875 the congregation sent him to Hamburg for a year to study theology. Gerhard Oncken, the leader of the continental Baptist movement, arranged for a tutor for Pavlov. Before he returned to Tiflis in 1876, Oncken ordained Pavlov as a missionary.⁷⁰ Immediately on his return, he began to travel around the Caucasus, preaching especially in Molokan communities. At first, the Baptists in Tiflis led a relatively unhindered life because in 1879 Baptists of

64. Mazaev, "Vospominaniia," 130.
65. Wardin, *On the Edge*, 256–57.
66. Fedot Petrovich Kostromin, *Baptist* 4 (15 February 1909) 22–23.
67. Steeves, "The Russian Baptist Union," 33, 41.
68. K. K. Martens, "Tri muzha Bozhiikh" (Three men of God), *Seiatel' istiny* (October 1929): n.p., quoted in "Mazaev, Dei Ivanovich (1855–1922), http://oni-proshli.ru/node/17; G. I. Mazaev, "Vospominaniia," 128.
69. Examples include I. Liasotskii, "Iz zapisok ssylnago" (From the notes of an exile), *Baptist* 2 (February 1908) 21–22; V. G. Pavlov, "Vozzvanie" (The call), *Baptist* 10 (October 1908) 24.
70. Pavlov, "Vospominaniia ssylnogo," 194–95; "Pravda o baptistakh" (The truth about the Baptists) in Karetnikova, *Al'manakh, vypusk 1*, 244–45.

nationalities other than Russian were granted freedom of confession, with the stipulation that their leaders had to be approved by the governor. The Tiflis Baptists put forward V. G. Pavlov and N. I. Voronin as candidates for pastor, and somehow their application was approved. Thus, although he was occasionally briefly detained by the authorities, generally Pavlov enjoyed the freedom of a legally recognized entity and for several years evangelized widely.[71] In 1886, however, Pavlov's situation quickly deteriorated.[72] In 1887 he was exiled to Orenburg for five years. Almost immediately upon his release in 1891, he was exiled there again for an additional five years. During this time one of his daughters drowned and just a few weeks later his wife and three other children died of cholera. Pavlov was left alone with his nine-year-old son Pavel.[73] When his second term of exile was over in 1895, Pavlov accepted the invitation to serve as the pastor of a Baptist congregation in Romania and remained there until 1901 when he returned to Tiflis.[74] In 1907 he went to Odessa at the invitation of the Baptist church.[75] During this time he suggested setting up an insurance fund for Baptist pastors.[76] In 1916 he accepted the invitation of the Baptists in Moscow to minister there.[77] He continued to serve as a traveling evangelist and died in Baku in 1924; he was buried in Tiflis.[78]

V. V. Ivanov also grew up in a Molokan community in the village of Novo-Ivanovka in Elizavetpol guberniia. In 1866 he was told by another Molokan that in order to fulfill the will of God, he had to be baptized. Evidently the man was one of the so-called "water Molokans" (*vodnye molokane*) who through studying the Scriptures had become convinced of the necessity of baptism.[79] This new information sent Ivanov on a search through the Bible and also caused him to seek out correspondents who could advise him.[80] In this way he learned of Molokan Nikita Voronin's baptism in Tiflis in 1867. Accordingly, in 1870 he went there and was finally

---

71. Pavlov, "Pravda o baptistakh," 245–47.

72. Ibid., 253–55.

73. Pavlov, "Vospominaniia ssylnogo," 199–203; 204–10.

74. Ibid., 218–19.

75. Ibid., 199–218.

76. *Bratskii listok* 10 (October 1910) 7.

77. J. H. Rushbrooke, "Velikii russkii baptist Vasilii Gur'evich Pavlov" (The great Russian Baptist Vasilii Gur'evich Pavlov) in Karetnikova, *Al'manakh, vypusk 1,* 192.

78. Ibid., 192–93.

79. VSEKhB, *Istoriia*, 42.

80. N. V. Odintsov, "Obrazets dlia vernykh" (An example for the faithful), *Baptist* 2 (1929) 10.

baptized in 1871 at the age of twenty-five.[81] He immediately became a traveling evangelist, especially active in the Caucasus, and is associated with the beginning of the Baptist community in Baku in 1880, where he later served as pastor from 1900–1917. In 1884 along with Pavlov he was designated one of the missionaries supported by the Baptists at their inaugural meeting in Novo-Vasil'evka.[82] Ivanov was an apologist and theologian for the Baptist movement, contributing to Prokhanov's first journal *Beseda* (The conversation, founded 1889) and later to *Baptist*. From 1895 to 1900 he and his family were exiled to Slutsk (then Poland, present-day Belarus).[83] During his career he is said to have baptized more than 1,500 people.[84] Of the three leaders profiled in this chapter, he wrote the most consistently about the Christian attitude to money and giving.

Mazaev, Pavlov, and Ivanov in various ways all contributed to the systematization of evangelical life in the post-1905 era. Mazaev represents the wealthy evangelicals who used their money for the good of the Christian community. Pavlov and Ivanov represent the experience of preachers who needed support in order to minister and who often suffered exile. All three retained a Molokan sensibility regarding the responsibilities of community members to one another. The three leaders promoted specifically Baptist Union funds to support evangelization, building construction, and also to serve Baptists in need. During the 1910s evangelical homes for orphans and the elderly were founded. As editors of *Baptist,* Mazaev, Pavlov, and Ivanov educated evangelicals concerning money and giving.

ASSISTANCE FUNDS

It must be noted that this portion of the history of compassionate ministry is closely connected to issues regarding evangelical unity and competing claims to authority that were in question at the time. Views on appropriate names for the movement (Evangelical Christian, Gospel Christian, Baptist, etc.),[85] church registration, baptism, open or closed communion, ordination, and personality clashes all played their part in a complex series of events as the various streams of the evangelical movement converged and regrouped during the first years of relative freedom. For the purposes of

81. Ibid.
82. VSEKhB, *Istoriia*, 101.
83. Ibid., 527.
84 *The Baptist World Alliance Second Congress*, 237.
85. A brief summary of the cultural and social issues connected with these names is given by Coleman, *Russian Baptists*, 95–96.

this chapter it is sufficient to remind the reader that by 1909 the evangelical movement was represented chiefly by two sizable and sometimes competing unions, namely the Russian Union of Evangelical Christians-Baptists (also referred to as the Russian Baptist Union), which was dominated by D. I. Mazaev, and the All-Russian Union of Evangelical Christians (that is, Evangelical Christian Union), which was officially registered by I. S. Prokhanov in that year.[86] Somewhat confusingly, Prokhanov also founded the Russian Evangelical Union in 1908, which was not a church union, but a coalition of like-minded individuals that was intended to function as the Russian counterpart of the Evangelical Alliance.[87] All three organizations (Russian Baptist Union, Russian Evangelical Union, All-Russian Union of Evangelical Christians) maintained funds designated for the assistance of people in need. The relationship between the funds of the Russian Evangelical Union and the All-Russian Union of Evangelical Christians is particularly difficult to untangle. In April 1909 the All-Russian Union of Evangelical Christians, that is, the church union, announced the formation of "circles" (*kruzhki*) for the support of different ministries, one of them being for "shelters and other charitable institutions," and warned that, "These circles ought not to be confused with the [already existing] funds of the Russian Evangelical Union,"[88] that is, the union conceived as the counterpart of the Evangelical Alliance. It was probably not so easy to make the distinction.

However, there is evidence that the assistance funds did not originate with church leadership at all, but were established in response to the initiative of individual evangelical believers. Months before there was any formal structure for receiving donations, believers anticipated possible needs by sending offerings for various causes to I. S. Prokhanov's journal *Khristianin*. At first Prokhanov seemed to be at something of a loss to direct these donations properly. *Khristianin* first appeared in January 1906 and already in May a gift of fourteen rubles, fifty-eight kopeks was sent to aid "brothers who had suffered during political disturbances." An appeal was made to the readership to identify someone who fit that category.[89] In the same is-

---

86 The differences between Baptists and the Evangelical Christians from a later, more antagonistic, Baptist point of view (1921) are outlined by N. I. Peisti and R. A. Fetler, "Raznitsa mezhdu Baptistami i tak nazyvaemymi 'Evangel'skimi Khristianami'" (The difference between Baptists and the so-called "Evangelical Christians"), *Blagovestnik*, Nos. 3–4 (1921) 47–49; for a detailed account of the issues surrounding the formation of the two unions see Steeves, "The Russian Baptist Union," 62–75.

87. VSEKh-B, *Istoriia*, 152–53.

88. "Ot Soveta SPBurgskoi obshchin Evangel'skikh khristian" (From the council of the St. Petersburg congregations of the Evangelical Christians), *Khristianin* 4 (1909) 47.

89. *Bratskii listok* 5 (1906) 32.

sue, *Khristianin* noted the receipt of an unsolicited contribution toward the founding of a clinic and another three rubles sent by two church members in Baku designated for a children's shelter.[90] At last, in August 1906, Prokhanov announced the organization of various funds to support a number of causes in the name of the "Temporary Council of the Russian Evangelical Union" (which was not formally organized until 1908). In particular, a charitable fund was designated "for the construction of hospitals, shelters, orphans' homes and other charitable institutions [to] be run in a purely evangelical spirit."[91] One of the purposes of *Khristianin* was to promote unity among "all the branches of living Christianity" in Russia,[92] and until World War I the journal continued faithfully to report news of the Russian evangelical world as a whole, regardless of the designation "Russian Baptist Union" or "All-Russian Union of Evangelical Christians."[93] As well, the funds administered by the Russian Evangelical Union served the entire evangelical community, Baptists included, until 1908. *Khristianin* (or, more precisely, the monthly supplement, *Bratskii listok*) published careful accounts of all funds collected by evangelicals to aid one another, including relief for the hungry that was distributed during the famine of 1907. It is worth noting that during the famine, assistance was distributed across the spectrum of evangelical groups and also to the Orthodox, and was largely administered by two Baptists, Iakov Iakovich Vins and V. P. Stepanov.[94] In 1908, D. I. Mazaev discouraged Baptists from contributing to the funds promoted in *Khristianin*. He admitted that they were "attractive," but maintained that they were actually antagonistic to Baptist interests, for example supporting the training of people in six-week Bible courses who had already been excluded from Baptist congregations. Mazaev did not specifically mention the compassionate fund, but it may be assumed that he did not encourage Baptists to contribute to it either.[95]

By the time Mazaev expressed his views on the Evangelical Union funds, he had seen to it that specifically Baptist funds were functioning. The Russian Baptist Union convened a series of annual congresses beginning in May 1905 that formalized the many activities that characterized the early

90. Ibid.

91. P[rokhanov], "Brat'ia! K molitve," 3.

92. Prokhanoff, *Cauldron*, 138–39.

93. See, for example, the detailed account of the Russian Baptist Union Congress in *Bratskii listok* 9 (September 1910) 11–24; 10 (October 1910) 5–24.

94. Accounts of donations to the various funds appeared regularly in *Bratskii listok*. For reports on famine aid in 1907, see *Bratskii listok* 2 (1907) 42; 5 (1907) 21–24; 7 (1907) 19–22; 8 (1907) 20; 9 (1907) 16; 10 (1907) 17.

95. *Baptist* 12 (December 1908) 2.

Aid within the Evangelical Community—Mazaev, Pavlov, and Ivanov

years of religious freedom. At a congress held in May 1907 at Rostov-na-Donu, the Baptist Union assigned all evangelism and church planting to a separately administered mission society under the direction of V. G. Pavlov. Meanwhile, the union was to take care of other matters including support for disabled preachers and their orphans.[96] A key element in the administration of Baptist Union funds was the denominational journal *Baptist*, which was also founded at the 1907 congress. It served as the main connecting point among Baptists as *Khristianin* did, ostensibly, for all evangelical groups, Baptists included. Besides managing the Disabilities Fund, the journal also published requests for aid that were intended to be sent directly to congregations or individuals.

Reflecting their ongoing concern for the now aging exiles, the first fund formally designated by the Baptists in 1908 was for disabled preachers, although it actually had a broader application, being for the support of "widows of our deceased workers in the Lord and also for . . . [workers] who because of their age are no longer able to work."[97] This priority is distinct from the Evangelical Union charitable fund started in 1906 for the construction of institutions to be run "in an evangelical spirit."[98] The latter suggests the startup of new projects, whereas the 1908 Baptist Disabilities Fund focused on believers' responsibility for the continued welfare of their own aged or ill preachers and their widows and orphans, a concern with roots in the pre-1905 era. No precise criteria were given for the eligibility of persons to receive help from this fund, nor were the people named who took responsibility for making such decisions. Ultimately the fund served as a form of insurance available more or less to all Baptists. In 1908 M. Iashchenko of Anapa wrote a lengthy letter to *Baptist* concerning the importance of giving to the Disabilities Fund. He frankly stated that believers should contribute regularly because:

> . . . who is this [money] for? For ourselves. Such a sum [i.e. the thousands of rubles that could be accumulated if all church members contributed systematically] can help not only the disabled and their widows and children, but it could help every orphan and every widow. . . None of us can dare say that he will never be widowed and no one can say that his children will

---

96. V. G. Pavlov, "Nashi sobraniia i torzhestva" (Our meetings and celebrations), *Baptist* 2 (August 1907) 16; *Baptist* 10 (May 1909) 18.

97. Pavlov, "Vozzvanie," 25.

98. P[rokhanov], "Brat'ia! K molitve," 3.

never be orphaned. And so, begin to contribute a kopek every day, and let anyone who can contribute more.[99]

Accordingly, numerous homely appeals for funds were published, such as the case of Gerasim Orlov, a church member in Kharkiv who could no longer work because he had lost an arm.[100] Some requests were for aid to entire congregations, such as a community in Ekaterinoslav guberniia that had experienced a flood.[101] New instances of discrimination on the part of the authorities were also cause for appeals. A request came from the village of Androsovka in Samara guberniia where five families were starving. The zemstvo (an elected governing body with oversight of local welfare) had refused to give them assistance on the grounds that "everyone [else] around them had had a good harvest." The people writing the letter, however, insisted that they were passed over precisely because they were Baptists.[102]

The well-being of exiles continued to be an important part of evangelical life even after 1905. A general government amnesty for prisoners of conscience was not automatic. I. S. Prokhanov and the same Dolgopolov who had carried money to the exiles in Gerusy personally petitioned Prime Minister Sergei Witte (1849–1915) for the exiles' return, an action which seems to have helped to facilitate their liberation.[103] The importance of exiles' stories to the growing historical memory of the evangelical movement is indicated by efforts to collect their memoirs. Accounts were published in the evangelical press, such as the stories of Ivan Liasotskii,[104] Feodot Petrovich Kostromin[105] and Daniil Martynovich Timoshenko.[106] As these heroes of the faith aged, it became a matter of concern to cultivate a sense of responsibility for their support on the part of the evangelical community. On the eve of his release in 1900, Ivan Liasotskii wrote to V. G. Pavlov asking for money for transportation back to his home where he hoped to gather his children together again, and for help finding employment. Presumably

99. M. Iashchenko (Anapa, Kuban oblast', 16 December 1908), *Baptist* 3 (1 February 1909) 9.

100. "Obrashchenie k dobrym serdtsam" (An appeal to kind hearts), *Baptist* 12 (December 1908) 38.

101. *Baptist* 8 (April 1909) 22–23.

102. *Baptist* 3 (February 1909) 23.

103. Prokhanoff, *Cauldron*, 136–37.

104. "Materialy dlia istorii russkikh baptistov iz zapisok ssyl'nago," *Baptist* 1 (January 1908) 20–22; No. 2 (February 1908) 19–23.

105. *Baptist* 4 (15 February 1909) 22–23.

106. *Baptist* 7 (April 1909) 6–10; 8 (April 1909) 12; 9 (May 1909) 13–17; 10 (May 1909) 6–9; for additional information see "Mikhail Danilovich Timoshenko (?1880–1938), www.blagovestnik.org/bible/people/p0020htm.

Pavlov helped him at the time; in 1908 he published the old letter in *Baptist* and reminded readers that by that time Liasotskii was an old man living in poverty in Nakhichevan-na-Donu.[107] One of the leadership responsibilities that Pavlov took especially seriously was to continue to assist former exiles. As Pavlov stated in 1908:

> I consider it unnecessary to prove that the worker who has dedicated his best strength to the proclamation of the gospel should not be left by his fellow [believers] after he has lost the ability to work, and in the event of his death his wife or children also should not be left without support."[108]

In summary, support for missionaries and prisoners of conscience had been a part of evangelical life since the 1880s. The development of dedicated assistance funds indicates, first of all, that after 1905 it became possible to take a more structured approach to a concern that had existed since the beginning of the movement. The existence of the funds and the medium of church publications also allowed evangelicals to give and receive information concerning their needs and respond with gifts, which built up a sense of mutual responsibility and community concern.

EVANGELICAL INSTITUTIONS

Another significant development in the post-1905 era is the establishment of specifically evangelical charitable institutions. Probably it was quite common for evangelicals to care for one another spontaneously, without formal structures, as did the Ovsiannikovs, a childless couple who adopted four orphans with plans to bring in six more.[109] However, following religious toleration as the evangelical movement grew and stabilized, there was also an impulse to establish church-supported institutions. The oddly-named *bebi khom* founded by Pashkovite Laura Grundberg continued to exist at least until 1909,[110] but other institutions were soon envisioned. As previously noted, in May 1906 a donation of three rubles was received by *Khristianin* in St. Petersburg from Andrei A. Timoshin toward support of a clinic.[111] There is no indication that such a clinic was ever established, but obviously some evangelicals were thinking early on in terms of new opportunities to

---

107. Liasotskii, "Iz zapisok ssylnago," 21–22.
108. Pavlov, "Vozzvanie," 24.
109. *Baptist* 11 (June 1912) 17.
110. *Molodoi vinogradnik* 6 (1909) 14–15.
111. *Bratskii listok* 5 (1906) 32.

offer help to society at large. Likewise, in May 1908 a motion was made at the annual congress of Evangelical Christians-Baptists (i.e. Russian Baptist Union) in Kyiv to establish a shelter or almshouse (*bogodel'nia*) specifically for church members who could not care for themselves. Those making the motion pointed out that many congregations were badly off because of a poor harvest and could not care for the disabled and other poor in their midst.[112] Again, it is not clear whether any steps were ever taken to found a shelter, although possibly this early proposal eventually developed into plans to organize the children's home/home for the elderly at Balashov in 1910. The latter proposal was directed toward caring for church members rather than the poor in general. Nevertheless, it indicates that evangelicals began quite early to envision founding more permanent compassionate institutions of their own.

Possibly the earliest example of a specifically evangelical institution started in the post-1905 era is a children's home founded by the Evangelical Christian congregation in St. Petersburg, possibly as early as the spring of 1906 when a donation of three rubles from "brother Chernikov" of Baku was received by *Khristianin*.[113] It is not clear whether such a home already existed, or whether the gift slightly predated it. The home was located at Raivola along the Finnish rail line. It is not known how many children lived at the home, nor the circumstances that brought them there, or how long it continued to function. A shadowy 1907 photo suggests that up to fifteen children and staff were in residence and that the home existed for at least a year.[114] The children were brought up to respond to the needs of others: in 1907 they sent a gift of three rubles for famine victims which they earned by selling their own handwork.[115]

The need for a charitable institution to accommodate orphans and the elderly from Baptist congregations was on the agenda of the Russian Baptist Union Congress held at E. I. Chertkova's palace in St. Petersburg in September 1910. Indeed, considerable attention was given to institutions in general at the congress. In his introductory address, Union president V. G. Pavlov stressed the need to demonstrate "practical Christianity" to the Russian people in order to show that evangelicals were presenting the gospel

---

112. "Protokol zasedanii s"ezda predstavitelei obshchin russkikh evangel'skikh khristian-baptistov," proiskhodivshikh v mae mesiatse 1908 g. v g. Kieve" (Minutes of the sessions of the congress of representatives of congregations of Russian Evangelical Christians-Baptists that took place in May 1908 in the city of Kiev), *Baptist* 8 (August 1908) 18.

113. *Bratskii listok* 5 (1906) 32.

114. *Bratskii listok* 10 (October 1907) n.p.

115. *Bratskii listok* 7 (July 1907) 19.

and were not a sect and that "we must . . . occupy ourselves with the founding of schools, shelters, prayer houses, etc."[116] Baptist-run schools were also on the agenda. A teacher named Elena Vasil'evna Beklemisheva reported on the need for improvements in the education of Baptist children who were frequently refused access to Orthodox village schools or were living on the city streets while their parents were working. She was in the process of organizing an agricultural school with preparation for Baptist teachers and requested support from the union.[117] Yet another motion was made for the union to start up a residence for the deaf, of whom there were many in the churches.[118]

The third day of the congress was specifically devoted to starting a shelter for orphans and the elderly. There were eighteen children for whom the Baptist Union had assumed responsibility, although their exact connection to the Union is not known. Seven children in Grigorievka and six in Pristen' (Kharkiv guberniia) were total orphans; five more children in Znamenka (perhaps near Elizavetgrad, present-day Kirovograd, Ukraine) could not be cared for adequately by their mother.[119] Efforts had already been made to place orphans and the elderly in the homes of church members and provide them with financial assistance from the union treasury. One delegate, I. P. Kushnerov, objected that because of the existing arrangement, there was no need for any special shelter. V. P. Stepanov then stated that, on the contrary, a shelter was necessary because people could not be "overseen" properly when they were scattered in separate households. Evidently he expressed the concern of many other delegates that there was no way of guaranteeing that the union's wards were being looked after properly unless they were all living in a single location.[120] It was agreed that the prominent Baptist church at Balashov in Saratov guberniia would make an excellent location for a children's home. William Fetler exclaimed that Balashov was the *zolotoe dno*, a figurative "gold mine," meaning that the congregation

116. *Bratskii listok* 9 (September 1910) 14.

117. *Bratskii listok* 10 (October 1910) 5–6. A resolution was passed at the congress that Beklemisheva be given "material and moral support" ("Izvlechenie iz protokola Vserossiiskago s"ezda evangel'skikh khristian baptistov s 1 po 9 sentiabria 1910 g. v S. Peterburge" [Excerpt from the minutes of the All-Russian Congress of Evangelical Christians-Baptists from 1–9 September 1910 in the city of St. Petersburg], *Baptist* 43 [20 October 1910] 342). There were other schools organized at about this time; for example, a "confessional mid-level trade school (*uchilishche*) for orphaned children established by Stundists in Kharkiv" (Bulgakov, *Nastol'naia kniga*, v. 2, 1678).

118. *Bratskii listok* 10 (October 1910) 7.

119. "Besedy 'Baptista'" (Conversations of *The Baptist*), *Baptist* 41 (6 October 1910) 324.

120. *Bratskii listok* 10 (October 1910) 7.

there had everything necessary for the project.[121] An unidentified Balashov delegate parried Fetler's enthusiasm by saying, "That gold mine has gone a bit rusty."[122] But I. A. Goliaev, the Balashov presbyter and delegate, affirmed that the issue had already been discussed in Balashov and the "brothers" there were in favor of establishing a union home. Goliaev concluded by saying, "If the proposal to build a union shelter in our city is from you, then it is our honor; if it is from the Lord, then it is a blessing."[123] Accordingly, a resolution was entered into the minutes: "The session of the All-Russian Union of Baptists decided to build a shelter for the elderly and orphans and asks the Balashov congregation to take upon itself the matter of building the shelter in its name and suggests that all congregations take part in this project."[124] At the same time, it was agreed that the existence of the shelter would not replace the Disabilities Fund, which would continue to be administered for the sake of preachers who were no longer capable of working or for their widows, "because it [would be] awkward to place such people in a shelter on the same level with other members."[125] In other words, the Disabilities Fund by this time was functioning something like a pension fund. A resolution was passed authorizing congress delegates to take up offerings in their home churches to support various projects, including the shelter in Balashov.[126]

Balashov was certainly chosen to set up the shelter because of its active, committed, and—at least by 1910—relatively well-to-do church membership. The area had been an important Molokan center where many initially resisted the first Baptist evangelists, P. G. Demakin, and N. M. Chetvernin, who probably arrived in the 1880s.[127] The Baptist community endured some early persecution; by about 1903 they were meeting for worship at the home of the merchant Z. I. Smirnov until a building was completed in 1909, largely

---

121. S. Belousov, "Vpechatleniia ot s"ezda" (Impressions of the congress), *Baptist* 47 (17 November 1910) 373.

122. Ibid.

123. *Bratskii listok* 10 (October 1910) 7.

124 Ibid., 7–8.

125. Ibid., 8

126. "Izvlechenie iz protokola," 343.

127. M. I. Goliaev, "Kak vel menia Gospod' (K 40-letnemu prebyvaniiu v tserkvi)" (How the Lord led me [On the 40th anniversary of (my) joining the church]), *Bratskii vestnik* 3 (1946) 13; see also Demchenko, "Missionerskoe sluzhenie," 2.

through his generosity.¹²⁸ It was an imposing building of red and white brick with fanciful towers and seating for nine-hundred worshippers.¹²⁹

The Balashov home received its charter in 1912. It was designated for orphaned children between the ages of two and sixteen and for the elderly. The Balashov church was responsible for supporting the home financially and for administering it through a committee elected by the congregation. Members of the committee could be of either sex. The residents of the home were all Baptists, "without regard for estate [position, class] or nationality."¹³⁰ Little else is known about the home, but it continued to exist at least until 1922 when it was last mentioned in the minutes of the Baptist Union Collegium. At that time it was overseen by a "Brother Matveev," and had been provided with supplies for several months.¹³¹ Presumably it was dissolved as were other private institutions for children in Soviet Russia in about 1922.¹³²

In addition to the centralized work undertaken by the national union, regional unions and congregations were also engaged in compassionate ministry. In November 1908, according to a letter from the church in Omsk to the journal *Baptist*: "God laid it on [our] hearts" to take up a special offering every week for the needs of orphans and widows. The church inaugurated its fund with a special celebration. Church members and visitors took communion together and heard several "speeches" based on James 1:27: "Religion that God our Father accepts as pure and faultless is this: to look after orphans and widows in their distress." They collected forty-four rubles and forty kopeks. The correspondent added, "All the brothers and sisters were in a cheerful frame of mind. How good it is for the soul when even the smallest thing is done in the name of God!" The letter concluded with an invitation to the wider Baptist community: "If there are orphans and widows in any congregation, or poor people without daily food, and the congregation is not able to help them because they are too poor, we ask you not to be shy [but] write to us [and] according to our means we will share from the fund we started."¹³³ Their efforts grew. On a journey to Siberia in 1909, V. G. Pavlov reported a meeting of the regional union at

---

128. V. G. Pavlov, "Pis'mo s puti" (A letter from the journey), *Baptist* 2 (8 January 1910) 15–16.

129. Ibid., 16.

130. *Baptist*, Nos. 1-2-3-4 (1914) 29–30.

131. SBHLA, The Historical Papers of Mrs. I. V. Neprash, "Zapis' 23, Zasedanie Kollegii Vserossiiskogo Soiuza" (Notation No. 23, Meeting of the Collegium of the All-Russian Union) 18 March 1922.

132 Kelly, *Children's World*, 206–7.

133. *Baptist* 2 (15 January 1909) 17.

Omsk where it was decided to get permission to found a home for orphans and the disabled. Land had been donated. To support it, church members on farms agreed to contribute a proportionate weight of all the wheat they harvested, while merchant members pledged one-fourth of a kopek of every ruble. Pavlov adds: "This is a wonderful decision and God grant that it would be realized soon."[134] How quickly the home was opened is unclear, but from the years 1917 to 1921 there was a home in Omsk for as many as one-hundred orphans, including children from within and outside of the evangelical movement, under the direction of the Siberian division of the Russian Baptist Union. It was located in Novo-Omsk, station Kulomzino, about ten kilometers from Omsk on the left bank of the Irtysh River.[135]

Like the assistance funds, the appearance of evangelical compassionate institutions after 1905 indicate a more structured response to caring for those within the community and the further development of a sense of mutual responsibility.

EDUCATING THE EVANGELICAL COMMUNITY ON MONEY AND GIVING

Thus, after 1905 evangelicals set up dedicated assistance funds and institutions to care chiefly for their own people in need. However, if the churches were to be able to sustain these efforts, they would need to develop a sense of community and mutual responsibility not unlike that of the Russian indigenous sectarian groups, chiefly the Molokans. Therefore, another important dimension of compassionate ministry after 1905 was teaching on the importance of supporting one another, indeed on the whole matter of the Christian's attitude to money. A 1907 editorial in *Baptist*, most likely by D. I. Mazaev, cited the case of the ingathering of one-hundred converts in Vladivostok. Surprisingly, given the great concern for evangelism, the writer stated that the number was too large: it meant that people were joining the church without adequate teaching. Significantly, the writer made the point that such people had no proper understanding of giving.[136] Indeed, between April 1905 and January 1912, both the Baptists and the Evangelical Christians grew by about one-third, for a total evangelical population of more than 95,000.[137] Clearly, people who perhaps had never been responsible for supporting institutions before had to be instructed in its importance. What

134. Pavlov, "Pis'mo s puti," 38.
135. Dik, *Svet Evangeliia v Kazakhstane*, 85.
136. *Baptist* 3 (September 1907) 36.
137 Coleman, *Russian Baptists*, 27.

is more, a sense of community had to be built among people from widely different backgrounds and geographic locations. Thus, Mazaev, Pavlov, and Ivanov used the pages of *Baptist* as their teaching tool to correct misconceptions and inculcate principles concerning money and giving. Other evangelical journals, such as *Khristianin* and *Bratskii listok, Slovo istiny*, and *Gost'* frequently presented similar ideas;[138] *Baptist*, however, is presented here as the most comprehensive and consistent.

First of all, *Baptist* regularly published the reports of evangelistic preachers supported by the Russian Baptist Union.[139] This emphasized the importance of the preachers' ministry and kept them in the mind's eye of church members. Then, the basic, repeated lesson for Russian evangelicals was that they carried the responsibility for financing their own ministries and were called to be both generous and systematic. The first issue of *Baptist* carried a report by evangelist F. P. Balikhin on his trip to attend the European Baptist Congress in 1903. Before he left Russia, D. I. Mazaev had instructed him as follows:

> . . . I ask you not to solicit from them [the European Baptists] any gifts for any needs. Praise God, we have multiplied significantly and consequently we have our own good resources and if we have not learned how to draw sufficient means from it, then it is our fault as leaders and God alone, who has given us many brethren, will give us the power to overcome stinginess and to extract the necessary water from the hard rock.[140]

The first step in "overcoming stinginess" was to label it as shameful. In 1908 V. V. Ivanov wrote: "It is painful to me and sometimes even strikes me as funny when I hear brothers and sisters weeping and loudly praying about the Kingdom of God and about pouring out blessings on our native land, while their cash boxes for missions are empty."[141] Sometimes stories were used to illustrate the spiritual consequences of stinginess. A wealthy but selfish woman had a dream in which she saw many houses being built in heaven. She noticed one poor, tiny house and asked who it was for. "You," responded

---

138. Just four of numerous examples include *Bratskii listok* 2 (1907) 43; *Gost'* 2 (December 1910) 12; V. G. Pavlov, "Khristianskoe upotreblenie deneg" (The Christian use of money), *Slovo istiny* 8 (1917) 116–18; A. Karev, "Kopilka Iisusa, ili kak nauchit'sia zhertvovat' dlia Khrista" (Jesus' money box, or how to learn to sacrifice for Christ), *Khristianin* 2 (1928) 12–14.

139. Examples from 1908 alone are found in *Baptist* 1 (January 1908) 15–16; 6 (June 1908) 23–28; 7 (July 1908) 20–22; 10 (October 1908) 16–18.

140. F. P. Balikhin, "Moia poezdka zagranitsu" (My trip abroad), *Baptist* 1 (July 1907) 16.

141. V. V. Ivanov, "Ispytaite menia" (Test me), *Baptist* 12 (December 1908) 3–4.

an angel. "And who is that big palace for?" she asked. "Your coachman," the angel answered. When she asked how that could be, the angel explained that the unimpressive size of her heavenly home was due to her failure to send the builders any materials (i.e. generous contributions) while her coachman, who gave away everything he had on earth, was constantly sending more and more heavenward. Thus, readers were given to understand, it is possible to have much money and be poor, mean, and unloving, while those without money may be rich in good deeds and generosity.[142]

If stinginess was to be avoided, generosity was to be praised. *Baptist* routinely printed lists of contributors, detailing who gave how much to which fund,[143] including a man named Fedor Dubovyi who was not even a church member, but who contributed toward the construction of a prayer house and also named it in his will.[144] Likewise, the obituary of Iakov Leontevich Matveev praised the deceased for leaving his money and land to the Baptist church even though he was poor. Mazaev as editor pointed out that Matveev's generosity and foresight distinguished him from certain other Baptists who, although they were rich and contributed during their lifetime, neglected to leave a will.[145] In addition, generosity was connected to spiritual benefits. In a 1908 article, V. V. Ivanov asked rhetorically why there was no revival in Russia when there was revival elsewhere in the world. Ivanov answered his own question, explaining that too many believers assumed that since they are saved by grace, they are obliged to do nothing at all, and so become "depressed, idle, and completely indifferent to any kind of charity at all, and as for the work of mission . . . they will only have beautiful words [and no action]."[146] To save the situation, Ivanov recommended a tithe (giving 10 percent) for all believers—rich and poor alike:

> Let all the brothers and sisters bring their ten percent to the business of missions . . . Let the poor bring their offering in *groshi* [i.e. the smallest monetary unit available], others in rubles, still others in tens or hundreds of rubles, and the wealthy in thousands, tens of thousands, and hundreds of thousands of rubles for the work of God, and then we will see the wonders of God in our congregations.[147]

142. *Baptist* 11 (November 1908) 16.
143. See, for example, *Baptist* 2 (15 January 1909) 18.
144. *Baptist* 6 (June 1908) 33.
145. *Baptist* 2 (August 1907) 25–26.
146. Ivanov, "Ispytaite menia," 3.
147. Ibid., 4.

Aid within the Evangelical Community—Mazaev, Pavlov, and Ivanov 111

Concern for preachers continued to be promoted, as when V. G. Pavlov, as editor, recommended that churches insure their pastors so that their families would have something to go on with in case of death.[148]

To undergird teaching on the importance of giving, *Baptist* also cited examples from the experience of evangelicals abroad. A 1908 article translated from English dealt with tithing.[149] Another article in a 1908 issue of *Baptist* described a meeting that took place in Liverpool, where there were complaints expressed about the low spiritual level of the Baptist churches and the lack of giving. However, when people began to give systematically, the atmosphere changed dramatically. The Russian commentator concluded, "The English Baptists now have twenty missionary doctors in the field . . . Let us be inspired as well!"[150] Besides citing examples of generosity from abroad, Russian Baptists were also encouraged to send help there. An earthquake in Italy led to an appeal from the editorship of *Baptist* to assist the Italian Baptist Union in aiding earthquake victims in that country in 1909,[151] again strengthening the sense of community and responsibility toward fellow believers, no matter how far away.

In addition to positive and negative examples and stories, giving was also systematized by means of regular reporting on funds and projects. Readers were alternately praised and criticized depending on progress. At the May 1908 congress it was decided to declare a special offering for all the churches for support of the Disabilities Fund on the first Sunday of October. At the same congress, specific sums were set aside for the widows of certain leaders.[152] The last issue of 1908 praised the churches for their generosity and pointed out the importance of reading *Baptist* regularly:

> We see that just one announcement in the journal gave us 502 rubles and 14 kopeks (and counting), which clearly shows that our brothers readily assist in good work once they know about it, so it would be desirable for all our brothers' congregations to become subscribers to our journal in the interest of the [common] good.[153]

---

148. *Baptist* 2 (5 January 1911) 13.
149. "O raspredelenii desiatiny" (On allocating the tithe), *Baptist* 3 (March 1908) 12.
150. *Baptist* 2 (February 1908) 23.
151. *Baptist* 4 (15 February 1909) 23–24.
152. *Baptist* 8 (August 1908) 18.
153. *Baptist* 12 (December 1908) 2.

A few months later another article complained that the Disabilities Fund was suffering for a lack of resources: "we have at the very least 10,000 Christian Russian Baptist souls, but why are there so few contributors?"[154]

Thus, *Baptist*, in particular, served as a teaching tool to present stories about the spiritual benefits of generosity both at home and abroad, to point to examples of generous evangelicals, and to keep readers focused on progress in maintaining evangelical ministries and institutions. Teaching on money and giving also contributed to the evangelicals' sense of responsibility to one another, including fellow believers in other countries.

CONCLUSION

From the early days of the movement, evangelicals showed concern for people in need. In particular, they took care of those in their midst who suffered for their convictions, especially exiles. Following the decree on religious toleration in 1905 it was possible to give more thought to building charitable institutions as a means of outreach, but the dominant trend was toward sustaining the existing evangelical movement, especially preachers and their families. Consequently, when it became possible to systematize giving, attention was paid very quickly to the establishment of church funds, including those intended for compassionate purposes. To educate and build up a sense of community and mutual responsibility among evangelicals, leaders such as D. I. Mazaev, V. G. Pavlov, and V. V. Ivanov used the journal *Baptist*. Essentially they promoted values that were important to the indigenous sectarian groups from which many of the evangelicals came, especially the Molokans.

---

154. M. Iashchenko, "O fonde invalidov" (About the disabilities fund), *Baptist* 3 (1 February 1909) 8–9.

4

Urban Rescue Ministry—W. A. Fetler

AID SHARED AMONG FELLOW evangelicals, expressed in the development of church-based funds and institutions, along with a sense of community and responsibility for one another, were among the many contributions of leaders such as D. I. Mazaev, V. G. Pavlov, and V. V. Ivanov. The second major trend in compassionate ministry among Russian evangelicals after 1905 was rescue ministry, which I will define as evangelization and practical assistance directed specifically at the urban poor—beggars, drunkards, prostitutes, and children from poor families.[1] There were groups of evangelicals in major Russian cities, such as Moscow, Kyiv, and Baku, and yet ministry of this kind evidently never spread much beyond St. Petersburg, and gathered most of its momentum between 1907, the year that William A. Fetler arrived in the capital, and 1915 when he was exiled from Russia. For this reason I will give special attention to Fetler, although he was not the only proponent of rescue ministry—I. S. Prokhanov is another important example. Yet it was largely because of Fetler's energy and vision that rescue ministry became part of Russian evangelical life, at least as an inspiration.

Compassionate outreach as practiced by the Pashkovites during the height of the movement from 1873 to 1884 had many components intended to benefit the urban poor. Thus, sewing cooperatives to employ women who might otherwise be driven to prostitution, tearooms for cab drivers, inexpensive dining rooms for poor students, and other forms of service, were all available in St. Petersburg. During the years following the exile of V. A. Pashkov and M. M. Korf in 1884, the Pashkovite movement assumed

---

1. In some sources "rescue" refers specifically to ministry devoted to reclaiming prostitutes; see Lamb, "Social Work of the Salvation Army," 122–26.

a quieter, semi-underground existence. Yet work among the urban poor was still an emphasis. Some unidentified evangelicals worked among poor children and families in St. Petersburg.[2] Jenny de Mayer set up a House of Industry on the island of Sakhalin[3]; Baron Paul Nicolay and Aleksandra Peiker worked in the prisons and among students.[4] By the early years of the twentieth century, however, it seemed to many in Russia that the grave problems of urban life called for a more vigorous response whether on the part of the state or on the part of private citizens.

During the second half of the nineteenth century, industrialization in Russia brought a steady stream of people into urban centers. Many laborers were temporary, migrating to factories or mines for shorter or longer periods while maintaining ties with their home villages; nevertheless, between 1890 and 1914 the number of urban, industrial laborers in Russia grew from about 1,424,000 to 3,743,800.[5] Cities, however, did not have adequate resources to accommodate so many; moreover, the newcomers did not always have sufficient skills or social support to enable them to survive, much less thrive, in an urban setting. Thousands were crowded into slum neighborhoods. An injury, an illness, or a pregnancy could render a worker unemployable, forcing many into begging, theft, or prostitution to survive. The term for "unsupervised" children, *besprizornye*, came into existence in the 1880s as child pickpockets, prostitutes, and alcoholics became a widespread feature of Russian life.[6] To help the urban poor, thousands of charities were founded in Russia during the second half of the nineteenth century.[7] A lively temperance movement, consisting of numerous government- and church-sponsored societies, sought to mitigate the effects of alcoholism, especially among the lower classes.[8]

For their part, Russian evangelicals had always assigned spiritual significance to social need. They believed that the first, essential step in changing people's lives for the better was to bring them to repentance, because they understood sin to be the ultimate cause of all misery.[9] They were moved by the plight of the poor, especially the moral degradation that accompanied

---

2. Duff, "Furlough Days in Russia," 255–56.
3. De Mayer, *Adventures with God*, 72–74.
4. Greta Langenskjöld, *Baron Paul Nicolay*, 75–81.
5 Engel, *Between the Fields and the City*, 102.
6. Kelly, *Children's World*, 159–61.
7 Ivanova and Ivanova, *Zarubezhnyi opyt*, 43–44.
8 Herlihy, *The Alcoholic Empire*, 9; Transchel, *Under the Influence*, 47.
9. "Drug iunoshi. Sotsialnyi vopros" (Friend of youth. The social question), *Molodoi vinogradnik* 1 (January 1911) 2.

poverty,[10] and depicted them in their publications as literally crying out for spiritual help: "From all sides ring out the screams for help of the dying, bare hands are stretched out for the bread of life, the people come in crowds to hear about the One who will bring rest to those who labor and are heavy laden."[11] At the same time, as the example of the Pashkovites demonstrates, the Russian evangelicals recognized the need to help people materially as well. However, whereas the largely upper-class Pashkovites were able to minister in ways that were typical for their station in life, serving as sisters of mercy or building charitable institutions on their own estates, by the early twentieth century there was interest in compassionate ministry that was accessible to the increasing numbers of evangelicals from the lower classes. What could ordinary people do to reach thousands of their fellow citizens in deep spiritual and physical need? Here the clearest example for the Russian evangelicals came from Great Britain in the form of rescue ministry, especially as it was practiced by the Salvation Army. Founded in London in 1878 by William Booth, the Salvation Army was already a worldwide movement by the time it reached Finland in 1889, which was then an autonomous Grand Duchy of the Russian Empire. Originally, the Army had been an exclusively evangelistic movement and only later moved into the area of social ministry, which was strongly disapproved of by some Salvationists.[12] However, a 1909 editorial by I. S. Prokhanov, doubtless expressed the thoughts of many Russian evangelicals: "It is my sincere conviction that the only genuine means of doing battle with the proletariat in Russia is the work of the Salvation Army, that is, the spiritual work of conversion united with social means."[13] Thus, the Russians' impulse to serve people in need met with a new model, represented by the Army's combination of preaching and service to reach the urban poor.

The Army experienced numerous setbacks in its attempts to minister within Russia itself[14] but many Russians were well aware of its existence nevertheless. William Booth's book, *In Darkest England and the Way Out* appeared in Russian in 1892 and made a strong impression.[15] A two-volume work entitled *Nastol'naia kniga dlia sviashcheno-tserkovno-sluzhitelei*

10. F. M. Trosnov, "Doklad F. M. Trosnova o poezdke v Finliandiu dlia oznakomleniia s Armiei Spaseniia" (Report of F. M. Trosnov about the trip to Finland to get acquainted with the Salvation Army), *Iunyi Khristianin* 1 (1909) 1.

11. Vil'gel'm Andreevich Fetler, "Molitvennyi dom baptistov v S.-Peterburge" (The Baptist prayer house in St. Petersburg), *Baptist* 1 (January 1908) 26.

12. Murdoch, *Origins of the Salvation Army*, 169–70; Aitken, *Blood and Fire*, 96–97.

13. *Bratskii listok* 4 (April 1909) 1.

14. Aitken, *Blood and Fire*, 95–138

15. Ivanova and Ivanova, *Zarubezhnyi opyt*, 62.

(Handbook for ministers of the Holy Church), published in 1913 gave more space to describing the Army than it did to describing Baptists and included a respectful assessment of the Army's work with alcoholics.[16] Russians traveling abroad, including some evangelicals, visited Salvation Army posts and brought back positive reports of its work. Prince Nicholas Golitsyn, son of the Pashkovite Princess Golitsyna studied the Salvation Army outside of Russia and became well acquainted with the Booth family—even to the point of reportedly falling in love with Booth's daughter Evangeline![17] Evangelist Fedor Balikhin visited the Salvation Army in Berlin in 1903 when he attended a German Baptist Congress.[18] The delegation of Russians who attended the European Baptist Congress in Berlin in 1908 again visited the local Army post.[19] The Salvation Army only operated officially in Russia itself between 1917 and 1923, although it was present in a semi-underground capacity beginning in 1910.[20] Throughout its time in Russia the Army depended on the hospitality of the local evangelical community. At the same time, the Army's focus on rescue ministry among the urban poor was certainly a powerful model for the Russian evangelicals, notably W. A. Fetler, who adopted many of its methods.

WILLIAM A. FETLER

Fetler's career has many parallels with that of I. S. Prokhanov.[21] Both men were based in St. Petersburg, a city that offered many opportunities for evangelical witness. Here were thousands of people in need of salvation through Jesus Christ, many of them uprooted from their traditional way of life and therefore open to hearing the gospel. Because of the previous generation of Pashkovites, St. Petersburg already had a large concentration of evangelicals, many of them wealthy and at least somewhat influential.[22] Both Prokhanov and Fetler were grounded in the Pashkovite community.[23]

    16. Bulgakov, *Nastol'naia kniga*, v. 2, 1598–1600.

    17 Aitken, *Blood and Fire*, 77–79.

    18. F. Balikhin, "Moia poezdka zagranitsu" (My trip abroad), *Baptist* 1 (June 1907) 16.

    19. *Baptist* 11 (November 1908) 35.

    20 Aitken, *Blood and Fire*, 132–34.

    21. Wardin, *On the Edge*, 368–69.

    22. Aitken questions the actual political influence wielded by aristocratic evangelicals or evangelical sympathizers in Russia (*Blood and Fire*, 73–74); however, W. A. Fetler's supporters were sufficiently influential to get his Siberian exile sentence changed to exile abroad (see J. Fetler, *Sluzhenie Rossii*, 46).

    23. V. Fetler, "Molitvennyi dom baptistov," 26–27; Popov, *I. S. Prokhanov*, 21–23.

Both studied in England. Prokhanov first came to St. Petersburg during the 1880s, attended Baptist College in Stokes Croft (Bristol) and the Congregationalist New College in London during the 1890s, and returned to St. Petersburg in 1901.[24] Fetler arrived in 1907 after completing the Pastors' College in London.[25] Both were active evangelists and worked hard during the 1910s to reach the urban population, an undertaking that included rescue ministry. Yet while Prokhanov mainly promoted rescue activity as a ministry for church youth,[26] Fetler himself was essentially a rescue preacher who consciously modeled himself after examples of such ministry he had experienced in England. According to his son John's biography, not only the ministry of William Booth, but also of C. H. Spurgeon, the Welsh Revival of 1904 to 1905, and the revival preaching tradition in general were formative for Fetler.[27]

Growing up in the family of a Baptist pastor in Latvia, Fetler was exposed at an early age to the ministry of C. H. Spurgeon, as he listened to translated sermons read aloud by his mother. For that matter, people throughout the Russian Empire had the same experience, because Spurgeon's sermons were known and respected, including in Russian Orthodox circles.[28] Spurgeon was, of course, especially admired by the evangelicals. In the summer of 1905 the small Russian delegation at the first Baptist World Congress in London (V. G. Pavlov, D. I. Mazaev, Baron Voldemar Uixkyll, V. V. Ivanov, and W. A. Fetler, then still a student)[29] made a special point of visiting Spurgeon's grave at West Norwood Cemetery. There they placed a wreath, sang a hymn, and prayed that the word Spurgeon had preached would continue to be spread around the world through his printed sermons and bear fruit to the glory of God.[30]

In 1898 at the age of fifteen Fetler experienced spiritual rebirth and was baptized late at night to avoid attracting the attention of the authorities. As a young man working as a clerk in Riga he sensed God's call to preach. He remembered that Spurgeon had founded a training college in London, and with the help of an English dictionary consulted in the public library managed to write out a postcard addressed simply to "College of Spurgeon,

24. Kahle, *Evangel'skie khristiane v Rossii i Sovetskom soiuze*, 13–14.
25. McCaig, *Wonders of Grace*, 12; J. Fetler, *Sluzhenie Rossii*, 10–13.
26. Kareva, "Moi vospominaniia" (My recollections), in Karetnikova, *Al'manakh, vypusk 2*, 176, 183–84.
27. J. Fetler, *Sluzhenie Rossii*, 12–15.
28. McCaig, *Wonders of Grace*, 82–88; Morden, *C. H. Spurgeon*, 114.
29. I. V. Kargel may have also attended the 1905 gathering; see Nichols, *Russian Evangelical Spirituality*, 188–90.
30. *Bratskii listok* 5 (1906) 27.

London, England." He was not aware that C. H. Spurgeon had died in 1892. The postcard reached its destination and Spurgeon's son Thomas, then the college president. On the basis of the correspondence that followed, the required interview was waived and Fetler was admitted to the Pastors' College in 1903.[31] As a student at the training school C. H. Spurgeon founded, Fetler was naturally influenced by his legacy. Spurgeon was an evangelical activist who believed that all genuine devotion to Christ would express itself in practical service.[32] According to Fetler, Spurgeon was convinced that social evils such as poverty could be remedied only by a wholehearted turning to God.[33] He would certainly have been aware of Spurgeon's concern for the general welfare of the poor, expressed in a lifetime of sacrificial giving, such as the founding of the Stockwell Orphanage in 1869. At a prayer meeting in 1866 Spurgeon proposed praying that God would show the Metropolitan Tabernacle congregation "a new work," and also provide the means to accomplish it. Within a few days, a donation of twenty thousand pounds was received for the purpose of founding an orphanage—evidently the "new work" about which the group had prayed. Spurgeon headed the board of trustees of this institution, which was greatly influenced by the work of George Mueller of Bristol, founder of the famous orphanage and a much-admired friend of Spurgeon's.[34] By the time Fetler was studying in London, the Stockwell Orphanage had been functioning for more than thirty years. Delegates to the Baptist World Congress in 1905, including the Russians, visited the orphanage, where the children greeted the visitors and sang.[35] In addition, Fetler probably modeled the sizable churches he founded in St. Petersburg (Dom Evangeliia [House of the Gospel], 1912) and Riga (Dom Golgofy [House of Golgotha], 1912 and Dom spaseniia [House of salvation], 1927) at least in part on the Metropolitan Tabernacle in London. Dom Evangeliia continued to function as a multi-purpose mega-church until it was closed down in 1930.[36] Dom spaseniia was confiscated in 1940 when the Soviet Union invaded Latvia.[37]

31. McCaig, *Wonders of Grace*, 12; J. Fetler, *Sluzhenie Rossii*, 10–13.

32. Morden, 'Communion with Christ,' 193.

33. J. Fetler, *Sluzhenie Rossii*, 29.

34. Details on the Stockwell Orphanage may be found in Morden,'Communion with Christ,' 204–18 and *C. H. Spurgeon*, 136–38.

35. *Bratskii listok* 5 (1906) 28, 31–32.

36. "Dom Evangeliia v Sankt-Peterburge" (Dom Evangeliia in St. Petersburg), Baptist.org.ru/read/article/672981; J. Fetler states that Dom Evangeliia was confiscated in 1928 (*Sluzhenie Rossii*, 57).

37. Fetler, Vil'gel'm Andreevich, baptistru.info/index.php/Fetler,_Vil'gel'm_Andreevich.

Also of great importance during his student years was Fetler's direct experience of the Welsh Revival of 1904 to 1905, at least one report of which circulated among Russian evangelicals.[38] In fact, the revival had important consequences for the Pastors' College and the Metropolitan Tabernacle in general. At the time of the revival, the Metropolitan Tabernacle held special prayer meetings and the congregation conducted evangelistic outreach in the Elephant and Castle area of London, with Pastors' College students taking a leading role. There were numerous conversions and an increase in church membership, while Pastors' College students were actively engaged in conducting meetings, preaching and praying. Processions of as many as five-hundred people, including college students, faculty, and church members would march through the streets singing.[39] The revival was endorsed and promoted by the college, especially by Archibald McCaig, the principal, who visited Wales in 1905 together with Thomas Spurgeon.[40] Fetler also visited Wales during the revival.[41] McCaig, who became a warm friend to Fetler and visited him in Russia four times, remembered in later years that during the revival the young Latvian preacher also "experienced a great quickening of his spiritual life."[42] In addition, Fetler picked up on the famous music of the Welsh Revival. On his first visit to Russia in 1910, McCaig noted the frequent singing in Russian of the Welsh refrain "Diolch Iddo,"[43] or "Thanks be to Him," the chorus of the hymn "Dyma Geidwad i bechadur," or "Here's a Saviour unto sinners."[44] The Welsh connection endured; in the 1920s when Fetler organized the Russian Missionary Society, Welsh missionaries were among those who came to minister in Eastern Europe.[45]

Significant in the Welsh Revival was the effect that it had on people from the lower classes of society. Jessie Penn-Lewis described the conversion of a thousand people in the Neath District who had never before attended church, including, "Many [who] had been to prison. Also drunkards, prize fighters, gamblers, and one clog dancer . . . Women quite drunk would stagger into the meetings and be soundly converted while standing in the hall." In particular, Penn-Lewis frequently mentioned the revival's effect on alcoholics, with the taverns standing empty because the people were

---

38. *Khristianin* 2 (February 1906) 53.
39. Randall, "'The Breath of Revival,'" 200–204.
40. Ibid.; McCaig, *Wonders of Grace*, 107.
41. Stewart, *A Man in a Hurry*, 20; J. Fetler, *Sluzhenie Rossii*, 13–14.
42. McCaig, *Wonders of Grace*, 12.
43. Ibid., 29–31.
44. Awstin, *The Religious Revival in Wales 1904*.
45. Rev. Noel Gibbard, "Remembering 1904–05."

all at church or chapel: "[A] man passing a public house saw the landlady come out and hold up a pint of beer saying, 'Come along,' but the convert held up his Bible and replied, 'No, we're going with this now. This is the key to heaven, and that to hell.'"[46] While it cannot be said that Russian evangelicals actually acquired their ideas on spiritual renewal and freedom from drunkenness through the Welsh Revival, it is certainly true that they were convinced that drunkenness was a spiritual problem that could be solved by repentance as will be described below. As with the outgoing, socially-involved influence of Spurgeon, his experience of the Welsh Revival would have confirmed Fetler's ideas about the power of the gospel to change lives and thus draw people out of poverty and its attendant vice.

In this connection, in London Fetler also participated in midnight meetings especially conducted for the benefit of prostitutes, the homeless, and drunkards.[47] The roots of midnight meetings go back to the 1840s when a small group of people who called themselves the "London by Moonlight Mission" went into the streets at night to talk to prostitutes and offer them the opportunity to change their way of life. This activity took on the character of a movement around the beginning of the winter of 1860, one of the results of the Prayer Revival of 1857. At that time many groups, such as the Female Aid Society, began to invite prostitutes to a hall or restaurant for tea and to hear a talk including an invitation to leave the streets. Such gatherings were backed up by a network of homes and other accommodations for women, including alternative employment opportunities and care facilities for children.[48] Possibly the first midnight meeting Fetler ever attended was one organized by Gypsy Smith and Dr. Campbell Morgan at the Westminster Chapel,[49] although certainly he was involved in the Pastors' College and Metropolitan Tabernacle meetings and at least knew of the Salvation Army's midnight meetings. In any case, midnight meetings became an important part of the rescue mission work Fetler organized in St. Petersburg some years later.

Thus, as a student in London, Fetler enthusiastically absorbed all that the evangelical world there could offer. He practiced the active, outward-looking evangelicalism of C. H. Spurgeon. He studied *Lectures on Revivals of Religion* by the American revivalist preacher, Charles Grandison Finney

---

46. Penn-Lewis, *The Awakening in Wales*, 76–77.

47. McCaig, *Wonders of Grace*, 107; Randall, "'The Breath of Revival,'" 202–203.

48. Randall, *Rhythms of Revival*, 116–17. For a detailed description of evangelical ministries to prostitutes in England, see Heasman, *Evangelicals in Action*, 148–68.

49. Stewart, *A Man in a Hurry*, 36–37.

(1792–1875).[50] He became acquainted with the preaching ministry of Gypsy Smith (1860–1947), which may have influenced his distinctive lively style and practice of singing from the pulpit,[51] as did the Spirit-led spontaneous singing and praying in Wales.[52] He learned first-hand about the work of William Booth and the Salvation Army.[53] He ministered to Russian sailors and immigrants to the United States in London's East End.[54] In summary, during his time in London, absorbing multiple models, Fetler wholeheartedly accepted the role of a rescue mission preacher in transforming lives and carried that ministry approach with him back to St. Petersburg.

RESCUE MINISTRY IN ST. PETERSBURG

Fetler returned to the Russian Empire in 1907[55] under the sponsorship of the Baptist independent Pioneer Mission. However, it appears that even then he may have still been somewhat undecided as to what shape his future ministry would take. After a few months in Latvia he answered an invitation to serve as pastor of the Latvian Baptist Church in St. Petersburg. He himself mentioned that he was still considering a missionary career in China at the same time, an idea that had been on his mind while in England.[56] Evidently, some Russian evangelicals even considered that Fetler had misled them by presenting himself as a missionary candidate for China at this time, but he eventually determined to stay in the capital where his powerful preaching contributed to the establishment of a Russian Baptist congregation in 1909.[57]

Fetler found a base among the remaining aristocratic Pashkovites. According to John Fetler's biography, as soon as he returned to St. Petersburg in 1907, W. A. Fetler made the acquaintance of Anna Ivanovna Pashkova,

---

50. Wardin, "William Fetler," 241.

51. Compare, for example, Smith, *Gypsy Smith* and the description of Fetler's preaching at the 1910 All-Russian Baptist Congress in *Missionerskoe obozrenie* (January 1911) 71–77; see also the description of worship at Dom spaseniia in Riga by Scottish evangelist James Stewart quoted by J. Fetler, *Sluzhenie Rossii*, 63–65.

52. Worship during the Welsh Revival is described and analyzed in Clarke, *Music and Theology*, 120–22.

53. J. Fetler, *Sluzhenie Rossii*, 13.

54. McCaig, *Wonders of Grace*, 12; Wardin, "William Fetler," 236.

55. Fetler's arrival was announced in *Bratskii listok* 8 (1907) 20.

56. V. Fetler, "Molitvennyi dom," 26.

57. See Saloff-Astakhoff's unmistakable description of "Mr. F." in *Christianity in Russia*, 134–35. It is interesting that Fetler's younger brother Robert served as a missionary with China Inland Mission at one point (Wardin, "William Fetler," 242).

the colonel's widow, who "saw him as continuing her husband's work."[58] She also is supposed to have introduced Fetler to Lord Radstock, although it is not clear when and where such a meeting might have taken place. Perhaps Fetler met Radstock in England in 1910 when he went there to raise funds to build a Baptist church in St. Petersburg.[59] In any case, he was firmly enough established in those upper class evangelical circles to enable him to rely on their help, as he did in 1915 when he was arrested. At different times he lived in the homes of Princess Natalia Liven[60] and also Elizaveta Chertkova, who later joined the Baptist congregation at Dom Evangeliia.[61] Even members of the royal family were curious about Fetler's ministry, such as Queen Olga of the Hellenes (Greece), formerly Grand Duchess Olga Konstantinovna Romanova (1851–1926).[62] Pashkovite Aleksandra Peiker was acquainted with Queen Olga, and a few years later, in 1915, the queen intervened to assist the Salvation Army when its members were threatened with fines and imprisonment after a police raid on one of their meetings.[63]

For his first few years in St. Petersburg Fetler conducted preaching meetings at numerous stations around the capital and as far away as Moscow. People from all walks of life attended; in total, about two- to three-thousand people were present at such meetings every week.[64] In at least two of Fetler's meeting locations—Tenishev Hall and a large room next to a bathhouse in Kazachii pereulok—probably beginning in late 1909, Fetler held night meetings of the type he had experienced in London. The pattern did not change significantly from what had been practiced at least since 1889 by the Manchester evangelist, Rev. S. F. Collier or Gypsy Smith[65] except that in St. Petersburg no processions, music, or singing to attract people were permitted by the authorities.[66] Following a regular evening meeting,

---

58. J. Fetler, *Sluzhenie Rossii,* 20; this assertion suggests that Anna Ivanovna returned to Russia after her husband's death.

59. McCaig, *Wonders of Grace,* 13–14; J. Fetler, *Sluzhenie Rossii,* 22.

60. V. Fetler, "Molitvennyi dom," 26–27.

61. Wardin, *On the Edge,* 375.

62. McCaig, *Wonders of Grace,* 46–47, 49. Queen Olga supported the translation of the Bible into Modern Greek. Published in 1900, it created such a controversy that it had to be withdrawn; see http://www.greekroyalfamily.gr/en/history-archotitatis-protis-vasillissas-ton-ellinon-olgas.html. According to McCaig, Fetler had a long conversation in 1910 with Queen Olga's private secretary "about his soul" (*Wonders of Grace,* 49). Possibly this was an interview with Ioulia Carolou, who had done the Greek Bible translation.

63. Karl Larsson, "The Army in Russia," 60–61; Aitken, *Blood and Fire,* 193–95.

64. V. Fetler, "Molitvennyi dom," 26–27.

65. Smith, *Gypsy Smith,* http://www.biblebelievers.com/gypsy_smith/.

66. McCaig, *Wonders of Grace,* 109–10.

church members would go out in the streets to cafes, taverns, and theatres, to invite people to the hall, although when word about the meetings spread, people would gather outside early, waiting to be admitted.[67] At a meeting in February 1910, an observer noticed mostly prostitutes in attendance, some very young, together with their "followers and admirers."[68] Archibald McCaig was present at another meeting that same year where most of the visitors were men.[69] An Australian visitor, J. A. Packer, described both men and women as "dissolute, drunken, ill-clad, cold, and hungry... [who]... came eagerly in the hope, at least, of finding warmth and rest." He added: "I have seen many midnight meetings for the reclamation of the submerged masses, but none that impressed me with such an overpowering sense of sadness as this one in St. Petersburg."[70] Delegates to the Russian Baptist congress in St. Petersburg in September 1910 attended one of Fetler's night meetings and were deeply moved: "All who attended... could not go to sleep for a long time and long after midnight exchanged impressions."[71]

When the hall was full—the room beside the bathhouse accommodated about three-hundred—the choir would begin to sing "quiet songs about rebirth and the joy of a pure life."[72] Then the preaching began, and the response was deeply emotional. As Fetler described the first night meeting he organized: "Weeping and sobbing began... Hardened hearts became as soft as children's and cries of repentance filled the air."[73] Besides words of comfort, the listeners also heard reprimands from the pulpit; Fetler decried the hypocrisy of men who used women and then blamed them for being sinners.[74] Of course, there was always an altar call. On the night J. A. Packer attended "a score or so professed to have found salvation."[75] Sometimes the conversions were dramatic: one night a woman who attended had a farewell letter and a bottle of poison in her pocket, but came to the meeting and found Christ instead.[76]

---

67. Packer, *Among the Heretics*, 39–40.
68. *Baptist* 15 (7 April 1910) 118–19.
69. McCaig, *Wonders of Grace*, 110.
70. Packer, *Among the Heretics*, 39.
71. S. Belousov, "Vpechatleniia ot s"ezda" (Impressions of the congress), *Baptist* 48 (1 December 1910) 388.
72. *Baptist* 4 (20 January 1910) 29.
73. *Baptist* 4 (20 January 1910) 29–30.
74. *Baptist* 15 (7 April 1910) 119.
75. Packer, *Among the Heretics*, 39.
76. *Baptist* 4 (20 January 1910) 30.

Baroness Maria N. Iasnovskaia testified that as a result of the night meetings many people converted from lives of drunkenness and dishonesty and "were completely changed." As word got around that Baptists made reliable workers and servants, it was not unusual for upper-class families to contact Fetler because they wished to employ "Baptist cooks, chamber maids, [and] coachmen."[77] In other words, an informal employment agency also became part of the ministry. Fetler expected that those who found work would, in turn, continue to spread the gospel to others. He charged them: "Brothers, go and drive the carriages; sisters, go and cook as well as you know how so that you may witness and praise the Lord!"[78] The poor were thus empowered to make their own way in life and also to spread the gospel.

It soon must have occurred to Fetler and others to wonder what would become of the people who attended the meetings. In his description of the first night meeting, Fetler stated that when it was over, "[The people] did not want to go back to their dreadful dwellings, and indeed they could not, because they did not have their earnings for the night,"[79] meaning, of course, that because of the meeting the prostitutes had not been able to make the minimum amount of money needed to pay for their keep. In a 1912 article Fetler stated that, "Many of our fallen sisters have been willing to leave their life of sin and degradation, but we have been in trouble to help them, not having a home where we could take them in, until they could find work."[80] One partial solution for offering long-term help for at least some of those who attended the midnight meetings—although evidently not, as it turned out, for prostitutes—was eventually found by acquiring a permanent property for the Baptist congregation of St. Petersburg. Meanwhile, ministry to women caught in the "white slave traffic" was carried on by Baroness Maria N. Iasnovskaia, a member of Dom Evangeliia who had been converted at age sixteen at one of Lord Radstock's meetings.[81] That other evangelicals were also interested in the fate of women is suggested by a brief account in *Baptist* of the All-Russian Congress against the Trafficking of Women held on 21 April 1910 in St. Petersburg.[82] Among the resolutions made at that congress was that an organization similar to the YMCA (represented by

77. Stewart, *A Man in a Hurry*, 39; compare Fetler's statement in a sermon during the All-Russian Baptist Congress in September 1910 quoted in *Missionerskoe obozrenie* (January 1911) 75.

78. J. Fetler, *Sluzhenie Rossii*, 29.

79. *Baptist* 4 (20 January 1910) 29.

80. Wilhelm Fetler, "Russia and the Gospel," *The Missionary Review of the World* (October 1912) 745.

81. *The Baptist World Alliance Second Congress*, 237.

82. *Baptist* 18 (28 April 1910) n.p

the St. Petersburg men's club *Maiak* [Lighthouse]) needed to be set up for the benefit of young women,[83] but it is not known whether any steps were actually taken.

The need to build a substantial church in St. Petersburg to accommodate the crowds of people who came to evangelistic meetings was expressed as early as 1907.[84] W. A. Fetler made the motion to build a specifically Baptist prayer house at the congress of Evangelical Christians-Baptists held in Kyiv in May 1908. The motion carried unanimously and a fund was set up to receive donations.[85] It took time and patience to navigate the bureaucracy, but eventually a suitable property for the construction of a sizable prayer house was attained on Vasilievskii Island, Line 24, Number 11. A groundbreaking celebration was held on 8 September 1910 as part of another Russian Union of Evangelical Christians-Baptists congress.[86] Many people contributed sacrificially to the expensive project. Elizaveta Chertkova gave a considerable sum;[87] those who were less well-off even went without sugar or necessary shoe repair in order to be able to give.[88] In spite of earlier scruples expressed against appealing to evangelicals abroad for support,[89] major funding was sought for the prayer house in England and the United States in 1911.[90] The effort to build a large meeting hall in the capital was not without its critics, who wondered if the expense was justified.[91] Indeed, special collection jars (*kopil'ki*) were distributed to church members for the next several years to raise money bit by bit to cover the debt.[92] Nevertheless, even before the church's adjoining mission house was finished, Fetler moved

---

83 *Baptist* 19 (5 May 1910) n.p.

84. See D. I. Mazaev's speech at the Evangelical Christian and Baptist congress in St. Petersburg in January 1907, reported in *Bratskii listok* 2 (1907) 23.

85. "Protokol zasedanii s"ezda predstavitelei obshchin russkikh evangel'skikh khristian-baptistov proiskhodivshikh v mae mesiatse 1908 g. v g. Kieve" (Minutes of the sessions of the congress of representatives of congregations of Russian Evangelical Christians-Baptists that took place in May 1908 in the city of Kiev), *Baptist* 8 (August 1908) 17.

86 *Bratskii listok* 10 (October 1910) 19–20; Belousov, "Vpechatleniia ot s"ezda," 397; *Gost'* 3 (January 1911) 23; recall that since 1903 the Russian Baptist Union was formally titled the Russian Union of Evangelical Christians-Baptists.

87. J. Fetler, *Sluzhenie Rossii*, 26.

88. *Gost'* 11 (November 1913) 260.

89. Balikhin, "Moia poezdka zagranitsu," 16.

90. Wardin, "William Fetler," 237.

91. *Gost'* 12 (October 1911) 242–43.

92. *Gost'* 2 (February 1915) 38.

into it, and at last the building was dedicated on Christmas Day (7 January) 1912.[93]

Parallels can be drawn between Dom Evangeliia and Spurgeon's Metropolitan Tabernacle (opened 1861) in London. Archibald McCaig, for one, cannot refrain from referring to Dom Evangeliia as "the New Tabernacle."[94] Both churches are early examples of "mega-churches," multi-purpose facilities that were used for mass meetings and more. Both could seat thousands (Dom Evangeliia could accommodate at least two thousand). Like the Metropolitan Tabernacle with its many rooms and adjoining buildings,[95] Dom Evangeliia had Sunday school classrooms, lecture halls, space for a publishing enterprise and book store, and later a garden open to the public.[96] An "inexpensive dining room, for the assistance of workers and students" called Ebenezer was advertised as adjoining the offices of the journal *Gost'* at the same address.[97] The dining room was frequented by some of the three thousand workers at a nail-making factory across the street. The church also maintained a convalescent home for members who were ill.[98] In short, Dom Evangeliia in St. Petersburg was intended to attract, accommodate, and involve people in much the same way that the Metropolitan Tabernacle did in London. It was assumed that one of the buildings' functions was to provide space for compassionate ministry.

Curiously, it was when Dom Evangeliia was briefly closed by the authorities in the late fall of 1913 that it became apparent that something needed to be done to provide temporary housing and help people find their way to a new life. As a writer for the journal *Gost'* observed:

> It isn't easy for a habitual drunkard or hooligan to become a sober, honest person; but if the Spirit of God has touched the heart and brought someone to the conscious decision to be done with sin, it is nevertheless dangerous to leave one who is still weak and wavering [to return to] his former drunken and dissolute companions.[99]

---

93. Wardin, "William Fetler," 237.
94. McCaig, *Wonders of Grace*, 119, 127.
95. Kruppa, "The Life and Times of Charles H. Spurgeon," 11.
96. Packer, *Among the Heretics*, 62; McCaig, *Wonders of Grace*, 174.
97. *Gost'* 3 (January 1911) 37; Oncken et al, "The Baptist Work in Russia," 188; Wardin, "William Fetler," 237;
98. Wardin, "William Fetler," 237.
99. E. N. K[uteinikova], "Iz nochlezhki v Dome Evangeliia" (From the night shelter in Dom Evangeliia), *Gost'*. 12 (December 1914) 303.

During the closure, meetings were held in a theater, with many "drunkards, hooligans, and all kinds of homeless people from a nearby night shelter"[100] in attendance. When it became possible to do so, Fetler opened one of the halls (called Bethany) in Dom Evangeliia as a kind of half-way house (*nochlezhka*, "night shelter") during the winter of 1913 to 1914. The first client was admitted in December 1913, a musician and singer whose face was swollen from the effects of alcohol. A week later he invited a friend to join him. By the next month there were eighteen residents and gradually the number climbed to fifty.[101]

Maria Petrovna Miasoedova (1872–1961), a Russian aristocrat who had joined the Salvation Army in France was the obvious person to lead this ministry, together with E. K. Aleksandrova, the two of them "like a real mother and sister."[102] In the morning the residents attended prayers; during the day work was found for them doing carpentry, wallpapering, or shoe repair. Some of them formed a choir. Church members contributed toward the needs of the shelter. Not all of the residents persevered. Seven or eight dropped out, but the organizers hoped that "God's seed" planted in their souls would someday bring results: "sooner or later, perhaps on a sickbed or at death, [the seeds] will spring up and Christ will receive to Himself those for whom He has waited so long."[103] This is significant in that apparently the Dom Evangeliia shelter was not geared to quick results. Rather, it was open to men who wanted to try to learn another way of living and did not make assistance contingent on making a commitment to Christ. The "experiment" lasted until the spring of 1914 when the group disbanded, some of them to fill permanent situations that had been found for them. Others had probably come to the city as seasonal workers and returned to their villages when it was time to plant crops. The beginning of World War I a few months later ended the project for good. Two of the residents, bound for the front, came back to visit. They requested Gospels to take along and also asked that Fetler would pray for them. Others sent letters.[104]

During this period Dom Evangeliia was also the venue for at least one other attempt to improve the lives of poor women. Continuing the idea of the Pashkovite sewing cooperatives of which she had been a part, Elizaveta Chertkova invited two-hundred women from a St. Petersburg slum area

100. Ibid.
101. Ibid.
102. Ibid.
103. Ibid., 304.

104 Ibid.; see also S. V. Sevasti'ianov, "Mariia Petrovna Miasoedova (Ocherk zhizni)" (Maria Petrovna Miasoedova [A life sketch]), in Karetnikova, *Al'manakh, vypusk 2*, 258–59.

to Dom Evangeliia. After telling the women about forgiveness in Christ, she demonstrated the operation of a sewing machine and presented each woman with a new Singer, so that they could begin to earn money.[105] The details of how Chertkova selected the women and whether any follow up was ever done to determine the effectiveness of this grand gesture are not known. Nevertheless, Dom Evangeliia was a focal point for evangelistic outreach and compassionate ministry intended to reach the urban poor of St. Petersburg in ways that were new to Russia.

THE SALVATION ARMY IN RUSSIA

A creative symbiosis existed between the Salvation Army and the Russian evangelicals. The Salvation Army served as an important model for the street mission and rescue work undertaken by Fetler and others, while the local evangelicals made it possible for the Army to get started in their country. There had been sympathy and appreciation between the two groups for a number of years. Brigadier Mildred Duff paid a holiday visit in 1899 to unnamed Russian friends whom she considered, "more than three-quarters Salvationists themselves."[106] Probably her hosts were Pashkovites with whom she had become acquainted abroad. The Salvation Army tried for years to work in Russia. Commissioner George Scott Railton (1849–1913) came to St. Petersburg once in 1904 and again in 1908 for the purpose of getting permission to enter Russia officially, although his formal applications to the emperor were ignored. Also in 1908 the newspaper editor W. T. Stead (1849–1912) met with Russian Prime Minister Petr Stolypin (1862–1911) in St. Petersburg on the Army's behalf and had a promising discussion, but this also came to nothing.[107] In March 1909 General Booth himself visited St. Petersburg for two days. At this time Booth met with government officials as well as a number of leading evangelicals in the city, including Baron Paul Nicolay, Elizaveta Chertkova, and Alexandra Peiker.[108] Once again, there were no results. I. S. Prokhanov commented on Booth's visit with some disappointment: "The General would like to begin the work of the salvation of perishing drunkards and the poor (*bosiaki*, "barefoot ones") of Russia and bring them to Christ, but for the time being he is not permitted to do so."[109]

---

105. J. Fetler, *Sluzhenie Rossii*, 29.
106. Duff, "Furlough Days in Russia," 255.
107. Karl Larsson, "The Army in Russia," 18–19.
108. Booth's visit is detailed in Aitken, *Blood and Fire*, 119–25.
109. *Bratskii listok* 4 (April 1909) 1.

Obviously, the Russian evangelicals desired and supported the Army's entrance. The writer of a 1910 article in *Baptist* remarked with some asperity that whereas the Army was widely active elsewhere in the world, "It seems that Russia alone is closed to the activity of the Salvation Army."[110] Yet, the Russians did not merely wait for the Army to arrive, as the involvement of Fetler and others indicates; rather, they themselves were active in rescue ministry. In 1908 I. S. Prokhanov sent F. M. Trosnov to visit the Salvation Army post in Helsingfors (Helsinki) with the idea of beginning rescue ministry in St. Petersburg. Like many Russians, Trosnov was at first slightly put off by the style of the Army meetings which he described as "theatrical and gay," in contrast to the reverent worship to which he was accustomed. However, he was much impressed by the highly disciplined, sacrificial, and devoted work of the Helsinki group. Accompanied by a translator, he visited a residence for prostitutes, and a day-care center, and gave a detailed description of Army work visiting families in the slums.[111] Trosnov returned to Helsinki later in 1909 when General Booth visited the city, and evidently had a personal meeting with him there.[112]

Finally, in 1910 Colonel Jens and Agnes Povlsen of Denmark came to St. Petersburg in another attempt to find a permanent way into the country.[113] They stayed until 1912 and relied on the existing evangelical network in the city for support, quietly doing door-to-door visitation, holding meetings in the homes of Pashkovite aristocrats, and preaching, almost certainly at the locations where Fetler regularly preached.[114] Influential evangelical friends, such as "Madame T.," surely Elizaveta Chertkova (from the transliteration of her surname as "Tchertkoff"), lobbied for the Army in high places, including with the Dowager Empress Maria Fedorovna, who had met William Booth together with her sister, Queen Alexandra, at Buckingham Palace shortly after his visit to St. Petersburg.[115] None of these efforts bore any permanent fruit, however. A formal application submitted by the Povlsens, requesting permission to begin work officially, was finally rejected in 1912.[116] A break came when, for several months in 1913, the Army was invited to participate in the All-Russian Hygiene Exhibition where they

---

110. "Parad p'ianits" (A parade of drunkards), *Baptist* 52 (22 December 1910) 416.

111. Trosnov, "Doklad," 1–8.

112. F. Trosnov, "Kratkii otchet o 2-i poezdke v Gel'singfors" (A brief account of the second trip to Helsingfors), *Molodoi vinogradnik* No. 5 (1909) 11–14.

113. Aitken, *Blood and Fire*, 132–34.

114. Ibid., 134–35.

115. Ibid., 125–29, 135.

116. Ibid., 136.

exhibited photos and items associated with the Army's social work in Finland, including an officer's uniform and a bed from a shelter. The exhibit won a prize and was made part of a permanent museum.[117] Here again, the St. Petersburg evangelicals were essential to the Army's success. Elizaveta Chertkova, by then over eighty years old and rather deaf, assisted Colonel Karl Larsson at the exhibit and arranged housing for him at Dom Evangeliia. There Larsson met Adam Pieshevskii,[118] a converted Jew who had encountered the Salvation Army in Germany and in England. Pieshevskii corrected the many grammatical mistakes in the pamphlet that Larsson was handing out in the exhibition booth and eventually became the editor of the Army's newspaper, *The War Cry*. Its sale became the Army's basic means of reaching the Russian population, publishing spiritual appeals and stories of Army work abroad. *The War Cry* was registered in Finland under the tamer title *Vestnik spaseniia* (Herald of salvation) and was publicly sold on the streets by official vendors who wore what was essentially a Salvation Army uniform, but with the name of the paper on the hat-band. Tom Aitken states that Fetler helped the paper get started by distributing *Vestnik spaseniia* as an enclosure in one of his own publications, but does not mention that the paper's address, at least on the first issue, was the same as that of Dom Evangeliia—V. O., 24-aia liniia, d. No. 11, kv. 3.[119] In other words, Fetler gave the Salvation Army a Russian home address.

The other main figure who, besides Fetler, typified the relationship of the St. Petersburg evangelicals to the Salvation Army, both supporting the organization and replicating its work, is the previously-mentioned Maria Miasoedova. She was living in Paris when she first heard a Salvation Army street preacher. In 1894 she joined the Army and served for six years in France, Switzerland, and England.[120] During his brief visit to St. Petersburg in 1909, General Booth attended a Duma session and met Miasoedova's father, Senator Petr Miasoedov, who then became acquainted with the Povlsens in 1910.[121] Many years later in a letter to friends, Miasoedova recalled a visit she made to her family in Russia in about 1913. At that time she met William Fetler, who challenged her to discontinue her ministry in France and return to Russia for good:

---

117. Larsson, "The Army in Russia," 20; Aitken, *Blood and Fire*, 143–47.

118. Larsson, "The Army in Russia," 57; Aitken, *Blood and Fire*, 168–69.

119. *Vestnik spaseniia* 1 (July 1913). Details on the hygiene exhibit and *Vestnik spaseniia* in Russia are given in Larsson, "The Army in Russia," 20–23; Ivanova and Ivanova, *Zarubezhnyi opyt*, 80–82; Aitken, *Blood and Fire*, 144–50.

120. V. A. Popov, "Kapitan Armii Spaseniia," 16.

121. Aitken, *Blood and Fire*, 132–34.

Are there so few sinners in Russia in need of salvation? Do the native Russian people have no need of revival? Or don't you love the Motherland and your own people? No, Maria Petrovna, you have no right to leave the Motherland. You are needed here. France has its own preachers and the Russian people are waiting for you.[122]

Accordingly, Miasoedova returned to Russia permanently. Besides Fetler's urging, she was well aware of the Salvation Army's efforts to enter Russia. In fact, she herself lobbied K. P. Pobedonostsev, Ober-prokuror of the Most Holy Synod, to allow the Army's entry.[123] She added that at some point when she was in London, "They were thinking of marrying me to a German [Salvation Army] officer in order to start work in Russia. But that was not God's will for me."[124] Did she take up Fetler's challenge because the Army had become too controlling? As described above, she performed a Salvation Army-type ministry at Dom Evangeliia, but it is not clear whether she was still considered "Army personnel" at that time. It is known that she translated some twenty gospel songs for inclusion in the Salvation Army's hand-sewn Russian songbook.[125] Miasoedova also continued to wear her Army uniform, albeit without the insignia of her rank, at least until 1924,[126] although the lack of insignia at that date can be explained because the Salvation Army was excluded from Soviet Russia in 1923.[127] As for the uniform, given the state of the economy at the time, Miasoedova almost certainly had to wear whatever clothing she had available. Whatever the case, the point is that urban rescue ministry was practiced energetically by Russian evangelicals who were close to, but not necessarily directed by the Salvation Army.

Some people with connections to the Russian evangelical movement joined the Army outright. Vera Gorinovich became the first Russian Salvation Army officer in 1913. She was the daughter of N. E. Gorinovich, the young Nihilist who was blinded and disfigured with sulfuric acid by fellow revolutionaries and later befriended by Colonel Pashkov.[128] The sec-

122. Sevast'ianov, "Miasoedova Mariia Petrovna," 8.
123. Ibid., 9.
124. Ibid.
125. Aitken, *Blood and Fire*, 172.
126. Sevast'ianov, "Miasoedova, Mariia Petrovna," 3.
127. SAIHC, item 7.0, folder EE/4/2/1-1913-1992, "Protokol No. 14, Zasedanie komissii po provedniiu otdeleniia tserkvi ot gosudarstva ri TSK RKP, 27 fevralia 1923 goda" (Minutes No. 14, Meeting of the Commission on the conduct of the separation of church and state, ri TSK RKP, 27 February 1923), gives instructions to dissolve the Salvation Army.
128 Trotter, *Lord Radstock*, 195; Larsson, "The Army in Russia," 23; Prokhanoff,

ond national officer was Clara Becker, the Russian adopted daughter of an Estonian lawyer, who participated in Baron Paul Nicolay's Student Christian Movement before she joined the Salvation Army in 1915.[129] In December 1914, Adam Pieshevskii, who had met Karl Larsson at Dom Evangeliia and edited *Vestnik spaseniia*, was among the eight men and women sworn in to the Salvation Army at their first enrollment in Russia.[130] At some point, William Fetler offered General Booth the members of his congregation as "ready-made" members of the Salvation Army. He did this because one of the objections raised by the authorities concerning allowing the Salvation Army to work in St. Petersburg was that the Army had no followers already in the city. John Fetler writes that, "It is not known whether General Booth made use of this suggestion."[131] Perhaps Fetler wrote his proposal to Booth in a letter, or perhaps he expressed it to Colonel Jens and Agnes Povlsen during their time in St. Petersburg (1910 to 1912). In any case, the offer implies not that Fetler wanted the Salvation Army to take over Dom Evangeliia, but rather that Fetler and the whole Russian evangelical community were pleased to welcome the Army as believers of their own kind who could add to the movement's critical mass in the capital. It is interesting that the affinity between the Russian evangelicals and the Salvation Army was never challenged, although the Army did not practice baptism or the Lord's Supper.[132] The absence of controversy suggests that for the Russians, evangelism and compassionate ministry were of more immediate importance than theology.

URBAN RESCUE MINISTRY AND THE ROLE OF ORDINARY PEOPLE

At the end of 1910 Fetler announced the founding of the Acts of the Apostles Brotherhood, the purpose of which was to encourage Christians to shake off their torpor and indifference and live a more devoted life of faith. Scores of people all over the country recommitted their lives to Christ through this

---

Cauldron, 69; Liven, *Dukhovnaia probuzhdenie*, 17–20; Aitken, *Blood and Fire*, 161–62. Aitken reports a mysterious meeting during the 1950s in Moscow between a Swedish tourist and a 73-year-old Russian woman who identified herself only as "Vera." She spoke at some length about her warm memories of the Salvation Army's early years in St. Petersburg. It is assumed that she was Vera Gorinovich (*Blood and Fire*, 301–2).

129. Aitken, *Blood and Fire*, 181–84.
130. Larsson, "The Army in Russia," 57; Aitken, *Blood and Fire*, 168–69.
131. J. Fetler, *Sluzhenie Rossii*, 35–36.
132. Murdoch, *Origins of the Salvation Army*, 66.

brotherhood. To join it was necessary to submit a written statement explaining one's reasons for wanting to join and detailing one's original conversion. Those accepted were given a biblical pseudonym.[133] In the months that followed, members of the Brotherhood wrote to *Gost'* describing their experiences of leading a life of total devotion to Christ. It is interesting that their renewed commitment frequently led them to involvement in service to the urban poor. True to Russian evangelical convictions about compassionate ministry, such activity was not reserved for "professionals," whether church leadership or those in the Salvation Army, but was open to all Christians. The overall impression is of ordinary people becoming aware of others and then simply responding to their needs in the process of sharing the gospel. Thus, a Brotherhood member who was a storekeeper described his experiences ministering to people in St. Petersburg with whom he came in contact: "Every day the unemployed, drunkards, prostitutes and lots of customers come to me. I tell them that there is an experienced Physician who can heal all spiritual wounds, and don't they want to get out of their situation?" The storekeeper called on other believers to provide clothing or a place to stay as he became acquainted with people's needs, thus establishing an informal circle of concern.[134] Yet another member of the Brotherhood began to visit a hard-labor prison (*katorzhnaia t'iurma*).[135] These kinds of involvements were difficult; ministries that had been tolerated in the past among the well-to-do were not always welcomed among simple people. A certain "Sister Lidia" wrote in 1911 about her inspiration to visit a hospital together with two other young girls to talk to the patients and distribute tracts. When word got around that they were on the premises, they were quickly ejected by a priest.[136]

Rescue ministry and street missions were also regarded by the Russian evangelicals as an appropriate activity for youth—witness the visit to the Salvation Army post in Finland arranged for the young F. M. Trosnov in 1908.[137] I. S. Prokhanov related that an unsealed envelope was handed to him by a participant at a St. Petersburg youth meeting in 1909. Inside was a description of "a true society of Christ's disciples" based on Matthew 25:31–46, in which Christ is identified with the poor and outcast. The message to Prokhanov stated that Christians must "go about to the hospitals, prisons, everywhere there is grief, poverty, suffering illness. They must dry

133. *Gost'* 2 (December 1910) 12.
134. *Gost'* 4 (February 1911) 61.
135. *Gost'* 6 (April 1911) 121.
136. *Gost'* 3 (January 1911) 26–27.
137. Trosnov, "Doklad," 1–8.

tears, comfort grief, carry light and joy everywhere . . . And only then will the Kingdom of God be built on earth."[138] That the topic of service to the poor came up at a youth meeting is revealing. Likewise, at the first meeting of Baptist youth in Rostov-on-Don in 1909, Mikhail Timoshenko gave a speech on organizing youth groups. One of the spheres of activity he mentioned for young people was visiting the sick and poor: "Visiting the poor, encouraging them, helping them by personally performing tasks, and by means of material assistance are all a part of the activity of the [youth] group."[139] The expectation that young people would practice rescue ministry even extended to children. Anna Iosifovna Gromova (born 1899), who later married Evangelical Christian leader Aleksandr Karev (1894–1971), was involved as a child in Sunday school activities in St. Petersburg. She was a member of a children's choir and sang a plaintive solo, "Papa, my papa, come home now," the plea of a child trying to persuade her father to come home from a tavern late at night.[140] After her baptism in 1915, Gromova was part of the Evangelical Christians' street mission group, visiting night shelters and jails. They also dropped in at taverns in pairs; the girl would sing and the boy would preach a brief message.[141] The young people involved in this ministry designed their own insignia of an embroidered white armband. They wore the armbands proudly until one occasion when the police rounded them up, confiscated their literature, and held them all night for questioning. After that, Prokhanov forbade the use of the insignia as it only drew unwanted attention.[142] After the February 1917 Revolution, street mission work was energetically developed among the Evangelical Christians by Aleksandr Karev, side by side with the Salvation Army.[143] Baptist youth in Irkutsk and St. Petersburg (Dom Evangeliia) also regularly visited taverns, restaurants, and tea houses to sing and distribute tracts. It was an unpredictable ministry because sometimes the visitors were received kindly and other

---

138. *Molodoi vinogradnik* 6 (1909) 2.

139. Timoshenko, *Pervyi vserossiyskiy s'ezd kruzhkov baptistskoi molodezhi,* 19.

140. This is almost certainly a translation of Henry Clay Work's (1832–1884) "Song of Little Mary" (1864), a temperance favorite; see http://ingeb.org/songs/fatherde.html and http://rpo.library.utoronto.ca/poem/2385.html.

141. Kareva, "Moi vospominaniia," 176, 183.

142. Ibid., 184.

143 AUCEC-B Archives, Drawer 5, Folder 21, Istoricheskiie vospominaniia (Historical recollections), N. Vysotskii, "Istoriia tserkvei Evangel'skikh khristian 1917–1929" (The history of the Evangelical Christian churches 1917–1929), (Moscow, 13 May 1981), 1.

times with insults. "In this work one has to completely forget about oneself," advised one reporter.[144]

Youth also concerned themselves with caring for children in the city. A girls' youth group at the Evangelical Christian Church of St. Petersburg held a sale of handmade items in 1909 and earned 231.45 rubles, which they set aside for the "baby home" at Kellomäki and another institution called the "Brothers' children's shelter." Perhaps this is a reference to the children's home at Raivola, of which mention was first made in 1906.[145] The report went on to state that the members of the youth group had spent a good deal of time with poor children and noticed how they suffered from their surroundings, especially the bad city air. Accordingly, they decided to begin praying about organizing a summer event for city children and requested donations and gifts of clothing to that end.[146] In the summer of 1909 they organized a summer "shelter" (*priut*) with a program intended to improve health and spiritual life for eight girls and three boys, aged four to nine. All were the children of "poor widows."[147] Also in 1910 the girls' group put on a Christmas party and program for the children of poor families.[148] In summary, care for the urban poor, was perceived by the Russian evangelicals as a collective calling, open to people in all walks of life, and especially the young.

THE RUSSIAN TEMPERANCE MOVEMENT

The rescue agenda also shaped the manner in which evangelicals participated in the Russian national conversation on temperance. Evangelicals were, however, latecomers to the national cause of temperance because the initial years of its popularity in the 1890s coincided with some of the worst years of their suppression. Part of a general European trend, literally thousands of organizations and associations devoted to promoting temperance were formed between 1895 and 1914 throughout the Russian Empire.[149] In particular, religious temperance societies began to flourish in 1889, when the Most Holy Synod of the Russian Orthodox Church granted permission

---

144 *Gost'* 11 (November 1917) 175; E. N. K., "Iz zhizni obshchiny Doma Evangeliia" (From the life of the Dom Evangeliia congregation), *Gost'* 10 (October 1917) 156.

145. *Bratskii listok* 5 (1906) 32.

146. *Molodoi vinogradnik* 6 (1909) 14–15.

147. A. N. "Sredi detei" (Among the children), *Molodoi vinogradnik* 12 (1909) 21.

148. *Iunyi khristianin* 2 (1909) 1–4; A. Maslei, "Elka dlia bednykh detei" (A Christmas tree for poor children), *Molodoi vinogradnik* 1 (January 1911) 20.

149. Transchel, *Under the Influence*, 47.

to bishops to organize temperance activities without waiting for Synod approval and directing them to encourage the preaching of temperance from the pulpit. A renewed call for sobriety on the part of the Orthodox churches was sounded in 1910, which was echoed in the evangelical press of the same period.[150]

While it was agreed that alcoholism was a serious social problem in Russia, there was no consensus as to its cause or cure. Among Orthodox temperance advocates there was some disagreement as to whether their objective should be to promote abstinence or moderation. In part, this was due to a faint "suspicion that sobriety was somehow un-Orthodox."[151] Certainly, sobriety was closely identified with sectarian groups, including evangelicals, who had apparently inherited the abstinent attitude of the Molokans.[152] In fact, sobriety was one of their most appealing characteristics, according to a study done by St. Petersburg Orthodox clergy in 1910.[153] For this reason, temperance societies were sometimes regarded as slightly dangerous, capable of leading unsuspecting Orthodox into sectarian groups.[154] Indeed, the authorities' fear that temperance societies could serve as a "cover" for sectarian activity was not unfounded. At some point during the time that St. Petersburg evangelicals were living a semi-underground existence following the exile of V. A. Pashkov and M. M. Korf in 1884, the Swedish missionary N. F. Höijer started the process of registering a temperance society to create a legal organization that could be used as a base for evangelistic work. Because of strict police surveillance he soon left the capital for Odessa, while the existence of the temperance society became something of a burden for St. Petersburg evangelicals.[155]

Generally, participants in a temperance society took a pledge to remain sober for a shorter or longer period of time, as briefly as three months or as long as a lifetime. Some temperance leaders, notably Father Aleksandr Rozhdestvenskii (1872–1905), who founded the Aleksander Nevskii Society in 1898, regarded temperance as a path leading to the formation of a morally responsible Christian life. Accordingly, groups such as the Nevskii Society sought to heighten members' awareness of the gospel and replace alcohol

---

150. Hedda, *His Kingdom Come*, 101–103.

151. McKee, "Sobering Up the Soul of the People," 225–26.

152. Sinichkin, *Vse radi missii*, 116; note, however, that at least in the early days of his ministry, Colonel Vasilii Pashkov served champagne after meetings at his home (Corrado, "Colonel Vasiliy Pashkov," 82).

153. Herrlinger, *Class, Piety, and Politics*, 314.

154. McKee, "Sobering Up the Soul of the People" 226.

155. Rev. N. F. Höijer, "Forty Years in Russia," in Brooks, *Good News for Russia*, 162–63.

use with spiritual and cultural pursuits, including choral singing, lectures and reading on religious themes, and pilgrimages.[156] Meanwhile, interest in the temperance cause quickly led to the organization of secular societies as well. In 1895, the state-supported Guardianship of Popular Temperance was organized and, ironically, funded by the government monopoly on vodka sales established by Finance Minister Sergei Witte in 1894. The Guardianship sought to reduce alcohol consumption by offering cultural and social alternatives to the taverns, but of a less serious nature than those sponsored by religious societies, such as theatrical performances, concerts, circuses, and other entertainments.[157]

Evangelicals supported the national temperance agenda and insisted on sobriety for church members. An editorial writer (probably V. G. Pavlov) stated, "I propose that every Baptist congregation should be a temperance society, if it wants to be the light of the world and the salt of the earth, and therefore its members must be complete abstainers, using absolutely no intoxicating beverages, because an example is stronger than teaching."[158] Selling alcohol was also discouraged: the journal *Baptist* recommended that a church member who opened a beer shop should be excluded from the community.[159] By 1910 evangelicals were interacting with the national temperance agenda, although they were never at its center. In their publications they readily pointed out things like US President Taft's teetotalism[160] and advertised temperance literature.[161] A story entitled "Zhertva Bakhusa" (The sacrifice of Bacchus) by Mikhail Timoshenko ran as a serial in the journal *Baptist* during the winter of 1910.[162] Notes for Sunday school lessons on temperance were published in their journals,[163] as were statistics on vodka consumption in the Russian Empire.[164] International events, such as an anti-alcohol congress held in Milan in 1913, were announced in the evangelical press.[165] Special mention was made of foreign visitors to the capital who were interested in the cause of temperance, such as some Danish Lutherans

156. Hedda, *His Kingdom Come*, 101–3.

157. Transchel, *Under the Influence*, 47–48.

158. "Beseda 'Baptista'" (Conversation of *The Baptist*), *Baptist* 3 (13 January 1910) 20.

159. "Beseda 'Baptista'" (Conversation of *The Baptist* 51 (15 December 1910) 407.

160. *Baptist* 9 (24 February 1910) 1.

161. *Bratskii listok* 1 (1908) 51; *Gost'* 2 (December 1910) 18; *Gost'* 3 (January 1911) 34, 45; *Gost'* 8 (August 1911) 167; *Gost'* 12 (December 1913) 290.

162. See, for example, the installment in *Baptist* 4 (13 January 1910) 28.

163. *Baptist* 19 (5 May 1910) 152–53; *Baptist* 46 (10 November 1910).

164. *Baptist* 39 (22 September 1910) n.p.

165. *Gost'* 10 (October 1913) 234.

who arrived in 1907.[166] The First All-Russian Congress on the Battle against Drunkenness held in January 1910 in St. Petersburg was also reported in some detail.[167] W. A. Fetler was a member of a temperance organization.[168]

However, in contrast to both secular and some Orthodox temperance advocates, Russian evangelicals understood alcoholism as a distinctly spiritual problem that could be overcome by giving one's life to Christ.[169] Such had been the case from the early days of the evangelical movement. Several peasants were brought to trial in Odessa during the 1870s on the charge of spreading Stundist teaching. They were accused of persuading people to leave the Orthodox Church, but witnesses had to admit that they were "good people" and especially that there were no drunkards among them.[170] In the same way, through Pashkov's ministry a certain worker named Kirpichnikov on one of his estates was cured of drunkenness when he repented. In 1887 Kirpichnikov and his wife were exiled to Siberia (Minusinskii krai) for their evangelistic activity.[171] Personal testimonies published in evangelical journals bear out the power of the repentance motif. Significantly, although they involve deliverance from alcohol, such testimonies were not specifically framed as anti-alcoholism stories, but focused instead on repentance and God's power to deliver people from drunkenness. A typical example was given in 1906 by a writer who described a conversation with an old woman who wept over her inability to stay away from vodka. Her interlocutor agreed that, of course, she did not have the strength to resist alcohol on her own, but assured her, "I know One Who is the source of strength . . . He has already healed many . . . drunkards, prostitutes and thieves," and then offered the woman the address of a "house"—presumably a prayer house—where she could go and "see many who have been just such drunkards as you and even worse. They now live a sober and upright life."[172] The presence of "many" former drunkards suggests that deliverance from alcohol was considered a rather commonplace occurrence in the evangelical community. Twenty years later the same theme of repentance sounded in an article in *Khristianin* by S. Baranov concerning the ways his poverty-stricken family tried to stop their father from drinking. They had him bathe

166. *Bratskii listok* 10 (October 1907) 2.
167. *Baptist* 3 (13 January 1910) 24–25; *Utrenniaia zvezda* 2 (8 January 1910) 1–2.
168. Wardin, "William Fetler," 237.
169. See, for example, *Gost'* 7 (1911) 138–39 and D. I. Mazaev, "P'ianstvo i ego lechenie" (Drunkenness and its treatment), *Baptist* 4 (February 1912) 10–12.
170. "K. M. Staniukovich o sudebnom protsesse M. Ratushnogo" (K. M. Staniukovich concerning the court trial of M. Ratushnyi), *Bratskii vestnik* 5 (1947) 52.
171. VSEKhB, *Istoriia*, 104, 125.
172. *Khristianin* 4 (1906) 71–72.

in a holy lake, gave him potions to drink, and even attempted hypnosis, but nothing helped. At last a co-worker at his job told the father that he needed to repent and begin a new life with Christ, which he eventually did and "completely changed." Again, the emphasis was on repentance and redemption, not drunkenness as such.[173]

Ultimately, therefore, the rescue model, which gave people the opportunity to respond to Christ and thus transform their lives, was the evangelicals' main contribution to the Russian temperance movement. W. A. Fetler publicly promoted its effectiveness in connection with the All-Russian Congress on the Battle against Drunkenness held January 1910 in St. Petersburg. On the night before the congress ended, participants were invited to a meeting in Tenishev Hall where Fetler spoke about the excellent record of believers in helping people leave drunkenness behind: "We evangelical Christians have been performing our task [combatting drunkenness] all along, and more than one person possessed by the foul vice has found healing with us." He asked for all those present who had been saved from the sin of drunkenness to raise their hand, and hundreds of hands went up. Fetler then went on to describe the practice of holding night meetings and calling people to repentance. The gathering concluded with a magic lantern show, "depicting the destruction and ruin of an honest working family by drunkenness."[174]

Thus, although the Russian evangelicals were in touch with the national temperance movement, they also asserted that their emphasis on turning to God alone was the only consistently effective solution for drunkenness. In a lengthy article published in *Baptist* in 1912, D. I. Mazaev depicted the temperance campaign as an illustration of the spiritual weakness of the Orthodox Church. Ultimately, he stated, all the government can do is limit alcohol sales or chase down and punish bootleggers.[175] Temperance societies, likewise, with their attempts to provide "moral" entertainment alternatives to the taverns could only have a temporary effect at best. Moreover, Mazaev asserted that they were actually harmful because they:

> . . . degrade the merit of the church, distract from Christianity, and positively strip away the prestige of the clergy, because they inevitably give the impression that the churches, with all their beauty and their worship services and their singing, reading, and preaching, in terms of their power to influence the human

---

173. S. Baranov, "Deian. Ap. 16,31" (Acts 16:31), *Khristianin* 8 (1925) 58–59.
174. *Baptist* 4 (20 January 1910) 29.
175. Mazaev, "P'ianstvo i ego lechenie," 11.

soul not only do not surpass or even equal, but are [actually] inferior to some worthless little suburban theater.[176]

In his article Mazaev called on the Orthodox Church to come against this state of affairs and reclaim the spiritual high ground that Christianity demands. He likened their situation to that of the disciples who failed to drive out a demon from a boy when his father appealed to them to do so. According to Jesus, the reason they could not is that "this kind [of demon] does not go out except by prayer (and fasting)" (Matthew 17:14–21; Mark 9:14–29). In other words, as far as evangelicals were concerned, people in bondage to drunkenness needed to come directly to Christ, and certainly not attend magic lantern shows or even go on pilgrimages to holy shrines.[177] Since repentance was the key, preaching the gospel was the way to transform people's lives, and thus, ultimately, to draw them out of poverty as well.

It is interesting that the Russian Orthodox "trezvennik" movement (based on the word *trezvyi*, meaning "sober"), which was begun in the mid-1890s by Ivan Alekseevich Churikov (1861–1933), used what appear to be forms and emphases typical of evangelical rescue ministry to help people overcome their addiction to alcohol. They experienced notable success. Like evangelicals, trezvenniki invited people to a hall to hear a sermon that included a call to sobriety presented by one of the group's "little brothers" (*bratsy*). Instead of making a commitment to abstain from alcohol for a certain period of time, which was typical of more mainstream temperance societies, the commitment of a trezvennik was for life. Like Stundists, trezvenniki met regularly outside of regular worship services to encourage one another, listen to sermons, pray and sing.[178] In 1922 one of the important trezvennik leaders, Ivan Koloskov, joined the Evangelical Christian Union.[179] Here again, repentance was expected to lead to social transformation.

FETLER'S EXILE AND LATER MINISTRY

William Fetler's practice of urban rescue ministry continued to inform his activities throughout the rest of his career. His work in St. Petersburg attracted a good deal of attention and comment, both favorable and unfavorable, in Russia and abroad. John Fetler hints that the opposition of the Empress's

---

176 Ibid., 12.
177. Ibid., 8–9.
178. McKee, "Sobering Up the Soul of the People," 218.
179. Prokhanoff, *Cauldron*, 216; for more information on Koloskov, see Martzinkovski, *With Christ in Soviet Russia*, 249–52.

mysterious and malevolent favorite, Grigorii Rasputin (1869–1916), directly led to Fetler's exile in 1915.[180] However, as early as 1909 Fetler had already been placed under police surveillance for unauthorized preaching in Moscow and in 1914 was charged with slandering the Orthodox Church. In addition, his numerous foreign contacts and the general suspicion of evangelicals propagating the "German faith" in wartime all endangered his position in Russia. In November 1914 he was arrested in the midst of a Saturday evening prayer meeting and sentenced to exile in Siberia. Because of sympathetic friends in high places however, and supported by the prayers of believers, Fetler's sentence was commuted to lifelong exile abroad.[181]

Fetler continued to do rescue work among Russian immigrants in the United States, intentionally targeting alcoholics. He served as dean of the Russian Bible Institute in New York City, sponsored by the American Baptist Home Mission Society. However, when he became convinced that too many of the American Baptists were modernists Fetler broke with them and departed for Philadelphia, accompanied by fifty students. There he founded his own non-denominational Bible and Educational Institute at the end of 1917. He claimed that some of the converts who later became his students knew nothing when they began except, "to drink and play cards and smoke tobacco and gamble and fight each other and live in sin."[182] In other words, ministry to people steeped in vice remained a priority for Fetler. In November 1920, he returned to Europe with more than twenty missionaries who planned to spread the gospel both among Russian-speaking refugees who had been displaced by war and revolution and also within Soviet Russia. In London he organized the Russian Missionary Society. Compassionate ministry was carried out among refugees with the establishment of a children's home in Poland, near Warsaw.[183] Riga became the mission's headquarters in 1923. There in 1927, with American and British financial support, Fetler established another mega-church, Dom spaseniia (House of salvation), in a working-class neighborhood. John Fetler compares his father to William Booth in that he was still above all concerned for the poor and working people, focusing his evangelistic efforts on Riga's industrial suburbs. As he had done in St. Petersburg nearly twenty years before, Fetler again held midnight meetings at various locations throughout Riga to attract prostitutes, the homeless, and alcoholics. In Salvation Army style he led a brass band

---

180. J. Fetler, *Sluzhenie Rossii*, 41–42.

181. Wardin, "William Fetler," 238–39; Fetler's firsthand account of his arrest appears in J. Fetler, *Sluzhenie Rossii*, 42–46.

182. Pastor William Fetler, "A Great Missionary Program for Russia," in Brooks, *Good News for Russia*, 125, 127–28.

183. J. Fetler, *Sluzhenie Rossii*, 55–56; Wardin, "William Fetler," 240.

through the streets of the city to attract people to evangelistic meetings. His own children were among the musicians. During the 1930s he formed all thirteen children of his children into the Fetler Family Band and toured Europe and the United States.[184] When the Great Depression brought economic hardship to Latvia, peasant members of the Dom spaseniia congregation brought produce to the city and a soup kitchen was organized in the sanctuary for the hungry.[185] In short, service to the urban poor remained one of Fetler's ministry priorities.

CONCLUSION

Service to the urban poor, of which there were increasing numbers as industrialization changed the demographics of the Russian Empire, was part of evangelical mission both before and after religious toleration was declared in 1905. The upper-class Pashkovites had ministered to city dwellers, but after 1905, new methods and opportunities presented themselves to believers of other social classes as well. William A. Fetler served as an important catalyst for the development of rescue ministry in the capital, drawing on his experiences as a student at the Pastors' College in London. Confirmed in the legacy of evangelical activism demonstrated by C. H. Spurgeon and inspired by the Welsh Revival and many examples of rescue ministry available in England, including that of the Salvation Army, Fetler served both spiritual and physical needs and helped others to do the same. He introduced night meetings to St. Petersburg and opened a men's shelter at Dom Evangeliia. Fetler and other evangelicals assisted the Salvation Army as it struggled for official admission to Russia even as they practiced rescue ministry themselves. In particular, it was assumed that young people would take the lead in reaching the urban poor. Evangelical youth were known to preach in taverns and also to organize events for poor children.

The rescue ministry approach, with its emphasis on social transformation through individual repentance, also informed the evangelicals' interaction with the Russian temperance movement. They regarded alcoholism as a spiritual problem and assumed that drunkards would become sober as a matter of course when they repented. Consequently, they geared their efforts to that end. At the same time, as the case of the Dom Evangeliia men's shelter suggests, the Russian evangelicals did not necessarily push people to decisions for the gospel, but allowed time for a natural response. It is impossible to tell with any certainty how many people were helped by

---

184. J. Fetler, *Sluzhenie Rossii*, 69.
185. Ibid., 58–61, 65.

the evangelicals' rescue efforts, but they probably number in the hundreds judging from articles in the press. At the same time, it would appear that extensive rescue ministry work only took place in St. Petersburg.

5

War, Revolution, and Famine, 1914 to 1923

THE PREVIOUS CHAPTERS HAVE described the two main directions that compassionate ministry took among Russian evangelicals soon after religious tolerance was decreed in 1905. Broadly speaking, they developed funds and institutions to support the needy within their own membership and also reached out to the urban poor. The evangelicals believed in the power of the gospel to transform lives and thereby mitigate suffering, and therefore considered that their main calling was to preach. However, during the years leading up to the First World War, compassionate ministry remained an integral part of their overall mission, just as it had been since the early days of the movement. This chapter will demonstrate that the evangelicals continued to hold to the same basic priorities even as their activities necessarily changed as they faced new and overwhelming social changes.

The years 1914 to 1923 consisted of almost uninterrupted war. During this decade the Russian autocracy fell and the Bolsheviks came to power. Cities emptied out as people fled to the countryside in search of food, and the national infrastructure was all but destroyed. Bandits sacked the villages and thousands succumbed to typhoid. The First World War (1914 to 1918), the revolutions of 1917, and the ensuing Civil War (1918 to 1920) and famine (1921 to 1923) carried a staggering human cost. In 1926 the first census since 1897 was taken in Russia. It was estimated that the total population would have been 175,000,000 if growth had continued unhindered since 1914. However, "The actual population was 147,028,000, indicating a deficit of approximately 28,000,000 persons."[1] An accurate breakdown of that number is impossible. Perhaps one-third of the deficit is accounted for by the unborn and those who were born between 1917 and 1921 but did not survive infancy.[2] Somewhere between 1.3 to two million may have been battlefield deaths, with another two to 3.5 million civilian deaths attributable to hunger, exposure, and disease.[3] According to Sheila Fitzpatrick, deaths from hunger and epidemics from 1921 to 1922 exceeded the combined total of casualties in the First World War and Civil War.[4]

The Russian evangelicals, of course, endured the same suffering as their fellow citizens. Throughout, they remained committed to compassionate ministry, although the needs among and around them were on an unprecedented scale. They adapted to rapidly changing conditions as best they could, sustaining their own membership, ministering to soldiers and their families, POWs, refugees, and finally the masses of starving. The 1921 to 1923 famine in particular demanded a new level of administrative skill as the evangelicals determined a course of action among their own churches and coordinated work with foreign aid agencies and individual donors while trying to steer a safe course under a new government.

EVANGELICAL COMPASSIONATE MINISTRY DURING WORLD WAR I AND THE CIVIL WAR

The First World War began with a surprising wave of patriotic enthusiasm that also swept over the Russian evangelicals. An English observer, Stephen Graham, described the atmosphere in Moscow at the beginning of the war:

> I found no depression of the national spirit . . . no strikes, no riots, no revolutionary propaganda or pessimism, but instead an all-pervading cheerfulness and national unanimity which even the most optimistic could not have foreseen. The peasants go to the front with great enthusiasm, and the *intelligentsia*, Radical and Conservative alike, cheer them on.[5]

---

1. William G. Rosenberg, "Introduction: NEP Russia as a 'Transitional' Society," in Fitzpatrick et al, *Russia in the Era of NEP,* 4.

2. Ibid., 5.

3. Compare Rosenberg, "Introduction: NEP Russia as a 'Transitional' Society," 4–5, with Pipes, *Russia under the Bolshevik Regime,* Kindle location 3362–3371.

4. Fitzpatrick, *The Russian Revolution,* 85.

5. Graham, *Russia and the World,* 20.

V. V. Ivanov wrote enthusiastically of the dedication of "sectarians" to the cause of helping "those who are battling at their posts for the integrity and honor of our dear Motherland (*Rodina*) and for our defense against the heavy and gloomy threat of the haughty Germans and the cruel Turks."[6] This was not out of character for the evangelicals, who had been active in supplying the front and caring for the wounded during the Russo-Turkish conflict of 1877.[7] Evangelicals served as soldiers in World War I in numbers proportionate to that of other citizens.[8] Some of the women, such as N. V. Rodionova and another identified only as "E. B." went to the front as nursing sisters.[9] In Odessa during the war years Baptists increased their visits to prisons and military hospitals.[10] Besides their genuine concern for the nation and the well-being of its soldiers and other citizens, the evangelicals hoped that their participation in the war effort would help to demonstrate that they were not subversives, but reliable citizens. According to an editorial in *Baptist* (probably authored by V. V. Ivanov), "The present difficult . . . time . . . opens a wide field of charity on which there is the opportunity for all true sons of Russia to show their faithfulness to the Fatherland and the Tsar."[11] Evangelicals joined thousands of private citizens who entered into the task of caring for the wounded, preparing supplies, and collecting money for the war effort. According to Stephen Graham, every available space was used to house and tend the wounded.[12] Sewing and knitting circles were formed in Baptist churches in Baku, Balashov, and elsewhere to provide articles to outfit the troops and supply military hospitals.[13] Evangelicals organized infirmaries (*lazarety*) to nurse the wounded. In Baku, Molokans and Baptists joined together to open one such infirmary in November 1914. The eight-room house donated by a Molokan family named Kolesnikov could accommodate up to thirty patients from the Turkish front. The staff consisted of a doctor, a medic (*feldsher*), and a nurse while "our young girls and ladies" cleaned and cooked on a voluntary basis.[14] Dom Evangeliia in

6. V. V. Ivanov, "Na pomoshch' ranenym voinam" (To the aid of wounded soldiers), *Baptist*, Nos. 15–16 (1914) 17–18.

7. Dalton, "Recent Evangelical Movements," 109–10; V. G. Pavlov, "Vospominaniia ssylnogo" (Recollections of an exile), in Karetnikova, *Al'manakh, vypusk 1*, 196.

8. Coleman, *Russian Baptists*, 116.

9 *Gost'* 1 (January 1915) 7; E. B., "Iz pis'ma sestry miloserdiia s fronta" (From a letter of a sister of mercy at the front), *Gost'* 5 (May 1917) 10–11.

10. *Gost'* 11 (November 1917) 175.

11 *Baptist*, Nos. 21–22–23–24 (1914) 6.

12. Graham, *Russia and the World*, 21, 25

13 *Baptist*, Nos. 21–22–23–24 (1914) 5–6.

14 Ivanov, "Na pomoshch," 17–18.

St. Petersburg also functioned as an infirmary for the wounded, supported by contributions sent to the specially designated "Good Samaritan Fund."[15] As the wounded left, however, they were not replaced by others, doubtless in relation to the restrictions leveled against sectarian groups at that time by the government.[16] By September 1915 all the wounded had been replaced by refugees, mostly youngsters who had been sent away to safety by their parents.[17] Most of the evangelical infirmaries were closed down along with their sponsoring churches after only a few months of activity.[18] In Samara, however, the Baptist church was evidently able to stay open until 1917, although the infirmary became a financial burden to the congregation.[19]

Besides the wounded, aid was also extended to prisoners. It is estimated that by 1918 there were up to three million Russian soldiers in captivity.[20] During the war believers were encouraged to make and ship hardtack (*sukhari*) to Russian prisoners in Germany and Austria, especially fellow Christians. It was explained that because the Christians were resolved not to steal to meet their own needs, they suffered hunger more than other prisoners without such scruples. A brother in Voronezh guberniia who owned a bakery dedicated himself to making hardtack especially for Russian POWs.[21] *Gost'* readers were encouraged to make hardtack and send it to Dom Evangeliia in St. Petersburg. From there it could be forwarded free of charge through a special arrangement with the city council.[22] Meanwhile, outside of Russia hundreds of churches and individuals in Europe involved themselves in evangelistic work among Russian POWs. During the war the German Baptists reported two thousand baptisms among converted Russian prisoners.[23] In particular, ministry among POWs in Germany and Austria led to the founding of the influential mission *Licht im Osten* (Light in the east) by Walter Jack and Jakob Kroeker.[24] From his new base in the United States following his 1915 exile, W. A. Fetler helped to establish the

15. *Gost'* 1 (January 1915) 8; "Fond miloserdnago samarianina" (The Good Samaritan fund), *Gost'* 1 (January 1915) 19–21.

16. Coleman, *Russian Baptists*, 121–23.

17. *Gost'* 1 (January 1915) 18; *Gost'* 2 (February 1915) 45; *Gost'* 9 (September 1915) 215.

18. Coleman, *Russian Baptists*, 122.

19. *Gost'* 7 (July 1917) 15.

20. This figure is cited by Brandenburg, *The Meek and the Mighty*, 158.

21. I. V. Neprash, *Gost'* 8 (August 1917) 1–3.

22. *Gost'* 12 (December 1917) 172–73.

23 Green, *Tomorrow's Man*, 74.

24. For a more detailed description of the impressive mission to Russian prisoners of war, see Brandenburg, *The Meek and the Mighty*, 157–65.

Gospel Committee for Work among Russian War Prisoners, which prepared thousands of brochures for distribution by evangelists and hundreds of prisoner volunteers.[25] Following the signing of the Treaty of Brest-Litovsk that ended the war between Germany and Soviet Russia in March 1918, returning Russian POWs made up a powerful missionary force. To this day there are churches that attribute their founding to returning Russian prisoners of war.[26]

Not surprisingly, the world war also quickly created a mass of social problems as men left their families to go to the front. The war also increased the incidence of homelessness in Petrograd as refugees came to the city. Evangelicals were among those who worked to alleviate their needs. In the summer of 1916, the young people of Dom Evangeliia expressed the wish to do something for the many homeless children in the capital. To raise money to rent an apartment and pay a woman to look after the children, they began to make items to sell at a Christmas bazaar, which was held in January 1917, and also solicited individual donations. By the summer of that year there were ten children living in a rented three-room apartment with two women to care for them. The home was supported by donations of cash, groceries, and volunteer services, such as doing the laundry or chopping wood. Typical of the evangelicals was the emphasis placed on not only the physical rescue of orphaned children in an exceptionally difficult time, but the ultimate aim to "plant seeds of righteousness and love for God and people" in the children's souls.[27] The home lasted only until November 1917, partly because of the difficulty of securing food in Petrograd and partly because the soldier fathers of the children returned from the front and again took over responsibility for their families. However, offerings were still accepted at Dom Evangeliia for the purchase of warm clothing, shoes, and food for the many children in the city in desperate need.[28] The youth groups of Dom Evangeliia also continued a variety of visitation and service activities during the war and after. They regularly visited military infirmaries and nursing homes, both for the newly wounded and for veterans who had been wounded as long ago as the 1905 war with Japan. In addition, they stayed in touch with a juvenile prison colony.[29]

25. J. Fetler, *Sluzhenie Rossii*, 49.

26. Based on personal conversations with Baptist pastors in Izmail and Berezovka, in Odessa oblast', Ukraine, November and December 2013.

27. E. N. K[uteinikova], "'Sem'ia' detei v Levashove" (The "family" of children in Levashov), *Gost'* 6 (June 1917) 86–87.

28. "Nechto o priiute v Levashove" (Something about the shelter in Levashov), *Gost'* 11 (November 1917) 175.

29. *Gost'* 10 (October 1917) 156.

The Salvation Army, by then made up of both foreign and Russian officers and recruits represented a major part of evangelical compassionate activity during the war. They primarily served the homeless and refugees. After four years of a semi-underground existence in St. Petersburg, the onset of World War I allowed the Army to engage openly in compassionate ministry, although officially it still had no legal status. It continued to rely on its close connection with the Russian evangelicals to navigate problems with the government. In October 1914 the Army opened a Slum Post outside Petrograd's Moscow Gate. The shelter they established cared for families in the area whose fathers were in the war. In early 1915 the Slum Post moved from its suburban setting to an inner city district known as Vasia's Village. Here they worked among the very poor, assisting the people who lived in overcrowded apartments. The Post fed eighty children every day, cared for the babies of unmarried mothers, and held children's meetings. In 1915 the Army sponsored a children's "summer colony" in Finland.[30] Another major effort begun in 1915 was the establishment of a shelter for refugees. The Salvation Army offered help to the Petrograd Committee for Finding Asylum for Refugees and was allowed to do so as the offer was conveniently understood as being from the Finnish Salvation Army, since no Russian Salvation Army officially existed. Accordingly, a fifty-bed facility was set up, which was then abruptly requisitioned by the military. Local evangelical friends again proved useful when Aleksandra Peiker took the Army's problem to the Dowager Empress Maria Fedorovna, who intervened to keep the property in the hands of the Salvationists. Presently, American citizens in Petrograd opened a similar home for refugees and asked the Army to run it. At about the same time a Salvation Army home for Russian children whose fathers were away at the front was opened in Finland.[31]

In October 1915 there was a police raid on a Salvationist meeting and the members of the post were threatened with either fines or prison stays. Just as they did before the war, the Army again went for help to the Russian evangelicals. Elizaveta Chertkova referred them to Aleksandra Peiker, who put them in touch with Olga, Dowager Queen of the Hellenes, who had had some contact with William Fetler.[32] She intervened on behalf of the Salvation Army and the charges were dropped.[33] Tom Aitken connects the police raid on the Salvation Army with the appointment of Aleksei Khvostov,

---

30. Larsson, "The Army in Russia," 57; Aitken, *Blood and Fire,* 169–74, 191.
31. Larsson, "The Army in Russia," 57–58; Aitken, *Blood and Fire,* 174–77.
32. McCaig, *Wonders of Grace,* 46–47, 49.
33. Larsson, "The Army in Russia," 60–61; Aitken, *Blood and Fire,* 193–94.

Rasputin's choice, as Minister of the Interior during the fall of 1915.[34] Perhaps Khvostov's appointment had some bearing on Fetler's exile as well, as John Fetler hints,[35] a process that began about a month after the incident at the Salvation Army meeting. In both cases, highly-placed friends interceded. Throughout 1916, however, the situation deteriorated for evangelicals in Russia. They were popularly perceived to be German sympathizers, practicing a "German faith"—an inaccurate, but not surprising connection to make, considering the ties between Russian Baptists, German Baptists, and Mennonites.[36] A 1922 letter described the overall situation for evangelicals during the war:

> During the war there were so many attacks on the part of the Orthodox clergy; they wanted to accuse us of being German spies. Many brothers were sent to Siberia; they closed down congregations; brothers and sisters were subjected to cruel persecution. They threatened us that after the war they would eat us alive.[37]

Already by early 1915 numerous prayer houses in the south were closed and their major leaders exiled to Siberia. By August of that year still more prayer houses in the region of Petrograd were closed as well. Dom Evangeliia was requisitioned as a barracks. By 1916 the Baptist Union and the Evangelical Christian Union were also closed down.[38] It is not surprising that the February Revolution of 1917 was initially greeted with joy by the evangelicals. The year began with the emperor's abdication and the institution of the Provisional Government. An editorial in *Slovo istiny*, based in Moscow, exulted:

> No, it is not a dream! Great Russia has actually shaken off the burden of the ancient domination of autocracy. The structure of the oppression of soul and spirit has collapsed; the chains of the evil, dark powers are broken. And now all of the past already seems like a dream, such a nightmare, bloody, suffocating and endless . . . The resurrection of that already stinking Lazarus—Russia—has been accomplished."[39]

---

34. Aitken, *Blood and Fire*, 192–93.

35. J. Fetler, *Sluzhenie Rossii*, 41–42.

36. For a detailed discussion of the evangelicals' perceived foreign connections, see Coleman, *Russian Baptists*, 92–123.

37. D. Pravover (Kiev) to A. Kolesnikov, 16 January 1922, *Seiatel' istiny* (March 1922) 11. Clearly, Pravover viewed the 1917 revolution as God's intervention.

38. Coleman, *Russian Baptists*, 121–22.

39. *Slovo istiny* 1 (May 1917) 1–2.

The biggest change in early 1917 was that evangelicals were able to minister publicly again. Gradually churches that had been closed were reopened and exiled pastors returned home.[40] Compassionate ministry was an immediate priority. In April 1917, the Russian Baptist Union held its first congress since 1911 in Vladikavkaz. To refill the empty cash box, a resolution was made to request that every individual church member set aside one day's pay and forward it to the Union so that missionary work could begin anew. An additional call was made to encourage church members to give to the orphanage and old people's home in Balashov. It needed to be expanded because it was overcrowded—evidently as a result of the war.[41] The Baptist church in Omsk held a bazaar to raise money for the congregation's own children's home and for the distribution of Christian literature when it opened again in July 1917 after a year's closure.[42] In 1920 a regional gathering of evangelists in Viatka made plans to organize a shelter for orphans and the elderly in the village of Riabka, Perm' guberniia.[43] Clearly, evangelical institutional life was making a comeback and leaders such as Baptist Union president Dei Mazaev emphasized the blessing of freedom that they now enjoyed.[44] The situation initially improved for the Salvation Army as well, which officially opened on 16 September 1917. While the American socialist journalist, John Reed (1887–1920), believed that at this point the Salvation Army was "admitted to Russia for the first time in history,"[45] in actual fact it had already been present since 1910. It continued to work closely with local evangelicals, such as Aleksandr Karev and others who participated in street mission work.[46] Commissioner Karl Larsson summarized the Army's ministry as consisting of its headquarters, seven corps, two children's homes, two slum posts and an "eventide home."[47] One of the Salvation Army's properties was a house on Vasilievskii Island donated by Elizaveta Chertkova, who by that time had resettled in Finland.[48] The coming of the Bolshevik

---

40. M. D. Timoshenko's account of his exile ran as a serial in *Slovo istiny* during 1917. For a brief biography of M. D. Timoshenko see www.blagovestnik.org./bible/people/p0020.htm.

41. *Gost'* 5 (May 1917) 3–4.

42. *Gost'* 7 (July 1917) 15.

43. Iarygin, *Evangel'skoe dvizhenie*, 59.

44. "Pervyi svobodnyi s"ezd russkikh baptistov vsei Rossii" (The first free congress of the Russian Baptists of all Russia), *Baptist* 1 (July 1917) 2.

45. Reed, *Ten Days that Shook the World*, 13.

46. AUCEC-B Archives, Drawer 5, Folder 21 Istoricheskiie vospominaniia (Historical recollections), Vysotskii, "Istoriia tserkvei" (History of the churches), 1.

47. Larsson, "The Army in Russia," 99.

48. Aitken, *Blood and Fire*, 230–31.

Revolution, however, and the deteriorating supply situation in Petrograd necessitated the evacuation of the two children's homes to locations outside the city before the end of 1917.[49] One of the homes, which moved several hundred kilometers south of Moscow to a village near the city of Orel, continued to exist for another three years, but then had to be abandoned.[50] The Salvation Army was officially "dissolved" by a government order in 1923.[51]

While their legal status initially improved, the material status of many evangelicals continued to deteriorate. The Bolsheviks came to power in October (November n.s.) 1917 and in 1918 although the war with Germany ended the Civil War began. Between 1917 and 1920 both Evangelical Christians and Baptists in Petrograd lost members as people starved, died of illness, or left the city in search of food and safety. I. S. Prokhanov's wife was one of the numerous casualties of 1919.[52] By 1920 each of the two Evangelical Christian churches in Petrograd were reduced in size from about 1500 members to two hundred.[53] Here again, compassionate ministry was a priority as evangelicals turned to one another for help. Despite its upbeat account of the 1920 Evangelical Christian congress in Moscow, the July issue of the journal *Utrenniaia zvezda* also issued a plea, "To the congregations located in grain-producing localities." It stated that people were hungry in the cities, especially Petrograd, and detailed how Christians could feed their fellows by sending packages of dried bread, potatoes, and vegetables to addresses in Petrograd and Moscow.[54] Similar arrangements must have been made at the Baptist Dom Evangeliia because the former Pashkovite, M. N. Iasnovskaia wrote in 1920, "We are alive thanks to the brothers who sent us dried bread all the time and supported us."[55]

Meanwhile, according to eyewitnesses who described their experiences as young people at Dom Evangeliia during the years of revolution and civil war, a full program of activity was carried out that focused on helping those in need. "We lived here," remembered E. G. Mamulina in 1971 concerning the amount of time she and others spent at Dom Evangeliia.[56]

49. Larsson, "The Army in Russia," 99.

50. Aitken, *Blood and Fire*, 242.

51. SAIHC, item 7.0, folder EE/4/2/1–1913-1992, "Protokol No. 14, Zasedanie komissii po provedniiu otdeleniia tserkvi ot gosudarstva ri TSK RKP, 27 fevralia 1923 goda" (Minutes No. 14, Meeting of the commission on the conduct of the separation of church and state ri TSK RKP, 27 February 1923).

52. Prokhanoff, *Cauldron*, 181–83.

53. Kahle, *Evangel'skie khristiane v Rossii i Sovetskom soiuze*, 225.

54. *Utrenniaia zvezda* 2 (July 1920) 11.

55. M. N. Iasnovskaia, *Blagovestnik* 11 (1920) 180.

56. Sevast'ianov, "Pleiada sluzhitelei," 1.

The youth gathered in the evenings for prayer and choir practice, but also to sew, knit, and construct items to be given away. True to the expectation that compassionate ministry was part of the calling of evangelical youth, specialized groups carried on visitation in the city. The "Bethany" group concentrated on the elderly and housebound, while the "Andrew" group focused on assisting those in educational institutions, hospitals, and at railroad stations.[57] During the Civil War, Dom Evangeliia also served as a shelter for its own staff and a few members. As was the case with the Evangelical Christian congregations, Dom Evangeliia lost many members who died or became refugees.[58] The pastor, I. N. Shilov, wrote in 1920 that every day Dom Evangeliia fed between twelve and eighteen people,[59] evidently the resident community. M. N. Iasnovskaia added that, "The Lord provides us with daily bread in an amazing way."[60] M. P. Miasoedova, the former Salvation Army captain who had managed the Dom Evangeliia halfway-house during the winter of 1913 and 1914 was living there herself in 1924.[61]

Thus, during the difficult years immediately following the revolutions of 1917, while many evangelicals struggled to help one another survive, compassionate ministry continued in the form of institutions and outreach to people in need. In addition, at least one innovative evangelistic project with elements of compassionate ministry was undertaken at this time, namely the so-called "Tent Mission." As its name suggests, the Tent Mission consisted of several itinerant bands of young men and women who visited towns and villages in various regions of Soviet Russia from spring to fall between 1918 and 1923, holding evangelistic meetings for the general public either under a large tent, or in whatever more permanent premises were available. The effort began as an outreach to soldiers. Its founder, Iakov Ia. Dik (1890–1919), was among the Mennonite men who served as medical orderlies during World War I. Following the February Revolution, when evangelistic work could be done openly, Dik and his cohorts organized the Christian Soldiers' Circle, first in Moscow and then in Petrograd. They published a newspaper, *Budil'nik sovesti* (Reveille of the conscience), held meetings for soldiers, and opened an inexpensive dining room for them. Moscow evangelical youth, such as Nikolai Salov-Astakhov, also took an active part in the work of the Circle.[62] They met four times a week, making

57. G. Babere, "Dom Evangeliia," *Golos istiny* 5 (44) (May 2003) 30.
58. Kahle, *Evangel'skie khristiane v Rossii i Sovetskom Soiuze*, 225.
59. I. N. Shilov, *Blagovestnik* 11 (1920) 181.
60. M. N. Iasnovskaia, *Blagovestnik* 11 (1920) 179.
61. S. V. Sevast'ianov, "Miasoedova, Mariia Petrovna," 3.
62. I. V. Neprash, "Iz deiatel'nosti soldatskogo khristianskogo kruzhka gor. Moskvy"

use of both Baptist and Evangelical Christian prayer houses and a rented hall. The group distributed thousands of brochures and Scripture portions on the streets, in hospitals, on trains, and anywhere soldiers could be found. It is estimated that a total of more than four thousand soldiers attended the Circle's first thirty-six evangelistic meetings.[63] The need for ministry among soldiers decreased when the Treaty of Brest-Litovsk (March 1918) brought Russia's participation in World War I to an end. However, the co-workers of the Christian Soldiers' Circle were reluctant to disband and hit on the idea of a traveling tent mission to continue their ministry. After a summer of work near Tambov in 1918, the group was ready for expansion and during the summer and fall of 1919 twenty-five more missionaries, including Mennonites, Russians, Jews, and one Latvian, divided into four groups that traveled throughout South Russia.[64] According to the goals enumerated in October 1918 in an article in the Mennonite publication *Friedenstimme* (Voice of peace), it was planned that the missionaries would also teach peasants about improving their farms and nurse the sick.[65] The Tent Mission was a strenuous and dangerous undertaking because the Civil War was at its height and anarchist bands led by Nestor Makhno (1888–1934) were active throughout the south. Frequently the missionaries were called upon to tend those who were suffering from typhus and influenza, including the very bandits who threatened them.[66] By late fall 1919, only seven of the twenty-five returned to their base in Ekaterinoslav (present-day Dnepropetrovsk). Some had been killed by bandits, others had fallen ill with typhus and could not travel.[67] Iakov Dik was one of a group of missionaries hacked to death by bandits in the Mennonite village of Eichenfeld (present-day Novopetrovka) in October 1919. Consequently, the Tent Mission's leadership passed to N. I. Salov-Astakhov.[68]

When the Civil War ended in 1920 it was possible to regularize the Tent Mission's work and subsequently it was registered by the People's Commissariat of Internal Affairs in Kharkiv. The missionaries thereby gained

---

(From the activity of the Christian Soldiers' Circle of the city of Moscow), *Gost'* 7 (July 1917) 1; Ia. Ia. Dik, "Ot rukovoditelei soldatskogo khristianskogo kruzhka Moskvy" (From the leadership of the Christian Soldiers' Circle of Moscow), *Gost'* 10 (October 1917) 155; N. I. Salov-Astakhov, *Palatochnaia missiia*, 11.

63. "Moskovskii soldatskii khristianskii kruzhok" (The Moscow Christian Soldiers' Circle), *Gost'* 6 (June 1917) 7; Neprash, "Iz" deiatel'nosti," 12–13.

64 Salov-Astakhov, *Palatochnaia missia*, 18.

65 Gislason, "The Tent Mission," 89.

66 Saloff-Astakhoff, *Judith*, 108; Salov-Astakhov, *Palatochnaia missiia*, 59, 89, 109.

67. Salov-Astakhov, *Palatochnaia missiia*, 80.

68. Ibid., 81–83.

the legal right to travel, present religious lectures, bring medical assistance, cooperate with government bodies to organize elementary schools and children's homes, and evangelize in night shelters, public dining rooms, hospitals, train stations, parks, and ports.[69] A home for orphaned children was operated by members or supporters of the Tent Mission in Schoenau (Molochna Colony, Ukraine).[70] Possibly it may be identified with the second of two children's homes overseen by the Abraham Harder family, the first having been founded for Mennonite children in Grossweide (Molochna Colony) in 1906.[71] These institutions functioned in relative freedom until 1922 when the Soviet authorities forbade all religious instruction and the personnel were replaced.[72] The atmosphere changed still more in 1923 when it became difficult to carry out the mission's work, even with legal documentation. Finally, in the summer of 1923 all religious organizations were required to re-register, but every effort to renew the Tent Mission's charter failed.[73]

In conclusion, the evangelicals' situation improved briefly with the February Revolution, but along with the rest of the country they endured great hardship during the Civil War. Nevertheless, compassionate ministry continued to be a significant part of their mission as they adapted themselves to a rapidly changing situation. The evangelicals cared for one another and worked to maintain their institutions for children and the elderly, as well as serving those in need around them. Young people continued to be particularly active in compassionate ministry. In addition, new avenues of service, such as the Tent Mission, were attempted in spite of extremely harsh and dangerous conditions. As had often been the case in previous decades, the evangelicals' efforts were not especially long-lived during the Civil War because of numerous hindrances, sometimes due to natural circumstances, such as hunger or disease, and sometimes due to government restrictions, as in the case of the Salvation Army.

---

69. Ibid., 101–2.

70. Saloff-Astakhoff, *Touching Heaven by Prayer*, 31–33; Toews, *Mennonite Martyrs*, 93–94.

71. H., Er. "Harder, Abraham A. (1866–1941). *Global Anabaptist Mennonite Encyclopedia Online*. 1956. http://www.gameo.org/encyclopedia/contents/harder_abraham_a._1866-1941.

72 Toews, *Mennonite Martyrs*, 93–94; see also Saloff-Astakhoff, *Little Lame Walter*; *Real Russia*, 71–72.

73 Salov-Astakhov, *Palatochnaia missiia*, 147–48.

EVANGELICAL COMPASSIONATE MINISTRY DURING THE 1921 TO 1923 FAMINE

Assistance in times of famine was a relatively familiar service activity among Russian evangelicals before 1921. During the famine of 1891 evangelicals sent a shipment of flour to exiles in Orenburg.[74] In 1907 evangelicals collected money for famine relief.[75] Funds were collected in 1911 as well, during a drought in the Orenburg region.[76] The vast scope of the 1921 to 1923 famine, however, surpassed the level of suffering the evangelicals had ever seen before. Droughts were part of the rhythm of agricultural life in central Russia, but they could be compounded into humanitarian disasters by government mismanagement. Such was the case in the famine of 1891 to 1892, which created considerable public criticism and pleas for organized emergency planning.[77] Similarly, the 1921 to 1923 famine in Soviet Russia was an example of natural and human factors magnifying one another. It is possible that people could have managed to feed themselves in spite of the destruction brought on by the preceding seven years of war, revolution, and civil war, or that they could have survived a major drought in normal times. They could not, however, endure both at once. Drought began to be felt especially in the Volga region by the fall of 1920. In southern Ukraine by March 1921 the grain seeded in the fall had become so dry that the wind was blowing it out by the roots.[78] Clearly, the coming harvest would be ruined, and Soviet Russia had few resources with which to meet the crisis. Thirty-five million people, that is, one-third of the total population of European Russia lived in the drought-stricken area designated by the government in the early summer of 1921.[79] The zone extended for eight-hundred miles along the Volga River from Viatka in the north to Astrakhan in the south, and three-hundred fifty miles from west to east between Penza and Ufa. An additional ten million faced starvation in southern Ukraine, a situation that would not be acknowledged officially until the end of 1921. By 1922 famine

---

74. V. G. Pavlov, "Vospominaniia ssylnogo" (Recollections of an exile) in Karetnikova, *Al'manakh, vypusk 1*, 208.

75. *Bratskii listok* 2 (1907) 42; 5 (1907) 21–24; 7 (1907) 19–22; 8 (1907) 20; 9 (1907) 16; 10 (1907) 17.

76 *Gost',* 10 (August 1911) 201–2; *Gost'* 11 (September 1911) 230; *Gost'* 12 (October 1911) 254.

77. Kniaz'kov, *Golod v drevnei Rossii*.

78 Arthur Slagel, "Organizing Feeding Operations in the Ukraine," in Hiebert and Miller, *Feeding the Hungry,* 205.

79. Fisher, *The Famine in Soviet Russia,* 51 n. 5.

conditions existed in the Caucasus as well.⁸⁰ In 1922 the executive body of the All-Russian Baptist Union counted forty-four thousand of its church members in the government-designated Volga famine zone, or 20 percent of all Baptists.⁸¹ As the extent of the famine in Ukraine became known and as it further extended into the Caucasus, the percentage of believers involved also increased. Later in 1922 the Southern Baptist Foreign Mission Board reported that fifty thousand Baptists and their families were in danger.⁸² Meanwhile, the Evangelical Christian Union sought assistance for at least forty congregations of unspecified size in the Volga region and ninety-one affected by the famine in Ukraine.⁸³

The 1921 to 1923 famine was also different in that it involved evangelicals in an immense international relief effort. In addition to working with their own resources, leaders were called on to coordinate the receipt and distribution of aid from abroad. A new level of organizational sophistication was required, both for rendering aid within congregations, and for maintaining contact between congregations and leadership at the center. Local committees did the demanding work of keeping statistics and managing local allocations. The famine also affected relationships between Evangelical Christians and Baptists as tensions developed concerning the principles according to which aid should be distributed. A Joint Commission for Assisting in the Distribution of Foreign Baptist Relief, consisting of representatives from both the Baptists and the Evangelical Christians was organized in 1923.⁸⁴

It took time to develop a response to the famine. Relief for the hungry and homeless of Europe after the First World War was a matter of concern for many people of good will around the world. Aid to Soviet Russia, however, was represented by "one thick, black question-mark."⁸⁵ There was sufficient information concerning the needs within the country; the problem was the difficulty of entering Soviet Russia to ease those needs. Political suspicions

---

80. Patenaude, *The Big Show*, 67.

81 SBHLA, The Historical Papers of Mrs. I. V. Neprash on Religion in Russia, "Zapis' No. 19 zasedaniia Kollegii Vserossiiskogo Soiuza" (Notation No. 19 of the meeting of the Collegium of the All-Russian Union), 24 February 1922.

82. SBHLA, "Foreign Mission Board Report," Southern Baptist Convention (1922) 307.

83. *Utrenniaia zvezda* Nos. 3–4–5 (March–April–May 1922) 2.

84. SBHLA, "Agreement between the council of All-Russian Union of Evangelical Christians and the Collegium of the All-Russian Baptist Union with regard to the Joint Relief Commission," Moscow, 8 February 1923.

85 J. H. Rushbrooke, "Russia: What Can Baptists Do?" *Baptist Times and Freeman* (16 September 1921).

ran deep between the capitalist nations that could offer help, especially the United States, and Soviet Russia. The Soviet government feared that massive foreign aid would serve as a pretext for counter-revolution, while many in the capitalist world worried that the Soviets would use aid for their own revolutionary purposes.[86] In the meantime, foreign groups that were seriously concerned about providing aid to Soviet Russia, such as Mennonites and Baptists, did relief work elsewhere while they exerted themselves to find a way into the country.[87]

The key point of contact for Baptists abroad became the recently reconstituted All-Russian Baptist Union which had moved to Moscow. The shifting political picture of the Civil War years had left Baptist leaders isolated from one another in different parts of the country. In 1917 Pavel V. Pavlov, the pastor of the Baptist church in Moscow, together with his father, V. G. Pavlov, and M. D. Timoshenko, began to reconstruct the Russian Baptist Union there.[88] A Baptist congress consisting of about sixty delegates convened in May 1920 and P. V. Pavlov was elected president of the Union's new executive board, or Collegium. Influential Russian Baptists outside of Moscow, notably D. I. Mazaev, protested the 1920 congress as non-representative and denied its legitimacy.[89] Nevertheless, during the spring and fall of 1921 Baptists abroad contacted the Union in Moscow to begin to make plans for sending famine aid. These included I. V. Neprash (1883–1957) of the Eastern Union of Russian and Ukrainian Evangelical Christian-Baptists in the USA, a former preacher at Dom Evangeliia who had immigrated to the United States in 1918,[90] and J. H. Rushbrooke who had been elected Commissioner for Europe at the July 1920 London meeting of the Baptist World Alliance.[91] Over the next few years the Baptist Union Collegium in Moscow oversaw the distribution of a significant amount of international aid. By September 1922 they reported the receipt, or at least the availability, of sixty-eight million rubles (US $160,000) in famine aid

---

86. Volkogonov, *Lenin*, 39–46.

87. For details on Mennonite famine aid, see Hiebert and Miller, *Feeding the Hungry*. Note that the Society of Friends (Quakers) had been doing relief work in Russia since 1916 (Asquith, *Famine*, 9).

88. Coleman, *Russian Baptists*, 138.

89. "Ob edinstve s brat'iami baptistami" (On unity with the Baptist brethren), *Utrenniaia zvezda*, Nos. 1–2 (January–February 1922) 4; Coleman, *Russian Baptists*, 192.

90. *The Christian Workers' Magazine* (August 1918) 970; see also http//: smsinternational.org/neprash4html.

91. "General Review of the Year," *American Baptist Foreign Missionary Society* (1923) 29;

from abroad.⁹² Most of it was from the international Baptist community (including the United States, Great Britain, Denmark, Sweden, Hungary, Czechoslovakia, and Argentina)⁹³ which contributed at least US $300,000 to famine relief between 1921 and 1924, including agricultural reconstruction projects and medical supplies. Used clothing and shoes worth at least that same amount were shipped from the United States to Russia as well in 1921 and 1922, for an approximate total of US $600,000 in foreign aid,⁹⁴ although not all of the international Baptist aid available was channeled through the Moscow Baptist Union.⁹⁵ Other foreign donors included the Eastern Union of Russian and Ukrainian Evangelical Christian Baptists in the USA, which contributed approximately US $10,000 throughout 1922.⁹⁶

However, not all the aid offered came from abroad. As early as 1920, according to O. Iu. Redkina, "not a few" Molokan, Evangelical Christian, and Mennonite congregations in Balashov, Samara, Omsk, and elsewhere, sent telegrams and letters to V. I. Lenin requesting that they be allowed to share their grain reserves both with their fellow believers in Petrograd and Moscow and with other hungry people as well. Some shipped entire boxcars of grain directly to Lenin.⁹⁷ By 1921 the government-designated famine zone encompassed most of these congregations, but their readiness to help is significant. That their generosity was sustained throughout the famine years is evidenced by the Russian Baptist Union's financial report or projection dated 25 September 1922,⁹⁸ in which the total amount of money listed for "Assistance" was ninety million rubles. After subtracting the foreign

92 SBHLA, The Historical Papers of Mrs. I. V. Neprash, "Zapis' No. 48," 25 September 1922. The dollar equivalent was computed by Steeves, "The Russian Baptist Union," 175–78.

93 J. H. Rushbrooke, "Russian Famine and Baptist Relief," *The Baptist Times and Freeman* (5 May 1922) 280; "British Baptists and Relief in Russia," *The Baptist Times and Freeman* (27 October 1922) 697.

94 "International Conference on Baptist Relief and Mission Work in Europe," Baptist World Alliance, 1 August 1922, 348; J. H. Rushbrooke, "European Relief," Foreign Missions Board Report, Southern Baptist Conference, 1923, 121; SBHLA, ABFMS Correspondence, J. H. Rushbrooke (London) to Rev. Dr. J. H. Franklin (New York) 20 December 1923; "General Review of the Year," American Baptist Foreign Mission Society, 1923, 25.

95. SBHLA, W. O. Lewis Papers, W. O. Lewis "Report," 12 May 1923, 3; J. H. Rushbrooke, "Report," October 1923, 11.

96 "Chto sdelano golodaiushchim?" (What has been done for the starving?), *Seiatel' istiny* (March 1922) 15; (October 1922) 13; (November 1922) 14.

97 GARF f. 130, op. 4, d. 462, quoted by Redkina, *Sel'skokhoziaistvennye religioznye trudovye kollektivy*, 129.

98 SBHLA, The Historical Papers of Mrs. I. V. Neprash, "Zapis' No. 48," 25 September 1922.

contribution (68,000,000 rubles), it means that Russian evangelicals collected or anticipated collecting an additional 22,000,000 rubles, or approximately US $39,000, for relief from within the country. It is likely that at least half of those funds were given in kind. In July 1922 the Collegium called for the establishment of a special famine fund with the goal of collecting two-hundred thousand puds (more than seven million pounds) of grain, which could be done if every single member gave at least ten funts, that is, nearly ten pounds. At five-hundred rubles a pud, that much grain would be worth ten million rubles.[99] If the Collegium did, indeed, manage to collect such an amount from the churches, it represents a strong commitment to mutual aid and a remarkable accomplishment, given the circumstances.

By the end of August 1921 the Soviet government signed agreements with the American Relief Administration (ARA), directed by Herbert Hoover (1874–1964), and the International Committee for Russian Relief, overseen by the Norwegian explorer and humanitarian Fridtjof Nansen (1861–1930).[100] A few weeks later the Russian Baptist Union issued its own general appeal for famine aid.[101] However, the Russians did not merely wait for aid to arrive from far away. Two weeks after the circular letter went out to the world, another was sent to the churches announcing the decision of the Collegium to take upon itself a united, and therefore more effective, famine response by organizing a special department. The letter acknowledged that although help was being sought from abroad, "upon us in Russia lies the obligation of mutual love—by our own efforts, although from our scant supplies, to give what we have for the relief of the suffering of our starving brothers."[102] The Collegium suggested the following measures: 1) Establish two- or three-member commissions in each congregation and regional association to handle foodstuffs and money. 2) Collect pledges for regular support of the hungry. The purpose of the subscription was to commit to giving help dependably until the next harvest without expending all

---

99 Based on Steeves's calculation, US $1=562.5 rubles; 22 million/562.5= $39,111; SBHLA, The Historical Papers of Mrs. I. V. Neprash, "Zapis' No. 34," [8?] July 1922, Item 180; "Zapis' No 48," September 1922.

100. Patenaude, *The Big Show*, 46–47.

101. SBHLA, The Historical Papers of Mrs. I. V. Neprash, P. V. Pavlov, M. D. Timoshenko, I. N. Shilov, "Tsirkuliarnoe pis'mo No. 3096" (Circular letter No. 3096),15 September 1921; "A Message from the Baptist Union of All Russia," *The Baptist and Reflector* (9 February 1922) 4; "A Message from Russian Baptists," *The Watchman-Examiner* (9 February 1922) 183; "A Message from Russian Baptists," *The Baptist* (11 February 1922) 54–55.

102. SBHLA, The Historical Papers of Mrs. I. V. Neprash, P. V. Pavlov, M. D. Timoshenko, I. N. Shilov, V. G. Pavlov, D. P. Stenin, I. M. Sirotin, A. I. Shal'e, I. I. Kul'man, "Circular letter No. 317010," 30 September 1921.

resources in a single burst of effort. 3) Repeat the subscriptions from time to time. Make special offerings for the starving on one Sunday or holiday gathering every month. Suggest that church members contribute a day's wages once a month for famine relief. Alternatively, establish a fast day once a month and contribute what would have been spent on food to famine relief, or hold an auction of valuables or other useful items and contribute the proceeds. 4) Finally, churches should inform the Collegium concerning what resources had been collected in order to know where to send it and ensure fair distribution. As for the local famine committees, they were to take a survey of their membership and inform the Collegium of the number of members in need and their dependents in each place.[103]

The leadership of the Evangelical Christian Union in Petrograd also gave instructions to its members concerning the famine, although not until 1922, perhaps because in recent years the focus had been on encouraging believers in grain-growing regions to supply the cities with food and not the other way around.[104] In the spring of 1922 the Evangelical Christian Executive Council circulated the addresses of relatively well-off congregations among their churches in the famine zone so that the latter could relocate. Churches with supplies were instructed to send food packages to congregations with none. The Executive Council asked to be notified at least by postcard of all food and money that were sent. Above all, church members were asked to pray.[105] A more formal survey of the needs among Evangelical Christians was commissioned after the Executive Council of that church union formally joined the national famine relief organization, Pomgol (abbreviated from *pomoshch,*' "help," and *golod,* "hunger, famine"), on 9 June 1922.[106] At that time the Evangelical Christian Union set up a three-member committee in Moscow to coordinate the Union's work with Pomgol.[107] Congregations were advised to select a local Pomgol representative and collect all the necessary information for the committee in Moscow: the degree and character of need, the number of hungry people, and the amount of help they were already receiving and its origin. All the Evangelical Christian departments and congregations were instructed to send their offerings of money and supplies to the Pomgol-Evangelical Christian

103 Ibid.

104. *Utrenniaia zvezda* 2 (July 1920) 11; cf. GARF f. 130, op. 4, d. 462, quoted by Redkina, *Sel'skokhoziaistvennye religioznye trudovye kollektivy,* 129.

105. *Utrenniaia zvezda,* Nos. 3–4–5 (March-April-May 1922) 1–2.

106. *Utrenniaia zvezda,* Nos. 6–7–8 (June–July–August 1922) 25.

107. Ibid.

committee.¹⁰⁸ This step may have been taken as the result of failed efforts on the part of I. S. Prokhanov, President of the Evangelical Christian Union, to attract an international sponsor. He had announced in the spring of 1922 that the ECU was seeking famine aid from believers abroad.¹⁰⁹ Since 1911 Prokhanov had been one of the ten vice-presidents of the Baptist World Alliance¹¹⁰ and very likely he personally contacted a number of foreign Baptist leaders. A response from Dr. J. H. Franklin, Secretary of the American Baptist Foreign Mission Society, however, discouraged Prokhanov from asking for help over and above what by that time was already being done through the Baptist Union in Moscow.¹¹¹ At their 1920 congress in London the Baptist World Alliance had assigned specific areas or countries to the particular care of the stronger Baptist unions and had established as a matter of policy that the Baptists in a given country were to operate as a single union and relate exclusively to their designated sponsor.¹¹² In the matter of giving famine assistance in Russia, the Baptist World Alliance, supported by the powerful American boards, acknowledged the Evangelical Christians, as "Baptist in faith though not in name."¹¹³ Besides, in May 1920 the Baptist congress in Moscow had overlapped for several days with an Evangelical Christian congress and the two church bodies had agreed in principle to the formation of a joint union and the publication of a journal.¹¹⁴ The essential unity of Baptists and Evangelical Christians, if not their leadership and organizational headquarters (Moscow and Petrograd, respectively) was thus affirmed during the early 1920s, although genuine administrative cooperation was not achieved at that time.¹¹⁵

Thus, basic lines of information gathering and communication were laid down, along with an organizational structure to meet the crisis. The main source of supply to the Baptist Union in Moscow and its relief committees throughout the country was extended through the American Relief

---

108 I. S. Prokhanov, "Tsirkuliarnoe pis'mo" (A circular letter), *Utrenniaia zvezda*, Nos. 6–7–8 (June–July–August 1922) 25.

109 *Utrenniaia zvezda*, Nos. 3–4–5 (March–April–May 1922) 1.

110. Coleman, *Russian Baptists*, 28, 46, 111.

111 SBHLA, ABFMS Correspondence, J. H. Franklin to I. S. Prokhanoff, 15 March 1922.

112 Wardin, "William Fetler," 241.

113. Everett Gill, "'Naked and Ye Clothed Me,' Southern Baptists Play the Good Samaritan," *Home and Foreign Fields* (April 1922) 12.

114 *Utrenniaia zvezda* 2 (July 1920) 2, 8.

115. *Utrenniaia zvezda*, Nos. 6–7–8 (June–July–August 1922) 6; Coleman, *Russian Baptists*, 162–63.

Administration,[116] which was set up to cooperate with smaller relief organizations that wished to gather their own support and direct it in a particular way. Thus, an organization such as the Baptist World Alliance or American Mennonite Relief could access ARA supplies, provided they could demonstrate that they had a workable plan for distributing aid.[117] There were three basic food programs. Through bulk food sales, staples worth US five-hundred dollars or more could be purchased directly from an ARA warehouse and distributed according to the plan of the organization that bought it. "Food drafts" allowed a donor to pay in advance for a designated recipient to receive a standard food package from an ARA warehouse. A US ten dollar parcel contained forty pounds of flour, twenty pounds of rice, ten pounds of sugar, ten pounds of lard, three pounds of tea, and twenty tins of milk. The third program, "Eurelcon," allowed cooperating organizations to buy food at cost from the ARA and use it to prepare and serve a daily balanced ration.[118] The Russian evangelicals made use of all three programs.

Typically, donors channeled money through the ARA apparatus to the Collegium of the Baptist Union for bulk sales and also the purchase of food packages. The Baptist Union, in turn, and its local committees acted as the distribution network.[119] For example, in May 1922 in response to an appeal from the North Caucasus, the Collegium ordered three-hundred packages from the ARA warehouse in Rostov.[120] Besides receiving and allotting standard packages and bulk food allotments, Baptists opened a Eurelcon public kitchen in Peski, near Voronezh on 22 May 1922. By the end of June it was feeding about one-thousand people every day, besides distributing about 350 units of dry rations in the neighborhood. In 1922 another kitchen was planned for Balashov.[121] Yet another kitchen opened in Moscow in July 1922

---

116. Sometimes the ARA/Moscow Collegium route was bypassed, as in the summer of 1922 when British Baptists cooperated with Save the Children and the Nansen Commission to buy and distribute grain and other supplies in Saratov and Melitopol (J. H. Rushbrooke, "Russian Famine and Baptist Relief," *The Baptist Times and Freeman* [5 May 1922] 280; "British Baptists and Relief in Russia" [27 October 1922] 697).

117. Fisher, *The Famine in Soviet Russia*, 163–164.

118 SBHLA, ABFMS Correspondence, P. Pavloff, Michael Timoshenko, N. Challing [Shal'e] (Moscow) to Rev. J. H. Rushbrooke (London), December 1921, 1; Slagel, "Organizing Feeding Operations," 209–10.

119 M. Timoshenko (Moscow) to P. I. Davidiuk, 3 February 1922, *Seiatel' istiny* (March 1922) 12; P. Pavlov (Moscow) to P. I. Davidiuk, 5 May 1922, *Seiatel' istiny* (July 1922) 12; N. Levandanto (Moscow) 19 August 1922, *Seiatel' istiny* (October 1922) 13.

120 SBHLA, The Historical Papers of Mrs. I. V. Neprash, "Zapis' No. 29," 10 May 1922.

121 SBHLA, W. O. Lewis Papers, H. E. Porter, "Additional Notes on Distribution thru A.R.A. in Russia, January–June 1922."

with at least three employees who were paid in rye flour.[122] In addition, the Baptist Union in Moscow fed "a few outside people, including children" in its own kitchen using groceries from ARA parcels.[123] Provision was also made for the Baptist orphanage at Balashov.[124]

Local church committees were a crucial element in distribution. They carried responsibility for requesting, allocating, and accounting for the aid they received both directly and from the center. First of all, the task involved keeping track of the number and needs of the people in their care. This was a complex task as church leaders died or became refugees themselves; one congregation might be absorbed into another as their numbers dwindled.[125] Once aid was allocated there was still the task of claiming it, and this could be the most difficult of all for committee members, involving long journeys in unheated boxcars full of typhus-carrying lice.[126] Mennonites in the Volga region formed caravans to travel to ARA warehouses that might be fifty miles away from their villages. Their horses were weak with starvation; blizzards could make travel impossible; there was always the danger of being robbed.[127] Distribution of food and clothing was also a committee matter. When international Baptist aid was focused on the Melitopol area (Ukraine) in July 1922, local committees carried out the food distribution there.[128] The Collegium of the Baptist Union gave specific instructions to the committee at the Moscow Baptist church concerning the way ARA food packages should be divided up to support seven church leaders for three months.[129] Concerning clothing, Dr. Everett Gill, European Representative of the Southern Baptist Convention Foreign Mission Board, recommended that the local famine committee chairman select "a sub-committee of Baptist women" to open and inventory the bales they had received. They would then prepare a list of those who were to receive clothing. Recipients were to sign their names on an order when they received their items. When the dis-

---

122 SBHLA, The Historical Papers of Mrs. I. V. Neprash, "Zapis No. 32," 28 June 1922, Item 170; "Zapis' No. 93," July 1922, Item 184.

123 SBHLA, W. O. Lewis Papers, H. E. Porter, "Additional Notes on Distribution thru A.R.A. in Russia, January-June 1922."

124 SBHLA, The Historical Papers of Mrs. I. V. Neprash, "Zapis' No. 23," 18 March 1922.

125 E. S. Ianchenko (Buzuluk, Samara), Seiatel' istiny (July 1922) 9–10.

126 Fisher, The Famine in Soviet Russia, 75.

127 A. J. Miller, "Unsealing the Closed Door," in Hiebert and Miller, Feeding the Hungry, 190–92.

128 "Foreign Mission Board Report," Southern Baptist Convention (1923), 122.

129 SBHLA, The Historical Papers of Mrs. I. V. Neprash, "Zapis' No. 30," 10 May 1922.

tribution was completed, a general receipt would be made out in triplicate and signed by the local committee chairman and the district ARA supervisor, to be filed with the ARA headquarters in Moscow, the Baptist Union, and the Southern Baptist Convention in Richmond, Virginia. Gill proudly claimed, "The plan combines simplicity and efficiency, and the distribution is made by the Baptists to Baptists and their neighbors and friends."[130] The system probably did work something like that, although perhaps not as smoothly as Gill envisioned. For one thing, the inventory alone was a daunting task. If an average bale contained four-hundred pieces of clothing,[131] it means that the 150 bales allotted to Saratov in 1922[132] possibly contained sixty thousand pieces to store, transport, and account for over a large geographical area. Also, committees might run afoul of the authorities. In 1923 a shipment of clothing and shoes sent by the American Baptists was turned over to Baptists in the Odessa area.[133] As soon as the members of the local committee set off with their load, they were detained by police.[134] Finally, disbursements of food and clothing had to be acknowledged either to the Baptist Union in Moscow or to other donors,[135] another complex task. In addition, the inevitable question arose as to whether and what kind of help should be given to those on the outskirts of the evangelical community, such as excommunicated church members or the non-believing children of church members. The Baptist Collegium left those decisions up to the local committees' discretion, but as a general rule recommended that only one-third of a church member's share be given to those who were more remotely connected to the community, and then only to the most needy.[136] One of their concerns was avoiding the charge that people joined the churches only for the sake of material aid.

130 Gill, "Naked and Ye Clothed Me," 13.

131. This estimate is based on the size of bales of clothing shipped by Mennonite Central Committee to Russia and Ukraine during the early 2000s.

132. General Review of the Year," *American Baptist Foreign Mission Society* (1922) 29–30; H. E. Porter, "In the Land of Bolshevism," *The Watchman-Examiner* (13 July 1922) 884.

133 SBHLA, Papers of W. O. Lewis, W. O. Lewis, "Report on the Distribution of Clothing in Russia. For Dr. Rushbrooke," 12 May 1923.

134 W. O. Lewis, "On the Way to Russia," *The Watchman-Examiner* (28 June 1923) 821.

135. Rushbrooke, "British Baptists," 697.

136 SBHLA, The Historical Papers of Mrs. I. V. Neprash, "Zapis' No. 16," 16 January 1922.

In summary, although the evangelicals had operated assistance funds since about 1884,[137] the 1921 to 1923 famine required more administrative skill, especially to coordinate aid from abroad. However it is unclear how efficiently the system actually functioned. Pleas from various famine areas continued to reach the outside world throughout 1922, suggesting that the centralized information and distribution structure could not be relied on for everything.[138] Of course, transportation and communication within Soviet Russia were so poor it is unlikely that any of the evangelical congregations counted on all the help they needed coming from abroad as channeled from the center. Certainly aid from the outside was a long time arriving. The Baptist World Alliance made initial contact with the Moscow Baptist Union in the fall of 1921,[139] but the first cash advance extended to the Baptists was only available in mid-January 1922, when Dr. Everett Gill came to Moscow.[140] Gill was prepared to help distribute a shipment of used clothing, but as P. V. Pavlov pointed out, "Yes, we need clothing, but what good will it do if our brethren die of starvation?" Indeed, while Gill was still in Moscow the Union was notified that a Baptist pastor had starved to death and others were reduced to eating their shoes. "One of the most blessed things I was ever permitted to do was to write out four thousand dollars' worth of food orders from Southern Baptists as a gift to our suffering brethren," Gill wrote.[141] The meeting minutes of the Collegium noted the receipt of US $4,000 from the United States and US $1,150 given on behalf of the British Baptists and directed, "Thank the foreign brethren, although compared with the need, it is not such significant help . . . ask them for further support."[142]

Consequently evangelicals endured by doing the same things others did to survive. People sold off or traded farm implements and furniture for food. They tore down wooden fences and grave markers to sell for firewood in order to buy something to eat. Many left their homes and joined the thousands of refugees on the roads in search of food. As a church member

---

137. Sinichkin, *Vse radi missii*, 79–85; Wardin, *On the Edge*, 146.

138 Kuz'ma I. Ziuzin and Mikhail N. Bronstein (Odessa), 13 February 1922, *Seiatel' istiny* (March 1922) 12.

139 See the numerous letters printed in *Seatel' istiny* March, July, and October 1922 issues.

140 SBHLA, W. O. Lewis Papers, H. E. Porter, "Additional Notes on Distribution thru A.R.A. in Russia, January-June 1922"; Gill, "Naked and Ye Clothed Me," 12.

141 Gill, "Naked and Ye Clothed Me," 13.

142 SBHLA, The Historical Papers of Mrs. I. V. Neprash, "Zapis' No. 16," 16 January 1922."

in Saratov guberniia wrote, "Most of us have gone."[143] Sometimes they carried along clothing and other items they hoped to sell or exchange for food. It was dangerous: starving robbers frequently waylaid starving refugees.[144] Others died at home. W. O. Lewis, the Special European Representative of the American Baptist Foreign Mission Society wrote: "In the village of Novo-Vasilievka the first of January last [1922], there were 6,000 inhabitants. Last winter 1,500 starved to death . . . One deacon in a Baptist church here told us that he had carried out on his own shoulders and buried 153 members of Baptist families who had died of starvation."[145] A church member wrote from Malye-Iagury, near Stavropol: "Our brothers are dying of hunger and we haven't the strength to stand at the pulpit to preach the gospel."[146] Yet many believers continued to try to help others during the famine, even though they were hungry themselves. It is impossible to survey the full extent of what was done without benefit of foreign aid, but there is evidence that many evangelicals gave faithfully and sacrificially, not only to their fellow church-members but to others as well. I. V. Neprash wrote that even in the famine zone some evangelicals fasted once a week, "in order to gather at least a few crumbs for the dying. Unbelievers come to them for help and say, 'We've been everywhere; we've asked everywhere; no one has given us anything. But you are believers, give something for the sake of Christ; don't let us perish.'"[147] A Mennonite family that began one day to give bread to everyone who asked gave away forty pieces in just a few hours.[148] Some churches served as sanctuaries for refugees who had left home in search of food. At a prayer house in Samara:

> deaconess Praskovia Ivanovna Kolesnikova is burdened with masses of the starving, the elderly, widows with children left behind after the death of the breadwinner. They sleep on the floor . . . The congregation can't feed them of course; members of the congregation who don't have enough for themselves and their children gather up scant offerings.[149]

143. *Seiatel' istiny* (July 1922) 10.

144 W. O. Lewis, "Famine Conditions in Russia," *The Watchman-Examiner* (28 December 1922) 1686; Arthur Slagel, "Organizing Feeding Operations," 207.

145 W. O. Lewis, "Famine Conditions in Russia," *The Baptist* (30 December 1922) 1496.

146 V. Savel'ev (Malye Iagury village, Stavropol guberniia), *Seiatel' istiny* (July 1922) 9.

147 I. Neprash, "Vopl' iz Samary" (A cry from Samara), *Seiatel' istiny* (March 1922) 15.

148 Arthur Slagel, "Organizing Feeding Operations," 207.

149 P. Chekmarev (Samara) to I. Neprash, 16 January 1922, quoted in I. Neprash,

In 1922 the Evangelical Christian journal *Utrenniaia zvezda* listed the addresses of relatively well-off congregations that were able to accommodate refugees from the famine zones (with the stipulation that they write ahead!).[150] With few exceptions, the addresses were far away from the worst famine areas and certainly would have been difficult to reach considering the hardship, unreliability, and danger of travel. Yet the sanctuary offer must have rescued at least a few because the next journal issue contains a letter from distant Smolensk guberniia that reported, "Concerning the starving brothers—we put up the families that arrived and the last Petrograd group among believing families. We would be happy to receive other brothers and sisters and their families. We will divide the bread we have with everyone."[151] Some churches sent packages of supplies to other churches or individuals in need.[152] In Perm' guberniia a Baptist received such a package prepared by a congregation in Kursk and forwarded through Moscow. When he went to pick it up, a postal worker made a little speech to the bystanders:

> Look here, comrades, lots of you are hungry or well-fed; but which one of you well-fed ones helped someone who was hungry? I know that no one has helped his friend because he's afraid to go hungry himself. But look what that Baptist Union does. They live in Moscow and they see that their Christian brother here is hungry and they help him.[153]

Several believers conducted an evangelistic trip in the Viatka area, the northernmost region of the Volga famine zone, sometime before summer 1922. When they saw how people were suffering, they sold their own clothing to buy bread before they began preaching.[154] Aid workers serving with American Mennonite Relief found a group of Mennonite villages in Nepliuev (Ukraine) where a committee had organized its own relief kitchen where those who still had food fed those who had none.[155] Others from the region around Petrograd held a meeting in a leper colony where they also

---

"Vopl' iz Samary," *Seiatel' istiny* (March 1922) 13.

150 *Utrenniaia zvezda* Nos.1–2 (January-February 1922) 1–2.

151 D. Poliachenkov (El'na, Smolensk guberniia), *Utrenniaia zvezda,* Nos. 3-45 (March-April-May 1922) 10.

152 *Seiatel' istiny* (July 1922) 10.

153 Ibid.

154 *Utrenniaia zvezda,* Nos. 3–4–5 (March–April–May 1922) 1–2

155 Arthur Slagel, "Visualizing Famine Conditions," in Hiebert and Miller *Feeding the Hungry,* 243.

distributed eighteen puds (about 650 pounds) of potatoes that had somehow been collected by the women in their church.[156]

Thus, the evangelicals did what they could to keep themselves and others alive. Yet, a 1922 article in *Utrenniaia zvezda* pointed out that even if all their measures—taking in refugees, sending food packages, and seeking and coordinating help from abroad—were successful, they would be useless if God did not intervene.[157] Even as they helped the hungry, the evangelicals were convinced that their true contribution during the famine was spiritual in nature. Faith in Christ, they believed, "gives a person the ability to endure the most awful deprivations and suffering and . . . helps him to maintain a firm faith in the One who creates and sustains everything even in the difficult, critical moments of life."[158] It was understood that preaching the gospel eased "spiritual famine"—depression, despair, cruelty, and indifference—to which believers also succumbed. "Soul-sick" is the way Arthur Slagel, a worker with American Mennonite Relief, described the Mennonites in Ukraine.[159] Still, the letters that reached Moscow, Petrograd, and the Slavic evangelical community abroad from Christians in the famine areas are remarkable for their humility and faith, as well as for the presence of mind they demonstrate on the part of writers who had somehow to secure paper, ink, and a method of sending mail. Of course, the famine necessarily hindered church work in the affected areas.[160] Yet Baptists in Saratov, in the middle of the Volga famine zone, at least occasionally held meetings in a public auditorium that attracted several hundred people at a time.[161] Church workers in Kyiv and Odessa reported the high price of food, the numbers of people dying, and their desperate need of clothes and shoes, but added that they needed Bibles, Gospels, and hymnals because so many people were turning to the Lord.[162] "The meetings are overflowing with thirsty souls, there are many repentant sinners, in many places there are new congregations being

---

156 "Iz Petrogradskoi guberniia" (From Petrograd guberniia), *Utrenniaia zvezda*, Nos. 3–4–5 (March–April–May 1922) 9.

157 *Utrenniaia zvezda*, Nos. 1–2 (January–February 1922) 1–2.

158. Ibid., 1.

159 Arthur Slagel, "Visualizing Famine Conditions," 223–25.

160 F. A. Bashkov (Ekaterinoslav) to P. Bartkov, 14 August 1922, *Seiatel' istiny* (October 1922) 13.

161 H. E. Porter, "In the Land of Bolshevism," *The Watchman-Examiner* (13 July 1922) 885.

162 Avraam Pritskiy (Kiev) to P. I. Davidiuk, 25 February 1922; the Odessa Russian congregation of Evangelical Christians-Baptists (Odessa) 13 February 1922, *Seiatel' istiny* (March 1922) 12.

formed," wrote P. V. Pavlov from Moscow.¹⁶³ In the winter of 1921 to 1922 two evangelists from Tsaritsyn traveled on foot through an area where they preached to as many as one thousand at a time.¹⁶⁴ As had been their practice since the early days of their movement, during the famine evangelicals gave particular attention to sustaining preachers and other church workers. The Second Petrograd Oblast' Congress of Evangelical Christians held on 24 February 1922 collected enough subscriptions in both money and food to support its four full-time evangelists until August.¹⁶⁵ F. A. Bashkov wrote that packages from abroad had been received in Ekaterinoslav (present-day Dnepropetrovsk) and divided among "needy workers in the churches of Christ."¹⁶⁶ Again, not all the help come from outside the country. A congregation where the people already had been eating bark for two months at first decided that they could not possibly give any support to the Evangelical Christian Union although they would pray fervently that the work of God would increase. But they changed their minds: "we discussed it a lot and somehow we couldn't bring ourselves not to participate, so little by little we scraped up twenty-five thousand [rubles] that we are sending with great joy for the growth of the activity of the Union."¹⁶⁷ Thus, the evangelicals' commitment to mutual aid and to supporting preachers, in particular, remained an important part of their practice of compassionate ministry even during the rigors of the famine.

However, famine relief was not always a straightforward matter for the Russian evangelicals: "Any large efforts to furnish food and clothing to suffering multitudes are always attended by perplexing problems and a degree of moral hazard."¹⁶⁸ In particular, receiving and distributing famine relief added to the tension between Baptists and Evangelical Christians. P. D. Steeves maintains that, "Baptists limited their aid to fellow Baptists, while Evangelical Christians were more open. As a result the Baptists accused them of distributing aid 'in order to win adherents to their union.'"¹⁶⁹ While

---

163 P. V. Pavlov (Moscow) to P. I. Davidiuk, 5 May 1922, *Seiatel' istiny* (July 1922) 12.

164 "Iz Tsaritsyna" (From Tsaritsyn), *Utrenniaia zvezda* Nos. 3–4–5 (March–April–May 1922) 9.

165 *Utrenniaia zvezda*, Nos. 1–2 (January–February 1922) 7.

166 F. A. Bashkov to Pavel Bartkov, 14 August 1922, *Seiatel' istiny* (October 1922) 13.

167 "Tugai oblast,'" 5 December 1921, *Utrenniaia zvezda*, Nos. 3–4–5 (March–April–May 1922) 10.

168 "General Review of the Year," American Baptist Foreign Mission Society (1922) 25.

169. Steeves, "The Russian Baptist Union," 178.

the statement is not inaccurate, the situation is somewhat more complex. True, the connection to Pomgol suggests more "openness" in sharing aid on the part of Evangelical Christians. However, much of the assistance the Baptist Union shared came through ARA channels, which required contributing a certain percentage for ARA committees and programs, which were intended to reach all sectors of the suffering population.[170] Thus, a consignment of used clothing sent to Odessa in 1923 by the American Baptists was shared with the university medical department, the Roman Catholic and Orthodox communities, orphans, and some Italians stranded in the city.[171] That is, it could be argued that the Baptists' contribution to the needs of the wider society was automatically taken care of by the mechanism of which they were a part. However, it could not be ignored that the focus of international Baptist famine work was in Moscow, not Petrograd, the former capital where the Evangelical Christian Union was still located. It was almost inevitable that the Evangelical Christian leadership would feel they were being bypassed. Eventually there was enough concern about the level of cooperation between the two unions that J. H. Rushbrooke called a meeting between them in Moscow in February 1923.[172] By that time the need for mass feeding operations was lessening. However, there was hope that Russian evangelicals and their supporters abroad would be able to continue relief work and also engage in reconstruction and development projects.[173] In addition to outlining the basis for fair cooperation between the two bodies, it was also necessary to lay the groundwork for possible future service opportunities. Certainly from the point of view of the Baptist World Alliance, if they were to continue working within Soviet Russia it was important to have a reliable, functional local partner organization. The agreement (in English), signed by P. V. Pavlov and I. S. Prokhanov, established a Joint Relief Commission. Its structure was intended to circumvent the complaints the two evangelical church unions had concerning one another's relief work and also guarantee that future efforts would be carried out in accordance with the desires of its contributors, above all.[174] As W. O. Lewis traveled around the country in 1923, following up on the allocation of used clothing sent by the American Baptists, he reported on the level of cooperation between Evangelical Christians and Baptists in nine different

170. Fisher, *The Famine in Soviet Russia*, 62.

171. SBHLA, Papers of W. O. Lewis, W. O. Lewis, "Report on the Distribution of Clothing in Russia. For Dr. Rushbrooke," (12 May 1923), 2.

172 W. O. Lewis, "The Ship that Rushed to Russia," *Missions* (September 1923) 470.

173 J. H. Rushbrooke, "The Russian Need: The Main Facts," *The Watchman-Examiner* (2 November 1922) 1396.

174 SBHLA, W. O. Lewis Papers, "Agreement," (Moscow) 8 February 1923.

places and found it adequate.¹⁷⁵ However, a letter of complaint dated August 1923 from an angry Evangelical Christian church member in Melitopol' to I. S. Prokhanov accused the local Baptists of creating a "bacchanalia" in the matter of distributing the very clothing Lewis was checking on.¹⁷⁶ Doubtless much depended on the specifics of each local situation.

However, the days of international cooperation only lasted a few years longer. Seeing that agricultural reconstruction was essential, Mennonites and Baptists abroad shipped Fordson tractors and Oliver gang ploughs to Russia in 1922 and 1923, respectively.¹⁷⁷ Efforts were also made to work with local believers to improve livestock and stimulate local clothing manufacture.¹⁷⁸ However, these projects were difficult to manage and financial support from abroad was dwindling.¹⁷⁹ By the summer of 1922 there was promise of a good harvest and much controversy ensued when the Soviet government began exporting grain abroad at the same time that grain was being brought in to feed the hungry.¹⁸⁰ By summer 1923 the relationship between the ARA and the Soviet government was officially dissolved.¹⁸¹ In 1924 J. H. Rushbrooke turned over the tractors to the Nansen Commission. Bratskaia pomoshch (Fraternal help), a Russian Baptist credit union established by P. V. Pavlov in 1922,¹⁸² was to act as intermediary between the Nansen group and local farmers, with the stipulation that if the Nansen enterprise was liquidated, the tractors would be transferred to the Baptist cooperative.¹⁸³ In 1926 J. H. Rushbrooke was still trying to collect debts incurred by the

---

175 SBHLA, W. O. Lewis Papers, W. O. Lewis, "Report on the Distribution of Clothing in Russia," May 1923.

176 AUCEC-B archives, drawer 2, folder 1, F. Sherenev to I. S. Prokhanov, 25 August 1923.

177. Hiebert and Miller, *Feeding the Hungry*, 293–307; J. H. Rushbrooke, "Russia," *The Baptist Times and Freeman* (29 September 1922) 621; SBHLA, ABFMS Correspondence, 1920–1929, J. H. Rushbrooke, "Report of the Baptist Commissioner for Europe," October 1923, 3.

178. Hiebert and Miller, *Feeding the Hungry*, 307–22; SBHLA, ABFMS Correspondence, J. H. Rushbrooke, "European Relief. Report of the Baptist Commissioner for Europe for the Quarter ended 30th September 1924," 2; "To the Members of the Committee of Supervision," 14 January 1925, 2–3.

179 "General Review of the Year," American Baptist Foreign Mission Society, (1923) 25.

180. Patenaude, *The Big Show*, 186–92.

181. Ibid., 194–96.

182. Coleman, *Russian Baptists*, 176.

183 SBHLA, ABFMS Correspondence, J. H. Rushbrooke, "European Relief. Report of the Baptist Commissioner for Europe for the Half-year Ending 1st December 1923."

Nansen Commission and some Baptist business initiatives.[184] In short, the transition from relief to development was not sustained.

CONCLUSION

Beginning with the First World War, Russian evangelicals, along with the rest of Europe, encountered human suffering on an undreamed of scale. Although their efforts to help were dwarfed by the immensity of the need, they were nevertheless of the same character as evangelical compassionate ministry practiced in the past. Evangelicals readily took part in caring for the wounded, refugees, orphans, and the starving during an era of great upheaval. No statistics are available concerning the number of people evangelicals may have helped to save during the famine. The American Relief Administration, however, is credited with keeping "millions" from starvation during the 1921 to 1923 famine and the Russian evangelicals certainly hold at least a small place in that undertaking.[185] Even under threat of starvation, many of them continued to give and serve sacrificially. At the center the Baptist Union and the Evangelical Christian Union worked to sustain reliable structures for receiving and directing aid which certainly surpassed the level of administrative sophistication ever required by the evangelicals before. New circumstances required new measures, and it can be said that the evangelicals tried to adapt to the challenges they faced. In the process, they demonstrated the same commitment to evangelism and compassionate ministry that characterized the Russian movement from the beginning.

---

184 SBHLA, ABFMS Correspondence, J. H. Rushbrooke, "Report of the Baptist Commissioner for Europe to the Committee of Supervision for the Half-year ended 31st December 1926," 28 January 1927.

185. Volkogonov, *Lenin*, 345; Patenaude, *The Big Show*, 196–99.

6

Christian Economic Communities—
I. S. Prokhanov

THE PREVIOUS CHAPTER OUTLINED the years of war and revolution, describing the ways in which those tumultuous events affected compassionate ministry among Russian evangelicals. This chapter will focus on the later phase of the Russian evangelicals' Golden Age, the 1920s, and particularly on another leader, I. S. Prokhanov, and one of his approaches to compassion. Before World War I, Prokhanov, like William Fetler, was interested in reaching the poorest members of urban society, along the lines of the Salvation Army.[1] Young people from the churches of the Evangelical Christian Union of which Prokhanov was president were active in rescue ministry.[2] Prokhanov is also remembered for his evangelistic work among students, organizing a young people's association similar to the YMCA during the first years of religious tolerance.[3] However, one of Prokhanov's significant areas of interest during the 1920s was the active promotion of Christian economic communities. Prokhanov saw such communities—helped along by early experiments in Soviet economic policy—as a way of realizing the description of the Jerusalem church in the Book of Acts: "All the believers

---

1. I[van] S[tepanovich] P[rokhanov], "O poezdke br. F. M. Trosnova v" Finliandiiu" (On brother F. M. Trosnov's trip to Finland), *Iunyi khristianin* 1 (1909) 1.

2. A. I. Kareva, "Moi vospominaniia" (My recollections), in Karetnikova, *Al'manakh, vypusk 2,* 176, 183–84.

3 I[van] S[tepanovich], "Iz zhizni kruzhkov khristianskoi molodezhi i vchastnosti—kruzhkov, stremiashchikhsia k dobru i pravde" (From the life of Christian youth groups and particularly of groups striving for goodness and truth), *Molodoi vinogradnik* 6 (1909) 2–11; *Molodoi vinogradnik* 11 (1909) 5–7; Prokhanoff, *Cauldron,* 189–206.

were together and had everything in common. Selling their possessions and goods, they gave to anyone who had need" (Acts 2:44–45) and "There were no needy persons among them. For from time to time those who owned land or houses sold them, brought the money from the sales and put it at the apostles' feet, and it was distributed to anyone as he had need" (Acts 4:34–35). Prokhanov believed that communal living would provide an all-encompassing solution to poverty among community members, as well as serve as a means of Christian witness and thereby ultimately transform all of society. Others shared Prokhanov's convictions, but he articulated the most comprehensive program for the organization of economic communities.

RUSSIAN EVANGELICALS AND THE NEP

O. Iu. Redkina has carried out an extensive assessment of the scores of agricultural communes and labor cooperatives that were set up across Soviet Russia by evangelicals during the 1920s. Hundreds more were organized by Old Believers, Tolstoyans, Orthodox, and other groups.[4] V. A. Popov states that by 1924 the Baptist Union alone had formed twenty-five agricultural communes, each composed of about twenty-five family groups in twelve different guberniias.[5] The background for the surge in communal living and cooperative labor in general was the New Economic Policy (NEP) introduced by the Soviet government at about the same time that the famine began in 1921. After seven years of destruction due to war and revolution, the Bolsheviks realized that they needed to introduce measures to rebuild agriculture and industry. To encourage farming, grain requisitions were abolished and after a fixed tax in kind was paid, peasants were entitled to market their surplus. Restrictions were also lifted on industry and "bourgeois" industrial managers, recast as "experts," were allowed to return to their pre-revolution employment. Private trade and production reappeared on the Russian economic scene.[6] Bolshevik party leader V. I. Lenin framed the NEP as a necessary "breathing space" rather than a setback for the revolution, as his critics feared.[7] With different theorists acting on differing interpretations of the way the revolution could be expected to work itself

---

4. Redkina, *Sel'skokhoziaistvennye religioznye trudovye kollektivy*.

5. V. A. Popov, "Khristianskie kommuny I. S. Prokhanova i gorod Solntsa" (Christian communes of I. S. Prokhanov and the City of the Sun), in Beliakova and Sinichkin, *105 let legalizatsii russkogo baptizma*, 136.

6. William G. Rosenberg, "Introduction: NEP Russia as a 'Transitional' Society," in Fitzpatrick et al, *Russia in the Era of NEP*, 1–6.

7. Patenaude, *The Big Show*, 106–107.

out, the 1920s proved to be a rather erratic time of experimentation in many spheres.

The evangelicals welcomed the NEP, indeed the revolution as a whole, as an opportunity to demonstrate what Christians could do, promoting the "revolution of the spirit,"[8] a non-violent undertaking which Prokhanov declared to be the essential prerequisite for the success of any political program: "to overthrow sin and give the first place to God in every heart."[9] The evangelicals experienced distinct benefits during the 1920s, including marked numerical growth. While exact statistics are lacking, Heather J. Coleman estimates that the Baptists and Evangelical Christians taken together probably at least tripled their 1912 count of 114,652, for a total of over 340,000 members by the end of the decade. Other estimates claim anywhere from 200,000 to 500,000 members, which, including family members and occasional attendees, could signify about one million people connected in some way with evangelical congregations.[10] During the early Soviet years, the evangelicals were to some extent accommodated by the Bolsheviks as people who had suffered under the tsars. In particular, Vladimir Dmitrievich Bonch-Bruevich (1873–1955), an associate of V. I. Lenin, regarded them as potential revolutionary material and intervened on their behalf from time to time.[11] At first, the new Soviet government focused its attacks on the Orthodox Church. In January 1918 a decree separated church and state, which had the most drastic consequences for the Orthodox. In theory, the evangelicals were in agreement with the separation of church and state, even as the decree also caused problems for them by prohibiting religious instruction for children and youth and depriving them of legal status, which made it difficult to hold property.[12] Remarkably, even as the Civil War raged, additional legislation in January 1919 permitted release from military service on religious grounds.[13] That policy continued until the mid-1930s,[14] although in 1923 the government demanded a definite renunciation of pacifism on the part of evangelicals.[15] In fact, by 1922 it was clear

8. P[avel] V[asilievich] P[avlov], "Politicheskiia trebovaniia baptistov" (Political demands of Baptists), *Slovo istiny,* 1 (May 1917) 2–3.

9. Prokhanoff, *Cauldron,* 172, 174.

10. Coleman, *Russian Baptists,* 162–63.

11. Prokhanoff, *Cauldron,* 175–76; Coleman, *Russian Baptists,* 158–59, 182.

12. Coleman, *Russian Baptists,* 156, 158.

13. Ibid., 155–56, 180–81.

14. Guy F. Hershberger, Albert N. Keim and Hanspeter Jecker, "Conscientious Objection," *Global Anabaptist Mennonite Encyclopedia Online.* 1990, http://gameo.org/index.php?title=Conscientious_Objection&oldid=103534.

15. Coleman, *Russian Baptists,* 191–97.

that government policy was no longer simply against Orthodoxy, but that it intended to discard religion itself.[16] In short, despite having certain advantages, the evangelicals quickly experienced the push-pull effect of living in a state that, while temporarily tolerating them, ultimately intended to abolish religion altogether. In fact, even as the movement expanded throughout the 1920s, evangelicals endured intermittent arrests, imprisonments, fines, beatings, and other setbacks.[17] Help for believers in prison continued to be part of their compassionate ministry profile.[18] Prokhanov published a small volume listing all the new laws and amendments concerning religion, which assisted believers in their legal negotiations with the authorities.[19]

The trend of the entire decade was toward the dismantling of all but government-sponsored organizations.[20] Of course, this affected private and faith-based compassionate institutions whose functions were taken over by the state. Initially, the demands of coping with overwhelming numbers of people in need, for example the thousands of children who had been orphaned and made homeless by war, disease, and famine, forced temporary cooperation between the Bolsheviks and private charities, even as the former decried "bourgeois philanthropy" and "voluntarism."[21] But the alliance was short-lived. Regarding children, the government set up hundreds of specialized facilities to house and train orphans during the 1920s.[22] In reality, this process meant the commandeering or closing of existing religiously-based children's institutions, including those established by evangelicals.[23] In short, by the mid-1920s compassionate ministry as the evangelicals had

---

16. Redkina, *Sel'skokhoziaistvennye religioznye trudovye kollektivy*, 525; Coleman, *Russian Baptists*, 190. An excellent, detailed study of Soviet atheism is Daniel Peris, *Storming the Heavens*.

17. A few examples include Prokhanoff, *Cauldron*, 189–98, 217–25; de Mayer, *Adventures with God*, 191–221; Sevast'ianov, "Pleiada sluzhitelelei," 5; Coleman, *Russian Baptists*, 156.

18. A. Mazina, "Pervyi prazdnik sester obshchin Kievskogo otdela V.S.E.Kh." (The first celebration of the sisters of the Kiev department of VSEKh congregations), *Bratskii listok* 3 (1926) 56–57.

19. Prokhanoff, *Cauldron*, 187.

20. Coleman, *Russian Baptists*, 197.

21. Kelly, *Children's World*, 196–97.

22. "Organizatsiia raboty s besprizornymi det'mi v 1920-e gody" (The organization of work with unsupervised children in the 1920s), http://miloserdie.ru/index.php?ss=2&s=12&id=55; Kelly, *Children's World*, 206–7.

23. SBHLA, The Historical Papers of Mrs. I. V. Neprash, "Zapis' No. 23, Zasedanie Kollegii Vserossiiskogo Soiuza" (Notation No. 23 of the meeting of the Collegium of the All-Russian Union), 18 March 1922; Toews, *Mennonite Martyrs*, 93–94; Kelly, *Children's World*, 196–97; see also Saloff-Astakhoff, *Little Lame Walter* and *Real Russia*, 71–72.

practiced it in the past was no longer viable. However, Prokhanov and others believed that evangelicals could still minister to human need by cooperating with certain aspects of the state's program, particularly the organization of economic communities. The evangelicals presented themselves as "naturals" for the new Soviet society, who were already practicing its ideals of equality, brotherhood, and justice. In a 1925 article P. V. Ivanov-Klyshnikov (son of V. V. Ivanov) described Baptists as a "hidden labor collective" and therefore well suited to working and living cooperatively because that had already been their way of life for decades, not on the basis of a mere legal charter, but on the basis of God's law.[24] In addition, according to Prokhanov, only evangelicals possessed the necessary spiritual power to live communally: "Only people who are 'one in heart and soul' and who are embraced by the flame of the Spirit of God can make this special life a reality."[25]

RUSSIAN EVANGELICALS AND ECONOMIC COMMUNITIES

Certainly by the time of the revolution Russian evangelicals already had experience with communes and cooperatives, or at least had given the subject serious thought. They were motivated both by spiritual expression and self-preservation. As early as 1870, Stundist leader Ivan Riaboshapka appealed to P. E. Kotsebu, governor of New Russia, for permission to form a new community of twenty families on the "free steppes," "according to the model of the first apostolic church of Christ."[26] Riaboshapka expressed a religious motivation for the request, which was, incidentally, denied. However, another likely reason for seeking land was the persecution Riaboshapka and his fellow believers were experiencing at the hands of their Orthodox neighbors.[27] Religious idealism and avoidance of persecution were also the reasons that inspired I. S. Prokhanov and a like-minded group to form an agricultural community in Crimea for several months in 1894.[28] Moreover,

---

24. P. V. Ivanov-Klyshnikov, "Nashi obshchiny, kak estestvennye kollektivy" (Our congregations as natural collectives), *Baptist* 1 (1925)14.

25. I. S. Prokhanov, *Evangel'skoe khristianstvo i sotsial'nyi vopros* (Evangelical Christianity and the social question), quoted by Popov, "Evangel'skie trudovye arteli" 28.

26 VSEKh-B, *Istoriia*, 111–15.

27. Based on a conversation with Pavel Nikolaevich Shapoval, pastor of the Baptist church in Pomoshchnoe, Kirovograd oblast,' Ukraine, 9 November 2012. The congregation in Pomoshchnoe is one of several in the area that were founded through Riaboshapka's preaching.

28 Prokhanoff, *Cauldron*, 87.

Russian evangelicals regarded communal living as a means of Christian witness. In 1908 *Baptist* published an article about a Romanian Baptist congregation that had recently started a farm. Their consistent Christian example in both word and deed proved so attractive to their neighbors that very quickly fifteen new people wished to be baptized—an appealing idea for the Russians.[29] Employment for believers was another motivation for forming economic communities. In 1911 V. V. Ivanov encouraged congregations to look after their own members by organizing agricultural or manufacturing work and sharing out the profits to provide a livelihood for those in need.[30] That such cooperative efforts enjoyed some success is indicated by the experience of N. Ia. Iakovlev, who set up a macaroni and baked goods factory in Moscow in 1907 and sold shares to fellow evangelicals. Two years later Iakovlev had fifty-three employees and twenty-five shareholders; his stated purpose was to provide employment for "brothers" and support the mission of the church.[31] Yet another motivation for communal activity was the establishment and support of evangelical institutions. In 1909 *Bratskii listok* presented the possibility of setting up a farming community near Kharkiv under the leadership of Arkadii Egorovich Alekhin.[32] Alekhin was identified as an "experienced brother" who proposed the purchase of an entire settlement (*khutor*) where up to twenty families could make a living raising grain, berries, cattle, and also doing some manufacturing, as there were work rooms and a brick factory available. In addition, Alekhin suggested that a school be set up, as well as a shelter for children "of the brotherhood," that is, orphaned or disadvantaged children from evangelical families. The requirements for entering into the proposed project included "communal feelings," a willingness to work, and capital in the amount of 1,500 rubles per family.[33] It is not known whether anything ever came of this scheme,[34] or the extent to which evangelicals were involved in similar efforts prior to the revolution. However it is clear that from the early days of their movement, Russian evangelicals were attracted to the image of the Jerusa-

---

29. *Baptist* 2 (February 1908) 23.

30. V. V. Ivanov, "Polozhenie Baptistov" (The situation of Baptists), *Baptist* 9 (23 February 1911) 70.

31. "Bratskoe predpriatie: 'Mamre'" (Fraternal enterprise: Mamre), *Bratskii listok* 6 (1909) 4.

32. *Bratskii listok* 5 (May 1909) 1–2.

33 "O poselenii veruiushchikh v Sibiri" (On the settling of believers in Siberia), *Bratskii listok* 4 (April 1909) 10–13.

34. This project may be identified with one that was discouraged by D. I. Mazaev and led to a church split with fifteen Baptists joining the Evangelical Christian Union; see VSEKh-B, *Istoriia*, 490.

lem church in Acts 2, and were at least interested in cooperative economic schemes to support their own membership and institutions and serve as a means of witness.

By 1921 when a special committee attached to the People's Commissariat for Agriculture, abbreviated as Narkomzem, invited sectarians and Old Believers to settle on newly nationalized lands,[35] the evangelicals responded with enthusiasm, but they were already ahead of the program. Almost immediately after the February Revolution, an agricultural colony with a shelter for children and the elderly was organized on the property of F. S. Savel'ev (1863–1947) near Moscow, although it is not known how long the community continued to exist.[36] Possibly it represented an effort to save lives by retreating to the countryside because of the desperate food shortages in the cities in the years immediately after the revolution.[37] Very early, however, Prokhanov envisioned a long-term role for communal living. In 1918 he published a brochure entitled *Evangel'skoe khristianstvo i sotsial'nyi vopros* (Evangelical Christianity and the social question), that outlined a pattern for the development of economic communities.[38] By 1919 evangelicals were discussing the formation of communes at regional congresses and the Gefsimaniia (Gethsemane) community in Tver' guberniia had already been organized.[39] In 1920 the representative of a Petrograd Baptist congregation (perhaps Dom Evangeliia, although that is not specified), V. G. Melis, proposed to the Council of People's Commissars that a network of artels be opened nationwide that would be called "Christian Labor." They would engage in various enterprises such as providing fuel and foodstuffs, the operation of small-scale repair, carpentry, and metal-working shops, and other agricultural and cottage industries, the proceeds of which would be used to finance the support of shelters and hospitals they planned to operate.[40] Indeed, scores of evangelical cooperatives did appear throughout the country, operating dining rooms and bakeries, building houses, repairing agricultural equipment, making shoes, and engaging in many other activities.[41]

---

35 GARF, f. 1235, op. 58, d. 50, l. 235–236, "K sektantam i staroobriadtsam, zhivushchim v Rossii i za granitsei" (To the sectarians and Old Believers living in Russia and abroad), quoted by Grachev, *Studencheskie gody*, 50.

36. Redkina, *Sel'skokhoziaistvennye religioznye trudovye kollektivy*, 83, 143–44, 161, 639; V. M. Khorev, "Istoriia Krasnovorotskogo dvizheniia."

37. Nikol'skaia, *Russkii protestantizm*, 70.

38. Popov, "Evangel'skie trudovye arteli," 28; Redkina, *Sel'skokhoziaistvennye religioznye trudovye kollektivy*, 126.

39. VSEKhB, *Istoriia*, 190.

40. Redkina, *Sel'skokhoziaistvennye religioznye trudovye kollektivy*, 129.

41. Popov, "Evangel'skie trudovye arteli," 27; Coleman, *Russian Baptists*, 175–76;

In 1922 a credit union, *Bratskaia pomoshch* (Fraternal help), was founded by P. V. Pavlov from the Baptist Union office in Moscow, with at least six other offices across the country, to assist these many enterprises.[42] In other words, communes and cooperative labor were spontaneously and immediately embraced by the evangelicals after the revolution. Especially at first, they represented a way for religious groups to survive in a turbulent time.[43] They also provided a basis for compassionate service in the form of shelter and support to vulnerable members. At the same time, many evangelicals, including Prokhanov, also saw successful communes as a way of witness, of embodying Christian principles. It was a distinct contribution that believing people could make to the building of a new society.[44]

PROKHANOV AND CHRISTIAN ECONOMIC COMMUNITIES

Sofia Liven's youthful impression of Prokhanov was that he was a leader who encouraged Christians to participate actively in society.[45] Throughout his life he demonstrated a commitment both to Christian unity across confessional lines and to Christian involvement in social issues. He grew up in a Molokan family in Vladikavkaz. His father, Stepan Antonovich, joined the Baptists, and Prokhanov himself was baptized in January 1887.[46] From 1888 to 1893 he studied in St. Petersburg at the Institute of Technology. During this time he related to the semi-underground evangelical circles in the capital.[47] To connect and inform the national evangelical community he published several journals—first the underground journal *Beseda* (The conversation, 1889), then *Khristianin* (1906) modeled on the non-denominational British journal *The Christian*,[48] and in 1910 the more political *Utrenniaia zvezda* (Morning star).[49] Prokhanov was inspired by the Evangelical Alliance[50] and

---

Redkina, *Sel'skokhoziaistvennye religioznye trudovye kollektivy*, 387.

42. Popov, "Evangel'skie trudovye arteli," 27; Coleman, *Russian Baptists*, 176.

43. Wesson, *Soviet Communes*, 74–75; Redkina, *Sel'skokhoziaistvennye religioznye trudovye kollektivy*, 114–15.

44. Redkina, *Sel'skokhoziaistvennye religioznye trudovye kollektivy*, 133.

45. Liven, *Dukhovnoe probuzhdenie*, 82–83.

46 Prokhanoff, *Cauldron*, 43–44.

47. Popov, *I. S. Prokhanov*, 21–23.

48 Puzynin, *The Tradition of the Gospel Christians*, 153.

49 Sinichkin, *Vse radi missii*, 163–64.

50. For a detailed history of the Evangelical Alliance, see Randall and Hilborn, *One Body in Christ*.

its vision of unity and cooperation.⁵¹ While in England in 1896 Prokhanov gave a speech at the fiftieth anniversary of the Alliance's founding.⁵² In 1908, he established an Evangelical Union in Russia in an attempt to bring together different kinds of evangelically-minded individuals in an Alliance-like organization.⁵³ He reached beyond evangelical circles to interact with reform-minded Orthodox in the early 1920s.⁵⁴ Prokhanov also participated in the organization of Christian political parties, once in 1905 (Union of Freedom, Truth, and Peace) and again in 1917 (Christian Democratic Party "Resurrection").⁵⁵ Both efforts only lasted for about a year, but the attempt again underlines Prokhanov's interest in Christian participation in the public sphere.

Prokhanov had many historical models to draw on as his ideas on communal living developed. The most familiar form of communal life in Russia was the ancient peasant *mir*, which might consist of anywhere from several dozen to a thousand households banded together to work the land. In the nineteenth century political theorists worked with the idea of the peasant commune as a natural instrument of social transformation. Conservative theorists idealized it: "[They] believed that the Russian peasant with his life firmly based on Russian Orthodox Christianity and the village commune, was destined to rejuvenate the world."⁵⁶ Radical Populist thinkers regarded the peasant commune as a means of carrying Russia into a prosperous and just future, completely bypassing industrialized capitalism. Broadly speaking, Populism envisioned an entirely communal society where people lived freely and equally as brothers.⁵⁷ One of the main theorists of the Populist movement was the writer and philosopher Nikolai Gavrilovich Chernyshevskii (1828–1889), whose 1863 novel *Chto delat'?* (What is to be done?) became a revolutionary classic and is one of the books Prokhanov remembered as being of importance to him in his youth.⁵⁸

Of course, Prokhanov grew up in the Molokan community and was familiar with their strong ethic of mutual support. Besides monastic

---

51. Nichols, *Russian Evangelical Spirituality*, 121–24, 243.

52. Arnold, *Jubilee of the Evangelical Alliance*, 310–13.

53. Prokhanoff, *Cauldron*, 149–52; for more analysis of the Evangelical Union in Russia, see Kahle, *Evangel'skie khristiane v Rossii i Sovetskom soiuze*, 102–106.

54. Prokhanoff, *Cauldron*, 210–16.

55. Vladimir A. Popov, "Evangel'skoe dvizhenie v Rossii i politicheskie partii" (The evangelical movement in Russia and political parties), in Raber and Penner, *History and Mission in Europe*, 163, 166.

56. Lawrence, *A History of Russia*, 98–99.

57. Wesson, *Soviet Communes*, 52–53.

58. Prokhanoff, *Cauldron*, 36.

communities, it was typical for religious groups in Russia, such as Old Believers, Dukhobors, Molokans, and others to live in close cooperation with one another, if not always in formal communes. In 1898 while living abroad, Prokhanov was called on to aid a group of Dukhobors stranded in Cyprus by an epidemic while in the process of immigrating to Canada. Prokhanov improved the ventilation and sanitation of the barracks where they were living before he himself succumbed to the disease.[59] The connection with the Dukhobors was one Prokhanov maintained[60] and it added to his experience of Christian communal living. In 1927 he visited the Dukhobors in Diamond, British Columbia. In a report he wrote admiringly of their spacious two-story houses, fruit orchards and jam factory, and their fine livestock.[61]

Another example close at hand for Prokhanov was the life of German-speaking Mennonite colonists in South Russia. Mennonite Hermann Fast and his wife Elizaveta Gorinovich, sister of the revolutionary who had converted to Christianity through the ministry of V. A. Pashkov,[62] worked with him to produce *Beseda* and later were members of the Vertograd commune that Prokhanov founded in 1894. From about 1909 Prokhanov partnered with Mennonites in a publishing enterprise called *Raduga* (Rainbow).[63] Although not specifically communal enterprises, the Mennonite villages were widely admired in Russia as examples of productivity, efficiency, and cleanliness, with a strong ethic of mutual assistance.[64]

Thus, the Evangelical Alliance, Populism, Molokans and Dukhobors, and Mennonites likely all had some influence on Prokhanov's ideas about the role of Christianity in the world. He wanted Christians to transcend doctrinal boundaries in order to bring their influence to bear on all aspects of life. He expected evangelicals to be active and exemplary citizens, supporting everything that contributed to progress and enlightenment.[65] Declaring a week of prayer for the nation in September 1906, Prokhanov called upon evangelicals to implore God to "save our native land" by means of political and economic reform. Such prayers, he wrote, are pleasing to the Lord, who rejects slavery because, "Where the Spirit of the Lord is, there is freedom"

59. Ibid., 110–12.

60. *Bratskii listok* 7 (1906) 2; *Bratskii listok* 2 (1907) 34.

61. "Iz puteshestvii Br. I. S. Prokhanova po severo-amerikanskim Soedinennym Shtatam i Kanade" (From the journey of Brother I. S. Prokhanov in the North American United States and Canada), *Khristianin* 5 (1927) 43–44.

62. Trotter, *Lord Radstock*, 195; Prokhanoff, *Cauldron*, 69; Liven, *Dukhovnaia probuzhdenie*, 17–20.

63. Kahle, *Evangel'skie khristiane v Rossii i Sovetskom Soiuze*, 44–45.

64. Urry, *None but Saints*, 113, 122.

65. Prokhanoff, *Cauldron*, 172.

(1 Cor. 7:21).[66] In other words, beyond evangelicals caring for their own or reaching out to the urban poor with the message of salvation, Prokhanov saw Christian compassion in broader terms, encompassing systemic change that would affect every aspect of society. For Prokhanov and other Russian evangelicals as well, the state-sanctioned opportunity to establish economic communities in the 1920s was not only a way of supplying their material needs, but also represented a chance to demonstrate the reality and effectiveness of their worldview.[67]

Yet probably the most direct example of communal living for Prokhanov was through an employer, Nikolai Nikolaevich Nepliuev. Although their association was brief and perhaps even rather antagonistic, Nepliuev's far-reaching ideas for social reform based on religious principles surely contributed to Prokhanov's thinking. Nepliuev was an Orthodox layman, deeply concerned with spiritual renewal. He belonged to an ancient Russian noble family and began a career of diplomatic service in Germany. He was dissatisfied with the luxurious, self-indulgent life of a Russian aristocrat abroad, however, and over a period of time had several vivid and joyous dreams in which he saw himself on his home estate surrounded by peasant children.[68] This was enough to move Nepliuev to resign from the diplomatic corps and return to his family home in Chernigov guberniia where, in 1880, he organized a school for ten orphaned peasant children where they received instruction in agriculture and Christian morality. Five years later he opened an agricultural school for men, and in 1891 a women's school.[69] Finally, the *Krestovozdvizhenskoe trudovoe bratstvo* (Elevation of the Cross labor brotherhood) was officially organized in 1895 with Nepliuev as patron.[70] Essentially it was a Christian agricultural cooperative based on commonly-owned goods. In 1901 he also turned over the rights to all his real estate to the brotherhood.[71] Nepliuev is said to have recognized himself in the character of Dmitrii Nekhliudov, the hero of Leo Tolstoy's final novel, *Resurrection* (1899).[72] In the novel, Nekhliudov experienced a profound spiritual transformation and turned over his estate to the peasants.

66 *Bratskii listok* 9 (1906)1.

67. Redkina, *Sel'skokhoziaistvennye religioznye trudovye kollektivy*, 125, 387.

68. N. N. Nepliuev, "Vozdvizhenskaia shkola. Kolybel' Trudovogo bratstva" (The elevation [of the Cross] school. The cradle of the labor brotherhood) in *Izbrannye sochineniia*, 29–30; *Besedy o bratstve*, 25–26.

69. Avdasev, *Trudovoe bratstvo*, 8–9.

70. Ibid., 9.

71. Ibid., 16.

72 According to a conversation with V. N. Avdasev, founder and curator of the Nepliuev museum in Sumskaia oblast' (Ukraine), 27 December 2011.

The brotherhood enterprise survived into the Soviet era but was eventually turned into a collective farm.[73]

After completing his engineering course in St. Petersburg, during the winter of 1893 to 1894 Prokhanov worked as assistant director of a sugar factory that belonged to Nepliuev in Chernigov guberniia. Prokhanov's friend Fedor Stavtsev took charge of another small factory in the same neighborhood. While they were employed by Nepliuev, Prokhanov and Stavtsev met regularly with members of the brotherhood as well as with the patron himself, but the style of their approach to Christianity was rather different from what Orthodox believers were used to. The two evangelicals attempted to instruct the community, including Nepliuev, in their own methods of Bible reading and spontaneous prayer.[74] It is easy to imagine that this would have been more than a little annoying to their employer. Prokhanov reported, "as for Neplueff... the priest, and other zealous Orthodox employees, we soon became dangerous men in their sight, so that our further stay... became impossible." They were let go in February 1894.[75] Yet the memory of his dismissal was recorded late in Prokhanov's life and is somewhat at variance with an obituary of Nepliuev that appeared in *Khristianin* in 1908:

> In the midst of the desert of *kulachestvo* [rich peasants] and exploitation, which has been the lot of the peasant population, he [Nepliuev] was one of the few who went to the people with the light of Christian love and created oases of liking for work [*trudoliubie*] and love for one's brothers in the form of independent and free brotherhoods... Of all the people whom I have met, I have never seen a single one who could carry such a great work on his own shoulders.[76]

Ultimately, Nepliuev's accomplishments meant more to Prokhanov than their differences in religious sensibility. It is significant that his first attempt at realizing the dream of communal living took place in 1894, just a few months after leaving Nepliuev's factory. According to V. A. Popov, during his student years in St. Petersburg, Prokhanov came across the "archives" of the exiled V. A. Pashkov and M. M. Korf. Reading their old letters, he learned that one of the reasons Pashkov and Korf traveled in the south in 1883 was to locate a suitable site for a Christian agricultural community,

---

73. Avdasev, *Trudovoe bratstvo*, 17–18.
74. Prokhanoff, *Cauldron*, 86.
75. Ibid., 86–87.
76. "Pamiati N. N. Neplieuva" (In memory of N. N. Nepliuev), *Khristianin* 1 (1908) 46.

which they found in Crimea.⁷⁷ Before Pashkov and Korf had time to carry out their plans, however, they had been forced to leave the country in 1884. Ten years later, with the impression of Nepliuev's Brotherhood still fresh, Prokhanov became one of a small group of evangelicals who attempted for a short time to bring the dream of an agricultural commune to life. Their intention was to replicate the lifestyle of the Jerusalem church described in Acts 2 and also to create a refuge from government repression.⁷⁸ The Crimean site Pashkov and Korf had selected was near Simferopol.⁷⁹ In his autobiography Prokhanov made no reference to any earlier exploration by Pashkov of the area, but identified the place where the group settled as an estate called "Kirk" that belonged to German colonists called the Jerusalem Brotherhood who had immigrated to Palestine.⁸⁰ Possibly they were connected with the Temple Society (*Tempelgesellschaft*), a German Pietist movement that promoted the resettlement of its adherents in Palestine.⁸¹ In any case, communal living already had a history in the area.

Hermann Fast and his family were the first to arrive. Other members of the community were Prokhanov's friend Fedor Stavtsev; peasant and beekeeper Egor Syromiatnikov; and Zinaida Nikolaevna Nekrasova (1851–1915), widow of the poet and publisher Nikolai Alekseevich Nekrasov (1821–1877), together with her two nieces.⁸² Rather like a literary allusion, Nekrasova's participation suggests at least an indirect association between the little community and the ideals of Populism. Her husband had edited the literary journal *Sovremennik* (The contemporary) and was known for his poems sympathizing with the suffering of Russian peasants and workers. Nekrasov was also an associate of the Populist theorist N. G. Chernyshevskii whose novel *Chto delat'?* appeared on the pages of *Sovremennik* in 1863. Nekrasova's two nieces had been impressed with evangelical worship in St. Petersburg and invited their aunt, who attended regularly.⁸³ Nekrasova was

---

77. Popov, *I. S. Prokhanov*, 134; "Khristianskie kommuny I. S. Prokhanova," 135.

78. Prokhanoff, *Cauldron*, 87.

79. AUCEC-B Archives, Drawer 3, ISP Folder 7.3a, A. Savchenko, "Ekspeditsiia," 1.

80. Prokhanoff, *Cauldron*, 88.

81. Rozhdestvenskii, *Iuzhnorusskii shtundizm* 18589; Urry, *None but Saints*, 169, 185–89.

82. Popov, "Evangel'skie trudovye arteli," 26; *I. S. Prokhanov*, 134.

83. Prokhanoff, *Cauldron*, 88; Kolesova, *I zhizn,'* 90. An article reprinted from *Saratovskii listok* (Saratov leaflet) states that she "gave herself mainly to religious life in the spirit of the sectarian-rationalists. Living in Petersburg, she attended meetings of the Pashkovites" (*Baptist* 39 [22 September 1910] 312).

a wholehearted participant in the agricultural commune venture and apparently contributed a substantial amount to finance the undertaking.[84]

Indeed, the spirit of all the participants was one of commitment. Prokhanov wrote: "One felt as though he had lost his 'self,' his freedom, his personality. But as it was done in accordance with the example of the Apostles and with the word of Jesus Christ concerning self-denial . . . joy filled our hearts and all the time we were in the brightest state imaginable spiritually."[85] The community was called Vertograd, an Old Church Slavonic word meaning "vineyard," or "garden." They divided up the work. Prokhanov took care of the cattle and horses, dug holes for planting grapevines, and hauled clay in a wagon. In the evenings the group gathered in a common room where the women knitted and sewed while Prokhanov delivered talks on the Bible and church history. Their peaceful, hardworking life did not last long, however. On 12 September 1894 a circular to provincial governors from the Ministry of the Interior declared Stundists to be dangerous to the state.[86] In connection with the new wave of persecution, Prokhanov received word that his father had been exiled and departed for Vladikavkaz and then St. Petersburg to intercede for him. Prokhanov decided to leave the country early in 1895 to try to organize help for believers from abroad.[87] It is not clear how much longer and in what form Vertograd lasted after his departure. V. A. Popov states that it existed for four years.[88] Mennonite historian Cornelius Krahn agrees that the Fasts lived on an estate near Simferopol until 1897, although he does not identify it with Vertograd.[89] Baptist historian Aleksandr Savchenko maintains that Vertograd continued until 1900.[90] In any case, the village built near the site after World War II was called Ukroinyi, perhaps a significant name since *ukroinyi ugolok*, or "little hidden corner," connotes a place of daily prayer.[91] Eventually, however, Fast sold off the property and left for Romania and then Canada in 1901, where his family settled in a Dukhobor village.[92] Stavtsev took a job on the railroad. Syromiatnykov went home to the Ekaterinoslav region, while Nekra-

---

84. Kolesova, *I zhizn*,' 90–91.

85. Prokhanoff, *Cauldron*, 88.

86. Ibid., 90; Coleman, *Russian Baptists*, 22.

87. Prokhanoff, *Cauldron*, 89–91.

88. Popov, *I. S. Prokhanov*, 135; "Khristianskie kommuny I. S. Prokhanova," 135.

89. Cornelius Krahn, "Fast, Hermann (1860–1935)," *Global Anabaptist Mennonite Encyclopedia Online*, 1956.

90. Savchenko, "Ekspeditsiia," 1

91. Ibid.

92. Krahn, "Fast, Hermann (1860–1935)."

sova lived in several different places before settling in Saratov, where she lived very simply and attended the Baptist church.[93] She was, sadly, excluded from the evangelical community at the end of her life, perhaps something to do with conflicts over money. Whatever the case, she was not well off when she died and was buried according to Orthodox tradition.[94]

ECONOMIC COMMUNITIES IN THE 1920S

Vertograd represents the first relatively successful attempt by Russian evangelicals to establish an economic community. Prokhanov kept its memory alive throughout his career.[95] The early days of Soviet Russia offered fresh opportunities. Three of the most well-known communes of the 1920s had roots in the Evangelical Christian Union: Gefsimaniia (1919), Utrenniaia zvezda (Morning star, 1922), and Vifaniia (Bethany, 1923), all in Tver' guberniia. All three survived until 1929.[96] Prokhanov's 1918 work, *Evangelical Christianity and the Social Question*, provided the organizational basis for their founding and he took a strong proprietary and pastoral interest in them.[97] In his tract, Prokhanov outlined the development of communities collectively titled *Sigor* or "Zoar" after the city to which Lot fled from the destruction of Sodom in Genesis 19:22.[98] Evidently, Prokhanov connected the formation of such communities with the idea of refuge, which would have been important in 1918 when much of the urban population abandoned the cities in search of food.[99] Besides being places of refuge, the purpose of the Sigor communities was to set up the necessary conditions that would allow members to embody the life of the Jerusalem church.[100] Prokhanov noted that there is no scriptural indication that community of goods in the early church was obligatory or permanent. Yet, he envisioned it as the height of

---

93. AUCEC-B Archives, Drawer 3, ISP Folder 7.3a, A. V. Karev, "I. S. Prokhanov—k 30-letiu so dnia ego konchiny" (I. S. Prokhanov on the 30th anniversary of his death), 3–4; "Iz zhizni vdovy N. A. Nekrasova" (From the life of the widow of N. A. Nekrasov), *Baptist* 39 (22 September 1910) 312.

94. Kolesova, *I zhizn,'* 91; see also, http://www.greatwomen.com.ua/2008/05/07/zinaida-nikolevna-nekrasova.

95. *Utrenniaia zvezda*, Nos. 6–7–8 (June–July–August 1922) 13; Prokhanoff, *Cauldron*, 87–89.

96. Redkina, *Sel'skokhoziaistvennye religioznye trudovye kollektivy*, 639.

97. *Utrenniaia zvezda*, Nos. 6–7–8 (June–July–August 1922) 13.

98. Ibid.

99. Ibid., 6; Kahle, *Evangel'skie khristiane v Rossii i Sovetskom Soiuze*, 225; Nikol'skaia, *Russkii protestantizm*, 70.

100. *Utrenniaia zvezda*, Nos. 6–7–8 (June–July–August 1922) 13.

Christian commitment: "Only people who are 'one in heart and soul' and who are embraced by the flame of the Spirit of God can make this special life a reality."[101] Furthermore, he saw communal living as a means of witness through concrete example:

> We firmly hold to the opinion that Christianity is not only a word, but a deed, not only teaching, but also transformed life. Therefore we believe that the evangelical movement in Russia must express itself not only in preaching, but in the creation of new forms of social-economic life. We know that among the followers of evangelical teaching there are people who wish to create the highest form of social life and are prepared to do it.[102]

The evangelicals had long acknowledged the importance of practical Christianity that expressed itself in concrete acts.[103] Before the revolution compassionate ministry had been a way for them to make their faith visible and to support people in need. After the revolution, as other forms of service were taken over by the state, Prokhanov essentially saw economic communities as filling the same purpose as a means of witness and of economic support. *Evangelical Christianity and the Social Question* gave practical pointers. Prokhanov proposed three different levels of involvement for Christians gathered in economic communities: 1) all property and land held in common (total community—*vseobshchina*); 2) common land and equipment with private household property (half community—*poluvseobshchina*); 3) common means of production, such as a windmill, factory, oil press, etc. (simple community—*prostaia obshchina*). He also created model charters for such cooperatives, detailing the responsibilities of members, the function of the governing body, proper accounting practices, the procuring of materials and so on. Each family wishing to join in a Sigor community was required to contribute two-thousand rubles; a community was to consist of between ten and twenty families.[104] Prokhanov warned that such a project was not a simple undertaking, but required both spiritual and physical exertion: "tireless labor, many deprivations and frustrations, and also the . . . highest Christian qualities: meekness, humility, longsuffering and self-sacrifice."[105] Prokhanov maintained that wherever evangelicals formed

---

101. Quoted by Popov, "Evangel'skie trudovye arteli," 28.

102. Quoted by Popov, "Khristianskie kommuny I. S. Prokhanova," 135.

103. V. V. Ivanov, "Polozhenie baptistov" (The situation of Baptists), *Baptist* 9 (23 February 1911) 69–70.

104. Quoted by Popov, "Evangel'skie trudovye arteli," 28; Redkina, *Sel'skokhoziaistvennye religioznye trudovye kollektivy*, 126.

105. Quoted by Popov, "Evangel'skie trudovye arteli," 28

economic communities, the results of their work would be of the highest quality: their grain yields would be the best, their cattle would be the finest, and their villages would be clean, attractive, and well-appointed. In other words, the superiority of the community would be its testimony.[106]

Gefsimaniia was the first commune organized according to Prokhanov's plan in 1919. The group was headed by Ivan Pavlovich Beliaev, a peasant who had been forced underground in 1916 because of his evangelical beliefs. With the revolution he had become a member of the Council of Workers' Deputies in Reval (present-day Tallinn, Estonia).[107] The group took over a derelict estate directly from the government authorities and quickly made significant improvements.[108] By 1924 Gefsimaniia worked fifty *desiatiny* (roughly 124 acres) and kept work horses, cattle and sheep. The community members lived in two houses and ate in a common dining room. Children lived separately from their parents from the age of seven. The Gefsimaniia members built an artesian well, an electrical station, and a bathhouse and shared their agricultural machinery with neighboring peasants. The community had its own metalwork and carpentry shops, a smithy, and tailoring and shoemaking shops. A council made up of the most mature members managed the commune.[109] On a visit to Gefsimaniia, Prokhanov observed the good spirit, noting that the members were always singing while they worked, and before and after meals.[110] In fact, the community inspired Prokhanov, who wrote and translated many hymns, to compose "Song of the First Christians."[111]

In 1923 five families (a total of forty-five persons) from Gefsimaniia formed another commune, Vifaniia (Bethany); A. I. Vorob'ev was founder and president. By 1928 there were 108 members, 88 percent of whom were poor peasants and workers. The group took over another collective that was located on a former estate called Koshelovo. The engineer M. P. Shop-Mishich described Vifaniia at length in a glowing 1928 report.[112] The community raised cattle, sheep, pigs, chickens, geese, and turkeys. There

---

106. Tash-Otlu, "Ekspeditsiia po izyskaniiu zemel' dlia goroda solntsa" (Expedition to seek out land for the city of the sun), *Khristianin* 2 (1928) 44.

107. Nikol'skaia, *Russkii protestantizm*, 70.

108. Redkina, *Sel'skokhoziaistvennye religioznye trudovye kollektivy*, 165.

109. Ibid., 377; Coleman, *Russian Baptists*, 174–75.

110. Prokhanov, "Novaia ili Evangel'skaia zhizn,'" 104.

111 I. S. P., "Pesnia pervo-khristian" (Song of the first Christians), *Utrenniaia zvezda*, Nos. 3–4–5 (March–April–May 1922) 4; "Pesn' pervykh khristian" (Song of the first Christians), *Bratskii listok* 3 (1925) 37–38; concerning Prokhanov's musical interest see Prokhanoff, *Cauldron*, 144–48.

112. M. P. Shop-Mishich, "Vifaniia" (Bethany), *Khristianin* 7 (1928) 28–29, 33.

were leatherwork, carpentry, and machine shops, a windmill, and an oil press. The members lived in five houses and ate in a communal dining room. There was a grade school and a library with five-hundred volumes. The community sold cattle and seed to local peasants and rented out its agricultural equipment. In 1924 photographs and descriptions of Vifaniia were part of the All-Russian Agricultural Exhibit, and several prizes and other official recognition of their achievements followed.[113] Vifaniia became an Evangelical Christian showpiece, an advertisement for communal living. It was open to visitors and also to people in need, "providing meals and hospitality to the hundreds of people who come to it from everywhere."[114] Shop-Mishich exclaimed:

> One would like to shout so that everyone who does not believe in the possibility of realizing brotherhood on earth could hear it: "come and live at Vifaniia." There you will be convinced that humanity has matured to a new way of living, where labor, joy, and happiness rule and where there is no personal property.[115]

Less is known about Utrenniaia zvezda, chronologically the second major Evangelical Christian commune; it began in 1922 but changed its status to *tovarishchestvo*, or partnership group, in 1926. It cooperatively owned some agricultural equipment. Redkina notes that a critical, anti-religious article about the community's failure as a commune nevertheless admitted that Utrenniaia zvezda worked eighty-four *desiatiny* (roughly 226 acres) and achieved better harvests than neighboring peasants.[116]

Thus, *Evangelical Christianity and the Social Question* presented a practical basis for the founding of economic communities, some of which were quite successful. There was enough interest in communal living on the part of the evangelicals for Prokhanov to develop his ideas further in the 1925 pamphlet, *Novaiia ili evangel'skaia zhizn'* (The new, or evangelical life). In it Prokhanov called attention to the error of regarding Christianity as something strictly spiritual and uninvolved with the world. He pointed out that Christ did not encourage his disciples to remain on top of Mount Tabor after the Transfiguration, but instead led them back into the world to battle against evil and labor with souls.[117] Prokhanov perceived the goal of the

---

113. Redkina, *Sel'skokhoziaistvennye religioznye trudovye kollektivy*, 378–79.
114. Shop-Mishich, "Vifaniia," 28.
115. Ibid., 32.
116. A. Nemkov, "Ne sumeli v svoiikh rukakh uderzhat'" (They couldn't keep it in their own hands), *Kollektivist* 3 (1928) 36–38, quoted by Redkina, *Sel'skokhoz-iaistvennye religioznye trudovye kollektivy*, 380.
117. Prokhanov, "Novaia ili evangel'skaia zhizn,'" 105.

Russian evangelical movement as that of "removing the spiritual shackles from people's souls and opening human hearts wide in order to receive the living beams of light from the never-aging spiritual sun—the Gospel."[118] In short, the goal of the Russian evangelical movement was a new life for all.[119] Prokhanov explained that evangelical life begins with inner transformation as people hear and accept the gospel, but that this inevitably leads to external transformation as well[120]—a conviction that had undergirded the evangelicals' ideas on compassion for decades.[121] Moreover, Prokhanov foresaw that there will be no poor, no beggars, no needy among those partaking of the new life because all "lawful" needs will be met—adequately, but without luxury or excess.[122] That is, living out the gospel was expected to do away with poverty altogether. Prokhanov described the new life as rational, hard-working, sober, clean, joyful, holy, beautiful, and "nearly perfect."[123] Then, with details that border on the absurd, he illustrated the new evangelical life. Some of his images seem drawn from Chernyshevskii's *Chto delat'?* In a famous dream sequence the novel's heroine visits clean, bright palaces furnished with aluminum and crystal. She sees happy, beautiful people working joyfully in fields and gardens abounding with rich produce. Their labor is made easy and pleasant by efficient machines. They spend their evening hours enjoying theatrical performances, orchestras, and choirs. In the same way Prokhanov depicted clean, modern, mechanized, and electrified agricultural villages populated by cultured, sober Christian people tending large flocks of healthy animals. They wear light colored clothing in keeping with their joyful state of mind. Their whitewashed houses are decorated inside with Scripture verses and flowers. Fruit trees line the roads. People's lives are organized according to a daily, rational schedule of work and leisure. No one swears or speaks rudely.[124]

Historian Tat'iana Nikol'skaia is dismissive of Prokhanov's all-encompassing plans for social transformation: "Prokhanov's ideal, although reinforced with biblical quotes differs little from other communistic utopias. At its base are collective labor and the standardization of all aspects of daily life ... Like every utopia, Prokhanov's project is completely impractical and

---

118. Ibid., 99.

119. Ibid.

120. Ibid., 99–100.

121. Dillon, "A Russian Religious Reformer," 332; V. V. Ivanov, "O delakh" (On works), *Baptist* 5 (March 1909) 7; Liven, *Dukhovnoe probuzhdenie*, 14.

122. Prokhanov, "Novaia ili evangel'skaia zhizn,'" 113.

123. Ibid., 102–12.

124. Compare Chernyshevskii, *Chto delat'?*, 331–38 with Prokhanov, "Novaia ili evangel'skaia zhizn,'" 113–24, and Tash-Otlu, "Ekspeditsiia," 44.

extravagant."[125] Yet in an autobiographical sketch in 2009 Anatolii Arsen'evich Berezhnoi recalled that his father became a believer during the First World War and joined a commune called Akhor after Isaiah 65:10: "the Valley of Achor [will become a] resting place for herds, for my people who seek me."[126] It would appear that at least some of Prokhanov's vision for the new evangelical life was realized there:

> They built a whole settlement, with straight streets, with fruit trees. Discipline was strict; you could be kicked out for lice and fleas. They went to work singing, they started with prayer. This is where [my] father got acquainted with [my] mom . . . She was a Baptist and he was an Evangelical Christian. They married and began to work actively in the commune and the church.[127]

Nikol'skaia continues: "It is interesting that the Christian Prokhanov approaches the issue of the transformation of life from a materialistic position, that is, considering that 'rude manners will be changed for the better' as an effect of correctly arranged labor and a healthy way of life (and not faith in God and spiritual renewal)."[128] Yet perhaps that assessment is unfair. Certainly, Prokhanov's depiction of the ideal evangelical life is curious to the point of being laughable, yet he never expected that close communal living could be achieved without faith in God and a willingness to sacrifice one's own interests.[129] On his visit to Vifaniia in 1928, Prokhanov reminded the community that their first concern was always spiritual, with practical problems being of secondary importance.[130]

Prokhanov continued to promote his ideas on communal living. At the tenth congress of the Evangelical Christians in November 1926, a far-reaching program entitled "The Gospel Standard of Life" was adopted by the churches. It called for evangelicals to live according to the example of Jesus Christ. Like *The New, or Evangelical Life*, "The Gospel Standard of Life" proposed that Christian excellence should be evident in science, the arts, industry, and agriculture.[131] The congress recommended improving the communes by sending Bible school graduates to the Caucasus to study

---

125. Nikol'skaia, *Russkii protestantizm*, 69–70.

126. This community is not listed by Redkina in her extensive catalog; see *Sel'skokhoziaistvennye religioznye trudovye kollektivy*, 636–73.

127. Berezhnoi, "Byt' souchastnikom Evangeliia," 6.

128. Nikol'skaia, *Russkii protestantizm*, 69–70.

129. Prokhanov, "Novaia ili evangel'skaia zhizn'," 112.

130. Shop-Mishich, "Vifaniia," 26.

131. Prokhanoff, *Cauldron*, 238.

agronomy.[132] In the midst of setting up model communities as a witness to Soviet society, however, the compassionate goal of providing for people's needs was not forgotten. Point ten of "The Gospel Standard of Life" reminded believers that according to Acts 4:34, "there were no needy persons" in the Jerusalem Church. Community members were to look diligently to one another's needs.[133] Again, an important goal of the economic communities was to abolish poverty.

In 1928 Prokhanov published a lengthy article entitled "Chto nam delat'?" (What must we do?). He was quoting John 6:38 when the crowd asks Jesus, "What must we do (Russian: *Chto nam delat'?*) to do the works God requires?" However, it seems unlikely that in the Soviet Union anyone could have read the title without recalling V. I. Lenin's political tract of 1902 entitled *Chto delat'?*, which in turn was taken from the title of Chernyshevskii's novel. In his article Prokhanov offered a series of answers for both unbelievers and believers to the question, "What are we to do?" For unbelievers the answer was to repent. For believers, as in *The New, or Evangelical Life*, Prokhanov again presented the answer to the question as found in the life of the Jerusalem church: devotion to the apostles' teaching, fellowship with God and their fellow believers, prayer, and evangelism (Acts 2:42–47; 4:33). Prokhanov outlined each of these tasks, and then indicated the fifth point of activity: "the restructuring of the labor and social life of the peoples on a new basis."[134] Again he repeated Acts 4:34, "there were none in need among them," and Acts 4:32, "no one called anything his own; they owned everything in common." Prokhanov depicted the Jerusalem church as an "island" in a "sea of need and injustice" and exulted, "What a miracle that congregation must have seemed to those around it!" He continued: "The task of the evangelical church in Russia is exactly the same." No one could deny that preaching was the essential task of the church, but according to Prokhanov's article preaching alone was not enough; instead, "evangelical Christians must bring the gospel to life in such a way that there would be no needy among them." Evangelical communities were to be "islands of well-being."[135] In short, economic communities were not to exist for self-aggrandizement, but as a witness by putting an end to need.

The crowning achievement in communal living was to have been Prokhanov's plan for building a much larger community called Gorod

132. Redkina, *Sel'skokhoziaistvennye religioznye trudovye kollektivy*, 544; Popov, "Khristianskie kommuny I. S. Prokhanova," 136.

133. Prokhanoff, *Cauldron*, 238.

134. I. S. Prokhanov, "Chto nam delat'?" (What are we to do?), *Khristianin* 1 (January 1928) 12.

135 Ibid., 12.

Solntsa (City of the sun) or Evangel'sk. V. A. Popov suggests that the name "City of the Sun" was drawn from a 1623 work by the Dominican theologian Tommaso Campanella, which became available in a Russian translation in 1907.[136] However, Prokhanov need not have looked even that far. The sun is an obvious metaphor for the gospel, which, according to *The New, or Evangelical Life* was for many years hidden from the Russian people much as the sun would be from prisoners in a dungeon. Nevertheless, the gospel, like the sun's powerful rays, managed to penetrate the walls of the prison and left its distinct traces.[137] The purpose of the City of the Sun was to allow the gospel to shine with its full power upon and through its inhabitants. The plans for the project were formally approved at the 1926 Evangelical Christian congress. They had been drawn up by a committee of engineers, agronomists, and other specialists who were part of the believing community.[138] The Evangelical Christians entered into negotiations with Narkomzem for permission to choose a site for settlers and to travel to visit suitable locations. Although their request was refused as a religious organization, the group was advised to apply for land as individual citizens.[139] Evidently, the project was supported by E. A. Tuchkov (1892–?1950), the head of the OGPU (United state political administration)[140] department that dealt with religious organizations.[141] Possibly Prokhanov's ambitious idea fell in with a plan originating with the OGPU, to resettle Baptists and Evangelical Christians in Siberia.[142] Be that as it may, in August 1927 Prokhanov, together with "Engineer of the Project Bureau of the Evangelical Christian Union" M. P. Shop-Mishich and some others, set off for the Altai region on the border with Mongolia. Along the way large groups of believers met their train with bouquets and songs.[143] In due course a site for the new city was selected, cedar trees and maples were planted, and experts from the University of Tomsk were engaged to assist with more specific plans for ongoing economic development. However, Emel'ian Iaroslavskii (1878–1943), who headed the Central Committee's anti-religious committee as well as the League of the Godless (renamed League of the Militant Godless in 1929), criticized

136. Popov, "Khristianskie kommuny I. S. Prokhanova," 136; see also Popov, "Sibirskaia utopia baptistov."

137. Prokhanov, "Novaia ili evangel'skaia zhizn,'" 98–99.

138. Tash-Otlu, "Ekspeditsiia," 44.

139. Savin, "'Gorod Solntsa,'" 20–21.

140. That is, the secret police.

141. Istoriko-analiticheskii otdel MSTsEKhB, *Tserkov' dolzhna ostavat'sia tserkov'iu*, 53.

142. Redkina, *Sel'skokhoziaistvennye religioznye trudovye kollektivy*, 545.

143. Tash-Otlu, "Ekspeditsiia," 46.

the project in the press. Just a few months later, in May 1928, the Politburo instructed Narkomzem "to liquidate the matter of the organization of the city of Evangel'sk in Siberia."[144] At about the time the project was closed down, Prokhanov was already abroad. He was not allowed to return to the Soviet Union after attending the 1928 Baptist World Alliance meeting in Toronto[145] and he died in Berlin in 1935.

THE END OF THE COMMUNES

The relationship between religiously-based economic communities and the Soviet government had been ambiguous from the beginning. During the second half of the 1920s the Bolshevik attitude to the organization of communes steadily moved from ambivalent to hostile. Although ostensibly communal living was encouraged by the state, and sectarian energy and commitment had been needed to rebuild agriculture, over time it became clear that religiously-based communes failed to produce "real" communism.[146] Furthermore, from the ideological point of view, communes were theoretically desirable, but socially radical, that is, potentially difficult to control. Communal living in Russia had always assumed an air of protest and separation; it was a way of life that had been sought by many different kinds of idealists and carried with it religious overtones as well. As the battle against all forms of religious expression gained momentum, communes formed by religious groups were targeted for dissolution. The press played a prominent role.[147] From the mid-1920s there were multiple attacks on religiously-based labor cooperatives and economic communities, accusing them of neglect and unfairness toward their poorer members, disregard of safety regulations, the exclusion of members on religious grounds, violations of the separation of church and state, and many other charges.[148] In addition, the economic gains made by religiously-based communities and cooperatives caused the government some concern. According to Redkina, especially poor and middle peasants experienced material improvement, which made religion attractive and consequently threatened the state.[149] F. M. Putintsev (1899–1947), an atheist propagandist who studied and criticized sectarian groups during the 1920s, asserted that both the number of sec-

---

144. Popov, "Khristianskie kommuny I. S. Prokhanova," 137.
145. Coleman, *Russian Baptists*, 218.
146. Wesson, *Soviet Communes*, 91.
147. Redkina, *Sel'skokhoziaistvennye religioznye trudovye kollektivy*, 561.
148. Ibid., 562.
149. Ibid., 549–50.

tarian communes and their claims of success were inflated. He maintained that Gefsimaniia, founded in 1919, had actually ceased to exist by 1925 and that Vifaniia's relative success was due to extensive support in the matter of tax breaks, provision of equipment, and the like.[150] Finally, he declared that communal living was merely a blind for rich sectarians who wanted to preserve their property at the expense of the state and of the poor who were obliged to work for them. "We are not against sectarian communes, but we are against sectarian hypocrisy," he concluded.[151]

By 1928 the "breathing space" of the NEP was over and the first Five Year Plan (1928 to 1932) had been declared. Intense industrialization and the collectivization of agriculture followed. These changes were accompanied by the Cultural Revolution, which sought to create a truly proletarian society by force. For religious groups this meant that policies calculated to accommodate them and ultimately convert them to the revolutionary cause were no longer practiced.[152] The heaviest blow, of course, came on 8 April 1929 with the new law "On religious associations," which brought to an end all activity except for worship by registered groups of believers. Attacks against religiously-based economic communities and cooperatives followed quickly. The communes were dismantled. Vifaniia was handed over to a Communist collective in 1929 and renamed in honor of a Civil War hero.[153] In September 1929 Gefsimaniia was forced by the authorities to take in eleven additional poor families, new leaders were assigned, and the community was also renamed.[154] In self-preservation some communities migrated to Central Asia or Siberia, where the Soviet government was not yet in control.[155] A. A. Berezhnoi described the end of the Akhor community:

> Soon the Bolsheviks began to restrict the Christian communes. They sent a Party leader to Akhor. He began to change things around. The brothers understood what was up and began to leave. A big group, including my parents, moved to Kazakhstan . . . They organized a new commune but soon Soviet power reached there, too. They had to move again, this time to the city of Zyrianovsk in eastern Kazakhstan . . . A church was formed in

---

150. F. Putintsev, "'Kommunizm' i 'pokazatel'nost'' sektantskikh kolkhozov," 27–28.
151. Ibid., 31–33.
152. Coleman, *Russian Baptists*, 215.
153. Ibid., 217.
154. Redkina, *Sel'skokhoziaistvennye religioznye trudovye kollektivy*, 572.
155. Ibid., 575, 584.

Zyrianovsk made up of exiles and re-settlers (*pereselentsy*) like my parents.[156]

The dissolution was uneven—some labor collectives continued to function for a few more years.[157] A few evangelical economic communities were able to continue by reorganizing as collectives.[158]

It should be noted that the communes were regarded with suspicion by some evangelicals and their demise was regarded as God's judgment. A letter from Russia dated about 1930 stated that the Christian communities everywhere "ended . . . lamentably . . . in ruin and disgrace," with members "dispersed as beggars." Not only that, but: "It was evident that on all communities, even the Christian ones, was a curse. Besides household and commercial failures, fate was fighting against the communities. The fertile districts were left bare. Deut. 28:15–30 [a curse for sin] is fulfilled."[159] It is interesting that some would single out the economic communities as under a curse at a time when disaster had overtaken the whole evangelical movement. A wave of arrests followed the 8 April 1929 legislation. Prayer houses were closed, as were the evangelical journals. By 1930 neither the Baptist Union nor the Evangelical Christian Union were functioning.[160]

CONCLUSION

During the 1920s economic communities and labor cooperatives were formed by evangelicals partly as a means of survival, but ultimately as a way of living according to the gospel that would put an end to poverty and serve as a means of witness. In particular, since the early days of the evangelical movement, a desire had been expressed to live according to the description of the Jerusalem church in the Book of Acts. There were many precedents for the evangelicals' involvement in communal enterprises, including peasant communes, the Populist movement, the experience of indigenous sectarian groups and Mennonite colonists, and the example of idealists such as N. N. Nepliuev. The evangelical leader who most consistently wrote about economic communities was I. S. Prokhanov. Following the Bolshevik Revolution, evangelicals spontaneously entered into communal life for the sake

---

156. Berezhnoi, "Byt' souchastnikom," 6.

157. Redkina, *Sel'skokhoziaistvennye religioznye trudovye kollektivy*, 574.

158. Ibid., 572, 589.

159. "Our Worker, Mr. Dobrinin, Sends Following Extracts Taken From Mail Received by Him from Russia," *The European Harvest Field* (April 1930) 20.

160. Coleman, *Russian Baptists*, 217–18.

of self-preservation. In 1921 when the government sought sectarian help to rebuild the economy, and especially agriculture, many evangelicals responded. They considered that in effect they had already been living communally for decades. Numerous labor cooperatives and agricultural communities were formed and enjoyed sufficient success to be perceived as a threat by the government. Their organization took place at a time when other types of compassionate ministry were disappearing because of government policy. The communes fulfilled some of the functions of compassionate ministry that evangelicals had practiced in the past, especially the support of church members in need. I. S. Prokhanov proposed that their ultimate goal was to eradicate poverty completely; communal living was a way of demonstrating Christian values and even superiority in all facets of life. In other words, Prokhanov envisioned evangelicals leading the way in systemic change that would transform society completely, and, presumably, although not directly stated, render traditional forms of compassionate ministry obsolete.

Conclusion
The Legacy of Russian Evangelical Ministries of Compassion

SOMETIME AFTER THE BOLSHEVIK Revolution, Barbara Fetler, W. A. Fetler's wife, wrote a revealing epilogue to a collection of her husband's poor English-language verses.[1] With great love she described the celebration of Easter during her childhood in a pious Orthodox household. The highest holiday of the Russian church year began with the forty-day Lenten fast and continued with careful ritual through the dramatic, candle-lit midnight procession. The climax came when the priest would fling open the doors to the empty church and proclaim, "Christ is risen!"[2] Days of joyous feasting and visiting followed. Yet in the end, Barbara Fetler continued, "little by little, even from the second day, disappointment slowly but surely crept into the heart." The letdown came because the purity and beauty of the holiday could not be sustained. The joy and promise of the celebration of Christ's resurrection turned into nothing more than a series of parties with tipsy guests and ordinary conversations. In short, nothing ever really changed because of the Easter observance.[3] However, a year would pass and somehow expectation would be renewed again in the spring. In other words, Fetler realized that the promise of the resurrection itself held true even if the reality of the holiday celebration disappointed. As evidence of this, she mentioned numerous conversions: "A woman saved from suicide . . . fifty souls converted in three meetings . . . Red Guards singing in the choir . . . The news . . . that . . . whole villages are turning to Christ."[4] Surely these

1. Fetler, *The Stundist*.
2. Barbara Fetler, "Epilogue, Memories of my Childhood: Easter in Russia," in Fetler, *The Stundist*, 95–99.
3. Ibid., 100.
4. Ibid., 101

were early signs of resurrection, "the first swallows of the coming spring." She concluded, "Oh, let us go and tell the Russian people that the resurrection of Christ means our resurrection to a wonderful new life."[5]

In a few paragraphs Barbara Fetler perfectly summarized the Russian evangelicals' understanding of their calling. First, they perceived a "wonderful new life" that could not be attained through the dead traditions of the past, no matter how beautiful. Second, they believed that the way to the new life was through repentance—people had to come to God for forgiveness from sin. The results of the transaction were expected to be deep and permanent, unlike a passing annual holiday. Moreover, the changes were not merely internal to the new believer, but would be apparent to everyone. At least ten years earlier, V. V. Ivanov had described the new life as follows:

> Through the preaching of the Gospel, thousands of drunkards have become sober; wantons [male and female] have become chaste . . . beggars have become rich. The Gospel, like the sun, drives away all darkness and ignorance and makes people useful to their families, to society, and to the Kingdom of God on earth.[6]

In other words, the evangelicals expected profound changes to take place in people's lives because of the gospel, and that those changes would transform life around them to the benefit of all. The change, they believed, was so great as to amount to resurrection. Such good news, of course, could not be kept quiet, and so the third part of the evangelicals' program as expressed by Barbara Fetler was the call to "go and tell" everyone about it.

During their Golden Age (1905 to 1929) the Russian evangelicals reenacted Barbara Fetler's scenario innumerable times. Disappointment and despair led to a thirst for God, which led to repentance, which led to a new life. It was the responsibility of those living the new life to spread the word. Their mission was to change lives through the gospel. Consequently, the Russian evangelicals were tireless evangelists. Their approach to Christianity differed from traditional Russian Orthodoxy. Especially their emphasis on repentance and salvation through faith distinguished them from millions of their fellow citizens. However, they also believed in the witness of transformed lives expressed in deeds. In 1906 I. S. Prokhanov asserted that the kind of prayer God loves is the kind that leads to action: "when a person is inspired by the Spirit of God, the spirit of righteousness, love, and the striving to serve one's neighbor (and thus the Lord) to the point

---

5. Ibid.
6. V. V. Ivanov, "O delakh" (On works), *Baptist* 5 (March 1909) 7.

of self-forgetfulness and self-denial."[7] The purpose of this study is to demonstrate that compassionate ministry, defined as uncompensated service to people in need, was an organic part of Russian evangelical witness from the early days of the movement. Compassion was an important way to "go and tell" and also to give evidence of the "wonderful new life" brought about by the gospel. Because of their relatively small numbers, comparative lack of wealth, numerous competing priorities, and minority status, the Russian evangelicals never built up large charitable institutions. Their efforts to help people in need never lasted longer than a few years. However, in spite of those things, and of occasionally active resistance on the part of the authorities both in imperial and Soviet times, the evangelicals nevertheless sustained a consistent and coherent vision of compassionate ministry as part of their calling.

SUMMARY

This study has presented a history of the Russian evangelical movement during its particularly active years between 1905 and 1929 from the point of view of compassionate ministry. Prior to that period, there was some historical precedent for the Russians to associate certain forms of non-Orthodox Christianity with compassion through the example of the Quakers, the dissenter John Howard, or the evangelicals John and Walter Venning. In the 1870s Lord Radstock influenced the Pashkovites in the direction of compassionate involvement as well, although many of them were already active in various forms of charitable work. Nevertheless, Radstock's contribution was to invest their existing service with evangelical urgency. Thus, their previous work in prison visitation, as sisters of mercy, or teaching literacy to the peasants on their own estates continued, but became in addition the platform for preaching repentance and conversion, which they were convinced was the way to lasting social transformation. In the same way, the next generation of Pashkovites after V. A Pashkov's own exile from Russia in 1884 also joined in with existing forms of compassionate ministry while filling them with evangelical content. Thus, Jenny de Mayer established a House of Industry on Sakhalin Island at the time that movement was widespread. Likewise, at a time when "People's kindergartens" were fairly common, Iuliia Karpinskaia set up several in Kyiv with an evangelical slant. Meanwhile, as members of the movement suffered imprisonment and exile for their faith, especially during the 1890s, it became the task of those in freedom to help

---

7. I.[van] S.[tepanovich] P.[rokhanov], "Brat'ia! K molitve!" (Brothers! To prayer!), *Bratskii listok* 8 (1906) 1.

them spiritually and financially. The Pashkovites and the generations of evangelicals that followed maintained an interest in compassionate ministry as it was practiced abroad by such figures as Thomas Barnardo or George Mueller, or by organizations such as the Salvation Army.

The situation of the Russian evangelicals improved rather suddenly in April 1905 when religious toleration was declared. Until April 1929, when the law "On religious associations" put an end to all religiously-based activity beyond actual worship, the evangelicals remained relatively free, although they continued to suffer intermittent arrests, harassment, fines, and the closure of their prayer houses, especially during World War I. They began many ambitious projects after 1905, including publishing, church building construction, theological education, and the sending of missionaries. Amid all this activity, compassionate ministry remained a strong commitment. As this study has shown, it is possible to discern three major patterns for compassion during the period 1905 to 1929. First, evangelicals developed dedicated funds and institutions for the purpose of meeting the needs of their own community members, especially preachers and evangelists; second, they carried on rescue ministry to transform the lives of the urban poor; and third, they organized economic communities whose ultimate purpose was to eradicate poverty altogether. Each of these basic trends can be identified with different leaders of the movement. D. I. Mazaev, V. G. Pavlov, and V. V. Ivanov represent compassion practiced among the evangelicals themselves; W. A. Fetler characterizes rescue ministry; and I. S. Prokhanov is distinguished by his vision for the potential of economic communities. The first two major streams of compassionate activity were separated from the third by the years 1914 to 1923, which were marked by war, revolution, and famine. During this time, the evangelicals of necessity were called on to respond to human need on an unprecedented scale. They developed a new level of administrative sophistication to receive and channel a significant amount of famine aid sent from abroad. These approaches to ministry are all quite different; nevertheless throughout the entire period of the so-called evangelical Golden Age, they were undergirded by the same basic set of assumptions. The Russian evangelicals taught that preaching the gospel was their primary calling. At the same time, they were convinced that their witness should consist of good works as well as words. They cultivated an attitude of concern and personal involvement in the needs of others, following the example of Christ. They taught that compassion was the concern of all members of the community, regardless of their economic status or age; they saw it as a basic element of their common Christian witness. In fact, compassion was often presented as the particular responsibility of women and youth. Generosity and simple living were encouraged; in their publications evangelicals devoted a good deal of teaching to the proper Christian attitude to money and giving. Compassionate models from the West were actively sought, particularly in the case of urban rescue ministry, which closely followed the example of the Salvation Army. However, Russian evangelicals also drew on their indigenous sectarian roots, especially the Molokans, for the development of ministries within their own community.

Except for W. A. Fetler, all the leaders profiled in this study were of Molokan background. To a certain extent, although they had intentionally separated themselves from certain aspects of that heritage, it may be said that leaders such as D. I. Mazaev, V. G. Pavlov, and V. V. Ivanov worked to instill a Molokan-type ethic of mutual support into the new Baptist community. Since the beginning of the evangelical movement, Stundists and others had routinely gathered dedicated funds for the support of preachers and church members in need. In the post-1905 era it became possible to establish funds in a more formal way to provide aid within the community, and especially for preachers who were no longer capable of working, and their families. Another important element of post-1905 compassion was the organization of evangelical institutions to care for orphans and the elderly. In addition, as the movement grew, it was essential to teach newcomers about good works and giving. While compassionate ministry within the believing community was important for survival in a rather hostile environment, it was also understood to be a means of outreach. If the gospel was the main source of hope for society, then it was essential first of all to support the people whose calling it was to preach.

Many changes came to Russia as the country industrialized. In particular, the urban population grew during the late nineteenth and early twentieth centuries, creating a number of serious social problems. Evangelicals, notably W. A. Fetler, were inspired to attempt to reach the urban poor with the gospel by means of methods learned in England, according to the example of C. H. Spurgeon, the Welsh Revival, and the Salvation Army. Fetler arrived in St. Petersburg in 1907 and from about 1910 began to hold night meetings specifically to reach prostitutes and alcoholics. For a few months in 1914, the Russian Baptist church in the capital, Dom Evangeliia, served as a half-way house for men who wished to leave their life on the streets. Fetler and others helped to establish the Salvation Army in Russia. Rescue ministry was considered an appropriate involvement for youth, who preached and sang in taverns and organized summer camps and events for children in the slums. Another aspect of rescue-type ministry was the involvement of evangelicals in the Russian temperance movement. The evangelicals approached alcoholism as a spiritual problem that could be overcome by surrendering one's life to Christ.

Conclusion

Drastic changes overtook the entire country with the beginning of World War I. At first the evangelicals joined their fellow citizens in setting up field hospitals, tending the wounded, and caring for refugees, but by 1916 many prayer houses had been closed and church leaders sent into exile. Nevertheless, different kinds of compassionate service were still carried on by evangelical youth in several places. Following the February Revolution in 1917, evangelicals revived their support of existing compassionate institutions and made plans for new ones. A ministry among soldiers developed into the Tent Mission, which sent teams of missionaries throughout towns and villages in Ukraine evangelizing, but also tending the sick. After the end of the Civil War the Tent Mission succeeded in operating a home for orphans for a brief time. Throughout the years of revolution and war, evangelical compassionate institutions continued to function, but were shut down by about 1922. New challenges were created by the 1921 to 1923 famine, which both threatened the lives of evangelicals and involved them in local and international aid programs. Evangelical churches gave generously to famine relief and also set up their own structures to distribute large amounts of help from abroad. Some plans were made to extend relief projects into long-term development programs, but by the mid-1920s these hopes were extinguished.

The New Economic Policy begun in 1921 signaled a pause in the Bolshevik Revolution when for a few years limited capitalism was tolerated. To rebuild agriculture, the government invited "sectarians," including evangelicals, to form communes and also permitted the organization of collective labor enterprises to provide goods and services. Evangelicals entered readily into these efforts; indeed, in many ways they understood themselves to have anticipated them because of the "communal" way of life they had been accustomed to practice for many years. In several tracts on the subject of communal living, I. S. Prokhanov outlined practical steps for the formation of economic communities and gave them a theological basis. His interest was in replicating the life of the Jerusalem church described in the Book of Acts, which owned goods in common and saw to it that none of its members experienced physical need. Prokhanov apparently anticipated that living according to the ideal of the early church would lead to the eradication of poverty altogether. In an era when other forms of compassionate ministry were being restricted by the state, the formation of communes and labor collectives to some extent took over the place they once occupied both as a way of sustaining the community and also serving as a means of witness.

COMPASSIONATE MINISTRY AND RUSSIAN EVANGELICAL IDENTITY

What does their commitment to compassionate ministry reveal about Russian evangelical identity and about their practical theology? Their compassionate activity serves more to confirm what has already been observed about the Russian evangelical movement than to suggest anything new. Compassion re-emphasizes the complex, typology-defying nature of Russian evangelicalism. Albert J. Wardin, Jr. describes it as simultaneously a sect and a revival movement, formally against sacramentalism, yet insisting on adult baptism by immersion, and drawing upon both German and Slavic influences.[8] Gregory L. Nichols helpfully employs the image of a tapestry woven together of many colors.[9]

David W. Bebbington has delineated the four distinguishing marks of the evangelical movement as conversionism, activism, and the centrality of the Bible and the cross.[10] Certainly the Russians exhibit all four of those features; in particular this study has emphasized their consistent activity as ministers to a range of human need and their high view of repentance and conversion. However, their specific historical situation makes the Russians' evangelicalism quite complex. They were committed to compassionate outreach and inspired by leading English evangelicals, such as Lord Radstock, George Mueller, Charles Spurgeon, William Booth, and others, yet they gave at least as much attention to building up support within their own community. According to Ernst Troeltsch, that characteristic would place the Russian evangelicals in the sect category.[11] Indeed, an important part of their historical background is sectarian, rooted among the Dukhobors and especially the Molokans. Yet as has been remarked on several times, even the Molokan-type commitment to supporting one another was ultimately missional in intent—it was needed to sustain the preaching that would bring many people to salvation and thus transform society. In their approach to compassionate ministry the Russian evangelicals also defy Troeltsch's image of Pietism, the "sect ideal within the Church." It is true that they were strongly influenced by Pietism, especially the Stundists, and like the Pietists the Russian evangelicals "aimed solely at Christianizing the hearts of men."[12] However, Troeltsch claims that the Pietists practiced charity without any

---

8. Wardin, *On the Edge*, ix.
9. Nichols, *Russian Evangelical Spirituality*, 308.
10. Bebbington, *Evangelicalism in Modern Britain*, 2–17.
11. Troeltsch, *The Social Teaching of the Christian Churches*, vol. 2, 695–96.
12. Ibid., 717–18.

concern for altering social conditions, and that is not entirely characteristic of the Russians. While they were not revolutionaries in a political sense, they were feared and repressed because they promoted teaching that to both the tsars and the Soviets seemed to threaten the very existence of the state. They did not reject government authority or seek to overturn the social order, but religious freedom was the one element of social justice that they insisted on. They believed that the free preaching of the gospel would lead to personal transformation, which they fully expected to carry social consequences. They perceived Russia as suffering and regarded themselves as bearing the necessary message to change their native land for the better.

Besides attesting to the complexity of Russian evangelicalism, their practice of compassionate ministry also confirms the outward-looking nature of the movement. Aleksei Sinichkin titled his book on the Russian evangelicals *All for the Sake of Mission* (*Vse radi missii*),[13] the point being that nearly everything they did was based on their concern for reaching out to others. It cannot be said that the evangelicals were suffering from anything like a "fortress mentality," at least not through the 1920s. They willingly entered into contact with the wider Russian society, as their involvement in the temperance movement, famine relief, and economic communities show. Moreover, at times they allowed seemingly important doctrinal points to be "trumped" by compassion. Thus, the Salvation Army was a valued ministry partner even though the Army did not administer sacraments (ordinances). In the same way, residents of the Dom Evangeliia halfway house in 1914 were not required to subscribe to a certain set of beliefs before they could benefit from the rehabilitation program. From the Pashkovite movement until the end of the 1920s the Russian evangelicals tended to emphasize engagement and action over formal theology.

Moreover, through the lens of compassionate ministry we may see that the Russians exhibited a basically positive attitude to the world. I. S. Prokhanov's autobiography is subtitled, "The Life of an Optimist in the Land of Pessimism."[14] Ernst Troeltsch describes the Baptists as detached and quiet, taking care of one another and treating the world as lost and of the devil, merely the scene of suffering.[15] Yet we have seen that the Russian evangelicals (including Baptists) expected inward transformation that would improve society. Their focus was not strictly on the joys of the world to come or on sustaining their own community, but on making everyday life worth living for everyone. Compassionate ministry highlights the Rus-

13. Irpen,' Ukraine: Assotsiatsiia "Dukhovnoe vozrozhdeniie," 2011.
14. Prokhanoff, *Cauldron*.
15. Troeltsch, *The Social Teaching of the Christian Churches*, vol. 2, 696.

sian evangelicals' expectation of change for the better. What is more, they anticipated that inner change was the catalyst for greater involvement in human society, not less.

Thus, the complexity of Russian evangelicalism and its essentially missionary nature are characteristics that are confirmed by their compassionate activity. Also worth noting is the organic, intuitive nature of their compassionate activity. The Pashkovites had engaged in many different kinds of compassionate service by adapting existing ministries to evangelical purposes. It might be assumed that this was simply characteristic of upper-class people for whom charitable work was part of their lifestyle. Yet almost as soon as religious tolerance was declared in 1905, small offerings were spontaneously sent to the journal *Khristianin* by simple people who apparently expected that the new freedoms meant that evangelicals would now be starting up compassionate institutions as a matter of course. Compassion was a natural part of their faith.

Compassion also shows the essential adaptability of the movement. Challenging situations require challenging measures, and the Russians appear to have accepted and even embraced innovations such as night meetings, halfway houses, agricultural communities, or famine committees—each appropriate to different circumstances—without fear or complaints about going against tradition. The evangelicals also developed new organizational and administrative skills as they were needed. They willingly studied and appropriated foreign models.

In this way, compassion highlights the worldwide connections of the evangelicals, for which they were sometimes punished as "foreign elements." At the same time, it also points to their self-reliance. The evangelicals admired and identified with the compassionate work of their counterparts abroad, although they never enjoyed the social leverage, financial support, or respectability to attempt ministries such as that of George Mueller, Thomas Barnardo, or Friedrich von Bodelschwingh. However, the difficulty of their situation did not stop the Russian evangelicals from engaging in compassionate ministry. Nor did they wait for foreigners to do the work. The Russians intervened to bring the Salvation Army into their country, but they also carried out their own rescue ministries. They sought famine aid from abroad, but also gathered their own resources to help their own people.

Compassion was part of the mechanism that helped the evangelicals to develop and retain a sense of community even as their numbers grew. Through journal articles, reports, and editorials, especially in *Baptist*, mutual responsibility and concern were systematically cultivated. The evangelicals also used compassion to reinforce their legitimacy in the eyes of the state. During the early days of World War I, they transformed prayer houses into hospitals for the wounded in part because they wished to underline their loyalty. During the 1920s they formed agricultural communes and labor cooperatives for their own support, but also to demonstrate their usefulness as citizens.

In summary, viewing the Russian evangelicals through the lens of compassionate ministry allows us to see their complexity as outward-looking, adaptable evangelists who absorbed multiple influences but who were also struggling for their survival and legitimacy. Their activities were necessarily shaped by the relatively hostile context in which they lived. According to David Bebbington, their fellow believers in the Anglo-American world achieved "dominance" and were numerous and powerful enough to "sway the direction of change in the English-speaking world."[16] In contrast, perhaps the Russians could be described as "evangelicals under stress," who never attained the respectability and influence of their fellow believers abroad. At the same time, compassion was always a consistent and organic part of their outreach.

AREAS FOR FURTHER STUDY

This research suggests several directions for further study. First of all, there is reason to enlarge the present study by continuing to document evangelical compassionate ministry. In large part, I have concentrated on information culled from contemporary journals, but it would be well worthwhile to investigate archival sources for additional material. Because they served a teaching function, the journals tended to spiritualize nearly everything, including compassion. Thus, the sparse accounts of the children's home organized and operated by the youth of Dom Evangeliia for a few months in 1917 focus on the importance of faithfulness and prayer in ministry at the expense of basic information about the operation of the home.[17] Also, in the case of the Baptist shelter for orphans and the elderly in Balashov, the researcher would like to know the identity and number of the residents and the people who cared for them, as well as the particulars of the way the shelter was finally closed down in about 1922. Perhaps that information is still waiting to be discovered. In addition, it is possible that archival study would reveal more data on compassionate ministry outside of St. Petersburg, which has tended to dominate this study. The work of I. N. Karpinskaia in Kyiv at

---

16. Bebbington, *The Dominance of Evangelicalism*, 234.

17. E. H. K[uteinikova], "'Sem'ia' detei v Levashove" (The "family" of children in Levashov), *Gost'* 6 (June 1917) 86–87.

the turn of the twentieth century surfaced through archival research,[18] and more searching might serve to fill out the existing picture.

Comparative study of the Russian evangelicals and the compassionate work of state-recognized confessions in Russia—Lutheran, Reformed, Mennonite—could be fruitful. In addition, the compassionate ministry of imperial-era foreign missionaries, such as Pastor Dalton or the Rev. N. F. Höijer of Sweden would be a valuable addition.

Continuing the study of compassionate ministry among evangelicals throughout Soviet times is another potential direction. For the purposes of this study, the legislation of 1929 established a logical cut-off date, yet Soviet power took longer to consolidate in Siberia and Central Asia and some ministry ventures, especially economic communities and labor cooperatives, endured into the 1930s at a distance from the political center. One of the exiled pastors of Dom Evangeliia, Aleksei Petrovich Petrov, succeeded in collecting sufficient funds to open a home for orphans in Kharbin that accommodated two-hundred children, an effort that continued well past the 1920s.[19] Just as their predecessors had done in World War I, Soviet evangelicals contributed to the needs of the wounded during World War II, and also supported the Soviet Peace Fund in later years. It is still traditional for post-Soviet Evangelical Christian-Baptist youth to take some responsibility for doing chores for elderly members of their congregations. However, interviews among evangelicals who remember the Soviet period and the systematization of that information would doubtless yield many insights into the character of the movement. Moreover, the wave of compassionate activity that was ushered in with the perestroika years is striking. With no organic connection to compassionate ministries of the past, what were the motivating factors that inspired post-Soviet evangelicals to undertake ambitious projects such as setting up rehabilitation centers for alcoholics or shelters for street children? It is also important simply to record the histories of these many undertakings.

In addition, the Russian Pentecostals have not yet been studied with regard to compassionate ministry. The period of their most significant growth began in 1921, which is close to the end of the Golden Age. Nevertheless, it would be interesting to compare Pentecostal experience in this area with that of other Soviet evangelicals, especially after the formation of the All-Union Council of Evangelical Christians-Baptists in 1944.

---

18. Golovashchenko, *Istoriia Evangel'sko-Baptistskogo dvizheniia*.
19. Sevast'ianov, "Pleiada sluzhitelei," 12.

Post-Soviet charismatic churches are also active in the area of compassion and their history should be documented.[20]

Finally, much more could be done to incorporate the Russian evangelical experience of compassionate ministry into the history of global evangelicalism, which has been explored extensively by Bebbington[21] and Mark Hutchinson and John Wolffe.[22] This study has called attention to the influence of certain English evangelicals, such as Lord Radstock, C. H. Spurgeon, George Mueller, and William Booth, on the Russians' practice of compassionate ministry. However, it would be useful to further analyze similarities and differences between Western and Russian evangelical approaches to compassion, their relative effect on their respective societies, the ways that compassionate ministry has changed in both settings since the mid-nineteenth century, and the way it is regarded today in Western and post-Soviet contexts. Another fascinating study would be to compare Russian evangelical compassion with its practice in other non-Western evangelical contexts.

CONCLUSION

Since the collapse of the Soviet Union, considerable attention has been given to the neglected role of religion, both in the USSR and in Imperial Russia. In particular, a new generation of Eastern European evangelical scholars has undertaken to document and analyze largely unexamined aspects of their history and theology. This study represents another part of that task, assembling a history of compassionate ministry among Russian evangelicals between 1905 and 1929 and reflecting on what it suggests about their legacy. Their practice of compassion during this period shows that while it is rather difficult to define Russian evangelicalism in terms of familiar categories, it was essentially an outward-looking, adaptable, and missions-minded movement with a sense of social concern.

Important changes took place among Russian evangelicals during the Soviet period. It was not possible to practice compassion in the same way as it was earlier. However, the natural gravitation of evangelicals toward compassionate ministry in post-Soviet times suggests that the movement's basically missionary orientation, with an interest in evangelism and service, may have been submerged, but was never lost.

20. Catherine Wanner has touched on this topic in *Communities of the Converted*.
21. Bebbington, *The Dominance of Evangelicalism*.
22. Hutchinson and Wolffe, *A Short History of Global Evangelicalism*.

During the early 1990s in Makiivka, a city in Donetsk oblast' (Ukraine), women from several different Baptist churches would gather for Bible study once a week in a church-sponsored library near the central market. Often a little girl from the streets turned up at their meeting, one of the thousands of Ukrainian children whose family had become a casualty of the economic collapse that accompanied independence. The child, named Natasha, made a living for herself and her alcoholic mother by begging, but although she was at least eight years old she had never learned her numbers sufficiently to be able to count the money she collected. She would ask the women at the Bible study to help her. Over time they agreed that something had to be done for this girl and others like her. The women prayed for about two years and, with the help of many volunteers from a number of churches and some assistance from abroad, established a shelter called Good Shepherd in 1996. In the absence of any government-funded institution, Good Shepherd functioned for several years as the only children's shelter in Makiivka. Good Shepherd is now the name of a charitable fund made up of several compassionate projects. As of this writing, thirty children from the Good Shepherd social rehabilitation center, "Our Home," have moved to the Kyiv suburbs out of the way of military action in the Donetsk region.

The spontaneous, yet thoughtful response of the women and the churches they represent has been replicated scores of times in the countries of the former Soviet Union, as evangelicals have attempted to help children, the elderly, the disabled, and people suffering from addictions.[23] Many of their efforts have proved unsustainable, but some have survived. There is no organic connection between them and the ministries of the earlier generations of Russian evangelicals whose activity is documented in this study, yet there are recognizable points of correspondence between them. Taking Good Shepherd as a contemporary example, it is possible to see that present-day Russian evangelicals, like their predecessors, have shown themselves to be aware of the world around them, concerned for the needs of people, and committed to sharing the gospel. According to the Good Shepherd website, "[The] goal [is] to satisfy the children's physical needs, tell them about God` and His love for them, teach them spiritual truth and impart love into hardship [sic, that is, introduce love into a situation of hardship]."[24] Such a purpose statement would not have been out of place in any of the ministries practiced by Russian evangelicals between 1905 and 1929.

23. Excerpts from longer studies on evangelical compassionate ministry in the former Soviet Union may be found in Raber, "Evangelical Social Ministries in Ukraine since Independence"; and Wanner, "Social Ministry and Missions in Ukrainian Mega-Churches."

24. V. S. Tsupko, Shelter Director, http://www.shelter.dn.ua/en/shelter.

Bibliography

ARCHIVES

All-Union Council of Evangelical Christians-Baptists Archives (AUCEC-B Archives)
Salvation Army International Heritage Centre (SAIHC)
Southern Baptist Historical Library and Archives (SBHLA)

PRIMARY SOURCES AND CONTEMPORARY WORKS

Periodicals

All the World
American Baptist Foreign Missionary Society
Baptist (The Baptist)
The Baptist and Reflector
The Baptist Times and Freeman
Blagovestnik (The evangelist)
Bratskii vestnik (Fraternal messenger)
The Catholic Presbyterian
The Century Illustrated Magazine
The Christian Workers' Magazine
Drug (The friend)
Friend of Russia
The Gospel Call
Gost' (The visitor)
Home and Foreign Fields
Iunyi khristianin (Young Christian)
Khristianin (The Christian) (with supplement *Bratskii listok* [Fraternal leaflet],
Kommunisticheskaia revolutsiia (The communist revolution)
Molodoi vinogradnik (The young vineyard])
The Missionary Review of the World
Missionerskoe obozrenie (Missionary survey)
Missions

214 Bibliography

Russkii vestnik (Russian herald)
Seiatel' istiny (Sower of truth)
Slovo istiny (Word of truth)
Utrenniaia zvezda (Morning star)
Voprosy nauchnogo ateizma (Issues of scientific atheism)
The Watchman-Examiner

Letters

The Pashkov papers (personal correspondence of V. A. Pashkov)

Books

Arnold, A. J., ed. *Jubilee of the Evangelical Alliance, Proceedings of the Tenth International Conference held in London, June-July 1896*. London: Shaw, 1897.

Asquith, Michael. *Famine: Quaker Work in Russia, 1921–1923*. London: Oxford University Press. 1943.

Awstin, Mr. T. Davies. *The Religious Revival in Wales 1904*. Issue 6. http://welshrevival.org/histories/aw.

Balikhin, Fedor Prokhorovich. *Kratkaia avtobiografiia presvitera-propovednika evangel'skikh khristian-baptistov Fedora Prokhorovicha Balikhina* (A short autobiography of the presbyter-preacher of the Evangelical Christians-Baptists, Fedor Prokhorovich Balikhin). Rostov-na-Donu: Tipografiia F. Pavlova, 1908.

Baptist World Alliance. Second Congress. Philadelphia, June 19–25, 1911. *Record of Proceedings*. Philadelphia, 1911.

Begbie, Harold. *Life of William Booth, the Founder of the Salvation Army*. 2 vols. London: Macmillan, 1926.

Belykh, G. and L. Panteleev. *Respublika SHKID* (The Republic of ShkiD). Kiev: Veselka, 1989.

Bercovici, Konrad. *Crimes of Charity*. New York: Knopf, 1917.

Berdyaev, Nicholas. *The End of Our Time*. New York: Sheed & Ward, 1933.

———. *Russkaia ideia* (The Russian idea). Moscow: Folio, 2000.

Bonch-Bruevich, Vladimir D. *Izbrannye sochineniia*. Tom 1. *O religii, religioznom sektanstve i tserkvi* (Selected works. Volume 1. On religion, religious sectarianism and churches). Moscow: Izdatel'stvo Akademii Nauk SSSR, 1959.

———. *Krivoe zerkalo sektanstva* (The crooked mirror of sectarianism). Moscow: Zhizn' i znanie, 1922.

———, ed. *Materialy k istorii i izucheniiu russkago sektanstva i raskola*. Vypusk 1 (Materials for the history and study of Russian sectarianism and schism, Publication 1). St. Petersburg: Tipografiia B. M. Vol'fa, 1908.

———, ed. *Presledovanie baptistov evangelicheskoi sekty. Materialy k istorii i izucheniiu russkago sektanstva*. Vypusk 6 (The persecution of Baptists of the evangelical sect. Materials for the history and study of Russian sectarianism, Publication 6). Christchurch: Izdanie "Svobodnago slova," 1902.

———. "Presledovanie baptistov v Rossii" (The persecution of Baptists in Russia). *Vestnik Evropy* (Herald of Europe) 45.6 (1910) 160–83.

Brooks, Rev. Jesse W., ed. *Good News for Russia: A Series of Addresses Delivered at the First General Conference for the Evangelization of Russia, at the Moody Tabernacle, Chicago, June 24th to 28th, 1918.* Chicago: Bible Institute Colportage Association, 1918.

Bryant, Louise. *Six Red Months in Russia. An Observer's Account of Russia before and during the Proletarian Dictatorship.* New York: Doran, 1918.

Bulgakov, S. V. *Nastol'naia kniga dlia sviashchenno-tserkovno-sluzhitelei,* 2 vols. (Handbook for ministers of the holy church). 1913. Reprinted, Moscow: Moscow Patriarchate, 1993.

Byford, Chas. T. *Peasants and Prophets (Baptist Pioneers in Russia and South Eastern Europe).* 3rd edition. London: Kingsgate, 1914.

Chernyshevskii, N. G. *Chto delat'?* (What is to be done?). 1863. Reprinted, Kiev: "Radians'ka shkola," 1984.

Conybeare, Frederick C. *Russian Dissenters.* Harvard Theological Studies 10. 1921. Reprinted, New York: Russell & Russell, 1962.

Dalton (pastor). "Recent Evangelical Movements in Russia. Lord Radstock and Colonel Pashkoff." *The Catholic Presbyterian* 32 (August 1881) 104–15.

de Mayer, Jenny E. *Adventures with God in Freedom and in Bond.* Toronto: Evangelical Publishers, 1948.

Deyneka, Peter. *Twice Born Russian: An Autobiography.* 2nd ed. Grand Rapids: Zondervan, 1944.

Dillon, E. J. "A Russian Religious Reformer." *The Sunday Magazine* 4 (1902) 330–36.

Dostoevskii, F. M. *Dnevnik pisatelia za 1876 g.* (A writer's diary for 1876). St. Petersburg: Tipografiia Iu. Shtaufa, 1879.

———. *Idiot* (The idiot). 1868. Reprinted, Krasnoiarsk, Russia: Izdatel'stvo krasnoiarskogo universiteta, 1982.

Dostoevsky, F. M. "Dostoevsky and Pobiedonoszev: Some Letters." In *Dostoevsky: Letters and Reminiscences,* 239–65. Translated by S. S. Kotelliansky and J. Middleton Murry. New York: Knopf, 1923.

———. "Mirages: Stundism and Redstockists." In *The Diary of a Writer,* 566–69. Translated by Boris Brasol. Vol. 2. New York: Charles Scribner's Sons, 1949.

Duff, Brigadier Mildred. "Furlough Days in Russia." *All the World* 20.5 (1899) 255–56.

Fetler, John. *Sluzhenie Rossii: Epicheskii ocherk o missionerskom sluzhenii Vil'iama A. Fetlera 1883–1957* (Service to Russia: An epic sketch of the missionary service of William A. Fetler 1883–1957). Translated by Tat'iana Stremetskaia. Odessa: Bogomyslie, 1997.

Fetler, William (Basil Malof). *The Stundist in Siberian Exile and Other Poems.* London: Morgan & Scott, n.d.

Fisher, Harold H. *The Famine in Soviet Russia, 1919–1923: The Operations of the American Relief Administration.* Hoover War Library Publications 9. Stanford: Stanford University Press, 1927.

Fry, Elizabeth Gurney, Katherine Fry, and Rachel Elizabeth Cresswell. *A Memoir of the Life of Elizabeth Fry with Extracts from Her Journal and Letters.* 2 vols. 1848. Rev. ed. Digital Quaker Collection, http://dqc.esr.earlham.edu.

(Gorenovich). *On" liubit" menia* (He loves me). Halbstadt, South Russia: Tipografiia G. Ia. Brauna, 1907.

Giliarovskii, Vladimir. *Moskva i moskvichi* (Moscow and Muscovites). St. Petersburg: Azbuka-klassika, 2004.

Golder, Frank, and Lincoln Hutchinson. *On the Trail of the Russian Famine*. Stanford: Stanford University Press, 1927.

Graham, Stephen. *Russia and the World: A Study of the War and a Statement of the World-Problems that Now Confront Russia and Great Britain*. New York: MacMillan, 1917.

———. *With the Russian Pilgrims to Jerusalem*. London: MacMillan, 1913.

Hiebert, P. C., and Orie O. Miller. *Feeding the Hungry: Russia Famine 1919–1925. American Mennonite Relief Operations under the Auspices of Mennonite Central Committee*. Scottdale, PA: Mennonite Central Committee, 1929.

Höijer, Rev. N. F. *Russia's Evangelization: A Record of Missionary Experience and Organization Work*. Compiled and translated by Prof. M. A. de Sherbinin. Chicago: Oak, 1918.

Iarosh,' K. P. "Zabota o blizhnem: Ocherki blagotvoritel'nosti" (Concern for the neighbor: Studies of charity). *Russkii vestnik* 213.3 (1891) 39–74; 214.5 (1891) 170–205.

Iasevich-Borodaevskaia, V. I. *Bor'ba za veru, istoriko-bytovye ocherki, i obzor zakonodatel'stva po staroobriadchestvu i sektanstvu v ego posledovatel'nom razvitii* (The struggle for faith, historical-domestic sketches, and a survey of law on Old Belief and sectarianism in its chronological development). St. Petersburg: Gosudarstvennaia tipografiia, 1912.

Kerenskii, A. F. *Rossiia v povorotnyi moment istorii* (Russia at a turning point in history). Translated by L. A. Igorevskii. Moscow: Tsentrpoligraf, 2006.

Kliuchevskii, V. O. *Dobrye liudi drevnei Rusi* (The kind people of ancient Rus'). Moscow, 1902.

Kniaz'kov, S. A. *Golod v drevnei Rossii* (Famine in ancient Russia). St. Petersburg: Tikhomirov, 1908.

Lamb, Edwin Gifford. "The Social Work of the Salvation Army." PhD diss., Columbia University, 1909.

Langenskjöld, Greta. *Baron Paul Nicolay, Christian Statesman and Student Leader in Northern and Slavic Europe*. Translated by Ruth Evelyn Wilder. New York: Doran, n.d.

Larsson, Karl. "The Army in Russia." Translated and abridged by Clara Becker. Reprinted in *The Officer* (February 1990) 18–23, 57–58, 60–61, 99.

Latimer, Robert Sloan. *Dr. Baedeker and His Apostolic Work in Russia*. London: Morgan & Scott, 1907.

———. *With Christ in Russia*. London: Hodder & Stoughton, 1910.

Liven, S. P. *Dukhovnoe probuzhdenie v Rossii* (Spiritual awakening in Russia). 4th ed. Korntal: Svet na vostoke, 1990.

Martsinkovskii, Vladimir. *Zapiski veruiushego* (Notes of a believer). St. Petersburg: Khristianskoe obshchestvo: "Bibliia dlia vsekh," 1995.

Martzinkovski, V. Ph. *With Christ in Soviet Russia*. Mount Carmel, Haifa, Palestine: the author, 1933.

Masaryk, Th. G. *The Spirit of Russia*. 2 vols. New York, 1918.

Maude, Aylmer. *A Peculiar People, the Doukhobors*. New York: n.p., 1904. Reprint, New York: AMS, 1970.

Mazaev, G. I. "Vospominaniia" (Recollections). Typewritten manuscript, n.d.

McCaig, Dr. A. *Grace Astounding in Bolshevik Russia: A Record of the Lord's Dealings with Brother Cornelius Martens*. Second edition. London: Russian Missionary Society, 1930.

———. *Wonders of Grace in Russia*. Riga: Revival, 1926.

Müller, George. *Autobiography of George Müller or A Million and a Half in Answer to Prayer*. 3rd ed. Compiled by G. Fred. Bergin. London: Nisbet, 1914.

Müller, Mrs. *Preaching Tours and Missionary Labours of George Müller (of Bristol)*. London: Nisbet, 1883.

Nepliuev, N. N. *Besedy o bratstve* (Conversations about the brotherhood). 1903. Reprinted, Moscow: Preobrazhenie, 2010.

——— *Izbrannye sochineniia* (Selected works). Edited by V. V. Tkachenko. Sumy, Ukraine: Foligrant, 2011.

———. *Polnoe sobranie sochinenii, Tom 1* (Complete collected works, Vol. 1). St. Petersburg: Tikhanov, 1901.

Oncken, William Sears, J. Bystrom, and Peter Olsen. "The Baptist Work in Russia." *Missions* (March 1912) 188.

Packer, J. A. *Among the Heretics in Europe*. London: Cassell, 1912.

Penn-Lewis, Jessie. *The Awakening in Wales and Some of the Hidden Springs*. Washington, PA: CLC, 1993.

Pike, G. Holden. *The Life and Work of Charles Haddon Spurgeon*. 2 vols. Edinburgh: Banner of Truth, 1894.

Pobedonostsev, Konstantin. *Pis'ma Pobedonostseva k Aleksandru III* (The letters of Pobedonostsev to Alexander III). Edited by M. N. Pokrovskii. Moscow, 1925.

———. *Pobedonostsev i ego korrespondenty. Pis'ma i zapiski* (Pobedonostsev and his correspondents. Letters and notes). Edited by M. N. Pokrovskii. Petrograd, 1923.

———. *Reflections of a Russian Statesman*. Translated by Robert Crozier Long. Ann Arbor: University of Michigan Press, 1965.

Poysti, N. J. "What Happened in Russia?" *The Gospel Call* 11.2 (1937) 17, 25–26, 28; 11.3 (1937) 37; 11.4 (1937) 56–57, 61; 11.5 (1937) 71–72, 77; 13.1 (1939) 7–8, 15.

Prokhanoff, I. S. *In the Cauldron of Russia, 1869–1933, The Life of an Optimist in the Land of Pessimism Together with an Interesting History of the Russian Evangelical Christian Union*. New York: All-Russian Evangelical Christian Union, 1933.

Prokhanov, I. S. "Novaia ili Evangel'skaia zhizn'" (The new, or evangelical life). In *Novaia ili Evangel'skaia zhizn',* tom II (The new or evangelical life, vol. II). Compiled by V. Popov, 96–124. Moscow: Khristianskii tsentr "Logos," 2009.

———. *Verouchenie evangel'skikh khristian* (Teaching of the Evangelical Christians). 1925. Reprinted, Cherkassy, Ukraine: Izdatel'stvo "Smirna," 2002.

Prugavin, A. S. *Raskol vverkhu, Ocherki religioznykh iskanii v privilegirovannoi srede* (Schism from above, Studies of religious seeking among the privileged). 1880. Reprinted, St. Petersburg: Obshchestvennaia pol'za, 1909.

Putintsev, F. "'Kommunizm' i 'pokazatel'nost'' sektantskikh kolkhozov" ("Communism" and the "good showing" of sectarian collectives). *Kommunisticheskaia revoliutsiia* 19 (October 1925) 26–35.

Raleigh, Donald. J., ed. *A Russian Civil War Diary: Alexis Babine in Saratov, 1917–1922*. Durham: Duke University Press, 1988.

Ransome, Arthur. *The Crisis in Russia*. London: Allen & Unwin, 1921.

———. *Russia in 1919*. New York: Huebsch, 1919.

Bibliography

Reed, John. *Ten Days that Shook the World*. New York: Boni & Liveright, 1919. Reprinted, New York: International, 1971.

Rozhdestvenskii, Arsenii. *Iuzhnorusskii shtundizm* (South-Russian stundism). St. Petersburg: Tipografiia departamenta udelov, 1889.

Rushbrooke, J. H. *Baptists in the U.S.S.R., Some Facts and Hopes*. Nashville: Broadman, 1943.

Saloff-Astakhoff, N. I. *Christianity in Russia*. New York: Loizeaux Brothers, 1941.

———. *Interesting Facts of the Russian Revolution or In the Flame of Russia's Revolution with God and the Bible*. New York: the author, 1931.

———. *Judith: Martyred Missionary of Russia, A True Story*. 1941. Reprinted, Grand Rapids: Zondervan, 1974.

———. *Little Lame Walter the Young Hero of Faith*. 1931. Reprinted, Ephrata, PA: Grace, 2007.

———. *Real Russia from 1905 to 1932 and Communism in America*. New York: the author, 1932.

———. *Touching Heaven by Prayer*. Westchester, IL: Good News Publishers, 1960.

Salov-Astakhov, N. I. *Palatochnaia missiia, istoricheskii ocherk nachala 20-go veka* (The tent mission, A historical sketch of the beginning of the 20th century). Zaporozh'e: Izdatel'stvo "Piligrim," 2006.

Smith, Rodney. *Gypsy Smith (1860–1947): His Life and Work by Himself* (London: 1901). http://www.biblebelievers.com/gypsy_smith/.

Snowden, Philip. *Socialism and the Drink Question*. Socialist Library Vol. 6. Edited by J. Ramsay MacDonald. London: Independent Labour Party, 1908.

Sorokin, Pitirim. *Leaves from a Russian Diary—and Thirty Years After*. 1924. Reprinted, Boston: Beacon, 1950.

———. *Man and Society in Calamity: The Effects of War, Revolution, Famine, Pestilence upon Human Mind, Behavior, Social Organization and Cultural Life*. New York: Dutton, 1942.

Srebrianskii, o. Mitrofan. *Dnevnik polkovogo sviashchennika sluzhashchego na Dal'nem Vostoke* (The diary of a regimental priest serving in the Far East). Moscow: Otchii dom, 1996.

Stadling, Jonas. "The Famine in Eastern Russia: Relief Work of the Younger Tolstoy." *The Century Illustrated Magazine (1881–1906)* 46.4 (1893) 560–71.

Stead, W. T. *Truth about Russia*. London: Cassell, 1888.

Sukhotina-Tolstaia, T. L. *Vospominaniia* (Recollections). Moscow: Khudozhestvennaia literatura, 1980.

Timoshenko, M. D. *Pervyi vserossiiskii molodezhnii kongress iunoshei i devits v Rostove-na-Donu 1909 goda* (The first all-Russian youth congress of youths and girls in Rostov-on-Don 1909). Rostov-na-Donu: T-va Pavlova i Slavgorodskago, 1909.

Tolstoi, L. N. *Voskresenie* (Resurrection). 1899. Reprinted, Kiev: Gosudarstvennoe izdatel'stvo khudozhestvennoi literatury, 1953.

Tolstoy, Countess Alexandra. *I Worked for the Soviet*. Translated by the author in collaboration with Roberta Yerkes. New Haven: Yale University Press, 1934.

Trotter, Mrs. Edward. *Lord Radstock: An Interpretation and a Record*. 2nd ed. London: Hodder & Stoughton, n.d.

Vins, Ia. Ia., ed. *Nashi baptistskie printsipy* (Our Baptist principles). Translated by the editor. Harbin, China: Abramovich, 1924.

Wuorinin, John H. *The Prohibition Experiment in Finland*. New York: Columbia University Press. 1931.

SECONDARY SOURCES

Aitkin, Tom. *Blood and Fire, Tsar and Commissar: The Salvation Army in Russia, 1907–1923*. Studies in Christian History and Thought. Milton Keynes, UK: Paternoster, 2007.

Avdasev, V. N., ed. *Svet pamiati, N. N. Nepliuev v vospominaniiakh sovremennikov* (The light of memory, N. N. Nepliuev in the recollections of [his] contemporaries). Kyiv: Foligrant, 2008.

———. *Trudovoe bratstvo N. N. Nepliueva, ego istoriia i nasledstvo* (The labor brotherhood of N. N. Nepliuev, its history and legacy). Sumy, Ukraine: RIO "AS-Media," 2003.

Averkii (Archbishop), ed. *Zhitie sviatogo pravednogo ottsa nashego Ioanna Kronshtadtstogo chudotvortsa, ko dniu proslavleniia, 19 oktiabria 1964 goda* (The life of our holy and righteous father Ioann Kronshtadtskii the miracle-worker, On the day of his beatification, 19 October 1964). Jordanville, NY: Holy Trinity Monastery, 1964.

Babere, G. "Dom Evangeliia" (House of the gospel). *Golos istiny* 44.5 (2003) 29–31.

Ball, Alan M. *And Now My Soul is Hardened: Abandoned Children in Soviet Russia, 1918–1930*. Berkeley: University of California Press, 1994.

Bebbington, David W. *The Dominance of Evangelicalism: The Age of Spurgeon and Moody*. Leicester, UK: Inter-Varsity, 2005.

———. *Evangelicalism in Modern Britain: A History from the 1730s to the 1980s*. Grand Rapids: Baker, 1989.

———. *The Nonconformist Conscience: Chapel and Politics, 1870–1914*. London: Allen & Unwin, 1982.

Beliakova, N. A. and A. V. Sinichkin, eds. *105 let legalizatsii russkogo baptizma. Materialy mezhdunarodnoi nauchno-prakticheskoi konferentsii. 5–7 aprelia 2011 goda* (105 years of the legalization of Russian Baptism. Materials of the international scholarly-practical conference, 5–7 April 2011). Moscow: RSEKh-B, 2011.

Berezhnoi, Anatolii Arsen'evich. "Byt' souchastnikom Evangeliia, vospominaniia sluzhitelia evangelsko-baptistskogo bratstva" (To be a participant in the Gospel, recollections of a minister of the Evangelical-Baptist brotherhood). *Gost'* 39.6 (2009) 6–7.

Bjartveit, John, Lieutenant-Colonel (Ret.). *Reopening of Russia 1990–1992. Responsibility of the Norwegian Territory*. Oslo: The Salvation Army Territorial Headquarters, 1996.

Blane, Andrew Q. "Protestant Sects in Late Imperial Russia." In Andrew Blane, ed. *The Religious World of Russian Culture. Russia and Orthodoxy*. Vol. 2, *Essays in Honor of Georges Florovsky*, 267–304. The Hague: Mouton, 1975.

———. "The Relations between the Russian Protestant Sects and the State, 1900–1921." PhD diss., Duke University, 1964.

Bowen, James. *Soviet Education: Anton Makarenko and the Years of Experiment*. Madison: University of Wisconsin Press, 1962.

Bozhe, Vladimir, and I. Nepein. *Zhatva smerti: Golod v Cheliabinskoi gubernii v 1921–1922 gg.* (Harvest of death: The famine in Cheliabinsk guberniia in 1921–1922). Cheliabinsk, Russia: Cheliabinskaia biblioteka, 1994.

Brackney, William H., with Ruby J. Burke, eds. *Faith, Life and Witness: The Papers of the Study and Research Division of the Baptist World Alliance, 1986–1990.* Birmingham, AL: Samford University Press, 1990.

Brandenburg, Hans. *The Meek and the Mighty: The Emergence of the Evangelical Movement in Russia.* New York: Oxford University Press, 1977.

Breyfogle, Nicholas B. *Heretics and Colonizers: Forging Russia's Empire in the South Caucasus.* Ithaca, NY: Cornell University Press, 2005.

Brooks, Jeffrey. *When Russia Learned to Read: Literacy and Popular Literature 1861–1917.* Princeton: Princeton University Press, 1985.

Buss, Andreas E. *The Russian-Orthodox Tradition and Modernity.* Studies in the History of Religions 100. Leiden: Brill, 2003.

Caldwell, Melissa L. *Not by Bread Alone: Social Support in the New Russia.* Berkeley: University of California Press, 2004.

Clarke, Martin V., ed. *Music and Theology in Nineteenth-Century Britain.* Farnham, Surrey, UK: Ashgate, 2012.

Coleman, Heather J. *Russian Baptists and Spiritual Revolution, 1905–1929.* Bloomington: Indiana University Press, 2005.

Corrado, Sharyl M. "The 'End of the Earth': Sakhalin Island in the Russian Imperial Imagination, 1849–1906." PhD diss., University of Illinois, 2010.

———. "The Philosophy of Ministry of Colonel Vasiliy Pashkov." M.A. thesis. Wheaton, IL: Wheaton Graduate School, 2000.

Corrado, Sharyl, and Toivo Pilli, eds. *Eastern European Baptist History: New Perspectives.* Prague: International Baptist Theological Seminary, 2007.

Davies, R. E. *I Will Pour Out My Spirit: A History and Theology of Revivals and Evangelical Awakenings.* Tunbridge Wells, UK: Monarch, 1992.

Davis, Donald E., and Eugene P. Trani. "The American YMCA and the Russian Revolution." *Slavic Review* 33 (1974) 469–91.

Davis, Nathaniel. *A Long Walk to Church: A Contemporary History of Russian Orthodoxy.* Boulder, CO: Westview, 1995.

Demchenko, Dmitrii. "Missionerskoe sluzhenie v evangel'sko-baptistskom bratstve (1867–1928 gg.)" (Missionary service in the Evangelical-Baptist brotherhood [1867–1928]). Prokhladnyi, Russia: Report to the Congress of EKhB churches of South Russia, 26–27 May 2011.

Dik, Viktor. *Svet Evangeliia v Kazakhstane, Istoriia vozvesheniia Evangeliia i rasprostraneniia obshchin baptistov i mennonitov v Kazakhstane (pervaia polovina XX veka)* (The light of the Gospel in Kazakhstan, History of the proclamation of the Gospel and the spread of Baptist and Mennonite congregations in Kazakhstan [first half of the 20th century]). Steinhagen, Germany: Samenkorn, 2003.

Doherty, Catherine de Hueck. *Poustinia: Christian Spirituality of the East for Western Man.* Glasgow: Collins, Fount, 1977.

Elliott-Binns, L. E. *Religion in the Victorian Era.* 2nd ed. London: Lutterworth, 1946.

Ellis, Geoff, and Wesley Jones. *The Other Revolution: Russian Evangelical Awakenings.* Abilene, TX: Abilene Christian University Press, 1996.

Engel, Barbara Alpern. *Between the Fields and the City: Women, Work, and Family in Russia, 1861–1914.* Cambridge: Cambridge University Press, 1996.

Fedirko, O. P. *Obrazovanie i prosveshchenie na rosiiskom dal'nem vostoke v gody grazhdanskoi voiny: Problemy sekuliarizatsii i sakralizatsii* (Education and enlightenment in the Russian Far East during the years of the Civil War: Problems of secularization and sacralization). Blagoveshchensk, Russia: Izdatel'stvo BGPU, 2010.

Fedotov, G. P. *The Russian Religious Mind.* Cambridge: Harvard University Press, 1966.

Fiedler, Klaus. *The Story of Faith Missions from Hudson Taylor to Present Day Africa.* Oxford: Regnum, 1994.

Figes, Orlando. *A People's Tragedy: The Russian Revolution, 1891–1924.* London: Cape, 1996.

Fitzpatrick, Sheila. Alexander Rabinowitch, and Richard Stites, eds. *Russia in the Era of NEP: Explorations in Soviet Society and Culture.* Bloomington: Indiana University Press, 1991.

Fitzpatrick, Sheila. *The Russian Revolution.* Oxford: Oxford University Press, 1994.

Fountain, David. *Lord Radstock i dukhovnoe probuzhdenie v Rossii* (Lord Radstock and spiritual revival in Russia). Translated by T. Boll. Mayflower, 1988. Reprint, Al'fom, 2001.

Freeze, Gregory L. *The Parish Clergy in Nineteenth Century Russia: Crisis, Reform, Counter-Reform.* Princeton: Princeton University Press, 1983.

———, ed. *Russia: A History.* Oxford: Oxford University Press, 2009.

Gibbard, Rev. Noel. "Remembering 1904–05: The International Impact of the Welsh Revival." Transcribed from an address delivered at Neath Church, 18 October 2004.

Gislason, Leona. "The Tent Mission in South Russia, 1918–1923." *Journal of Mennonite Studies* 15 (1997) 80–97.

Golovashchenko, S. I. comp. *Istoriia Evangel'sko-Baptistskogo dvizheniia v Ukraine* (The history of the Evangelical-Baptist movement in Ukraine). Odessa: Bogomyslie, 1998.

Goroshko, Anton. *N. I. Peisti, Biograficheskiy ocherk.* (N. I. Peisti, A biographical sketch). Kyiv: Izdatel'stvo Khristianskogo bibleiskogo bratstva sv. apostola Pavla, 2010.

Grachev, Iu. S. *Gerusy-Giriusy (Goris).* Wheaton, IL: Evangelical Word, 1996.

———. *Studencheskie gody: Povest' o studencheskom khristianskom dvizhenii v Rossii* (Student years: A story about the student Christian movement in Russia). St. Petersburg: Bibliia dlia vsekh, 1997.

Green, Bernard. *Tomorrow's Man: A Biography of James Henry Rushbrooke.* Didcot, UK: Baptist Historical Society, 1997.

Harlampieva, Tsvetelina. "Scottish Missionaries in Karass and Their Role in the Russian Colonisation of the North Caucasus in the First Quarter of the XIX Century." *Almanakh via Evrasia* (2013,2) 1–22. http://www/viaevrasia.com.

Haykin, Michael A. G. and Kenneth J. Stewart, eds. *The Advent of Evangelicalism, Exploring Historical Continuities.* Nashville: B & H Academic, 2008.

Heasman, Kathleen. *Army of the Church.* London: Lutterworth, 1968.

———. *Christians and Social Work.* London: SCM, 1965.

———. *Evangelicals in Action: An Appraisal of their Social Work in the Victorian Era.* London: Geoffrey Bles, 1962.

Hedda, Jennifer. *His Kingdom Come: Orthodox Pastorship and Social Activism in Revolutionary Russia.* DeKalb: Northern Illinois University Press, 2008.

Heier, Edmund. *Religious Schism in the Russian Aristocracy*. The Hague: Nijhoff, 1970.
Herlihy, Patricia. *The Alcoholic Empire: Vodka and Politics in Late Imperial Russia*. New York: Oxford University Press. 2002.
Heretz, Leonid. *Russia on the Eve of Modernity: Popular Religion and Traditional Culture under the Last Tsars*. Cambridge: Cambridge University Press, 2008.
Hollingsworth, Barry. "John Venning and Prison Reform in Russia, 1819–1830." *Slavonic and East European Review* 48.113 (1970) 537–56
Hopkins, C. Howard. *John R. Mott 1865–1955: A Biography*. Grand Rapids: Eerdmans, 1979.
Hosking, Geoffrey A., ed. *Church, Nation and State in Russia and Ukraine*. London: Macmillan, 1991
Husband, William B. *Godless Communists: Atheism and Society in Soviet Russia, 1917–1932*. De Kalb: Northern Illinois University Press, 2000.
———., ed. *The Human Tradition in Modern Russia*. The Human Tradition around the World 1. Wilmington, DE: Scholarly Resources, 2000.
Hutchinson, Mark, and John Wolffe. *A Short History of Global Evangelicalism*. Cambridge: Cambridge University Press, 2012.
Iarygin, Nikolai. *Evangel'skoe dvizhenie v Volgo-Viatskom regione* (The evangelical movement in the Volga-Viatka region). Moscow: Akadmicheskii proekt, 2004.
Istoriko-analiticheskii otdel MSTsEKhB, comp. *Tserkov' dolzhna ostavat'sia tserkov'iu: Neobratimye desiatiletiia 1917–1937 gody v istorii evangel'skogo i baptistskogo dvizhenii. Dokumental'nyi material ob istorii tserkvi EKhB v Rossii* (The church must remain the church: The irreversible decades 1917–1937 in the history of the Evangelical-Baptist movement. Documentary materials on the history of the EKhB churches in Russia). Mezhdunarodnyi sovet tserkvei Evangel'skikh Khristian Baptistov, 2008.
Ivanova, E. V. and Zh. E. Ivanova, *Zarubezhnyi opyt sotsial'noi raboty v ramkakh rossiiskoi blagotvoritel'nosti* (Foreign experience of social work in the framework of Russian charity). Moscow: Mezhdunarodnaia akademiia informatizatsii, 2001.
Kahle, Wilhelm. *Evangel'skie khristiane v Rossii i Sovetskom Soiuze: Ivan Stepanovich Prokhanov, 1869–1935 i put' evangel'skikh khristian i baptistov*. Translated by P. I. Skvortsov. Original title: *Evangelische Christen in Russland und der Sovetunion. Ivan Stepanovich Prokhanov (1869–1935) und der Weg der Evangeliumschusten und Baptisten*. Wuppertal: Izdatel'stvo Onken, 1978. CD Disc: Istoriia Evangel'skogo dvizheniia v Evrazii, materialy i dokumenty, 4.0. Odessa: Euro-Asian Accrediting Association, Elektronnaia khristianskaia biblioteka.
Kalinicheva, Z. V. *Sotsial'naia sushchnost' baptizma 1917–1929 gg.* (The social essence of Baptism 1917–1929). Leningrad: Nauka, 1972.
Kappeler, Andreas et al. *Culture, Nation and Identity: The Ukrainian-Russian Encounter (1600–1945)*. Edmonton: Canadian Institute of Ukrainian Studies Press, 2003.
Karetnikova, M. S., ed. *Al'manakh po istorii russkogo baptizma, vypusk 1* (Almanac on the history of Russian Baptism, issue 1). St. Petersburg: Bibliia dlia vsekh, 1997.
———. *Al'manakh po istorii russkogo baptizma, vypusk 2* (Almanac on the history of Russian Baptism, issue 2). St. Petersburg: Bibliia dlia vsekh, 2001.
Kelly, Catriona. *Children's World: Growing Up in Russia, 1890–1911*. New Haven: Yale University Press, 2007.
Kerzum, A. P."Evangelichesko-missionerskoe blagotvoritel'noe obshchestvo" (Evangelical-missionary charitable society), http://encblago.lfond.spb.ru .

Khorev, V. M. "Istoriia Krasnovorotskogo dvizheniia: 1923–1951" (The history of the Krasnovorotskii movement). Report presented 14 April 2013 in Tsaritsyno, Russia, http://rusbaptist.livejournal.com/64796.html.

Kimberley, Page Herrlinger. *Class, Piety and Politics.* Berkeley: University of California Press, 1996.

Kizenko, Nadiezda. *A Prodigal Saint: Father John of Kronstadt and the Russian People.* University Park: Pennsylvania State University Press, 2003.

Klibanov, A. I. *Istoriia religioznogo sektanstva v Rossii (60-e gody XIX v.–1917)* (The history of religious sectarianism in Russia [1860s–1917]). Moscow: Nauka, 1965.

Kolesova, Ol'ga. *I zhizn,' i slezy, i liubov'. . .* (And life, and tears, and love. . .). St. Petersburg: Bibliia dlia vsekh, 2009.

Kozlov, V. I. and A. P. Pavlenko, eds. *Dukhobortsy i molokane v Zakavkaz'e* (Dukhobors and Molokans in the Transcaucasus). Moscow: Rossiiskaia akademiia nauk, Institut etnologii i antropologii im. N. N. Miklukho-Maklaia, 1992.

Kruppa, Patricia Stallings Kruppa. "The Life and Times of Charles H. Spurgeon." *Christian History* Issue 29 (10.1) 11.

Kuznetsova, Miriam R. "Early Russian Evangelicals (1874–1929): Historical Background and Hermeneutical Tendencies Based on I. V. Kargel's Written Heritage." PhD diss., University of Pretoria, 2009.

Lalleman, Pieter J., et al, eds. *Grounded in Grace: Essays to Honour Ian M. Randall.* London: Spurgeon's College; Didcot, UK: Baptist Historical Society, 2013.

Latourette, Kenneth Scott. *The Nineteenth Century in Europe: The Protestant and Eastern Churches.* Christianity in a Revolutionary Age, A History of Christianity in the Nineteenth and Twentieth Centuries, Vol. 2. Grand Rapids: Zondervan, 1959.

Lawrence, John. *A History of Russia.* New York: Farrar, Strauss & Giroux, 1957; 2nd revised ed. Mentor, 1969.

Lialina, G. S. *Baptizm: Illiuzii i real'nost'* (Baptism: Illusions and reality). Moscow: Izdetel'stvo politicheskoi literatury, 1977.

———. "Liberal'no-burzhuaznoe techenie v baptizme (1905–1917 gg.) (The liberal-bourgeois current in Baptism [1905–1917]). *Voprosy nauchnogo ateizma*, I (Issues of scientific atheism) I (1966) 312–40.

Lindenmeyr, Adele. *Poverty is not a Vice: Charity, Society, and the State in Imperial Russia.* Princeton, N.J.: Princeton University Press, 1996.

———. "Public Life, Private Virtues: Women in Russian Charity, 1762–1914." *Signs: Journal of Woman in Culture and Society* 18.3 (1993) 562–91.

Litsenberger, O. A. *Evangelichesko-liuteranskaia tserkov' v rossiiskoi istorii (XVI–XX vv.)* (The Evangelical Lutheran church in Russian history [XVI–XX cents.]). Moscow: Liuteranskoe kul'turnoe naslediie, 2003.

McCarthy, Kathleen D., ed. *Lady Bountiful Revisited: Women, Philanthropy and Power.* New Brunswick, NJ: Rutgers University Press, 1990.

McCarthy, Mark. "Religious Conflict and Social Order." PhD diss., Notre Dame University, 2004.

McFadden, David, and Claire Gorfinkel. *Constructive Spirit: Quakers in Revolutionary Russia.* Pasadena, CA: Intentional, 2004.

McKee, W. Arthur. "Sobering Up the Soul of the People: The Politics of Popular Temperance in Late Imperial Russia." *The Russian Review* 58 (1999) 212–33.

McLean, Hugh. *Nikolai Leskov: The Man and His Art.* Cambridge: Harvard University Press, 1977.

McLoughlin, William G. *Revivals, Awakenings, and Reform: An Essay on Religion and Social Change in America, 1607–1977.* Chicago History of American Religion Series. Chicago: University of Chicago Press, 1978.

Men', Aleskandr. *Russkaia religioznaia filosofiia.* Moscow: Khram sviatykh bessrebrennikov Kosmy i Damiana v Shubine, 2003.

The Mennonite Encyclopedia. Vol. 4. Scottdale, PA: Mennonite Publishing House, 1959.

Miller, Matthew Lee. "American Philanthropy among Russians: The Work of the YMCA, 1900–1940." PhD diss., University of Minnesota. 2006.

Minus, Paul M. *Walter Rauschenbusch: American Reformer.* New York: Macmillan, 1988.

Morden, Peter J. *C. H. Spurgeon—The People's Preacher.* Farnham, Surrey, UK: CWR, 2009.

———. *'Communion with Christ and his People': The Spirituality of C. H. Spurgeon.* Centre for Baptist History and Heritage Studies 5. Oxford: Regent's Park College, 2010.

Murdoch, Norman H. *Origins of the Salvation Army.* Knoxville: University of Tennessee Press, 1994.

Nesdoly, Samuel John. "Evangelical Sectarianism in Russia: A Study of the Stundists, Baptists, Pashkovites, and Evangelical Christians, 1855–1917." PhD diss., Queen's University, 1971.

Nichols, Gregory. *The Development of Russian Evangelical Spirituality: A Study of Ivan V. Kargel (1849–1937).* Eugene, OR: Pickwick Publications, 2011.

Nikitin, V. A. ed. *Sotsial'naia pedagogika* (Social pedagogy). Moscow: Gumanitarnyi izdatel'skii tsentr VLADOS, Moskovskii gosudarstvennyi sotial'nyi universitet, 2002.

Nikol'skaia, Tat'iana. *Russkii protestantizm i gosudarstvennaia vlast' v 1905–1991 godakh* (Russian Protestantism and state power 1905–1991). St. Petersburg: Izdatel'stvo Evropeiskogo Universiteta, 2009.

———. "Russkii protestantizm na etape utverzhdeniia legalizatsii (1905–1917 gg.) (Russian Protestantism at the stage of the confirmation of [its] legalization [1905–1917])." *Bogoslovskie razmyshleniia* 4 (2004) 161–81.

Orr, J. Edwin. *The Fervent Prayer: The Worldwide Impact of the Great Awakening of 1858.* Chicago: Moody, 1974.

Parker, Michael. *The Kingdom of Character: The Student Volunteer Movement for Foreign Missions (1886–1926).* Lanham, MD: American Society of Missiology and University Press of America, 1998.

Patenaude, Bertrand M. *The Big Show in Bololand: The American Relief Expedition to Soviet Russia in the Famine of 1921.* Stanford, CA: Stanford University Press, 2002.

Payne, Ernest A. *Out of Great Tribulation: Baptists in the U.S.S.R.* London: Baptist Union of Great Britain & Ireland, 1974.

Peris, Daniel. *Storming the Heavens: The Soviet League of the Militant Godless.* Ithaca, NY: Cornell University Press, 1998.

Petrochenkova, Kristina. "Dom trudoliubiia sv. Ioanna: 'Uchrezhdenie pervykh khristian vremen apostol'skikh" (House of labor of St. John: "An establishment of the first Christians of apostolic times." http://www.miloserdie.ru.

———. "Kniaginia-svoboda i ee sestry" (Princess freedom and her sisters). http://www.miloserdie.ru/index.php?ss=2&s=12&id=9896.

Pierard, Richard V., ed. *Baptists Together in Christ, 1905-2005. A Hundred-Year History of the Baptist World Alliance*. Falls Church, VA: The Baptist World Alliance, 2005.

Pipes, Richard. *Russia under the Bolshevik Regime*. New York: Vintage, 1994.

Pivorovich, V. B. and S. A. Diachenko. *Ulitsami starogo Khersona* (By way of the streets of old Kherson). Kherson: Letopis' Prichernomor'ia, 2003.

Popov, V. I. "Evangel'skie trudovye arteli" (Evangelical labor cooperatives). *Bratskii vestnik* 2 (1990) 26–32.

———. *I. S. Prokhanov, Stranitsy zhizni* (I. S. Prokhanov, Pages of a life). St. Petersburg: Bibliia dlia vsekh, 1996

———. "Kapitan Armii Spaseniia" (The Salvation Army captain). *Mirt* No. 79.2 (2012) 16.

———. "Sibirskaia utopia baptistov" (The Siberian utopia of the Baptists). *Nezavisimaiia gazeta* (20 October 2010), www.ng.ru/search/?9=Sibirskaia+utopiia+baptistov+s=poisk.

———. *Stopy blagovestnika* (Footsteps of an evangelist). St. Petersburg: Bibliia dlia vsekh, 1996.

Porter, Cathy, trans. *The Diaries of Sofia Tolstoy*. New York: HarperCollins, 2009.

Puzynin, Andrei. *The Tradition of the Gospel Christians: A Study of Their Identity and Theology during the Russian, Soviet, and Post-Soviet Periods*. Eugene, OR: Pickwick Publications, 2011.

Raber, Mary. "Evangelical Social Ministries in Ukraine since Independence." *East-West Church & Ministry Report* 1 (Winter 2006) 4–5.

Raber, Mary, and Peter F. Penner, eds. *History and Mission in Europe: Continuing the Conversation*. Schwarzenfeld: Neufeld, 2011

Randall, Ian and David Hilborn. *One Body in Christ: The History and Significance of the Evangelical Alliance*. Carlisle, UK: Paternoster, 2001.

Randall, Ian M. "'The Breath of Revival': The Welsh Revival and Spurgeon's College." *Baptist Quarterly* 41 (2005) 196–205.

———. *Communities of Conviction: Baptist Beginnings in Europe*. Schwarzenfeld: Neufeld, 2009.

———. *Rhythms of Revival: The Spiritual Awakening of 1857–1863*. Milton Keynes, UK: Paternoster, 2010.

———. *Spirituality and Social Change: The Contribution of F. B. Meyer (1847–1929)*. Carlisle, UK: Paternoster, 2003.

Redkina, O. Iu. *Sel'skokhoziaistvennye religiozyne trudovye kollektivy v 1917-i-1930-e gody na materialakh evropeiskoi chasti RSFSR* (Agricultural religious labor collectives 1917–1930s based on materials of the European part of the RSSR). Volgograd: Izdatel'stvo Volgogradskogo gosudarstvennogo universiteta, 2004.

Reimer, Johannes. *Evangelizatsiia pered litsom smerti: Iakov Dik i Russkaia palatochnaia missiia*. Translated by Rudolf Stainke. Harsewinkel: Bild & Medien, 2002.

Reshetnikov, Iu. E. *Ukrainskie baptisty i rossiiskaia imperiia: Tserkovno-gosudarstvennye otnosheniia mezhdu Rossiiskim pravitel'stvom i evangel'sko-baptistskim bratstvom na Ukraine vo vtoroi polovine XIX-nachale XX vv.* (Ukrainian Baptists and the Russian empire: Church-state relations of the Russian government and the Evangelical-Baptist brotherhood in Ukraine during the second half of the XIX and the beginning of the XX centuries). Odessa: Bogomyslie, 1997.

Riasanovsky, Nicholas V. *A History of Russia*. 2nd ed. London: Oxford University Press, 1969

———. *Russian Identities, A Historical Survey.* Oxford: Oxford University Press, 2005.
Samarina, Ol'ga Ivanovna. "Obshchiny Molokan na Kavkaze: Istoriia, kul'tura, byt, Khoziastvenaia deiatel'nost'" (Molokan communities in the Caucasus: History, culture, everyday life, household management). Candidate diss., Severo-kavkazskii Gosudarstvennyi tekhnicheskii universitet, 2004.
Saul, Norman E. *Friends or Foes? The United States and Russia, 1921–1941.* Lawrence: University Press of Kansas, 2006.
Savchenko, A. "Ekspeditsiia v kommunu Vertograd" (Expedition to the Vertograd commune). Typewritten manuscript. 29 August 1986.
Savin, Andrei. "'Gorod Solntsa,' ili Evangel'sk, K istorii odnoi religioznoi utopii v Sovetskoi Rossii" (The City of the Sun, or Evangel'sk, Toward a history of one religious utopia in Soviet Russia). *Gost',* 40.1 (2010) 20–22.
Savinskii, S. N. *Istoriia russko-ukrainskogo baptizma: Uchebnoe posobie* (History of Russian-Ukrainian Baptism: A textbook). Odessa: Bogomyslie, 1995.
Sawatsky, Walter. "Prince Alexander N. Golitsyn (1773–1844): Tsarist Minister of Piety." PhD diss., University of Minnesota, 1976.
———. *Soviet Evangelicals since World War II.* Scottdale, PA: Herald, 1980.
Scharpf, Paulus. *History of Evangelism: Three Hundred Years of Evangelism in Germany, Great Britain, and the United States of America.* Translated by Helga Bender Henry. Grand Rapids: Eerdmans, 1966.
Semenov-Tian-Shanskii, Ep. A. *Otets Ioann Kronshtadtskii* (Father John of Kronstadt). 1955. Reprinted, Paris: YMCA Press, 1990.
Serbyn, Roman. "The Famine of 1921–1923: A Model for 1932–1933?" In *Famine in Ukraine: 1932–1933,* edited by Roman Serbyn and Bohdan Krawchenko. Canadian Library in Ukranian Studies. Edmonton: Canadian Institute of Ukrainian Studies, University of Alberta, 1986.
———. "The Origin of the Ukrainian Famine of 1921–23 in the Light of Recent Research." In *Famine—Genocide in Ukraine 1932–1933: Western Archives, Testimonies and New Research,* edited by Wsevolod W. Isaijiw, 165–85. Toronto: Ukrainian-Canadian Research and Documentation Centre, 2003.
Seton-Watson, Hugh. *The Russian Empire, 1801–1917.* Oxford: Clarendon, 1967.
Sevast'ianov, S. V. "Miasoedova Mariia Petrovna, k stoletiiu so dnia rozhdeniia (Miasoedova Mariia Petrovna, on the hundredth anniversary of [her] birth). Typewritten manuscript.
———. "Pleiada sluzhitelei Doma Evangeliia, Leningrad 1924–1937 gody" (The constellation of ministers at Dom Evangeliia, Leningrad 1924–1937). Riga: Typewritten manuscript, ?1973.
Severiukhin, D. Ia. "Dondukova-Korsakova Mariia Mikhailovna, Kniazhna." http://encblago.lfond.spb.ru/showObject.do?object=2823338564.
Shevzov, Vera. *Russian Orthodoxy on the Eve of Revolution.* New York: Oxford University Press, 2004.
Shnaider, Ivan. *Evangel'skie obshchiny v Aktiubinskoi stepi, Sto let pervoi obshchine baptistov v Aktiubinske* (Evangelical congregations in the Aktiubinsk steppes, One-hundred years [since the] first Baptist congregation in Aktiubinsk). Steinhagen, Germany: Samenkorn, 2006.
Shubin, Daniel. H. *A History of Russian Christianity.* Vol. 3, *The Synodal Era and the Sectarians, 1725–1894.* New York: Algora. 2005.

Sinichkin, Aleksei. *Vse radi missii* (All for the sake of mission). Irpen,' Ukraine: Assotsiatsiia "Dukhovnoe vozrozhdenie," 2011.
Sinii, V. S. *Korotkii ogliad istorii baptizmu na Khersonshchini* (A brief look at the history of Baptism in the Kherson region). Kherson, Ukraine: n.p., 2003.
Southwood, Martin. *John Howard, Prison Reformer: An Account of His Life and Travels.* London: Independent, 1958.
Steeves, Paul D. "The Russian Baptist Union, 1917–1935: Evangelical Awakening in Russia." PhD diss., University of Kansas, 1976.
Steinberg, Mark D. and Heather J. Coleman, eds. *Proletarian Imagination: Self, Modernity and the Sacred in Russia, 1910–1925.* Ithaca, NY: Cornell University Press, 2002.
———. *Sacred Stories: Religion and Spirituality in Modern Russia.* Bloomington: Indiana University Press, 2007.
Stepniak-Kravchinskiy, S. *Shtundist Pavel Rudenko* (The Stundist Pavel Rudenko). Cherkassy, Ukraine: Madzhuga, 2004.
Stewart, James Alexander. *A Man in a Hurry: The Story of the Life and Work of Pastor Basil A. Malof.* Orebrö, Sweden: Evangelipress, 1968.
Suny, Ronald Grigor. *The Soviet Experiment: Russia, the USSR, and the Successor States.* New York: Oxford University Press, 1998.
Tarasoff, Koozma J. and Robert B. Klymasz, eds. *Spirit Wrestlers: Centennial Papers in Honour of Canada's Doukhobor Heritage.* Canadian Centre for Folk Culture Studies, Mercury Series Paper 67. Hull, Quebec: Canadian Museum of Civilization, 1995.
Taylor, Dr. and Mrs. Howard. *Hudson Taylor's Spiritual Secret.* Chicago: Moody Press, 1989.
Toews, A. A., "Dyck, Jakob J. (1890–1919)." *Global Anabaptist Mennonite Encyclopedia Online.* 1956, http://gameo.org/index.php?title=Dyck,_Jakob_J._(1890–1919)&oldid=94462.
———. *Mennonite Martyrs: People Who Suffered for their Faith, 1920–1940.* Translated by John B. Toews. Perspectives on Mennonite Life and Thought. Winnipeg: Kindred, 1990.
Toews, John B. *Lost Fatherland: The Story of the Mennonite Emigration from Soviet Russia, 1921–1927.* Studies in Anabaptist and Mennonite History 12. Scottdale, PA: Herald, 1967.
Transchel, Kate. *Under the Influence: Working-Class Drinking, Temperance, and Cultural Revolution in Russia, 1895–1932.* Pitt Series in Russian and East European Studies. Pittsburgh: University of Pittsburgh Press. 2006.
Treadgold, Donald W. *Twentieth Century Russia.* 3rd ed. Chicago: Rand McNally, 1972.
Tretyakov, Vitali. *Philanthropy in Soviet Society.* Moscow: Novosti, 1989.
Troeltsch, Ernst. *The Social Teaching of the Christian Churches.* 2 vols. Translated by Olive Wyon. 1931. Reprinted, Louisville:Westminster John Knox, 1992.
Urry, James. *None but Saints. The Transformation of Mennonite Life in Russia, 1789–1889.* Winnipeg, ON: Hyperion, 1989.
Volkogonov, Dmitri. *Lenin: A New Biography.* Translated and edited by Harold Shukman. New York: Free Press, 1994.
VSEKH-B. *Istoriia Evangel'skikh khristian-baptistov v SSSR* (History of the Evangelical Christians-Baptists in the USSR). Moscow: VSEKH-B, 1989.
Wanner, Catherine. *Communities of the Converted: Ukrainians and Global Evangelism.* Ithaca, NY: Cornell University Press, 2007.

Bibliography

———. "Social Ministry and Missions in Ukrainian Mega-Churches: Two Case Studies." *East-West Church & Ministry Report* 18 (Fall 2010) 12–14.

Wardin, Albert W., Jr. *Gottfried F. Alf: Pioneer of the Baptist Movement in Poland*. Nashville: Baptist History and Heritage Society, 2003.

———. *On the Edge: Baptists and Other Free Church Evangelicals in Tsarist Russia, 1855–1917*. Eugene, OR: Wipf & Stock, 2013.

———. "William Fetler: The Thundering Evangelist." *American Baptist Quarterly* 25 (2006) 235–46.

Wesson, Robert G. *Soviet Communes*. New Brunswick, NJ: Rutgers University Press, 1963.

Williams, A. E. *Barnardo of Stepney, the Father of Nobody's Children*. London: Allen & Unwin, 1943.

Winston, Diane. *Red-Hot and Righteous: The Urban Religion of the Salvation Army*. Cambridge: Harvard University Press, 1999.

Wright, J. F. C. *Slava Bohu: The Story of the Dukhobors*. New York: Farrar & Rinehart, 1940.

Zakhonov, I. *Nikolai Pirogov: Khirurg, pedagog, reformator* (Nikolai Pirogov: Surgeon, pedagogue, reformer). http://www.triz-ri.ru/themes/profi/profi13.asp.

Zhuk, Sergei I. *Russia's Lost Reformation: Peasants, Millennialism, and Radical Sects in Southern Russia and Ukraine, 1830–1917*. Baltimore: Johns Hopkins University Press, 2004.

Zvereva, N. K., comp. *Avgusteishie sestry miloserdiia* (Most august sisters of mercy). Moscow: Veche, 2008.

Electronic Sources

Arkhiv i bibliotechka sviashch. Iakova Krotova (Archives and small library of the priest Iakov Krotov). http://krotov.info

Entsiklopediia blagotvoritel'nosti Sankt-Peterburg. http://encblago.lfond.spb.ru

Global Anabaptist-Mennonite Encyclopedia On-line. www.GAMEO.org

Istoriia EKhB, Put' russkogo baptizma (History of the ECB, The way of Russian Baptism). http://ecbarchive.org

Istoriia Evangel'skogo dvizheniia v Evrazii (History of the evangelical movement in Eurasia), Nos. 1.1, 2.0, 3.0, 4.0, 5.0. *Elektronnaia khristianskaia biblioteka*. Odessa: E-AAA.

Pravoslavnyi portal o blagotvoritel'nosti i sotsial'noi deiatel'nosti (Orthodox portal on charity and social activity). http://miloserdie.ru

Index

Abraham Harder family, children's home overseen by, 155
Acts of the Apostles Brotherhood, 132–33
administrative skill, required for 1921 to 1923 famine relief, 166
agricultural colony, after the February Revolution, 180
agricultural communes, 59, 65–66
agricultural communities, 199
agricultural reconstruction, international cooperation supporting, 172
aid
   within the evangelical community itself, 61
   from the outside, 166
   task of claiming, 164
Aitken, Tom, 44, 80, 130, 149
Akhor commune, 193, 197
alcoholism
   fight against, 64
   as a spiritual problem, 204
   Welsh Revival's effects on, 119–120
Alekhin, Arkadii Egorovich, 179
Aleksander Nevskii Society, 136
Aleksandrova, E. K., 127
Alekseev, Savelii Alekseevich, 45
Alexander I (emperor), 27, 28, 88
Alexander III (emperor), 24, 93
Alexandra, (queen), 129
Alexis I (emporer), 27

All for the Sake of Mission (Vse radi missii) (Sinichkin), 207
All-Russian Agricultural Exhibit, 191
All-Russian Baptist Union, 157, 158
All-Russian Congress against the Trafficking of Women, 124
All-Russian Evangelical Christian Union, 14
All-Russian Hygiene Exhibition, 80, 129–130
All-Russian Union of Baptists, 106
All-Russian Union of Evangelical Christians (Evangelical Christian Union), 99
All-Union Council of Evangelical Christians-Baptists (AUCEC-B), 15, 17, 210
Al'manakh po istorii russkogo baptizma (Almanac on the history of Russian Baptism, 1997 and 2001), 17
almsgiving, 25
American Mennonite Relief, 163, 168
American Relief Administration (ARA), 160, 162–63, 172, 173
anarchist bands, active during the Civil War, 154
Anderson, Paul B., 81n134
"Andrew" group, 153
Anglo-American "prayer revival," 30
archival sources, needing further investigation, 209

aristocratic women, serving as voluntary nurses, 34
assistance funds, 98–103
assistance ministries, 77
Atav, S., 89
attitude, to compassionate ministry, 70
AUCEC-B (All-Union Council of Evangelical Christians-Baptists), 15, 17, 210
authorities. *See* government
Avdasev, V. N., 184n72

"baby home" (*bebi khom*), 47, 103
Baedeker, Friedrich, 45, 81, 93
Balashov home, 107
Baliaev, Ivan Pavlovich, 190
Balikhin, Fedor Prokhorovich, 44, 91n36, 109, 116
baptism, importance of, 3
Baptist(s)
  concerned with establishing a recognizable denomination, 13
  differences with Evangelical Christians, 99n86
  held meetings in a public auditorium in Saratov in the middle of the Volga famine zone, 169
  limited their aid to fellow Baptists, 170
  missionaries supported by, 98
  Molokans helpful to, 89
  repairing and redecorating *dom maliutki* (home for children up to the age of three), 9
  resettling in Siberia, 195
  sharing through ARA, 171
  situation more difficult for, 45
  threatened by the famine in the Volga region, 59n26
Baptist children, education of, 105
Baptist church in Syktyvkar (Komi, ASSR), held concerts to benefit victims of the 1988 earthquake in Armenia, 9
Baptist community
  endured early persecution, 106–7
  international contributed to famine relief between 1921 and 1924, 159
Baptist denominational organization, building, 61
Baptist journal, 61
  editors of, 95
  published reports of evangelistic preachers supported by the Russian Baptist Union, 109
  served as a teaching tool, 109, 112
  served as the main connecting point among Baptists, 101
Baptist movement, apologist and theologian for, 98
Baptist pastors, insurance fund for, 97
Baptist Union
  administration of funds, 101
  assistance through ARA channels, 171
  behind founding of communes and cooperatives, 66
  closed down by 1916, 58, 150
  helping Christian brothers, 168
  leaders of, 66
  main source of supply to, 162
  no longer functioning by 1930, 198
  sustained reliable structures for receiving and directing aid, 173
Baptist Union Collegium in Moscow. *See* Collegium of the Baptist Union
Baptist World Alliance, 158
  accessing ARA supplies, 163
  cash advance from, 166
  on Evangelical Christians, 162
  wanted a local partner organization, 171
Barnardo, Thomas, 30, 78, 79, 203
Barnardo Homes for children, 30, 78

Index 231

Bashkov, F. A., 170
battlefield deaths, 145
Bebbington, David W., 12, 206, 209, 211
bebi khom ("baby home"), 47, 103
Becker, Clara, 132
Beklemisheva, Elena Vasil'evna, 105, 105n117
believers. *See* evangelical believers
Bellow, John, 46, 93
Berdyaev, Nicholas, 23
Berezhnoi, Anatolii Arsen'evich, 193, 197–98
Beseda (The conversation), 98, 181, 183
"Bethany" group, 153
Bible, power and sufficiency of, 2
Bibles, circulated among the population, 30
Blackwood, Stevenson Arthur, 32
blind children, shelter for, 40
Bobrinskii, Vladimir Alekseevich (count), 32, 40, 42
Bodelschwingh, Friedrich von, 79
Boichenko, Grigorii Akimovich, 72
Bolshevik Revolution
  ideological changes, 67
  opportunities for communal living, 65
Bolsheviks
  accommodated evangelicals at first, 176
  attitude to the organization of communes, 196
  destruction of Orthodox Church as first concern, 58
  realizing need to rebuild agriculture and industry, 175
Bonch-Bruevich, Vladimir Dmitrievich, 176
Booth, Evangeline, 116
Booth, William, 79–80, 115, 128
  Fetler learned first-hand about, 121
  founder of the Salvation Army, 30
  ministry of, 117
  Trosnov visited with, 129
"bourgeois" industrial managers, recast as "experts," 175
Bratskaia pomoshch (Fraternal help) credit union, 62, 172, 181
Bratskii vestnik (Fraternal messenger), 17
Breyfogle, Nicholas B., 7, 87
British Baptists, cooperated with Save the Children and the Nansen Commission, 163n116
Budil'nik sovesti (Reveille of the conscience), 153
Buksgevden, Baron Otto O., 48
bulk food sales, from an ARA warehouse, 163
Byford, Chas. T., 46, 57

call, to "go and tell" everyone, 201
Campanella, Tommaso, 195
care for the poor
  giving way to private charitable organizations, 25
  traditional notions of versus "scientific" charity, 50
Carolou, Ioulia, 122n62
Catherine II (empress)
  granted Mennonites special rights, 11
  invited Quaker Dr. Thomas Dimsdale, 27
the Caucasus, 12
Central Baptist Church in Moscow, volunteers caring for geriatric patients, 9
Cernyshevskii, Nikolai, 23n3
challenging situations, required challenging measures, 208
charitable organizations. *See also* evangelical institutions
  cooperation between the Bolsheviks and private, 177
  establishment of, 64, 103–8

charitable organizations *(continued)*
  founded on Pashkovite estates, 44
  Soviet society transcended the need for, 5
charity (*blagotvoritel'nost',* or "creating good"), disappeared during the Soviet period, 6
Chernyshevskii, Nikolai Gavrilovich, 36, 182, 186
Chertkova, Elizaveta Ivanovna, 28, 32, 33, 35, 64, 122, 125, 129, 130
  continued the idea of the Pashkovite sewing cooperative, 127–28
  house on Vasilievskii Island donated by, 151
  protected by Emperor Alexander III, 80
Chetvernin, N. M., 106
children
  Bernardo Homes for, 30
  Dom Evangeliia offerings for, 148
  education of Baptist, 105
  evangelicals attempted to help, 212
  Karpinskaia taught the Gospels to sectarian, 50
  Kellomaki home for orphaned, 47
  Olga Zenkova began a clandestine school for Stundist, 50
  orphaned, home for operated by the Tent Mission, 155
  orphaned, physical rescue of, 148
  raising to serve as missionaries, 47
  shelter for blind, 40
  shelter for, established in Makivka (Ukraine) in 1996, 212
  shelter for, founded by the St. Petersburg Evangelical Christians in Raivola, 53
  summer colony for, in Finland sponsored by the Salvation Army in 1915, 149
  "unsupervised" (*besprizornye*), 114
  youth caring for in St. Petersburg, 135

children's homes
  Baptists repairing and redecorating, 9
  Dom Evangeliia youth staffing a small, 78
  founded by the Evangelical Christian congregation in St. Petersburg, 104
  overseen by Abraham Harder family, 155
China Inland Mission, expansion of the work of, 30
The Christian. See Khristianin (The Christian) journal
Christian agricultural cooperative, 184
Christian compassion, encompassing systemic change, 184
Christian Democratic Party "Resurrection," 182
"Christian Labor" artels, 180
Christian labor exchange, 39
Christian political parties, 182
Christian Soldiers' Circle, 78n112, 153–54
Christian teaching, regarding good works, 69
Christian witness, communal living as a means of, 179
Christianity, Dukhobors and Molokans rejected all material manifestations of, 62
Christians, having spiritual capacity to realize a new society, 66
Christ's love, appropriated by faith, not by good works, 23
Chto delat'? (Lenin), 194
Chto delat'? (What is to be done?) (Cernyshevskii), 23n3, 36, 182, 192
"Chto nam delat'?" (What must we do?), published by Prokhanov, 194

church committees, crucial in distribution, 164
church leaders, sent into exile by 1916, 205
church members
   aid practiced among, 61–62
   contributions sent to *Khristianin*, 53
church unions, formalizing and strengthening, 53
Churikov, Ivan Alekseevich, 140
"circles" (*kruzhki*), formation of, 99
citizenry, shaping change, 25
Civil War
   anarchist bands active during, 154
   beginning of, 152
   Dom Evangeliia helping those in need during, 152–53
   religious grounds for release from military service during, 176
civilian deaths, attributable to hunger, exposure, and disease, 145
class, fellowship transcended, 41
clinic (*lechebnitsa*), "for the sick of all social classes," 52
clothing and shoes, shipped from the United States to Russia, 159
Coleman, Heather J., 7, 10, 56, 176
Collegium of the Baptist Union, 158–59
   instructions concerning ARA food packages, 164
   money sent through the ARA apparatus to, 163
   suggested famine aid measures, 160–61
Collier, S. F., 122
common proprety, Dukhobor practice of holding, 88
communal living
   assumed an air of protest and separation, 196
   as blind for rich sectarians, 197
   as a means of witness through concrete example, 189
   as part of an all-embracing social transformation, 66, 175
   as a way of demonstrating Christian values, 199
communes
   agricultural, 59, 65–66
   Akhor, 193, 197
   end of, 196–98
   Gefsimaniia, 190
   improving, 193–94
   in Kazakhstan, 197–98
   peasant, 24, 182
   Popov on Baptist Union's, 175
   Redkina's assessment of, 175
   regarded with suspicion by some evangelicals, 198
   religiously-based, 20, 196
   roots in Evangelical Christian Union in the 1920s, 188
   "sectarians" invited to form, 205
   as socially radical, 65
   Vertograd, 183
communism, practised by the Dukhobors, 88
communities
   establishment of ideal, 82
   migrated to Central Asia or Siberia, 197
community, building a sense of, 109
community members, meeting their own needs, 203
compassion
   as the concern of all members of the community, 203
   evangelicals developing and retaining a sense of community, 208
   highlighting the worldwide connections of the evangelicals, 208
   as an important way to "go and tell," 202
   as a natural part of faith, 208

compassion *(continued)*
    re-emphasizing complex nature of Russian evangelicalism, 206
    three major patterns for, 203
    transformed into "philanthropy" (*chelovekoliubie*), 27
    translating the Russian word *miloserdie* as, 11
compassionate goal, of providing for people's needs not forgotten, 194
compassionate intervention, necessity for new, mass forms of, 54
compassionate ministry
    accessible to evangelicals from the lower classes, 115
    approaches to among evangelicals, 61
    basic commitment to, 4
    as a common task, 76–82
    confirming the outward-looking nature of the movement, 207
    considered essential by Russian evangelical believers, 69
    continued after the 1884 exile of V. A. Pashkov and M. M. Korf, 50
    evangelicals' reputation for neglecting, 70
    exposing upper classes to realities of life among the poor, 41
    factors informing, 86
    during the famine (1921 to 1923), 156–173
    highlighting evangelicals' expectation of change for the better, 207–8
    history of, by Russian evangelicals, 5
    integral for Russian evangelicals, 3
    main emphases, 1905 to 1929, 60–67
    memoirs of practitioners of, 18
    no longer viable by the mid-1020s, 177–78
    as an organic part of Russian evangelical witness, 202
    remained a strong commitment during the Golden Age, 203
    Russian evangelical identity and, 23–27, 206–9
    uniting divided social classes, 26
    during World War I and the Civil War, 145–155
compassionate models, actively sought from the West, 204
compassionate outreach, among evangelicals, 8
concrete acts, practical Christianity expressing itself in, 189
congregations
    engaged in compassionate ministry, 107
    Molokan, Evangelical Christian, and Mennonite readiness to help with famine aid, 159
convalescent home, at Dom Evangeliia for members, 126
conversion, united with social means, 115
Conybeare, Frederick C., 89
cooperative labor enterprises, evangelicals experimenting with, 59
cooperatives, model charters for, 189
Corrado, Sharyl M., 10, 19, 43
Council of People's Commissars, 180
Council of Worker's Deputies in Reval, 190
credit union, founded in 1922 for church members, 62
Crimean War, Russia's humiliating defeat in, 24
criminals, outreach to, 46
Cultural Revolution, creating a proletarian society by force, 197
cultural-economic improvement, useful for the present life only, 85

Dalton, Hermann F., 34, 36

Dalton, Pastor, 210
Davydov, Denis, 35
de Mayer, Evgeniia (Jenny), 47–49, 50, 114, 202
deaconesses, ministry of, 77
deaths
  battlefield, 145
  civilian, 145
  of missionaries, 154
  by starvation, 167
debt, burdening the rural population with, 24
Decree of 17 April 1905, on religious toleration, 10
Demakin, P. G., 106
"deserving poor," identifying and helping, 26
Dik, Iakov Ia., 153, 154
Dillon, Emile J., 31, 38
Dimsdale, Dr. Thomas, 27
dining room
  at Dom Evangeliia, 126
  organized to accommodate poor students, 38–39
"Diolch Iddo" ("Thanks be to Him"), 119
Disabilities Fund
  administered for the sake of preachers or their widows, 106
  importance of giving to, 101–2
  managing, 101
  special offering for support of, 111
  suffering for a lack of resources, 112
Doherty, Catherine de Hueck, 33
doing good, expressing gratitude to God, 70
Dom Evangeliia (House of the Gospel), 58, 118
  conection with Salvation Army, 80–81
  focused on helping those in need during years of revolution and Civil War, 152–53
  functioned as an infirmary for the wounded, 146–47
  offerings accepted for the purchase of warm clothing, shoes, and food for children, 148
  parallels with Spurgeon's Metropolitan Tabernacle, 126
  requisitioned as a barracks, 150
  served as a half-way house, 204, 207
  served as a shelter during the Civil War, 153
  shelter not geared to quick results, 127
  youth of, staffing of a small children's home, 78
Dom Golgofy (House of Golgotha), 118
Dom spaseniia (House of salvation), 118, 141
Dondukova-Korsakova, Maria Mikhailovna, 8–9, 35
Dostoevsky, Fyodor, 31, 39
drought
  part of the rhythm of agricultural life in central Russia, 156
  in the Volga region by the fall of 1920, 156
drunkenness. *See also* alcoholism, as a spiritual problem, 120
Dubovyi, Fedor, 110
Duff, Mildred, 44, 78, 128
Dukhobors, 62
  group stranded in Cyprus aided by Prokhanov, 183
  maintained communal proprety, 90
  mutual support practiced among, 87
  origins of, 87
  rejected all material manifestations of Christianity, 87
  settled in isolated areas, 88
  from which the Molokans descended, 86

"Dyma Geidwad i bechadur" ("Here's a Saviour unto sinners"), 119

East End Juvenile Mission, founder of, 78

Eastern European evangelical scholars, new generation of, 211

Eastern Union of Russian and Ukrainian Evangelical Christian Baptists, in the USA, 159

economic communities
- creating, 65–66
- establishment of, 61
- as a means of witness and of economic support, 189
- in the 1920s, 188–196
- pattern for the development of, 180
- with the purpose to eradicate poverty, 203
- singled out as under a curse, 198
- viable from about 1921, 66
- as a witness by putting an end to need, 194

economic gains, by religiously-based communities and cooperatives, 196

educated elite, new initiatives from, 25

emancipation, reinforcing ancient land tenure patterns, 24

Emigrants' Home in London, 31

employment, as motivation for forming economic communities, 179

employment agency, as part of Fetler's ministry, 124

"Engineer of the Project Bureau of the Evangelical Christian Union," 195

English evangelicalism, sources on the history of, 21

Entsiklopediia blagotvoritel'nosti Sankt-Peterburga (Encyclopedia of St. Petersburg charity), 7, 8

Era of Great Reforms (approximately 1861 to 1880), in Russia, 24

"Eurelcon," allowed cooperating organizations to buy food at cost from the ARA, 163

Eurelcon public kitchen, in Peski, in 1922, 163

Euro-Asian Accrediting Association (E-AAA), 18

"evangelical," containing many layers of meaning, 12

Evangelical (*evangel'skie*) Christians, 13
- with a capital "E," capital "C," 14
- more open with aid, 170
- Pashkovite movement descendants identifying themselves as, 43
- resettling in Siberia, 195
- street mission group, 134
- thanking God for compassionate ministries, 9–10

Evangelical Alliance
- Prokhanov inspired by, 181–82
- Russian counterpart of, 99

evangelical approaches, to social need in Russia, 66

evangelical aristocrats, work during the Russo-Turkish War (1877–1878), 34

evangelical aspirations, of Pashkovites, 36

evangelical believers. *See also* Russian evangelicals
- attempted to help children, the elderly, the disabled, and people suffering from addictions, 212
- called to live according to the example of Jesus Christ, 193
- commitment to supporting preachers and their families, 62
- compassionate ministry considered essential by, 69
- concurred on performing deeds that God has given people to do according to the Bible, 70

continued to try to help others during the famine, 167
contributed to Russian society in times of national need before 1905, 84
created new patterns for religious life, 25
dealt with intermittent persecution, 56
demonstrated they were not subversives, 146
endured intermittent arrests, imprisonments, fines, beatings, and other setbacks in the 1920s, 177
expected profound changes to take place in people's lives because of the gospel, 201
expected the church to be a community of mutual support, 86
expected to give to everyone as freely as their circumstances permitted, 72
expected to live simply, 74
fasted once a week even in the famine zone, 167
help for, in prison, 177
historical precedent in Russia for identifying with compassionate ministry, 28–29
insisted on sobriety for church members, 137
material status continued to deteriorate in 1917 and in 1918, 152
ministered publicly again in early 1917, 151
ministries of compassion practiced by, 83
not welcomed as participants in the wider Russian society, 86
numerical growth during the 1920s, 176
organized designated funds, 56
Pavlov helped with a supply of flour sent by, 94
as people of means, 73
perceived to be German sympathizers, 150
present-day unaware of evangelical compassionate ministry, 9
"prison ministry" came to mean caring for fellow members, 45–46
reminded by "The Gospel Standard of Life" program that "there were no needy persons" in the Jerusalem Church, 194
represented by two alternately cooperating and competing unions, 14
"Russian" applied to, 11
as Russians who had chosen a non-Russian path, 13
sending offerings to *Khristianin* (The Christian) journal, 99
status changed abruptly in 1905, 55
supported their own missionaries, 91
survival methods during the famine, 166–67
sustained preachers and other church workers during the famine, 170
tended to emphasize caring for their own, 57
took part in caring for wounded, refugees, orphans, and the starving during an era of great upheaval, 173
took responsibility for caring for their own exiles and prisoners, 94
turned to one another for help in 1919 and 1920, 152
uncertain status in the wider community, 57

evangelical believers *(continued)*
  understanding of money, 83
  wealthy expected to look to the needs of the those less well off, 74
  welcomed the NEP, 176
evangelical charitable institutions. *See* charitable organizations
Evangelical Christian Executive Council, 161
Evangelical Christian Union, 14
  communes having roots in, 188
  growth of, 56
  leadership of, 66, 161
  no longer functioning by 1930, 198
  shut down by 1916, 58, 150
  sought for congregations in the Volga region and in Ukraine, 157
  sustained reliable structures for receiving and directing aid, 173
Evangelical Christianity and the Social Question (Prokhanov), 66, 180, 188, 189, 191
Evangelical Christians-Baptists (Russian Baptist Union), 104
evangelical communities, as "islands of well-being," 194
evangelical community
  educating on money and giving, 108–12
  help given to those on the outskirts of, 165
evangelical compassionate ministry. *See* compassionate ministry
evangelical congregations, formal registration of, 55
evangelical content, to traditional compassion, 47
evangelical cooperatives, 180
evangelical dilemma, words or work, 69–70
evangelical economic communities, some continued by reorganizing as collectives, 198

evangelical emphases, list of, 12
evangelical institutions. *See also* charitable organizations
  establishment and support of, 179
  organized to care for orphans and the elderly, 204
evangelical leaders
  imprisonments under the Soviets, 58
  involved briefly in politics, 67
evangelical life, systematization of post-1905, 98
evangelical movement
  distinguishing marks of, 206
  goal of removing the spiritual shackles from people's souls, 192
  growing historical memory of, 102
  growth in the 1920s, 60
  rallied again with the February Revolution of 1917, 58
  regional histories of, 8
  represented by two competing unions by 1909, 99
evangelical press, 53
Evangelical Society for the Religious and Moral Education of St. Petersburg Protestants (*Evangelicheskoe obshchestvo religioznogo i nravstvennogo popecheniia protestantov v Peterburge*), 36–37
Evangelical Union, Prokhanov established, 182
evangelical youth. *See* youth
evangelicalism
  complexity of Russian, 206
  English, 21
  global, 211
  Golden Age (1905 to 1929) of Russian, 4, 54–60, 201
  modern expression in Russia, 54
evangelicals abroad, *Baptist* cited examples from the experience of, 111

"evangelicals under stress," Russians as, 209
evangelism
  as the answer to "What is to be done?," 26
  first importance to support, 85
  preaching the good news of Jesus Christ, 67
  as the ultimate act of compassion, 82
evangelistic trip, in the Volga famine zone before summer 1922, 168
evangelists, fully-supported, 91
Evangel'sk (City of the Sun), 66
evangel'skii, translating the word, 12
exiles, well-being of, 102
"experts," 175

faith
  essence of, 69
  without works as dead, 82
"faith alone," Protestant tenet of, 69
famine
  assistance in times of, 156
  contribution during as spiritual in nature, 169
famine (1891), 156
famine (1906), 68n71
famine (1921 to 1923), 145
  affected relationships between Evangelical Christians and Baptists, 157, 170
  assistance distributed across the spectrum of evangelical groups and also to the Orthodox, 100
  evangelicals involved in international relief effort, 157
  natural and human factors magnifying one another, 156
  new challenges created by, 205
  Russian evangelicals coordinated the distribution of food and material aid, 59

farming community, setting up near Kharkiv, 179
Fast, Hermann, 46, 93, 183, 186, 187
Father John of Kronstadt, 48n124
"Father of Continental Baptism," 13n50
February Revolution of 1917, initially greeted with joy by the evangelicals, 150
Fedorovna, Alexandra (empress), 34, 48, 49
Fedorovna, Dowager Empress Maria, 28, 48, 129, 149
fellowship, transcended class, 41
Female Aid Society, 120
Fetler, Barbara, summarized the Russian evangelicals' understanding of their calling, 200–201
Fetler, John, 117, 121, 141, 150
Fetler, Robert, 121n57
Fetler, William A., 11, 15, 45, 56, 61, 62, 64, 66, 116–121, 149
  at All-Russian Congress on the Battle against Drunkenness, 139
  arrival and exile of, 113
  on Baptist church at Balashov, 105–6
  challenged Miasoedova to return to Russia, 130–31
  characterizing rescue ministry, 203
  churches founded in St. Petersburg and Riga, 118
  conducted preaching meetings at numerous stations in St. Petersburg, 122
  exile and later ministry, 140–42
  exile of, 150
  gave the Salvation Army a Russian home address, 130
  helped establish Gospel Committee for Work among Russian War Prisoners, 147–48
  inspired to attempt to reach the urban poor with the gospel, 204

Fetler, William A. *(continued)*
   member of a temperance organization, 138
   motion to build a specifically Baptist prayer house, 125
   offered General Booth the members of his congregation, 132
   Salvation Army meetings set up by, 80
   served as an important catalyst for the development of rescue ministry, 142
   studied in England, 117
   supporters got his Siberian exile sentence changed to exile abroad, 116n22
   visited Spurgeon's grave, 117
Fetler Family Band, 142
field hospital (*lazaret*), at the beginning of World War I, 90
Figner, Vera, 35
Finney, Charles Grandison, 120–21
First All-Russian Congress on the Battle against Drunkenness, 138
First World War. *See* World War I
Fitzpatrick, Sheila, 145
Five Year Plan (1928 to 1932), 197
food and clothing, distribution of, 164
"food drafts," 163
food orders, from Southern Baptists, 166
"fool for Christ" (*iurod*), 33
"foreign elements," evangelicals punished as, 208
foreign evangelicals, observations and reports on the ministries of, 78
foreign observers in Russia, contemporary accounts of, 18
Fox, George, founder of the Religious Society of Friends (Quakers), 27
Franklin, J. H., 162
Friedenstimme (Voice of peace), Mennonite publication, 154
Fry, Elizabeth, 28

further study, directions for, 209–11

Gagarina, Vera Fedorovna (princess), 32, 35, 45, 80
Gavrilich, 90
Gebetstunde (prayer hour), 55
Gefsimaniia (Gethsemane) community, 188
   ceased to exist by 1925, 197
   first commune organized according to Prokhanov's plan in 1919, 190
   forced by the authorities to take in eleven additional poor families, 197
   in Tver' guberniia organized by 1919, 180
generosity
   connected to spiritual benefits, 110
   evangelicals' preference to err on the side of, 71
German Baptists
   baptisms among converted Russian prisoners, 147
   compassionate activity of, 11
   patterns of worship and organization set by, 90
German *Bibelstunde* (Bible hour), 55
"German elements," evangelicals as, 58
"German faith," 141, 150
German-speaking colonists, religious revival among, 54
Gerusy, rocky soil almost impossible to cultivate, 92
Gil'debrandt, Aleksandra Egorovna, 44
Gill, Everett, 164, 166
giving
   done "in secret" before God, 70
   good works and, 69
   systematized, 111
glasnost' ("openness"), 6

Index 241

global evangelicalism, incorporating Russian evangelical experience into, 211
goal, of bringing to faith the entire population of Russia, 29
Golden Age (1905 to 1929), of Russian evangelicalism, 4, 54–60, 201
Goliaev, Il'ia Andreevich, 74, 106
Golitsyn, Aleksandr, 27
Golitsyn, Prince Nicholas, 116
Golitsyna, Princess K., 80, 116
Golovashchenko, S. I., 18
Good Samaritan, parable of, 71
"Good Samaritan Fund," at Dom Evangeliia, 147
Good Shepherd charitable fund, 212
good works, as fruit of salvation, 23
Gorbachev, Mikhail, 5–6
Gorinovich, Elizaveta, 183
Gorinovich, N. E., 40, 46, 131–32
Gorinovich, Vera, 131, 132n128
Gorod Solntsa (City of the sun) or Evangel'sk, 194–95
gospel
  penetrating the walls of the prison, 195
  presentation of the message of as central, 40
  transforming power of, 67–69
Gospel Christians, 13
Gospel Committee for Work among Russian War Prisoners, 148
"The Gospel Standard of Life" program, 193, 194
government. *See also* Soviet government
  distribution by committees running afoul of, 165
  mismanagement compounded into humanitarian disasters, 156
  policy by 1922 intended to discard religion itself, 177

government-sponsored organizations, dismantling of all but, 177
Grachev, Iu. S., 17
Graham, Stephen, 145, 146
Great Reforms, in the 1860s, 24–25
Gromova, Anna Iosifovna, 134
Grundberg, Laura, 47, 50, 103
Guardianship of Houses of Industry and Workhouses, 48
Guardianship of Popular Temperance, 137

half community- *poluvseobshchina*, common land and equipment with private household property, 189
half-way house (*nochlezhka*, "night shelter"), in Dom Evangeliia, 127
Handbook for ministers of the Holy Church (*Nastol'naia kniga dlia sviashcheno-tserkovno-sluzhitelei*), 115–16
hard-labor prison (*katorzhnaia t'iurma*), visiting, 133
hardtack (*sukhari*), to Russian prisoners in Germany and Austria, 147
Hedda, Jennifer, 37
Heier, Edmund, 29, 33, 38
"hidden labor collective," Baptists as, 178
Hilton, Edward and Henry, 39
historical models, for ideas on communal living, 182
Höijer, N. F., 136, 210
Holiness teaching, influence of, on the Russian evangelicals, 20
home visitation, as appropriate for the young, 77
Hoover, Herbert, 160
House of Industry, on the island of Sakhalin, 114, 202
House of Industry (*Dom trudoliubiia*), for discharged prisoners, 48
Howard, John, 28, 202

human beings, responsibility to one
    another, 72
Hutchinson, Mark, 211

Iakovlev, N. Ia., 179
Iaroslavskii, Emel'ian, 195
Iashchenko, M., 101
Iasnovskaia, Maria N. (baroness),
    44–45, 58n22, 64, 124, 152, 153
Il'ich, Ivan, 41
Imperial Philanthropic Society, 27
Imperial Russia, sectarian life in, 7
In Darkest England and the Way Out
    (Booth), 115
In His Steps (Sheldon), 79
industrial laborers, in Russia between
    1890 and 1914, 63
industrial revolution, in Russia, 63
industrialization, brought people into
    urban centers, 114
infirmaries (*lazarety*), to nurse the
    wounded, 146
inner transformation, leading to ex-
    ternal transformation, 192
intellectuals, "going to the people," 33
International Committee for Russian
    Relief, 160
international relief effort, 1921 to
    1923 famine involved evangeli-
    cals in, 157
inward transformation, improving
    society, 207
*Istoriia Evangel'skikh khristian-
    baptistov v SSSR* (History of the
    Evangelical Christians-Baptists
    in the USSR, 1989), 17
*Istoriia Evangel'sko-Baptistskogo
    dvizheniia v Ukraine* (The history
    of the Evangelical-Baptist move-
    ment in Ukraine), 18
Italian Baptist Union, aiding earth-
    quake victims, 111
Ivanov, Stepan Ivanovich, 69

Ivanov, V. V., 55–56, 61, 66, 69, 86, 92,
    97–98
  on Christians doing good with
    whatever money they have, 73
  critical of Mazaev for his control-
    ling leadership and affluent
    personal lifestyle, 96
  on dedication of "sectarians" for
    defense against the haughty Ger-
    mans and the cruel Turks, 146
  described the new life, 201
  encouraged congregations to look
    after their own members, 179
  on evangelicals' reputation, 70
  on giving, 72
  on indifference to charity, 110
  on the joy of the gospel, 68
  on Molokan practice of placing
    offerings under a towel, 70
  raised as Molokan, 94–95
  representing compassion practiced
    among the evangelicals, 203
  seeking to preserve spirituality, 90
  on stinginess, 109
  on support of twenty evangelists, 68
  visited Spurgeon's grave, 117
  worked to instill a Molokan-type
    ethic of mutual support, 204
Ivanov, Vasilii Nikolaevich, 45, 93
Ivanov-Klyshnikov, P. V., 178

Jack, Walter, 147
Jerusalem Brotherhood, 186
Jerusalem church
  answer to the question as found in
    the life of, 194
  in the Book of Acts, 66, 86
  depicted as an "island" in a "sea of
    need and injustice," 194
  described in the Book of Acts, 82
  desire expressed to live according
    to the description of, 198
  embodying the life of, 188
  no needy persons in, 194

Index   243

replicating the life of described in the Book of Acts, 174–75, 205
replicating the lifestyle of and creating a refuge from government repression, 186
Jesus, works of compassion, 72
John Chrysostom (saint), quote from, 76
Joint Commission for Assisting in the Distribution of Foreign Baptist Relief, 157
Joint Relief Commission, 171
juvenile prison colony, 148

Kal'veit, Martin, 92
Kalweit, Martin, 13n50
Kapranova, Agaf'ia Ivanovna, 75–76
Kapranova, Ekaterina, 84
Kapustin, Savelii, 88
Kapustinskii, Sozont Evtikhievich, 92–93, 94
Karetnikova, M. S., 17
Karev, Aleksandr, 134, 151
Kargel, Ivan Veniaminovich, 13n45, 45, 80
Karpinskaia, Iuliia Nikolaevna, 49
    declared guilty of "spreading Stundism," 50
    set up "People's kindergartens" in Kyiv, 202
    taught the Gospels to "sectarian children," 50
    work of surfaced through archival research, 209–10
Karpovich von Mayer, Karl, 37
Kartashev, Anton, 81n134
Kashchenko Psychiatric Hospital, 6
Kazakhstan, communes organized in, 197–98
Kellomäki home for orphaned children, 47
Kherson, Ukraine, street named for John Howard, 28

Khristianin (The Christian) journal, 16, 181
    believers sending offerings to, 99
    the first legal evangelical publication since *Ruskii rabochii* (The Russian workman), 52
    promoting unity among "all the branches of living Christianity" in Russia, 100
Khvostov, Aleksei, 149–150
"Kirk" estate, 186
Kirpichnikov, 138
Kolesnikov Molokan family, 146
Kolesnikova, Praskovia Ivanovna, 167
Koloskov, Ivan, 140
Koloskov, M. D., 95
Korf, Modest Modestovich (count), 22–23, 32, 41
    "archives" of, 185–86
    exile of in 1884, 23, 42, 55
    pursued the idea of economic communities, 65
    on sewing groups, 35
Kostromin, F. P., 89, 92, 96, 102
Kotsebu, P. E., 178
Kozlianinova, Konstantsiia Sergeevna, 42–43
Kozmin, Gavriil, 69
Kozyrev, V. N., 6
Krahn, Cornelius, 187
Krestovozdvizhenskoe trudovoe bratstvo (Elevation of the Cross labor brotherhood), 184
Kroeker, Jakob, 147
Kropotkin, Pyotr, 33
Kruze sisters, 32
kulaki (rich peasants), 73
Kupriianov, Ivan, 93–94
Kushnerov, Ivan Petrovich, 56, 105

labor and social life, restructuring of, 194
"labor brotherhood" (*trudovoe bratstvo*), agricultural, 33

labor cooperatives, 199
Larsson, Karl, 80, 130, 151
Latvian Baptist Church, in St. Petersburg, 121
"law of love," 68
leaders
    of the Baptist Union, 66
    biographies of Russian, 18–19
    of the Evangelical Christian Union, 66, 161
    exiled to Siberia, 150
    involved briefly in politics, 67
    Molokan background of, 204
    sent into exile by 1916, 205
    Stundist, 73
    suffered multiple imprisonments under the Soviets, 58
League of the Militant Godless, 195–96
Lectures on Revivals of Religion (Finney), 120
Lenin, V. I., 23n3, 175, 194
Leningrad, 58n22
leper colony, potatoes distributed to during the famine, 168–69
Leskov, Nikolai, 31, 39
Lewis, W. O., 167, 171
Liasotskii, Ivan, 92, 102–3
Licht im Osten (Light in the east) mission, 147
"The Life of an Optimist in the Land of Pessimism" (Prokhanov), 207
Lindenmeyr, Adele, 5, 7, 25
"little brothers" (*bratsy*), 140
Livanov, F. V., 89
Liven, Natalia, 32, 41, 80, 122
Liven, Sofia, 32, 38, 41, 42, 58n22, 181
"London by Moonlight Mission," 120
Lutheran community, charitable outreach of, 37
Lutheran Evangelical Hospital, 37

Madonna House Apostolate in Canada, 33

Maiak (Lighthouse), 81, 125
Makhno, Nestor, 154
Makiivka (Ukraine), children's shelter established in 1996, 212
"Malachite Hall," in the Liven palace, 36
Malof, Basil, 62–63
Mamontov, V. G., 96
marsh land, reclaimed for agriculture, 27
material assistance to the poor, as appropriate for the young, 77
material wealth, generosity regarding, 72–73
Matveev, Iakov Leontevich, 110
Mazaev, D. I., 14, 61, 66, 86, 89, 93, 99
    avoided exile and imprisonment, 91n36
    depicted temperance campaign as spiritual weakness of the Orthodox Church, 139–140
    discouraged Baptists from contributing to the funds promoted in *Khristianin*, 100
    emphasized the blessing of freedom in 1917, 151
    example of a wealthy evangelical, 95–96
    instructions to Balikhin in 1903, 109
    as missions committee president, 2
    on the opening of a Molokan-sponsored library and reading room in Tiflis, 85
    president of the Baptist Union, 95
    protested the 1920 congress, 158
    raised as Molokan, 94–95
    representing compassion practiced among the evangelicals, 203
    visited Spurgeon's grave, 117
    wealthy rancher, 73
    worked to instill a Molokan-type ethic of mutual support, 204
Mazaev, Gavriil, 95

Index   245

McCaig, Archibald, 119, 123, 126
McCarthy, Mark, 28
Meehan-Waters, Brenda, 34
"mega-churches," early examples of, 126
Melis, V. G., 180
Men', Aleksandr, 33
Mennonite Central Committee, in Ukraine, 9n35
Mennonite colonists, in South Russia close at hand for Prokhanov, 183
Mennonite family, gave bread away during the famine, 167
Mennonite villages, widely admired in Russia, 183
Mennonites
   compassionate activity of, 11
   practical experience of, 91
   remained separate, 11
   spoke German and maintained their own church life, schools, hospitals, and other charitable institutions, 12
   in the Volga region formed caravans to travel to ARA warehouses, 164
Metropolitan Feognoz of Kyiv, 49
Metropolitan Tabernacle, 118, 119
Miasoedov, Petr, 130
Miasoedova, Maria Petrovna, 127, 130, 153
midnight meetings, 120. *See also* night meetings
miloserdie
   regained ground since the 1980s, 6
   translated as "mercy" or "compassion," 6
   word officially banned in 1920, 6
ministry
   of compassion, 83
   new forms of in the post-1884 era, 46–50
   to people steeped in vice, 141
   to students, 81
missionaries
   hacked to death by bandits, 154
   raising children to serve as, 47
missionary activity, led to exile, 91
missionary preachers, support for, 91
Missionerskoe obozrenie (Missionary review), an Orthodox publication, 69
missions committee, church members supporting, 91
Molokan background
   of leaders profiled, 204
   of main architects of compassionate ministry, 85
Molokans, 62
   emphasis on mutual support, 3, 10, 87, 90, 182–83, 206
   had no institution comparable to the Orphan Home, 89
   participated in national compassionate campaigns, 90
   placed emphasis on the centrality of the Bible, 88–89
   practiced hospitality to strangers, 90
   rejected all material manifestations of Christianity, 87
   rejected sacraments, but held a high view of Scripture, 3
   separated from the Dukhobors in the 1770s, 88
   situation more difficult for, 45
   tended to be more affluent than their Orthodox neighbors, 89
   welcomed exiles and strangers, 90
money
   believer's understanding of, 83
   not lasting for eternity, 76
money and giving, Christian attitude to, 98
Moody, Dwight L., 33
moral degradation, accompanied poverty, 114–15
Morgan, Campbell, 120

Motorin, Ivan, 79
Mott, John R., 81
Mueller, George, 78–79, 118, 203
Museum of Entrepreneurs, Patrons, and Charitable Workers in Moscow, 6–7, 6
mutual aid
 among Russian evangelicals after 1905, 94–98
 among Russian evangelicals prior to 1905, 87–94
 motivated by concern for preservation, 86
 practiced within the evangelical community, 82
 strong commitment to, 160
Mutual Aid (Kropotkin), 33
mutual support, established among Molokans, 86

Nansen, Fridtjof, 160
Nansen Commission, 172, 173
Narkomzem (People's Commissariat for Agriculture), 180, 196
Naryshkina, Madame, 49
Nastol'naia kniga dlia sviashcheno-tserkovno-sluzhitelei (Handbook for ministers of the Holy Church), 115–16
Natasha, 212
national infrastructure, all but destroyed, 144
Neive, Joseph, 46, 93
Nekhliudov, Dmitrii, hero of Leo Tolstoy's final novel, *Resurrection* (1899), 184–85
Nekrasov, Nikolai Alekseevich, 186
Nekrasova, Zinaida Nikolaevna, 186, 187–88
Nepliuev, Nikolai N., 6, 7, 33, 65, 79, 184–86
Neprash, I. V., 158, 167
Nevskii Society, 136

New Economic Policy (NEP), 175, 197, 205
new life, foundation of, 38
new life for all, as goal of the Russian evangelical movement, 192
Nezdolyi, S. K., 93
Nicholas II (emperor), 10
 abdication of, 58
 acquiesced to a series of political and social concessions, 55
 Decree of 17 April 1905 on religious toleration, 52
Nichols, Gregory L., 206
Nicolay, Paul, 45, 46, 80, 81, 114, 128
night meetings. *See also* midnight meetings
 conducted by Fetler, 122–24
 intended to draw drunkards and prostitutes, 64
Nikol'skaia, Tat'iana, 19, 192–93
Novaiia ili evangel'skaia zhizn' (The new, or evangelical life) (Prokhanov), 191
Novo-Vasilievka, in 1922 1,500 of 6,000 residents starved to death, 167

Ober-Prokuror of the Most Holy Synod, 92
 to Emperor Alexander III, 43
 Prince Aleksandr Golitsyn, 27
Obshchestvo pooshchreniia dukhovno-nravstvennogo chteniia (Society for the encouragement of spiritual-moral reading), 29–30
October Manifesto (1905), 55
OGPU (United state political administration) department, 195
Olga of the Hellenes (Greece) (queen), 122, 122n62, 149
Omsk, home for orphans, 108
"On religious associations" Soviet law, 4, 10–11, 197

Oncken, Johann Gerhard, 13, 13n50, 96
Orlov, Gerasim, 102
Orphan Home fund, 88
orphanage and old people's home, expanded in 1917, 151
orphans
  government set up hundreds of specialized facilities to house and train during the 1920s, 177
  home for operated by the Tent Mission, 155
  physical rescue of, 148
orphans and the elderly, starting a shelter for, 105
Orthodox Church
  accusing evangelicals of being German spies, 150
  affected by changes, 25
  approaches to compassionate ministry, 20
  brotherhoods and parish societies, 25
  call for sobriety on the part of, 135–36
  evangelicals differences from, 12–13
  gaining merit by doing good works, 69
  inspired by Pashkovite activities, 37
  interacting with reform-minded, 182
  Mazaev called on to reclaim the spiritual high ground, 140
  practices of doing good dismissed by Ivanov, 70
  schism in the seventeenth century, 87
  Soviet government focused its attacks on, 176
  temperance socieities, 25
  "trezvennik" movement, 140
  website of Moscow Patriarchate, 6

Ovsiannikovs, adopted four orphans, 103

pacifism, government demanded that evangelicals renounce in 1923, 59
Packer, J. A., 123
Pashkov, Vasilii Alekseevich, 8, 65, 183
  abandoning a life of refinement and giving away money to the poor, 31
  "archives" of, 185–86
  continued to be involved in the Russian evangelical movement, 43
  exiled from Russia in 1884, 23, 42, 55
  holding evangelistic meetings drawing people from all social classes, 29
  owned several estates, 39
  variety of people attracted to the evangelistic meetings held by, 40
Pashkova, Aleksandra Ivanovna, 35
Pashkova, Anna Ivanovna, 121–22, 122n58
Pashkovism, 33, 43
Pashkovite activity, 32, 36, 37
Pashkovite community, Prokhanov and Fetler grounded in, 116
Pashkovite ministries, 38, 39, 42–46
Pashkovite movement, 8, 10
Pashkovite Society for the Encouragement of Spiritual Moral Reading, 37
Pashkovites
  aided poorer evangelicals, 46
  anticipated the total transformation of society, 38
  compassionate outreach practiced by, 113
  continued to reach out to their communities and country after 1884, 43

Pashkovites *(continued)*
    continuity with existing ministries of compassion, 32–37
    dining room, 39
    Fetler found a base among the remaining aristocratic, 121–22
    gave attention to compassionate ministry practiced adroad, 23
    giving emphasis to Bible reading, 30
    goal of a transformation of Russia on an ethical and moral basis, 38
    inspired in compassionate ministry by Lord Radstock, 22
    proposed an alternative based on spiritual transformation, 51
    Soviet-era study of, 19
    worked for the transformation of individual lives, 38
patriotic unity, with the start of World War I in 1914, 57
Paul I (emperor), 87–88
Pavlov, Pavel V., 158, 166, 169–170, 172, 181
Pavlov, Vasilii Gur'evich, 13n50, 41, 44, 57, 61, 66, 73, 86, 90, 101, 158
    advocate for former exiles and for pastoral support, 96–97
    changed attitudes as the only lasting solution, 68
    continued to assist former exiles, 103
    daughter drowned and wife and three other children died of cholera, 92, 97
    experience of exile, 61
    helped with a supply of flour sent by believers, 94
    on human beings all descended from Adam and Eve, 72
    letter to, 102
    on love as an active, outgoing principle, 71
    on preaching the Gospel, 84–85
    president of the Baptist Union, 95
    raised as Molokan, 94–95
    recommended that churches insure their pastors, 111
    reported a meeting of a regional union in Siberia, 107–8
    representing compassion practiced among the evangelicals, 203
    stressed need to demonstrate "practical Christianity," 104–5
    visited Spurgeon's grave, 117
    worked to instill a Molokan-type ethic of mutual support, 204
Pavlova, Anastasiia, 84
Pavlovna, Liudmila, 42
peasant commune, as an instrument of social transformation, 182
peasant *mir*, banded together to work the land, 182
peasant Stundist, classic example of, 1
peasants
    bounding to their traditional village communes, 24
    entitled to market their surplus, 175
Peiker, Aleksandra, 32, 39, 42–43, 44, 80, 81, 114, 122, 128, 149
Peiker, Maria Grigorievna, 28, 29, 32, 33
Peisti, N. I., 35
Penn-Lewis, Jessie, 119
pension fund, Disabilities Fund functioning like, 106
Pentecostal experience, comparing with that of other Soviet evangelicals, 210
Pentecostals, compassionate ministry of, 12
people
    as equal before God, 76
    joining the church without adequate teaching, 108

Index   249

People's Commissariat for Agriculture (Narkomzem), 180, 196
"People's kindergartens" (*Narodnye detskie sady*), 49
perestroika (reconstruction), 6
perestroika years, compassionate activity in, 210
Perovskaia, opened a hospital on her property, 39–40
personal commitment, of Pashkovite compassionate ministry, 40
"Pesnia pervo-khristian" (Song of the first Christians), Prokhanov's musical interest, 190n111
Petrograd, homelessness in, 148
Petrograd Committee for Finding Asylum for Refugees, 149
Petrov, Aleksei Petrovich, opened a home for orphans, 210
Petrov, Father Grigorii, 79
"philanthropy," evangelical connection and, 27–32
"The Philosophy of Ministry of Colonel Vasiliy Pashkov" (Corrado), 10, 19
Pieshevskii, Adam, 130, 132
Pietism, Troeltsch's image of, 206, 206
Pietists, practiced charity without any concern for altering social conditions, 206–7
Pobedonostsev, Konstantin Petrovich, 43
  as Ober-prokuror (Director General) of the Most Holy Synod from 1880 to 1905, 4, 92, 131
Podin, Adam Karlovich, 46
Pomgol- Evangelical Christian committee, 161–62
Pomgol national famine relief organization, 161, 171
poor relief. *See also* urban poor; *specific ways of assistance*, views of, 25–26, 50

poor women, ministry of caring for, 35
Popov, M. A., 89
Popov, V. A.
  on Baptist Union's twenty-five agricultural communes, 175
  on "City of the Sun," 195
  on Prokhanov's student years, 185–86
  on Vertograd, 187
Popov, Vladimir, 19
Populism, envisioned an entirely communal society, 182
Poroshin, Nikolai, 84
post-Soviet charismatic churches, active in the area of compassion, 211
post-Soviet Evangelical Christian-Baptist youth, taking some responsibility for doing chores for elderly members, 210
poverty
  goal to abolish, 194
  living out the gospel expected to do away with, 192
  no barrier to giving, 73
Poverty is not a Vice: Charity, Society, and the State in Imperial Russia (Lindenmeyr), 7
Povlsen, Jens and Agnes, 129, 132
Poysti, N. J., 35
practical service, commitment to, 53
prayer houses
  closed by 1916, 205
  closed by early 1915 and leaders exiled to Siberia, 150
prayer meetings, Pashkov's practice of handing out food and money following, 41
Prayer Revival of 1857, 120
prayers, "save our native land" by means of political and economic reform, 183–84

Index

preachers
  Baptist fund for disabled, 101
  concern for continued to be promoted, 111
  evangelicals attention to supporting, 85
  meeting the needs of, 68
preaching, as an act of compassion, 3
press, multiple attacks on religiously-based labor cooperatives and economic communities, 196
prison, help for believers in, 177
Prison Guardian Society, 28, 33
"prison ministry," came to mean caring for fellow believers, 45–46
prison visitation
  continued by Friedrich Baedeker, 45
  as Dondukova-Korsakova's special calling, 35
prisoners
  aid extended to, 147
  in transport, 92
prisons, study of Russian, 28
Prokhanov, Ivan Stepanovich, 14, 16, 52, 61, 64, 67, 69–70, 79, 80, 90, 93, 99, 102, 129, 171
  articulation of a broader social agenda, 65
  autobiography, 207
  background of, 181–82
  on Booth's visit, 128
  Christian economic communities and, 181–88
  on Christ's command to "Give to anyone who asks," 71–72
  on communal living, 66, 180, 189, 193
  died in Berlin in 1935, 196
  failed efforts to attract an international sponsor, 162
  formed an agricultural community in Crimea in 1894, 178
  letter of complaint from an angry Evangelical Christian church member, 172
  outlined practical steps for the formation of economic communities, 205
  parallels with William Fetler, 116
  on prayer God loves leading to action, 201–2
  project as completely impractical, 192–93
  promoted rescue activity as a ministry for church youth, 117
  promotedf Christian economic communities, 174–75
  proposed ultimate goal to eradicate poverty completely, 199
  published new laws and amendments concerning religion, 177
  on Salvation Army, 115
  on service at a youth meeting, 133–34
  studied in England, 117
  vision for the potential of economic communities, 203
  wanted Christians to transcend doctrinal boundaries, 183
  wife a casualty of 1919, 152
  on women's ministry as broadly "charitable," 77
  worked as assistant director of a sugar factory, 185
Prokhanov, Stepan Antonovich, 91–92, 181
Protestant churches in St. Petersburg, focused services on people in their own communities, 37
Prugavin, A. S., 40, 41–42
public kitchens, opened by Baptists in 1922, 163–64
Putintsev, F. M., 196–97
Pvlov, P. V., 171

Quakers, example of, 202

Radstock (lord), 8, 22–23
  arrived in Russia at the height of the Populist movement, 33
  contribution of, 29
  converted to both personal faith and compassionate ministry, 31
  descended from two generations of Christians with evangelical interests, 30–31
  evangelical influence on the Russians encompassed compassionate activity, 30
  influenced the Pashkovites in the direction of compassionate involvement, 202
  modeled practical Christianity for his Russian followers, 31
Radstock movement, became known as "Pashkovism," 29
Raduga (Rainbow), 183
Railton, George Scott, 128
Rasputin, Grigorii, 141, 149
Red Cross, came to Russia in the 1860s, 34
Redkina, O. Iu., 7, 159, 175, 196
Reed, John, 151
refuge, communities connected with the idea of, 188
refugees, establishment of a shelter for, 149
regional unions, engaged in compassionate ministry, 107
religion, neglected role of in the USSR and in Imperial Russia, 211
religious awakening, simultaneously in several locations in the Russian Empire, 55
religious confession, freedom of but not "propaganda," 60
religious expression, battle against all forms of, 196

religious freedom, insisted on by Russian evangelicals, 207
religious grounds, release from military service on during the Civil War, 176
Religious Society of Friends (Quakers), 27
religious temperance societies, flourishing in 1889, 135
religious toleration, introduction of, 52
Religious-Educational Union, 37
religiously-based communes. *See also* communes
  failed to produce "real" communism, 196
  proliferation of during the 1920s, 20
Renberg, Anna (Agneta or Aniuta), 47
repentance
  as the key, 140
  social transformation through, 142
  theme of, 138–39
  as the way to the new life, 201
"repentant nobleman," a familiar figure in Russia, 33
"rescue," referring to ministry devoted to reclaiming prostitutes, 113n1
rescue ministry
  defined, 113
  emphasis on social transformation, 142
  in St. Petersburg, 121–28
  transforming the lives of the urban poor, 203
rescue model, 139
re-settlers (*pereselentsy*), 198
restrictions, introduced in 1910, 57
resurrection, promise of, 200
Resurrection (Tolstoy), 184–85
"revolution of the spirit," Christians promoting, 176

Riaboshapka, Ivan Grigor'evich, 1, 92, 178
  founder of numerous Baptist congregations in Ukraine, 1n2
  interest in Mazaev's reception of a stranger, 3
  prospered, 73
  test of Mazaev's hospitality, 2
rich persons, spiritual state of, 76
robbers, waylaid starving refugees during the famine, 167
Rodionova, N. V., 146
Romanian Baptist congregation, started a farm around 1908, 179
Romanova, Olga Konstantinovna (grand duchess), 122
royal family, members converted, 37
Rozhdestvenskii, Aleksandr, 136
RSCM (Russian Students' Christian Movement), 81, 81n134
Rushbrooke, J. H., 158, 171, 172–73
"Russian," as applied to evangelical believers, 11
Russian approach to charity, traditional, 26
Russian Baptist evangelists, Riaboshapka as an example, 1
"Russian Baptist history," with greater emphasis on Evangelical Christians, 20
Russian Baptist Union, 14, 61
  congress in April 1917, 151
  congresses, convened a series of annual, 100–101, 104
  famine aid, general appeal for, 160
  focus on establishment of denominational institutions, 62
  founding of, 11n37, 91
  nucleus of, 2
  reconstruction of, 158
  Siberian division of, 108
  support of twenty evangelists, 68
Russian Baptists
  encouraged to send help abroad, 111
  growth of between April 1905 and January 1912, 56
Russian Baptists and Spiritual Revolution, 1905–1929 (Coleman), 7, 10
Russian Bible Institute in New York City, 141
Russian Bible Society, founded in 1813, 27
Russian Empire, history of *miloserdie* in, 6
Russian evangelical leaders, biographies of, 18–19
Russian evangelical movement. *See* evangelical movement
Russian Evangelical Union, 14, 99, 100
Russian evangelicalism. *See* evangelicalism
Russian evangelicals. *See also* evangelical believers
  attracted to the image of the Jerusalem church in Acts 2, 179–180
  belief in requirement to care for people, 3
  declared religious toleration in April 1905, 203
  desired and supported the Salvation Army's entrance, 129
  economic communities and, 178–181
  embraced innovations appropriate to different circumstances, 208
  emphasizing engagement and action over formal theology, 207
  exhibited a basically positive attitude to the world, 207
  important changes during the Soviet period, 211
  joined the Salvation Army, 131
  limitations imposed on by the wider society, 4

Index   253

longest continuous period of relative freedom, 11
maintained a consistent intent and effort to serve people in need, 21
maintained a consistent understanding of compassionate ministry, 67
maintained definite ideas about how to "go about doing good," 4
never at the center of the debate over the best methods of charity, 26
never built up large charitable institutions, 202
New Economic Policy (NEP) and, 175–78
present-day showing themselves to be aware of the world around them, 212
as prolific writers and publishers, 16–17
recognized the need to help people materially, 115
regarding stinginess as a sin, 73
searching out the contributions of, 7
sustained a lively awareness of foreign compassionate ministry, 78
taught that preaching the gospel was their primary calling, 203
as tireless evangelists, 201
turning to God as the only consistently effective solution for drunkenness, 139
understood alcoholism as a distinctly spiritual problem, 138
wave of patriotic enthusiasm at beginning of First World War, 145
Russian identity, compassionate ministry and, 23–27
Russian Missionary Society organized by Fetler, 141
Welsh missionaries came to minister, 119
Russian New Testament (1862), 12, 54
Russian Orthodox. *See* Orthodox Church
Russian Pentecostals, not yet studied with regard to compassionate ministry, 210
Russian POWs, evangelistic work among, 147
Russian sectarians. *See* sectarians
Russian Students' Christian Movement (RSCM), 81, 81n134
Russian temperance movement, 135–140
  flourished between 1895 and 1914, 64
  involvement of evangelicals in, 204
  to mitigate effects of alcoholism, 114
Russian Union of Evangelical Christians-Baptists (Russian Baptist Union), 17, 18, 99, 125, 125n86
Russkii rabochii (The Russian workman), modeled after *The British Workman*, 29
Russo-Turkish conflict of 1877, 146
Russo-Turkish War, 84

sacrificial lifestyle, practicing, 33
Salov-Astakhov, Nikolai I., 153, 154
salvation, by faith alone, 69
Salvation Army, 63, 79–81
  back door into Russia in 1899, 80
  "dissolved" by a government order in 1923, 152
  evangelical compassionate activity during the war, 149
  as an example, 203, 204
  excluded from Soviet Russia in 1923, 81
  Fetler learned first-hand about, 121
  Fetler's approach like that of, 64
  meeting, police raid on, 149

Salvation Army *(continued)*
  officially opened on 16 September 1917, 151
  operated officially in Russia between 1917 and 1923, 116
  rescue ministry practiced by, 115
  in Russia, 53, 128–132, 204
  Russian, 40
  Russian evangelicals well aware of, 79
  Russians intervened to bring into their country, 208
  took over Pashkovite dining rooms, 44
  as a valued ministry partner, 207
samizdat (self-published materials), 17, 18
Savchenko, Aleksandr, 187
Savel'ev, F. S., 180
Savinskii, S. N., 17
schools, opened by Nepliuev, 184
"scientific charity," beginning during the reign of Alexander I (emporer), 27
"scientific" compassion, 26
Scripture, in a variety of languages from about 1813, 54
sect category, placing Russian evangelicals in, 206
sectarian communes, founded by evangelicals, 65
sectarian groups, sobriety closely identified with, 136
sectarians
  aided the starving among the Russians, 90
  emphasized responsibility to well-being of members of their own group, 62
  invited to form communes, 205
  patterns established among indigenous, 62
  practices of mutual support practiced among, 87
  tended to turn inward and work together as a community, 87
self-sustaining community, creation of, 87
Sergiev of Kronstadt, Father Ioann, 48
service, right attitude to, 70–76
sewing circles' main function, 77
sewing cooperatives
  continuing but unwilling to draw attention of authorities, 44
  different from the women's "missionary circles" or sewing circles, 77
  founding of, 34
  for poor women, 35–36
Shapoval, Pavel Nikolaevich, 178n27
sheep and the goats, parable of, 2
Sheldon, Charles, 79
shelter for children, founded by St. Petersburg Evangelical Christians in Raivola, 53
Shilov, Ivan Nikitovich, 58, 153
Shop-Mishich, M. P., 190, 191, 195
shtundisty (Stundists), systematic suppression in 1894, 55
Shuvalova, Elena Ivanovna (countess), 45, 93
Sigor communities, 188, 189
Sigor or *Zoar*, city to which Lot fled, 188
simple community- *prostaia obshchina*, common means of production, 189
sin
  overthrowing, 176
  as root of all misery, 67
  as ultimate cause of all misery, 114
Sinichkin, Aleksei, 207
sinners, repentant and turning to the Lord, 169–170
Sirotskii dom (Orphan home), common fund, 88
sisters of mercy (*sestry miloserdiia*), in hospitals and military units, 34

Skorokhodov, Emel'ian, 84
Slagel, Arthur, 169
Slum Post outside Petrograd's Moscow Gate, opened by the Salvation Army, 149
Smirnov, Z. I., 73, 74, 106–7
Smirnova, Anna (Aniuta), 47
Smirnova-Goliaeva, A. I., 74–75
Smith, Rodney "Gypsy," 63, 120, 121, 122
sobriety, as un-Orthodox, 136
social attitudes, development of new, 24
social changes, unprecedented between 1905 and 1929, 53
social classes, Christianity holding the solution to alienation between, 68
social differences, traditional charity as a way of eradicating, 26
social disasters, making new demands on evangelicals, 67
social egalitarianism, added to the identity of Pashkovite compassionate ministry, 42
social evils, remedied only by turning to God, 118
social experiments, innovative in Russia, 46–49
social ills, remedied through the gospel, 85
social need, Russian evangelicals assigned spiritual significance to, 114
social problems, created by the world war, 148
social reconciliation, not always happening, 41–42
"social service" or "social ministry," suggesting professional status, 11
social solutions, search for in Russia, 23–24
social welfare, understood to be the responsibility of the state, 5

Society for Support of Poor Women in St. Petersburg, 36
Society for the Dissemination of Moral-Religious Enlightenment in the Spirit of Orthodoxy, counteracting the spirit of Pashkovism, 37
Society for the encouragement of spiritual-moral reading (*Obshchestvo pooshchreniia dukhovno-nravstvennogo chteniia*), 29–30
Society for the Improvement of Housing for the Working and Needy Population of St. Petersburg, 32
Society of Agricultural Colonies and Industrial Shelters, 32
Solov'ev, Vladimir, 39
"Song of First Christians" (Prokhanov), 190
"soul-sick," Mennonites in Ukraine described as, 169
South Russia (Ukraine), 12
Southern Baptist Convention Foreign Mission Board, European Representative of, 164–65
Southern Baptist Foreign Mission Board, reported fifty thousand Baptists and families in danger, 157
southern Ukraine, famine began by March 1921, 156
Soviet evangelicals, contributions of, 210
Soviet government. *See also* government
  exporting grain abroad while grain was being brought in to feed the hungry, 172
  regarded evangelicals as something like allies, 58
Soviet law of 8 April 1929, "On religious associations," 54
Soviet Russia, difficulty of entering, 157–58

Soviet times, study of compassionate ministry among evangelicals during, 210
Soviet Union
   religious groups not permitted to care for the sick in hospitals, visit prisoners, or help orphans, 5
   sectarian life in, 7
Sovremennik (The contemporary) literary journal, 186
spiritual consequences, of stinginess, 109–10
"spiritual famine," preaching the gospel eased, 169
spiritual-moral development, consequences in the present as well, 85
Spurgeon, C. H., 63
   admired by the evangelicals, 117–18
   evangelical activist, 118
   example of, 204
Spurgeon, Thomas, 118
St. Petersburg, 12
   changed to "Petrograd," 58n22
   large concentration of evangelicals, 116
   need to build a substantial church in, 125
   rescue ministry in, 121–28
St. Petersburg Prison Guardian Society, 28
Stadling, Jonas, 90
Stalin, Josef, 60
state archives, opening of, 18
Stavtsev, Fedor, 185, 186, 187
Stead, W. T., 128
Steeves, P. D., 170
Stepanov, Iakov, 72
Stepanov, Simon, 92
Stepanov, V. P., 100, 105
stinginess, labeling as shameful, 109–10
Stockwell Orphanage, founding of, 118

Stolypin, Petr, 128
strangers, receiving simple, 1–2
Student Christian Movement, 132
Student Christian Volunteer Movement, 81
Student Volunteer Movement, 30
study, areas for further, 209–11
Stundism, curbing the spread of in the 1890s, 45
Stundists
   communities, similar practices to sectarians, 91
   declared to be dangerous to the state, 187
   defined, 1n1
   evangelicals influenced by, 206
   gathering in Karpinskaia's apartment, 49
   interest of Ukrainian in education, 50
   leaders prospered, 73
   peasant, 1
   situation more difficult for, 45
   in Ukraine, 13
"summer colony," for children in Finland sponsored by the Salvation Army in 1915, 149
"summer *priut*" ("summer shelter"), 77–78, 135
sun, as an obvious metaphor for the gospel, 195
Syromiatnikov, Egor, 186, 187

Taft, President, teetotalism of, 137
Tarajantz, Patwakan, 45
teaching, on the importance of supporting one another, 108
temperance, Russian national conversation on, 135
temperance movement. *See* Russian temperance movement
temperance societies
   participants in, 136

providing "moral" entertainment alternatives, 139
religious flourishing in 1889, 135
serving as a "cover" for sectarian activity, 136
sometimes regarded as slightly dangerous, 136
Temple Society (*Tempelgesellschaft*), a German Pietist movement, 186
"Temporary Council of the Russian Evangelical Union," 100
tension, between Baptists and Evangelical Christians, 170
Tent Mission
  described, 153–55
  not re-registered in 1923, 155
  registered by the People's Commissariat of Internal Affairs in Kharkiv, 154–55
  sending teams of missionaries throughout towns and villages in Ukraine, 205
theology, evangelism and compassionate ministry of more immediate importance, 132
Tiflis Baptists, 73, 97
Timashev, A. E., 30
Timoshenko, Daniil Martynovich, 102
Timoshenko, Mikhail Danilovich, 77, 134, 137, 151n40, 158
Timoshin, Andrei A., 103
tithe, recommended by Ivanov, 110
Tolstoy, L. N., 90
Tolstoy, Leo, 23n3, 29, 33
total community-*vseobshchina*, all property and land held in common, 189
transformation of life, approaching from a materialistic position, 193
transformative power, attributed to the gospel, 85
treasures on earth, true-life fable on not storing up, 74

Treaty of Brest-Litovsk (March 1918), 148, 154
Trepov, General, 30
"trezvennik" movement, 140
Troeltsch, Ernst, 206, 207
Trosnov, F. M., 129, 133
Trotter, Mrs. Edward, 30
Tsiglerova, Anastasiia, 93
Tuchkov, E. A., 195

Uixkyll, Baron Voldemar, 117
Uklein, Simeon, 88
Ukroinyi, 187
Union of Freedom, Truth, and Peace, 182
"unsupervised" children (*besprizornye*), 114
urban poor. *See also* poor relief
  assistance to, 113
  service to as one of Fetler's ministry priorities, 142
  service to open to all Christians, 133
  serving the needs of, 64
urban population, in Russia, 204
urban rescue ministry, 61, 63–64
  reaching people who were suffering the most, 82
  role of ordinary people and, 132–35
urbanization, social consequences of, 63
USSR, reappearance of charitable organizations in, 5
Utrenniaia zvezda (Morning star), 181, 188
  changed status to *tovarishchestvo*, or partnership group, in 1926, 191
  listed addresses of relatively well-off congregations able to accommodate refugees, 168

Venning, John, 28
Venning, John and Walter, 28, 202

Vertograd commune, 187
   evangelical community in Crimea in 1894, 65
   as first relatively successful attempt by Russian evangelicals to establish an economic community, 188
   Prokhanov founded in 1894, 183
Vestnik spaseniia (Herald of salvation), 130
Vettlers, Wilhelms Andreis. *See* Fetler, William A.
Victoria Hostel for Women in London, 31
Vifaniia (Bethany), 188
   formation of, 190–91
   handed over to a Communist collective in 1929, 197
   success due to extensive support, 197
Vins, Iakov Iakovich, 100
Vladivostok, ingathering of converts in, 108
voluntary organizations, for philanthropic or educational purposes, 24
von Mayer, Karl Karpovich, 48
Vorob'ev, A. I., 190
Voronin, Nikita Isaevich, 13n50, 73, 92, 97

Waldegrave, William Granville (Lord Radstock). *See* Radstock (lord)
war, almost uninterrupted from 1914 to 1923, 144
The War Cry, Salvation Army's newspaper, 130
war effort, evangelicals joined thousands of private citizens, 146
Wardin, Albert J., Jr., 206
"water Molokans" (*vodnye molokane*), 97
wealth
   not to be hoarded, 75
   right attitude to, 70–76
   theme of judgment for hoarding, 75
wealthy believers, expected to look to the needs of the those less well off, 74
Welsh Revival of 1904 to 1905, 117–18
   effect on people from the lower classes of society, 119
   example of, 204
   Fetler's direct experience of, 119
   practices of, 63
Wenberg, Mrs., 47
Western and Russian evangelical approaches to compassion, analyzing further similarities and differences, 211
Western religious groups, contact with the Russian ruling class, 27
"what is to be done?," debate on, 50
Wheeler, Daniel, 27
"white slave traffic," ministry to women caught in, 124
"the widow's mite," references to, 73–74
Wieler, Johann, 91, 95
Wieler, Johann (Ivan), 91
Wieler, Johannes (Ivan), 2
Witte, Sergei, 102, 137
Wolffe, John, 211
women, called to minister to those in need, 77
"wonderful new life," perceived by Russian evangelicals, 201
"workers' brotherhood" (*trudovoe bratstvo*), creation of, 7
World War I
   drastic changes overtook all of Russia, 205
   evangelical compassionate ministry during, 145–155
   evangelicals transformed prayer houses into hospitals, 209
   field hospital (*lazaret*) set up, 90

social problems created by, 148
Treaty of Brest-Litovsk (March 1918), 154
wave of patriotic enthusiasm, 57, 145

YMCA/RSCM, connected Russian evangelicals with the wider world, 81
Young Men's Christian Association (YMCA), 53, 79, 81
youth
    caring for children in St. Petersburg, 135
    compassionate ministry part of the calling of, 153
    of Dom Evangeliia continued visitation and service during the war and after, 148
    of Dom Evangeliia staffing small children's homes, 78
    first meeting in Rostov-on-Don in 1909 for Baptist, 134
    forms of ministry suitable for groups of, 77
    post-Soviet taking some responsibility for elderly members, 210
    Prokhanov promoted rescue activity as a ministry for, 117
    rescue ministry and street missions as appropriate activity for, 133
    visiting the sick and poor, 134

Zasetskaia, Iuliia Denisovna, 8, 35, 39
zemstvo, founding of, 24
Zenkova, Olga, began a clandestine school for Stundist children in her Kyiv home in 1903, 50
"Zhertva Bakhusa" (The sacrifice of Bacchus), 137
Zhuk, Sergei, 50
Zinov'ev, Count, assisted peasants, 40

www.ingramcontent.com/pod-product-compliance
Lightning Source LLC
Chambersburg PA
CBHW051517230426
43668CB00012B/1644